iPolitics

Citizens, Elections, and Governing in the New Media Era

iPolitics provides a current analysis of new media's effects on politics, both at home and abroad. Politicians rely on Twitter, Facebook, and YouTube to exercise political power. Citizens also use these tools to vent political frustrations, join political groups, and organize revolutions. Political activists blog to promote candidates, solicit and coordinate financial contributions, and provide opportunities for volunteers.

iPolitics describes the ways in which media innovations change how politicians and citizens engage the political arena. Most importantly, the volume emphasizes the implications of these changes for the promotion of democratic ideals. Among other things, contributors to this volume analyze whether the public's political knowledge has increased or decreased in the new media era, the role television still plays in the information universe, the effect bloggers have had on the debate and outcome of health care reform, and the manner in which political leaders navigate the new media environment. Although the majority of contributors examine new media and politics in the United States, the volume also provides a unique comparative perspective on this relationship using cases from abroad.

Richard L. Fox is Associate Professor of Political Science at Loyola Marymount University. He is coauthor of *It Still Takes a Candidate: Why Women Don't Run for Office* (Cambridge 2010) and *Tabloid Justice: The Criminal System in the Age of Media Frenzy*, 2nd edition (2007), as well as coeditor of *Gender and Election*, 2nd edition (Cambridge 2009).

Jennifer M. Ramos is Assistant Professor of Political Science at Loyola Marymount University. Her research focuses on understanding the causes and consequences of political change, with an emphasis on the role of ideas, norms, and identity. Her current interests include public opinion and foreign policy, sovereignty issues, and media and politics. She has published in *Journal of Politics, Public Opinion Quarterly, International Studies Perspectives*, and *Journal of Political Ideologies*.

iPolitics

Citizens, Elections, and Governing in the New Media Era

RICHARD L. FOX
Loyola Marymount University

JENNIFER M. RAMOS
Loyola Marymount University

CAMBRIDGE
UNIVERSITY PRESS

CAMBRIDGE UNIVERSITY PRESS
Cambridge, New York, Melbourne, Madrid, Cape Town,
Singapore, São Paulo, Delhi, Tokyo, Mexico City

Cambridge University Press
32 Avenue of the Americas, New York, NY 10013-2473, USA

www.cambridge.org
Information on this title: www.cambridge.org/9781107667655

© Cambridge University Press 2012

First published 2012

Printed in the United States of America

A catalog record for this publication is available from the British Library.

Library of Congress Cataloging in Publication Data
iPolitics : citizens, elections, and governing in the new media era / [edited by]
Richard L. Fox, Jennifer M. Ramos.
    p. cm.
Includes bibliographical references and index.
ISBN 978-1-107-01595-1 (hardback) – ISBN 978-1-107-66765-5 (paperback)
    1. Political participation – Technological innovations – United States.   2. Communication
in politics – Technological innovations – United States.   3. Internet in political
campaigns – United States.   4. Internet – Political aspects – United States.   5. Mass
media – Political aspects – United States.   6. Internet in public administration – United
States. I. Fox, Richard Logan. II. Ramos, Jennifer.
JK1764.I75   2011
320.0285′4678–dc23   2011025061

ISBN 978-1-107-01595-1 Hardback
ISBN 978-1-107-66765-5 Paperback

Contents

List of Tables and Figures

TABLES

FIGURES

Contributors

EDITORS

Richard L. Fox is Associate Professor of Political Science at Loyola Marymount University. He is coauthor of *It Still Takes a Candidate: Why Women Don't Run for Office* (Cambridge 2010), coeditor of *Gender and Election*, 2nd edition (Cambridge 2009), and coauthor of *Tabloid Justice: The Criminal Justice System in the Age of Media Frenzy*, 2nd edition (2007). He has published articles in *Political Research Quarterly, The Journal of Politics, American Journal of Political Science, Political Psychology, Public Administration Review, Women and Politics*, and *Legislative Studies Quarterly*. His primary research and teaching inter ests are political ambition, women and politics, congressional politics, and media and politics.

Jennifer M. Ramos is Assistant Professor of Political Science at Loyola Marymount University. Her research focuses on understanding the causes and consequences of political change, with an emphasis on the role of ideas, norms, and identity. Her current interests include public opinion and foreign policy, sovereignty issues, and media and politics. She has published in *Journal of Politics, Public Opinion Quarterly, International Studies Perspectives*, and *Journal of Political Ideologies*.

CONTRIBUTORS

Matthew A. Baum is Marvin Kalb Professor of Global Communications and Professor of Public Policy at Harvard University's John F. Kennedy School of Government and Department of Government. His research focuses on delineating the effects of domestic politics on international conflict and cooperation in general and American foreign policy in particular, as well as on the role of the mass media and public opinion in contemporary politics. His research has appeared in more than a dozen leading scholarly journals such as the *American Political Science Review*, *American Journal of Political Science*, and *Journal of Politics*. His books include *Soft News Goes to War: Public Opinion and American Foreign Policy in the New Media Age* (Princeton University Press 2003) and *War Stories: The Causes and Consequences of Public Views of War* (Princeton University Press 2010). He has also contributed op-ed articles to a variety of newspapers and magazines in the United States and abroad. Before coming to Harvard, Baum was associate professor of political science and communication studies at UCLA.

Tom Carlson is Associate Professor and Head of Research in Political Science at the Department of Politics and Administration, Åbo Akademi University, Finland. His primary areas of research focus on political communication, in particular political advertising and Web campaigning. He has published in international journals such as *European Journal of Communication, Journal of Information Technology & Politics, Journal of Political Marketing*, and *The Harvard International Journal of Press/Politics*.

Ann Crigler is Professor of Political Science at the University of Southern California. She is coauthor, editor, or coeditor of *Common Knowledge: News and the Construction of Political Meaning* (University of Chicago Press 1992); *Crosstalk: Citizens, Candidates and the Media in a Presidential Campaign* (University of Chicago Press 1996; winner of the 2003 Doris Graber Best Book Award given by the American Political Science Association's Political Communication Division); *The Psychology of Political Communication* (University of Michigan Press 1996); and *Rethinking the Vote: The Politics and Prospects of American Election Reform* (Oxford University Press 2004) as well as numerous articles and essays on political communication, elections, and emotions and political behavior. Her most recent book is a coedited volume, *The Affect Effect: Dynamics of Emotion in Political Thinking and Behavior* (University of Chicago Press 2007). In 2006, Professor Crigler was awarded the first David Swanson Award for Service to Political Communication Scholarship by the Political Communication Division of the American Political Science Association. Professor Crigler received her PhD in Political Science from the Massachusetts Institute of Technology.

Richard Davis is Professor of Political Science at Brigham Young University. He is the author of several books on American politics and the media including *Typing Politics: The Role of Politics in American Politics* (Oxford 2009); *Politics Online: Blogs, Chatrooms, and Discussion Groups in American Democracy* (Routledge 2005); and *The Web of Politics: The Internet's Impact on the American Political System* (Oxford 1999).

Urs Gasser is the Executive Director of the Berkman Center for Internet & Society at Harvard University. He is the coauthor of *Born Digital: Understanding the First Generation of Digital Natives* (Basic Books 2008). His research and teaching focus on information law and policy issues. Current projects – several of them in collaboration with leading research institutions in the United States, Europe, and Asia – explore policy and educational challenges for the future generation of digital natives, the regulation of digital media and technology (with emphasis on IP law), ICT interoperability, information quality, the institutional settings for fostering entrepreneurship, and the law's impact on innovation and risk in the ICT space. He graduated from the University of St. Gallen and Harvard Law School.

Jan Gerlach is the Executive Director of the Research Center for Information Law at University of St. Gallen. He worked at the Institute for Information Management at the University of St. Gallen as a junior research assistant during his studies and was granted the Freedom of Information Project at the Open Society Justice Initiative, Budapest (fall 2007). He is currently completing his doctoral thesis in the field of information law.

Parker Hevron is a PhD student in Political Science and International Relations at the University of Southern California. He studies the intersection of political communication and public law.

Lauren Hume is a law student and an editor of the *Law Review* at the New York University School of Law. She is a graduate of Wellesley College.

Jeffrey Jones is Director of the Institute of Humanities at Old Dominion University. He is the author of *Entertaining Politics: Satiric Television and Political Engagement*, 2nd edition (Rowman & Littlefield 2010), and coeditor of *Satire TV: Politics and Comedy in the Post-Network Era*

(NYU Press 2009) and *The Essential HBO Reader* (University Press of Kentucky 2008). With Geoffrey Baym, he is coeditor of the forthcoming collection *Not Necessarily the News? News Parody and Political Satire Across the Globe* (Routledge).

Marion Just is the William R. Kenan, Jr. Professor in Political Science at Wellesley College and an associate of the Joan Shorenstein Center on Press, Politics and Public Policy at Harvard's Kennedy School of Government. She is a consultant to the Project for Excellence in Journalism. Professor Just is a coauthor of *We Interrupt This Newscast: How to Improve Local News and Win Ratings, Too* (Cambridge University Press 2007); *Crosstalk: Citizens, Candidates and the Media in a Presidential Campaign* (University of Chicago Press 1996); and *Common Knowledge: News and the Construction of Political Meaning* (University of Chicago Press 1992). She coedited *Rethinking the Vote: The Politics and Prospects of American Electoral Reform* (Oxford University Press 2003) and *Framing Terrorism: News Media, Government and the Public* (Routledge 2003). Her research has been supported by grants from the National Science Foundation, the Pew Charitable Trusts, and the Ford Foundation. She is a member of the American Political Science Association, where she has received the Murray Edelman Distinguished Career Award from the Political Communication Section and an Excellence in Mentoring Award from the Women's Caucus.

Matthew R. Kerbel is Professor of Political Science at Villanova University. Over the past two decades, he has written extensively about the relationship between television and politics, a subject that first caught his interest when he worked as a television news writer for public broadcasting. His books on the subject include *Remote and Controlled: Media Politics in a Cynical Age* and *If It Bleeds, It Leads: An Anatomy of Television News*, which explore the impacts of television on the political process. In *Netroots*, his seventh book, Kerbel considers the possibility that Internet politics will rekindle the relationship between politicians and ordinary people that was largely lost in the television age.

Jennifer L. Lawless is Associate Professor of Government at American University, where she is also the Director of the Women & Politics Institute. She specializes in women and politics, public opinion, and political representation. She is coauthor (with Richard L. Fox) of the books *It Takes a Candidate: Why Women Don't Run for Office* (Cambridge 2005) and *It Still Takes a Candidate: Why Women Don't Run for Office*

(Cambridge 2010). Professor Lawless has published numerous articles in academic journals such as the *American Journal of Political Science, Perspectives, Journal of Politics, Political Research Quarterly, Legislative Studies Quarterly, Social Problems,* and *Politics & Gender.* She is a nationally recognized speaker, and her scholarly analysis and political commentary have been quoted in various newspapers, magazines, television news programs, and radio shows. Since 2010, she has been the editor of *Politics & Gender.*

Jesse Mills is a PhD student in Political Science and International Relations at the University of Southern California.

Lauren Mintz graduated with distinction from the U.S. Naval Academy with a BS in Political Science. She received an MA in Government in Politics with a concentration in American Politics from the University of Maryland, College Park. She has previously collaborated with Deborah Wheeler on the impact of the Internet in the Middle East. Her primary focus is the application of statistical methods in political science. She was commissioned in May 2010 from the U.S. Naval Academy and is currently serving as an Ensign in the U.S. Navy.

Zoe M. Oxley is Associate Professor of Political Science at Union College. Her research interests include the effects of the media on public opinion, media coverage of politics, political psychology, and women in electoral politics. She is the coauthor of *Public Opinion: Democratic Ideals, Democratic Practice* (CQ Press 2008) and *Conducting Empirical Analysis: Public Opinion in Action* (CQ Press 2011). Her work has also been published in the *American Political Science Review, Journal of Politics, Politics & Gender, Political Research Quarterly, Political Behavior,* and *PS: Political Science and Politics.*

Kim Strandberg is Senior Researcher at the Social Science Research Institute at Åbo Akademi University, Finland. His research focuses on political uses of the Internet. He has published in several international journals such as *Information Polity, New Media & Society, Party Politics,* and *Scandinavian Political Studies.*

Deborah L. Wheeler holds a PhD in Political Science and Middle Eastern Studies from the University of Chicago. Her areas of research include information technology diffusion and impact in the Arab world, gender and international development, and the Palestinian-Israeli conflict. She has published widely on the Internet and its impact in the Arab World including *The Internet in the Middle East: Global Expectations and Local Imaginations in Kuwait* (State University of New York Press 2006). In addition to her academic work, Dr. Wheeler is an international consultant and has most recently completed work for the United Nations Development Program and the Digital Opportunity Trust focused on using information technology in boosting human development.

Preface and Acknowledgments

As we complete this manuscript, countries in the Middle East and North Africa are experiencing protests and riots against ruling regimes. Despite government efforts to block them, new media tools such as YouTube, Twitter, and Facebook are enabling citizens to organize and share their frustrations with one another and the world. Amid antigovernment demonstrations in Egypt, for instance, the regime shut down the Internet for days. Of course, it was too late; President Hosni Mubarak stepped down after almost 30 years in power. The situation in Egypt is only one example of how new media and communication tools are being used to transform politics. By the time this book reaches readers, it is likely that there will have been additional events in which new technologies played a pivotal role in determining political outcomes. In this volume, we have endeavored to put together a collection of works that provides a context for understanding how these changes in the media and information environment are affecting politics today and how they may continue to transform politics in the future.

In spring 2010, the Institute for Leadership Studies at Loyola Marymount University, Los Angeles (LMU), invited leading scholars to its eighth annual Dilemmas of Democracy conference focused on new media and politics. As conference organizers, we were particularly interested in compiling analyses of both U.S. and non-U.S. new media environments as they relate to politics. We are pleased to have the contributions of those who participated in the conference: Matthew Baum, Ann Crigler, Richard Davis, Urs Gasser, Jan Gerlach, Lauren Hume, Jeffery Jones, Marion Just, Parker Hevron, Matthew Kerbel, Jennifer Lawless, Jesse Mills, Lauren Mintz, and Deborah Wheeler. We were also able to add contributions from Tom Carlson and Kim Strandberg, and Zoe Oxley. We thank these scholars for their time and effort.

Behind the scenes, we had much support from our faculty, administrative, and student colleagues at Loyola Marymount University. Foremost, we thank Michael Genovese, the Director of the Institute for Leadership Studies, who offered us the opportunity to put on this conference. Michael was extraordinarily kind and generous with his support and was invaluable as a mentor and facilitator of funds for the conference. In addition, we are grateful to LMU's Bellarmine College of Liberal Arts Dean Paul T. Zeleza who has continued to support the Institute for Leadership Studies by providing the funds to make the conference, and volume, possible. Our department colleagues also were an excellent support – from marshalling students to attend the conference to reading drafts of our manuscript, they remind us how lucky we are to be in this department; thus, we thank Lance Blakesley, Jodi Finkel, Evan Gerstmann, Fernando Guerra, John Parrish, Janie Steckenrider, Seth Thompson, and Cassandra Veney. We would like to point out, though, that the conference proceedings would not have gone as smoothly as they did had it not been for Mercedes Adams, our undergraduate student assistant. She has moved on to law school, so we miss her tireless good cheer and efficiency.

As for the manuscript, we are grateful to have Robert Dreesen at Cambridge University Press, who has been very supportive of this project from the beginning. Finally, we would like to thank our student research assistants: Elysia Galindo-Ramirez, who provided great assistance in putting together the final version of the manuscript, and Samantha Hay, who did a fantastic job creating the index.

We dedicate this book to Jennifer's daughter, Isabelle, who waited just long enough for the conference to be done to come into this world, and Richard's children, Lila and Miles.

Richard L. Fox
Jennifer M. Ramos
February 13, 2011
Los Angeles

Introduction

Politics in the New Media Era

Richard L. Fox and Jennifer M. Ramos

In the ever-changing news and information environment of the early 21st century, citizens and politicians are eagerly adapting new technologies to exercise political power. In the United States, some analysts attribute Barack Obama's success in the 2008 presidential election to the rise of social networking media.[1] Politicians abroad such as Israeli prime minister Benjamin Netanyahu adopted Obama's social networking media strategies to promote his own accomplishments and garner citizen support after seeing its success in the United States.[2] In 2010, Gavin Newsom, the mayor of San Francisco, became the first politician to announce his candidacy (for governor) on Twitter.[3] Netroots activists and bloggers, such as those affiliated with *Daily Kos*, promote progressive candidates across the United States, solicit and coordinate financial contributions, and provide opportunities for volunteers. On the other side of the political spectrum, conservative "Tea Party" activists capitalize on these

---

[1] Although presidential elections are dynamic endeavors and outcomes rely on numerous factors, Talbot (2008) makes a compelling case that the Internet propelled the Obama campaign in terms of fundraising, coordinating volunteers, and generating excitement for his candidacy.

[2] Ethan Bronner and Noam Cohen, "Israeli Candidate Borrows a (Web) Page from Obama," *New York Times*, November 14, 2008. Retrieved from http://www.nytimes .com/2008/11/15/world/middleeast/15bibli.html.

[3] Newsom initially declared that he was running for governor, but eventually pulled out of the race and decided to run for lieutenant governor. See James Eskenazi, "Newsom Announces Lt. Gov Candidacy in Old Media Blitz. Sorry Twitter," *SF Weekly*, March 12, 2010. Retrieved from http://blogs.sfweekly.com/thesnitch/2010/03/newsom_announces_ lt_gov_candid.php.

strategies as well.[4] In addition, most members of the U.S. Congress, as well as almost all U.S. candidates for any major political office, promote themselves and their accomplishments on Facebook or Twitter.

Political change around the world has also been propelled by new media tools. YouTube, Facebook, and Twitter have been critical organizing tools in the recent citizen protests in Northern Africa and the Middle East. These protests compelled the long-time leader of Tunisia, Zine al-Abidine Ben Ali, to resign and flee the country and forced Egyptian president Hosni Mubarak to step down. These protests are reminiscent of the situation in Iran in 2009, in which citizen-generated videos and commentary played a crucial role in promoting and exposing the presidential election protests. In fact, in the summer of 2009, the U.S. State Department asked Twitter to postpone a network upgrade so as not to disrupt citizen activism in Iran.[5] Yet the use of social media as a tool of citizen rebellion started before Iran. In 2007, the Burmese government tried to block Internet sites, blogs, and cell phone videos from exposing antigovernment protests to the outside world and publicizing the plight of dissidents who suffered under the harsh crackdown by the military government.[6] Clearly, the digital age has drastically transformed the method and style of political communication and mobilization.

Yet the degree to which the new media environment fundamentally alters political outcomes and brings citizens closer to democratic ideals – such as increased levels of political participation, a more responsive government, and freedom of expression – is much less clear. Initially, many political leaders and commentators assumed that new information and communication technologies would not only increase citizen involvement in longstanding democracies but also unleash a wave of democratization around the world. Yet early empirical analyses did not uncover the results many expected. Although the quantity of news and information sources has dramatically increased worldwide, the evidence suggests diminished citizen interest in "serious" news, as well as a decline in the overall quality of news (Baum 2003; Prior 2007). In addition, several studies find

---

4 See David Wiegal, "Talking tea parties at AEI, and on C-Span, 2 p.m. ET." *Washington Post* blog. June 9, 2010. Retrieved July 1, 2010, from http://voices.washingtonpost.com/right-now/2010/06/talking_tea_parties_at_aei_and.html.

5 Lev Grossman, June 17, 2009. "Iran's Protests: Twitter, the Medium of the Moment." *Time Magazine*. Retrieved from http://www.time.com/time/world/article/0,8599,1905125,00.html.

6 Mark Glasser, October 8, 2007. "Can Internet, Blogs Sustain the Saffron Revolution?" Retrieved from http://www.pbs.org/mediashift/2007/10/can-internet-blogs-sustain-the-saffron-revolution281.html.

that the Internet exerts little effect on mass-level political participation or citizen engagement (Bimber 2003; Galston 2002; Norris 2002).

By "new media" and "new media environment," we refer to the rise of the Internet and other technologies that promote the immediacy of communication and information gathering. We use these terms to capture how changes in the universe of news, information, and communication have exerted an impact on how traditional news outlets cover news, how citizens participate politically, and how candidates and elected officials campaign and govern.[7] Because changes in new technologies occur so quickly, scholars of political communication must continue to examine the transformative effects of the new media environment on politics. After all, since 2004, alone, we have witnessed the ascendance of social-networking sites, the advent of YouTube, widespread use of hand-held devices with full Internet capabilities, and numerous news websites, such as *The Huffington Post* and *Mashable*. These new media sources and tools provide citizens with new opportunities to express and organize themselves around their political interests.

Our goal in this volume, therefore, is two-fold. First, we aim to determine the degree to which recent changes in the news and information environment alter the form and substance of both domestic and foreign politics; that is, do citizens and politicians engage differently in the political arena as a result of new media? Scholars in this volume take up this question by examining topics such as how political leaders utilize Twitter and Facebook, whether YouTube plays a significant role in elections, and the Internet's impact on political participation and attitudes in non-democratic, developing countries. Second, we seek to ascertain whether the most recent changes in the news and information environment promote democratic ideals. Contributors in this volume assess whether citizens' political knowledge has increased or decreased over the past 20 years, whether "netroots" activism affected the debate over and outcome of health care reform in the United States, and the manner in which political leaders must navigate the new media environment to communicate

---

[7] Scholars have had difficulty pinpointing a definition of what constitutes the "new media." Media scholars Richard Davis and Diana Owen (1998, 7) comment that arriving at a definition is difficult because media in the current era are so multifaceted. The Pew Research Center for the People and the Press offers a purely technological definition, originally identifying the Internet and cable news as the new media, before adding cell phone applications. In this volume, we use the term to refer both to the new technological innovations over the last 20 years and the changes that the new technologies have brought about in society.

effectively with their constituents and the general public. Although the majority of chapters focus on politics in the United States, several chapters do address the influence of the new media environment in other areas of the world, including Europe and the Middle East. Together, the chapters allow us to provide a rich contextual assessment of the way in which the continually changing media environment influences political outcomes.

THE EVOLVING MEDIA LANDSCAPE AND ITS EFFECTS ON POLITICS

It would be difficult to overstate the rate of change the world has recently witnessed in terms of communications and information technology. Writing in the early 2000s, political communication scholar Bruce Bimber (2003, 1) asserted that "at no time in the history of American Democracy has a new set of communication and information-handling capacities been so rapidly assimilated by the political system." Writing from a global perspective, John Palfrey and Urs Gasser (2008, 3) characterized the period between 1991 and 2008 as exhibiting "the most rapid period of technological transformation ever," at least in terms of the delivery of information. These changes fundamentally affect the way in which citizens gather and receive news and information. In the early 1990s, the average citizen in an advanced society usually kept abreast of political events by listening to the radio, reading a newspaper, or watching a televised news broadcast. By the early 2000s, newspapers and television news broadcasts still existed, but citizens began accessing information through a myriad of new tools and sources. Newer, more sophisticated technologies continue to infiltrate the market; for example, tech-savvy news consumers now debate the costs and benefits of accessing news and information through iPads, iPhones, and Droids, just to name a few.

Beyond the Internet, the cable news industry provides around-the-clock political news and commentary. Often characterized by a partisan or ideological viewpoint, cable news programs and websites have flourished over the course of the last 20 years. Even entertainment and "soft news" programs now represent a significant source of political news. Programs such as the _The View_, _The Daily Show with Jon Stewart_, _The Colbert Report_, and _The Tonight Show with Jay Leno_ serve as important sources of political information in the United States and abroad (Gray, Jones, and Thompson 2009). And in this new environment, there is no such thing as missing a show; with a few clicks of the mouse, one can easily watch the programs of one's choosing and catch up on the events of the day.

The expansion of the Internet serves as the driving force behind the changes in the media and information environment. Certainly, a "digital divide" continues to exist, characterized by substantial discrepancies in Internet penetration exist around the world.[8] However, as the data presented in Table I.1 make clear, all regions of the globe have experienced dramatic growth in Internet usage between 2000 and 2009, a growth that will undoubtedly continue.

TABLE I.1. *Increased Internet Use Worldwide, 2000–2009*

Region	Population (estimated 2009)	% Population Using the Internet, 2000	% Population Using the Internet, 2009	% Growth in Internet Use, 2000–9
Africa	991,002,342	0.1	8.7	1,809.8
Asia	3,808,070,503	3.1	20.1	568.8
Europe	803,850,858	14.5	53.0	305.1
Middle East	202,687,005	–	28.8	1,675.1
North America	340,831,831	33.9	76.2	140.1
Latin America	586,662,468	3.5	31.9	934.5
Oceania/Australia	34,700,201	24.6	60.8	177.0

Sources: Internet World Stats www.internetworldstats.com/stats.htm, 2009; population estimates for 2000 are from the United Nations World Population Prospects database.

Accompanying the increase in access to the Internet has been a dramatic rise in the rates and usage of Internet-based tools and activities, such as blogging, social networking, and YouTube (see Table I.2). In addition, many citizens now rely on information via mass e-mail, cell phone applications, and Web browsers.[9] As we might expect, generational differences characterize how citizens access information. According to a 2010 Pew Center study, 72% of U.S. citizens between the ages of 18 and 29 use at least one social networking site, such as Facebook or MySpace, as compared to only 40% of women and men over the age of 30 who use these technologies.[10]

---

[8] The disparity in communication and information technologies between developing and developed countries has become known as the "digital divide" (Norris 2001).

[9] A Pew Research Center Report identifies the emergence of podcasts, Web browsers, and cell phones as sources of information. See "Maturing Internet News Audience – Broader than Deep," *Pew Research Center for the People and Press*, July 30, 2006. Retrieved from http://people-press.org/reports/pdf/282.pdf.

[10] Amanda Lenhart, Kristen Purcell, Aaron Smith, and Kathryn Zickuhr, "Social Media & Mobile Internet Use Among Teens and Young Adults," *Pew Research Center for*

TABLE I.2. *Use of New and Emerging Media through 2010*

New Media Format	Startup Date	Members or Uses Per Day (in 2010)
Total Number of Blogs	March 2003 (first tracked by Technorati)	112.8 million separate blogs
LinkedIn	May 2003	70 million members
MySpace	January 2004	67 million members
Facebook	February 2004	400 million members
YouTube	December 2005	2 billion view per day
Twitter	July 2006	83.6 million monthly users 2 billion tweets per month

Note: All views and members are based on worldwide figures.
Source: For data on blogs, see Gary M. Stern, "Keeping Track of the Ever-Proliferating Number of Blogs." Retrieved February 15, 2010, from http://www.infotoday.com/linkup/ludo21510-stern .shtml. For LinkedIn membership numbers, see Leena Rao, "LinkedIn Tops 70 Million Users; Includes over One Million Company Profiles," *TechCrunch*. Retrieved June 20, 2010, from http://techcrunch.com/2010/06/20/linkedin-tops-70-million-users-includes-over-one-million-company-profiles. For Facebook membership information, see http://www.facebook.com/press/ info.php?statistics. For MySpace facts, see Jeremiah Owyang, "A Collection of Social Network Stats for 2010." Retrieved January 19, 2010, from http://www.web-strategist.com/blog/2010/01/ 19/a-collection-of-social-network-stats-for-2010/. For YouTube hits, see Ben Parr, "YouTube Surpasses Two Billion Video Views Daily." Retrieved May 17, 2010, from http://mashable.com/ 2010/05/17/youtube-2-billion-views/. And for Twitter data, see Laurie Sullivan, "Twitter Acquires Analytics Startup, Supports Promoted Tweets." Retrieved June 11, 2010, from http://www .mediapost.com/publications/?fa=Articles.showArticle&art_aid=129994.

As citizens have come to rely more on online news sources, traditional media outlets, such as newspapers, national network broadcasts, and local television, have experienced concomitant declines. Table I.3 presents data regarding news habits in the United States. Between 1993 and 2008, the proportion of U.S. citizens who came to rely on online news as a regular news source grew from zero to nearly 40%. As data on newspaper readership reveals, these patterns are not unique to the United States. Between 2007 and 2009, newspaper readership in the United Kingdom fell by 25%.[11] Over the same time period other countries saw similar downward trends in newspaper circulation: Readership in Greece is down by 20%, Italy has seen an 18% decrease, and Canada's circulation is down 17%.[12]

the People and Press, February 3, 2010. Retrieved from http://pewinternet.org/Reports/ 2010/Social-Media-and-Young -Adults.aspx.

[11] James Robinson, "UK and US See Heaviest Newspaper Circulation Declines," *The Guardian*, June 17, 2010. Retrieved from http://www.guardian.co.uk/media/2010/jun/ 17/newspaper-circulation-oecd-report.

[12] Ibid. Newspapers, however, are not in decline everywhere and are actually on the rise in developing countries where Internet access remains limited. See "Not All Bad News:

TABLE I.3. *Changing News and Information-Gathering Habits in the United States, 1993–2008*

	1993	1996	2000	2004	2008
% of People who Regularly Watch, Read, or Listen:					
Newspapers	58	50	47	42	34
Radio News	47	44	43	40	35
Cable News	–	–	33	38	39
Local TV News	77	65	56	59	52
Nightly Network News	60	42	30	34	29
Network Morning News	–	23	20	22	22
Online News	–	2	23	29	37

Notes: "Regularly" means that the medium is used daily or at least three times a week. For newspapers and radio news, the data in the 1993 column are actually 1994 data and the 1996 column data are actually from 1995.
Source: Adapted from "Key News Audiences Now Blend Online and Traditional Sources Audience Segments in a Changing News Environment," *Pew Research Center for the People and the Press.* Retrieved August 17, 2008, from http://people-press.org/report/444/news media.

In this new information environment, engagement and participation have changed for the politically minded citizen. The citizen of 2011 texts regularly, sends pictures via cell phone, posts to Facebook daily, accesses news and political information from the Web, makes online financial contributions to political candidates, and organizes online communities on behalf of a cause. The technological revolution can even extend into the realm of voting. Citizens of Estonia became the first to cast ballots over the Internet in national elections when the government instituted e-voting in 2007.[13] These developments represent sharp contrasts from only a few years ago, when engaged citizenship meant writing a letter to an elected official, joining an interest group, or participating in a rally.

These new technologies also affect politicians, who have generally embraced them and capitalized on their power, particularly in the United States. In the 2004 U.S. Democratic presidential primary election, for instance, Howard Dean, the relatively obscure Democratic governor of Vermont, became the first candidate to harness on the power of the Internet. He used it to tap into a grassroots, viral constituency and ultimately raised more money than his much better known opponents

Newspapers Are Thriving in Many Developing Countries," *The Economist,* July 26, 2008, p. 80.

[13] David Mardiste, "Estonians Will Be First to Allow Internet Votes in National Election – Technology & Media – International Herald Tribune," *New York Times,* February 22, 2007.

(Hindman 2007). In 2008, presidential candidate Barack Obama took modern campaigning to a new level when he used new media strategies to mobilize and connect supporters; for example, his campaign developed lengthy inspirational videos that were watched by millions on YouTube,[14] and he announced his vice presidential selection via text message to several million supporters' cell phones.

In addition to political campaigns, politicians now use the new media to engage in issue advocacy. The 2009 debate over health care reform in the United States serves as a prime example. Former Republican vice presidential candidate Sarah Palin used her Facebook page to charge that Democratic health care proposals would put senior citizens in front of "death panels" who would decide whether the sick and elderly would receive health care. Relying on new media technology, Palin communicated her message to her more than 500,000 Facebook "friends."[15] These dubious charges, which were transmitted through an unfiltered social networking site, came to dominate news and analysis of the health care reform discussion for several weeks.

Even in nondemocratic countries, the ruling elite have adapted the new media to help maintain their authority. In Cuba, the government banned full access to the Internet so as to block potential challenges to the state, creating a limited version of the Internet that allows citizens to send text messages through a national e-mail system. Although citizens cannot access search engines or foreign websites, and even though access does not extend to individual homes, state-controlled "Intranet" cafes are increasingly prevalent.[16] Other authoritarian regimes have also become quite savvy with new media. China pays a hand-picked group of citizens 50 cents for every pro-government comment they post online.[17] To control Internet content the Russian government uses "web brigades," which criticize opposition leaders and praise the government.[18]

---

[14] As of July 1, 2010, "Yes We Can – Barack Obama Music Video," with more than 20 million views ranked as the most watched video in the YouTube category of "politics and news."

[15] For a full transcript of Palin's initial statement, which she issued on August 7, 2009, go to http://www.facebook.com/note.php?note_id=113851103434.

[16] Daniel Wilkinson, "Can the Internet Bring Change to Cuba?" *New York Review of Books* blog, July 6, 2010. Retrieved from http://www.nybooks.com/blogs/nyrblog/2010/jul/06/can-internet-bring-change-cuba/.

[17] Ki Mae Heussner, "Why Tyrants Like Twitter," *ABC News*, October 26, 2009. Retrieved from http://abcnews.go.com/Technology/AheadoftheCurve/tweeting-tyrants-authoritarian-regimes-media/story?id=8917868&page=2.

[18] Web brigades are groups of government-hired Internet users. See Andrew Wilson, "Russia's Over-Managed Democracy," *European Council on Foreign Relations*,

In addition, human rights activists suggest that Iran allowed access to Facebook – although not to other websites – before the 2009 presidential election in order to identify dissenters.[19]

Put simply, we would be hard-pressed to identify any region of the world that has not been touched by the new media, the rapid changes in technology, and the broader access to information these technologies and media provide.[20] In some countries, the new media offer citizens and politicians at the local and national levels an opportunity to engage more easily with one another. In other less democratic countries reformers and activists battle with repressive regimes as both sides try to harness the power of new technologies. However, in both democratic and nondemocratic contexts, the question remains: Do changes in the information and media environment actually promote democratic ideals?

DEMOCRACY AND THE NEW MEDIA

Initially politicians, pundits, and journalists anticipated that the Internet and new media environment would enhance democratic practices in existing democracies and loosen the reins of government in authoritarian regimes. As early as 1989, U.S. President Ronald Reagan predicted, "The Goliath of totalitarianism will be brought down by the David of the microchip."[21] In 1999, presidential candidate George W. Bush remarked, "Imagine if the Internet took hold in China. Imagine how freedom would spread."[22] That same year, UN Secretary General Kofi Annan pronounced, "With their power to promote openness and transparency,

---

December 4, 2007. Retrieved from http://www.ecfr.eu/content/entry/commentary_wilson_on_russia_election_results. See also Joshua Kurlantzick, "The Web Doesn't Spread Freedom," *Newsweek*, May 10, 2010. Retrieved from http://www.newsweek.com/2010/04/30/the-internet-helps-build-democracies-oh-no-it doesn-t.print.html.

[19] Ibid.

[20] The United Nations has actively sought to bridge the digital divide, meeting with some success through the UN Information and Communication Technology (ICT) Task Force (see http://unicttaskforce.org). In addition, projects such as One Laptop Per Child aim to decrease the gap by developing low-cost, low-power connected laptops to children in developing countries (see http://www.laptop.org).

[21] Reagan is quoted in Sheila Rule, "Reagan Gets a Red Carpet from British," *New York Times*, June 14, 1989. Retrieved from http://www.nytimes.com/1989/06/14/world/reagan-gets-a-red-carpet-frombritish.html.

[22] Bush at Phoenix, Arizona GOP Debate on December 7, 1999, quoted in Lokman Tsui, "Internet Opening up China: Fact or Fiction?" Paper presented at Media in Transition Conference, Boston, May 10–12, 2002. Retrieved from http://web.mit.edu/cms/Events/mit2/Abstracts/LOKMANTSUI.pdf.

telecoms are leaving tyrants, polluters and ineffective governments fewer places to hide."[23] More recently, Tom Brokaw, the legendary anchor of the *NBC Nightly News*, asserted that bloggers represented the "democratization of the news."[24] And U.S. Senator Mark Warner, a former telecom executive, contended that bloggers can "potentially creat[e] a new public square for democracy" (Davis 2009, 5).

This is not to say that political actors and media personalities are not cognizant of the costs associated with the power of the Internet. In speaking to a group of journalism students at New York University, Brian Williams, the current anchor of the *NBC Nightly News*, famously condemned bloggers as newsmakers: "Now I'm up against a guy named Vinny in an efficiency apartment in the Bronx who hasn't left the efficiency apartment in two years." Confirming Williams's criticism, his own blog – *The Daily Nightly* – at one point received fewer daily hits than the website *tvnewser.com*, which was started by a 19-year-old Towson State University student.[25] Overall, however, most pronouncements about the Internet and new media environment's democratizing potential have been cast in general and positive terms.

Matthew Hindman, in *The Myth of Digital Democracy* (2009), argues that evaluations of the democratizing role of the Internet depend on how democratization is defined. He notes that many commentators adopt an "Internet is good" perspective and therefore assume that it enhances the quality of democracy without identifying exactly how (Hindman 2009, 5). Indeed, general pronouncements of the positive influence of the Internet and digital age are difficult to refute normatively. However, the empirical evidence provided by political scientists who gauge improvement in democratic practices by looking at specific outcomes – including a more informed citizenry, increased political participation, greater freedom of expression in the marketplace of ideas, and the ease with which political leaders and organizations can mobilize citizens on behalf of an electoral candidate or political cause – is decidedly mixed.

---

[23] ITU Telecom Opening Ceremony, October 9, 1999. Retrieved from http://www.itu.int/telecom-wt99/press_service/information_for_the_press/press_kit/speeches/annan_ceremony.html.

[24] Brokaw is quoted in Julian Guthrie, "Fellow Anchors Defend Rather on Forged Papers," *San Francisco Chronicle*, October 3, 2004. Retrieved from http://articles.sfgate.com/2004-10-03/news/17450092_1_anchor-seat-tom-brokaw-media-critic-ken-auletta.

[25] See Kristen O'Gorman, "Brian Williams Weighs in on the New Media," *We Want Media*, April 6, 2007. Retrieved from http://journalism.nyu.edu/pubzone/wewantmedia/node/487. See also "Why Brian Williams' Blog is Striking," *cyberjournalist.net*, August 25, 2005. Retrieved from http://www.cyberjournalist.net/news/002840.php.

Let us turn first to the claim that the new media environment embodies a more *participatory culture* and therefore enhances democratic practices. For the last two decades, citizens have become increasingly able to interact with the news. With the growth of talk radio in the United States in the early 1990s, several programs began to incorporate citizen callers into their regular programming (Tolchin 1996). Following radio's lead, news websites began to ask readers to participate in online polls and provide their opinions on the issues of the day. More recently, many news stories posted online – whether in a traditional news outlet like the *Washington Post* or an online source like *slate.com* – allow readers to provide their feedback and debate their views with other readers. Further, most news websites, even traditional outlets such as *bbc.co.uk* or *latimes.com*, track and identify the most popular stories for readers to follow. In essence, news websites promote not only the stories identified as important by professional editors or journalists but also those in which viewers are most interested. The wide emergence of blogs in the early 2000s furthered this participatory trend by encouraging citizens to begin their own online publications as sources of news and commentary (Davis 2009; Kerbel 2009). These changes represent a dramatic shift from a time in which the average citizen's news and information gathering was a passive endeavor.

Although we might think that lower costs of political information and the ease of mobilization over the Internet will lead more people to participate in politics, no scholarly consensus has emerged on this issue. On the one hand, some investigators find that gathering political knowledge on the Internet leads to higher levels of turnout in U.S. presidential elections (Tolbert and McNeil 2003); that Internet mobilization can lead some inactive citizens to participate (Krueger 2002); and that the Internet has enabled nongovernment organizations (NGOs) to facilitate global civil society in countries around the world (Warkentin 2001). Yet somewhat surprisingly, most broad studies of the Internet and the digital age arrive at a different conclusion. Bruce Bimber (2003), one of the first scholars to analyze the connection between new media and politics, concludes that the Internet does not generate higher levels of political participation in the United States. M. Kent Jennings and Vicki Zeitner (2003) uncover no evidence of a positive relationship between Internet use and civic engagement. In fact, the results of Pippa Norris's (2001) cross-national study suggest that the Internet simply engages those who are already engaged. The same is true in the United States, where Markus Prior (2007) has argued that the Internet increases levels of political knowledge and engagement among those who are already politically active. Prior finds that many other citizens now turn away from politics and public affairs because of the ever-growing menu of entertainment options in the new media environments.

In addition to the mixed research on the extent to which the new media environment promotes a participatory culture, investigators have identified two troubling aspects of the new media environment. First and foremost, many scholars identify potentially problematic *personalized spheres of information*. Most notably, Cass Sunstein (2007) refers to the "Daily Me," Columbia journalism professor Todd Gitlin (1998) references citizens' "public sphericules" of information, and Farhad Manjoo (2008) writes about the "personal infosphere." Broadly speaking, each of these authors identifies as a central component of the new information atmosphere the ability of citizens to tailor very specifically the news and information they receive to their own personal interests and ideologies. In other words, people can navigate to the news in which they are interested and completely avoid information or viewpoints that run counter to their preexisting perspectives.

Consider, for instance, a politically liberal citizen in the United States. She can begin her day by reading the op-ed pages of the *New York Times* and return home from work to watch liberal-leaning MSNBC's evening news program, with hosts such as Rachel Maddow or Lawrence O'Donnell. Contrast her with a conservative who listens to talk radio show host Rush Limbaugh during the day and watches an hour or two of Fox News programming in the evening. Both citizens spend considerable time keeping up with public affairs. Yet they are presented with fundamentally different agendas and issue frames (Jamieson and Capella 2008). In fact, they likely will not be able to agree even on what might seem like a simple set of facts regarding political issues (Manjoo 2008). In terms of international politics, news consumers receive a very different take on the political affairs in the Middle East, for example, depending on whether they rely on the BBC, CNN International, or Aljazeera for their information.

Customizing the news to meet one's political views and preferences does not stop with the average politically interested citizen: Tailoring the news applies to policy makers as well. For instance, a leaked report of former U.S. Vice President Dick Cheney's travel guidelines revealed that he required all hotel rooms in which he stayed to have the television set tuned to the conservative Fox News channel.[26] Although choosing

---

[26] "Website Details Cheney's Hotel Comforts: 68 Degrees, Diet Sprite," *cnn.com*, March 24, 2006. Retrieved from http://www.cnn.com/2006/POLITICS/03/23/cheney.hotel/index.html.

news sources that reinforce one's perspective is not new, the new media environment expedites and reinforces this phenomenon.

An even more dramatic potential repercussion of the Daily Me, however, is the possibility that many citizens will remove politics and world affairs from their infosphere altogether (Prior 2007). As Cass Sunstein (2007, 7–8) posits, citizens may eventually reach a point in which they no longer have a common frame of reference for debate and deliberation of the most important issues of the day. Joseph Nye (2002, 10) goes so far as to argue that this type of "narrow-casting" of the news can "fragment the sense of community and legitimacy that underpins central governments . . . The greater agility of younger generations with the new technologies may further erode deference to age, authority and existing institutions."

The second unfavorable consequence of the new media environment that some scholars have focused on involves the *decline of conventional journalistic norms*. As traditional journalistic outlets shrink and blogs and other Internet outlets ascend to greater levels of prominence, citizens experience increasingly unfiltered news and information. Many blogs lack a traditional journalistic hierarchy in which an editor, who has the power to withhold publication, can demand writer accountability and accuracy (Davis 2009). Several news blogs and websites actually relish publishing unconfirmed rumors.[27] In 2004, for instance, *The Drudge Report* published the rumor that Democratic presidential nominee John Kerry had had an affair with a 20-year-old intern, a story that ultimately proved to have no validity.[28] Online and nonstop cable television news also loosens many of journalism's foundational principles, such as requirements for multiple sources and fact-checking, because traditional journalists must compete in this environment (Fox, Van Sickel, and Steiger 2007). Certainly network news divisions and big city newspapers that purport to have a commitment to objective and in-depth reporting have not always delivered accurate information on critical issues (Bennett, Lawrence, and Livingston 2007). Yet the new media environment's often unfiltered mass of information makes deciphering the quality of news far more difficult (Palfrey and Gasser 2008).

---

[27] In a National Press Club Speech on June 2, 1998, Matt Drudge asserted that he determined what to publish by "follow[ing] my conscience." Drudge said that he publishes rumors and gossip from "reliable" or "sincere" sources. For a transcript of the full speech, go to http://www.libertyroundtable.org/library/essay.drudge.html.

[28] Alexandra Polier, "The Education of Alexandra Polier," *New York Magazine*, May 21, 2005.

Clearly, the new media environment has changed radically the very nature of the production and distribution of news. What is less clear is the extent to which – if at all – these changes better inform consumers of news. Moreover, although the research does not substantiate claims about the democratic-enhancing effect of the new media on politics, much of this research was conducted before the advent of some of the newest tools, such as YouTube, Twitter, and Facebook. As the new media era continues to evolve and tech-savvy younger generations replace their older counterparts, it is critical to continue to examine the extent to which the new media environment advances political information and democratic ideals.

ORGANIZATION AND CONTRIBUTIONS TO THE VOLUME

We group the chapters in this volume into three sections, each of which addresses an aspect of the relationship between new media and politics. The first section focuses on the shifting media universe as it examines the political knowledge of citizens, the evolving role of television as a source of information, and the interplay between journalists and bloggers. In the second section of the volume, we turn to the manner in which the new media affect campaigns and elections. The final section assesses the relationship between the new media and governance; we cover topics such as citizen mobilization, elected officials' communication with their constituents, and new media integration into nondemocratic societies. Each chapter speaks to several of the following critical questions:

- Does the new media environment facilitate an informed and active citizenry?
- Has the new media environment altered the tone or substance of political discourse?
- Has the quality of news and information improved in the new media age?
- Have changes to the news and information environment affected the ease of governing?
- How does the new information environment affect political norms and practices?
- Has government accountability increased or decreased in the new media environment?

Our examination of the shifting media universe within the context of American politics begins with Zoe Oxley's chapter, "More Sources,

Better Informed Public? New Media and Political Knowledge." Oxley argues that a larger number of media sources and increased access do not lead to a more informed citizenry. Relying on survey data over the past 20 years, she finds that citizens have not gained higher levels of political knowledge and actually may be more easily misled in the new media environment. Oxley's evidence and analysis reveal that the purported democratic ideals of an increasingly informed citizenry have yet to be realized.

Whereas Oxley focuses on changes in political knowledge in the new media era, Jeffrey Jones addresses changes in the tone and content of the old media – television – in this new era. In Chapter 2, "Rethinking Television's Relationship to Politics in the Post-Network Era," Jones reminds us that television remains the most relied on source of information for most U.S. citizens. However, he argues that the conceptions of news, entertainment, and audience have changed dramatically over the last 20 years. More specifically, television news organizations are brands, traditional entertainment programming has become an important outlet for public affairs, and the audience has been transformed from passive receivers of information into active users. Together, these changes in the tone and substance of political discourse on television affect how citizens come to know the news of the world.

Richard Davis concurs that political discourse has changed, but contends that it is not clear whether this change translates into higher quality political information. In Chapter 3, "Interplay: Political Blogging and Journalism," Davis systematically investigates the relationship between traditional journalists and the new media's bloggers. He demonstrates that bloggers shape journalism, but at the same time, garner much of their information from mainstream news. Davis concludes that although the style of news and information has changed, in part because of bloggers, the quality of information has seen little, if any, improvement.

Ultimately, these three chapters pertaining to the shifting media universe highlight changes in the form and substance of news. Citizens receive information from a multitude of sources, television news has been substantially transformed over the past few years, and bloggers represent a critical influence on the information environment. Yet even though citizens have more sources and easier access to information, nothing suggests that these transformations have resulted in widespread changes in political awareness.

The second section of the volume focuses on the ways in which the media environment influences the electoral process, both in the United

States and Europe. In "YouTube and TV Advertising Campaigns: Obama versus McCain in 2008," Ann Crigler, Marion Just, Lauren Hume, Jesse Mills, and Parker Hevron examine campaign advertising in the 2008 U.S. presidential election, the first election in which presidential candidates could use YouTube. They find that politicians tailor their advertising strategies based on differences between television and Internet audiences. Although presidential elections in the United States are certainly dynamic endeavors, the findings in this chapter highlight how the Obama campaign used new technology to reach out to and mobilize citizens more effectively than did other recent presidential campaign, thereby suggesting that citizen mobilization can more readily occur in the new media era.

In Finland, candidates also actively integrate new media into their campaigns, particularly in national elections. As Tom Carlson and Kim Strandberg reveal in Chapter 5, "The Rise of Web Campaigning in Finland," however, engagement with voters has not reached the same levels as in the United States. In their analysis of national and European Parliamentary elections, Carlson and Strandberg find that most politicians now incorporate some form of new media into their campaigns, but still very few offer any kind of interactive features, such as chats and discussion boards. This is the case regardless of the demographic profile of the candidate. The authors conclude, therefore, that the evolution of website adoption by candidates in Finland has been "less than revolutionary."

The integration of new media into other European campaigns and elections lies in even starker contrast to their use in the United States. In Chapter 6, "E-Campaigns in Old Europe: Observations from Germany, Austria, and Switzerland" Urs Gasser and Jan Gerlach focus on the slow adaption of new media in some highly advanced democracies. Although they uncover a technology-enabled trend toward better distribution of political information in those countries, Gasser and Gerlach also find that, in contrast to the rampant use of these new technologies in politics in the United States, German-speaking countries surprisingly continue to rely on traditional forms of media for political campaigns. The limited implementation of new technology, they argue, is likely based on the entrenched cultural values that emphasize tradition. Thus, the new media have done little to transform democratic practices in these countries.

Overall, this section of the volume demonstrates that, even across advanced democracies, politicians do not uniformly integrate the new media into their political campaigns. Not all nations use new media technologies to the same extent, and cultural norms that emphasize tradition over change, the presence of strong party systems, and different incentives for adopting new technologies can affect the implementation of new media tools.

The final section of the volume analyzes the extent to which new media positively influence political engagement, discourse, and knowledge. The first two chapters in this section focus specifically on how elected leaders navigate the new media environment to communicate with constituents. In Chapter 7, "Preaching to the Choir or Converting the Flock: Presidential Communication Strategies in the Age of Three Medias," Matthew A. Baum finds that the expansion of the Internet, along with digital cable technology and the rise of "soft news," further fragments the media landscape. More specifically, it ushers in a proliferation of partisan niche media that allow consumers to limit their news exposure to information that largely confirms their preexisting beliefs. Politicians who master the various media can achieve success, as in the case of Barack Obama's 2008 presidential election win. However, when the context moves from campaigning to legislating, presidents must adopt a multipronged strategy to deal with the increasingly distinct components of the news and information environment. Ultimately, Baum argues that political leaders must recognize the different ways in which citizens learn about public affairs and then develop more targeted communication strategies accordingly.

Complementing Baum's work on presidential communication, Jennifer Lawless turns to the legislative branch of government and discusses how members of Congress are using social media tools in Chapter 8. In "Twitter and Facebook: New Ways for Members of Congress to Send the Same Old Messages?," Jennifer L. Lawless examines how members of Congress use social networking sites to communicate with their constituents. Her detailed analysis of every tweet and Facebook post issued by every member of Congress over an eight-week period in summer 2009 provides a nuanced assessment of the content of the messages transmitted through these new media. Lawless does find that Republicans are more likely than Democrats to rely on these new forms of communication, but ultimately, she concludes that Twitter and Facebook simply provide new ways to communicate with constituents: They have yet to significantly alter the substance of political communication.

Turning from communication strategies to policy making, Matthew R. Kerbel in Chapter 9, "The Dog That Didn't Bark: Obama, Netroots Progressives, and Health Care Reform," discusses the ways in which netroots activists influenced the health care debate in the United States. Kerbel argues that the inclusion of a public health care option in the reform proposals that emerged can be attributed in large part to the net-roots activists' shrewd use of the Internet to pressure congressional pro-gressives. These activists demonstrated that a self-selected Internet-based elite could successfully alter the political calculations of a Washington-based political elite by applying to governance the social networking tech-niques that proved effective during political campaigns. Kerbel concludes that Obama's strategic decision to eschew a health care strategy built around the Internet and his netroots supporters was understandable, but it also highlights the distinction between Internet politics in campaigns and in the policy-making process.

The final chapter of this section offers a comparative perspective on the new media and governance. In "New Media and Political Change: Lessons from Internet Users in Jordan, Egypt, and Kuwait," Deborah L. Wheeler and Lauren Mintz argue that new media enhance the ability of citizens in the Arab world to voice their political opinions and organize for more accountable and representative governments. Their case studies of Jordan, Egypt, and Kuwait provide evidence of changing norms and social practices that contribute to a more knowledgeable and active citizenry. Wheeler and Mintz assert that these changes, largely enabled by new media, empower citizens to challenge non-democratic regimes in a new way. Their findings help us to understand the foundations of the 2011 "Twitter revolutions" in the Middle East and North Africa. While these new media-driven changes and events might lead us to expect more citizen participation in government, Wheeler and Mintz conclude that we must be cautious about such optimism.

In its entirety, this volume extends our knowledge and understanding of how changes in the media environment continue to affect politics in the United States and around the globe. More specifically, three central lessons emerge from the contributions we include. First, scholars and commentators must present information about the effects of new media on politics in a nuanced fashion that accounts for different modes of communication. As the findings in this volume indicate, we have reached the point in the digital age in which generalizations are no longer useful; rather, we must focus on specific components, such as YouTube, Twitter, Facebook, or blogs, if we are to assess accurately their effects on politics. Second, context matters when evaluating how citizens and politicians use the new media. When we consider "context" in terms of types of political regime, for example, it becomes clear that politicians in democracies use new media tools quite differently than do leaders in authoritarian regimes. Even within democracies, the use of new media varies. Together, chapters in this volume demonstrate that whereas the new technologies can often organize and mobilize supporters during a political campaign, they are often less successful in affecting the policy-making process.

Finally, the majority of contributors to this volume suggest, that while the form and tools of politics and communication have changed, the new media environment has been limited in the extent to which it has improved the quality of democratic practices. In democracies and non-democracies, the perceived changes brought about by new technologies may be more superficial than genuine. It is still unclear whether or not new media are sufficient or necessary to enact real political change. For example, as of this writing, the social-media savvy protesters who toppled the Egyptian authoritarian regime led by Hosni Mubarek are now skeptical that the current military rulers will cede power to civilians after the scheduled elections in November 2011.[29]

Adding to the uncertainty of whether or not new media bring us closer to democratic ideals is the fact that *more* information does not necessarily mean *better* information. While we may strive for better informed and politically active citizens, they are faced with a plethora of information that they must sift through to form their opinions – a task not only time-consuming, but also potentially frustrating. Moreover, just because new media provide more pathways to interact with others, does not mean the quality of those relationships increases. While these new media may seem like they better connect politicians with their constituents, politicians may be more restrained in their communications (e.g., the potentially viral consequences as seen in the 2011 fall of U.S. Congressman Anthony Weiner).

The information and technological revolution that began in the early 1990s continues in earnest. As new devices and modes of communication regularly emerge on the political scene, it is critical for scholars to monitor and assess their effects. This volume serves that role and offers the most recent snapshot of the relationship between new media and politics.

References

Baum, Matthew A. 2003. *Soft News Goes to War*. Princeton, NJ: Princeton University Press.

Bennett, W. Lance, Regina G. Lawrence, and Steven Livingston. 2007. *When the Press Fails: Political Power and the News Media from Iraq to Katrina*. Chicago: University of Chicago Press.

---

[29] Marwa Awad, "Egypt protesters fear army resisting real change," Reuters, July 28, 2011. Retrieved from http://af.reuters.com/article/commoditiesNews/idAFL6E7ISoD 920110728?pageNumber=2&virtualBrandChannel=0.

Bimber, Bruce. 2003. *Information and American Democracy: Technology in the Evolution of Political Power*. New York: Cambridge University Press.

Davis, Richard. 2009. *Typing Politics*. New York: Oxford University Press.

Davis, Richard, and Diana Owen. 1998. *New Media and American Politics*. New York: Oxford University Press.

Fox, Richard, Robert W. Van Sickel, and Thomas L. Steiger. 2007. *Tabloid Justice: Criminal Justice in the Age of Media Frenzy*, 2nd ed. Boulder, CO: Rienner.

Galston, William A. 2002. "The Impact of the Internet on Civic Life: An Early Assessment." In Elaine C. Kamarck and Joseph S. Nye (eds.), *Governance.com: Democracy in the Information Age* (pp. 1–16), Washington, DC: Brookings.

Gitlin, Todd. 1998. "Public Sphere or Public Sphericules?" In Tamar Liebes and James Curran (eds.), *Media, Ritual and Identity* (pp. 175–202), London: Routledge.

Gray, Jonathan, Jeffrey P. Jones, and Ethan Thompson. 2009. *Satire TV: Politics and Comedy in the Post-Network Era*. New York: New York University Press.

Hindman, Matthew. 2007. "Reflections on the First Digital Campaign." In Doris Graber (ed.), *Media Power in Politics*, 5th edition (pp. 192–201), Washington, DC: CQ Press.

Hindman, Matthew. 2009. *The Myth of Digital Democracy*. Princeton, NJ: Princeton University Press.

Jamieson, Kathleen Hall, and Joseph N. Capella. 2008. *Echo Chamber: Rush Limbaugh and the Conservative Media Establishment*. New York: Oxford University Press.

Jennings, M. Kent, and Vicki Zeitner. 2003. "Internet Use and Civic Engagement: A Longitudinal Analysis." *Public Opinion Quarterly* 67: 311–34.

Kerbel, Matthew R. 2009. *Netroots: Online Progressives and the Transformation of American Politics*. New York: Paradigm.

Krueger, Brian. 2002. "Assessing the Impact of Internet Political Participation the United States: A Resource Approach." *American Political Research* 30: 476–98.

Manjoo, Farhad. 2008. *True Enough: Learning to Live in a Post-Fact Society*. Hoboken, NJ: Wiley.

Norris, Pippa. 2001. *Digital Divide: Civic Engagement, Information Poverty, and the Internet in Democratic Societies*. New York: Cambridge University Press.

Norris, Pippa. 2002. "Revolution, What Revolution? The Internet and U.S. Elections, 1992–2000." In Elaine C. Kamarck and Joseph S. Nye (eds.), *Governance.com: Democracy in the Information Age* (pp. 59–80), Washington, DC: Brookings.

Nye, Joseph. 2002. "Information Technology and Democratic Governance." In Elaine C. Kamarck and Joseph S. Nye (eds.), *Governance.com: Democracy in the Information Age* (pp. 1–16), Washington, DC: Brookings.

Palfrey, John, and Urs Gasser. 2008. *Born Digital: Understanding the First Generation of Digital Natives*. New York: Basic Books.

Prior, Markus. 2007. *Post-Broadcast Democracy*. New York: Cambridge University Press.

Sunstein, Cass. 2007. *Republic.com 2.0*. Princeton, NJ: Princeton University Press.

Talbot, David. 2008, September/October. "How Obama Really Did It: The Social-Networking Strategy that Took an Obscure Senator to the Doors of the White House." *Technology Review*. Retrieved from http://www.technology review.com.

Tolbert, Caroline J., and Ramona S. McNeil. 2003. "Unraveling the Effects of the Internet on Political Participation." *Political Research Quarterly* 56: 175–85.

Tolchin, Susan J. 1996. *The Angry American: How Voter Rage is Changing the Nation*. Boulder, CO: Westview.

Warkentin, Craig. 2001. *Reshaping World Politics: NGOs, the Internet, and Global Civil Society*. Lanham, MD: Rowman and Littlefield.

THE SHIFTING MEDIA UNIVERSE AND NEWS CONSUMERS

More Sources, Better Informed Public? New Media and Political Knowledge

Zoe M. Oxley

In fall 1993, early in President Bill Clinton's tenure, he proposed a major overhaul of the nation's health care system. Debate over this proposal received sustained attention from media organizations throughout 1994 until congressional leaders announced that the reforms did not have enough support to pass. Fast-forward 15 years and a similarly high level of attention was placed on President Barack Obama's attempt to reform the health care system. Again, a rancorous political debate broke out, and intense media attention and scrutiny followed.

These two health care policy debates occurred in considerably different media environments.[1] To keep on top of political developments in 1993, most Americans relied on ABC, CBS, or NBC evening news broadcasts, daily newspapers, or both. Some consulted cable television channels, radio, and newsmagazines for political news, although these media audiences were considerably smaller than for network television and newspapers. An important development in radio had been the resurgence of political radio, or talk radio. Rush Limbaugh, a conservative who had frequently criticized Clinton's health care reform proposals, hosted one of the most popular talk radio shows in the nation.

By 2009, the American public had access to many more political news outlets. In 15 years, the number of cable news channels had increased, the format of these shows had diversified, and political topics had become more common on entertainment-focused cable television shows. More

---

[1] Descriptions of media consumption in these introductory paragraphs draw primarily from chapters 3–5 of Prior (2007) and Pew Research Center for the People and the Press (2009).

people tuned into cable television shows than in the early 1990s, partly because of cable expansion to previously unserved areas. Limbaugh's show was still on the airwaves, as were other liberal and conservative talk radio shows. More significant, however, the Internet had emerged as an important source of political information, approaching newspapers in the percentage of the public turning to it for national and international news.

These changes in the media environment made following the intricacies of the health care reform debate in 2009–10 very easy. One could still read about yesterday's news in the morning newspaper and listen to radio news headlines or political talk radio during the commute. At home, the network evening news shows still carried a summary of the day's events. However, for those unable to catch, or who were uninterested in watching, network evening news shows, coverage of the day's happenings appeared on various cable channels all evening long. Some shows presented headlines and straight news reporting, whereas other programs, such as *The O'Reilly Factor* on Fox News or *The Rachel Maddow Show* on MSNBC, evaluated the developments from different political perspectives. Over on Comedy Central, policy debates received coverage on the satirical "fake news" shows, *The Daily Show with Jon Stewart* and *The Colbert Report*. In addition, information could be accessed 24/7 from a computer, BlackBerry, iPhone, or other portable electronic device. The variety of websites covering political events was staggering, ranging from online versions of other news media outlets to Internet-only news sites (such as Google news) to official government sites (e.g., www.whitehouse.gov) to blogs written by people from all political persuasions and with every level of expertise.

As the health care example and discussion of media changes in the Introduction reveal, the United States is in the midst of a news and information revolution. New media allow the public more choices for news today than ever before: News consumers can choose when to access news, how to access news, the presentation mode (print, audio, audiovisual, interactive, etc.), and content (e.g., factual reports versus political commentary, in-depth reports versus headline news, serious coverage versus humorous presentations). Yet has this explosion in the number and variety of outlets for political information resulted in a better informed public? Whether these changes to the media environment have resulted in higher levels of political knowledge among the American public is the focus of this chapter.

The public's knowledge of political matters is a topic of longstanding interest among scholars of American public opinion, mass media, and communication as well as among democratic theorists. The following two quotations succinctly summarize one normative view of this topic: "[D]emocracy functions best when its citizens are politically informed," and "[p]olitical information is to democratic politics what money is to economics: it is the currency of citizenship" (Delli Carpini and Keeter 1996, 1, 8). This view holds that people who are knowledgeable about politics are better able to determine their preferences, connect their interests to specific public policies, communicate their views to political leaders, and hold leaders accountable on Election Day. Fulfilling the responsibilities of citizenship in a democratic society is easier for people who are politically knowledgeable.

However, not all agree that democracy requires a highly knowledgeable public. Instead, some democratic theorists would prefer that only interested and knowledgeable people engage in politics; they believe that most people do not know enough about politics to participate meaningfully (Berelson, Lazarsfeld, and McPhee 1954; Schumpeter 1976). Other scholars have argued that the public can make reasonable political decisions (whether to support a specific policy proposal, which candidate to vote for, etc.) even if they cannot correctly answer factual questions about political issues and leaders (Graber 2001). Cues abound in the environment, such as the issue positions of trusted leaders and groups, to help the public fulfill its democratic duties (Ferejohn and Kuklinski 1990; Popkin 1994; Sniderman, Brody, and Tetlock 1991).

Despite these varying conclusions about the necessity for democracy of a well-informed public, in one way or another, these arguments focus on the role that public knowledge can and should play in a democratic society. Thus regardless of one's normative position, understanding the levels and sources of political knowledge among the public is important for evaluating the state of democracy. Later sections of this chapter present research findings from others, as well as original analyses, to illustrate the ways in which changes in the media and information environment have influenced political knowledge. However, to provide important background for this examination of new media and public knowledge, the next section provides a brief overview of political knowledge in the traditional (old) media environment.

POLITICAL KNOWLEDGE IN THE TRADITIONAL MEDIA ERA

Among scholars of politics, political knowledge generally refers to factual political information held by members of the public. As Michael Delli

Carpini and Scott Keeter (1996, 10) put it, political knowledge is "the range of factual information about politics that is stored in long-term memory." Similarly, Markus Prior (2007, 28) defines political knowledge as "knowledge of specific political facts and concepts as well as knowledge of recent noteworthy political events."

Within these broad definitions, it is useful to distinguish among specific types of political knowledge. In their classic study of political knowledge, Delli Carpini and Keeter (1996) identify three categories: (1) rules of the game, (2) substance of politics, and (3) people and players. Rules-of-the-game knowledge focuses on the structure of government, such as the duties of each branch of the federal government, what civil liberties are contained in the Bill of Rights, and how the Electoral College works. Knowledge of the substance of politics emphasizes activities of government, most notably, "what the issues are, what their history is, what the relevant facts are, what alternatives are proposed" (Berelson, Lazarsfeld, and McPhee 1954, 308). Finally, knowing political people and players entails awareness of current leaders of the United States and other nations as well as where these leaders and important political groups (e.g., the Democratic and Republican parties) stand on key issues of the day. Although knowledge of all three types of information can be gleaned from the news media, knowledge of the second and third types – the substance of politics, and people and players – is especially likely to come from the media. In contrast, many people learn about the first kind of knowledge, rules of the game, in educational settings rather than from the news. Thus this chapter focuses on the second two categories of knowledge.

Levels of knowledge vary across individuals, of course, and understanding this variation has been a key topic pursued by scholars of political knowledge. Not surprisingly, many individual characteristics, such as race, sex, age, education, and income, relate to knowledge (Bennett 1989; Delli Carpini and Keeter 1996; Jerit, Barabas, and Bolsen 2006; Neuman, Just, and Crigler 1992; Prior 2007). Among these, the single best predictor of knowledge is education. Citizens with more years of formal education tend to possess higher levels of political knowledge because education increases both the cognitive ability to learn about politics and one's interest in politics. The more people are interested in politics, the more they are motivated to learn political information.

Beyond individual ability and motivation, the opportunity to learn about politics influences political knowledge. Recognizing this fact naturally draws our attention to the broader political context, notably the information environment. All else being equal, when news media devote more attention to politics and government, levels of political knowledge among the public are higher (Barabas and Jerit 2009; Jerit et al. 2006). Furthermore, people who are more attentive to news media coverage of politics are more knowledgeable (Delli Carpini and Keeter 1996; Neuman et al. 1992; Prior 2007). These two findings make perfect sense, given that most of us learn about current political topics through the news media. Because knowledge expands when the news media devote more attention to politics, the recent explosion in the number of news sources presumably should have increased public knowledge of politics. Furthermore, in the new media environment, it is easier to access many new news sources. With 24-hour cable television news shows and countless online political sites available any time of the day or night, political information is readily accessible for many. Therefore, would not a better informed public result?

Perhaps, but the relationship between the new media environment and political knowledge might be more complex. In fact, research on knowledge in the old media environment suggests such complexity. For example, as the news environment provides more political information to the citizenry, the same knowledge gains do not occur in all people. Better educated citizens tend to learn more from this extra media attention than the less educated, which further increases the knowledge gap between these two groups (Barabas and Jerit 2009; Jerit et al. 2006). Why? The well educated are better able to process new information gleaned from the news as well as to integrate this information with their existing knowledge.

Furthermore, the effect of traditional news media on public knowledge varies by medium, particularly print versus television. The presentation of news on television is easier to digest than news in print, perhaps because of television's audiovisual format, the factual and less explanatory focus of print, or a combination of both (Eveland and Scheufele 2000; Graber 2001; Neuman 1976). Put another way, compared with television news, newspapers use "more cognitively taxing news formats" (Jerit et al. 2006, 268). Thus among newspaper readers, knowledge gains are greatest for those who have higher levels of education (Jerit et al. 2006) or cognitive skill (Neuman et al. 1992). Knowledge gains from television viewing do not vary as much by education level, although they vary by cognitive skill; gains are greatest for viewers with high cognitive ability (Neuman et al. 1992). These conclusions remind us that news sources vary in important ways that have implications for knowledge gain. Analyses of new media and knowledge should therefore consider differences across media sources in how political topics are covered and presented.

HAVE KNOWLEDGE LEVELS INCREASED IN THE NEW MEDIA ENVIRONMENT?

To explore whether public knowledge is higher now with recent developments in new media, we turn first to a 2007 political knowledge survey conducted by the Pew Research Center for the People and the Press. This survey included nine questions comparable to those asked on earlier surveys (most from 1989). Respondents were asked to name the vice president, their governor, and the leader of Russia and to identify the Speaker of the House of Representatives, the secretary of defense, and an administration official involved in a scandal (specifically, John Poindexter and Lewis "Scooter" Libby). They were also asked whether they knew that the United States had a trade deficit, which party was the majority party in the House, and the ideology of the chief justice of the Supreme Court.

As demonstrated in Table 1.1, the percentage of the public that correctly answered these questions declined over time for five items and increased for four items. For two items, the percentage point changes in knowledge were substantial: The percentage of the public correctly identifying the Speaker of the House increased from 14% to 49%, whereas the percentage able to identify the official involved in a scandal declined

TABLE 1.1. *Knowledge of Political Leaders and Events, 1989 and 2007*

	1989	2007	Difference
Percentage Who Correctly Named:			
The U.S. vice president	74%	69%	−5
Their state's governor	74	66	−8
The president of Russia*	47	36	−11
Percentage Who Knew:			
U.S. has a trade deficit	81	68	−13
The party controlling the House	68	76	+8
The chief justice is conservative	30	37	+7
Percentage Who Correctly Identified:			
Tom Foley/Nancy Pelosi	14	49	+35
Richard Cheney/Robert Gates	13	21	+8
John Poindexter**/Scooter Libby	60	29	−31

Notes: *Earlier data from 1994; **Earlier data from 1990.
Source: Pew Research Center for the People and the Press (2007, 1).

from 60% to 29%. Both of these changes are likely due to differences in media attention paid to these individuals, thus confirming what we already know: Media coverage can be related to political knowledge. Yet the overall conclusion from these survey data seems clear: "[C]hanging news formats are not having a great deal of impact on how much the public knows about national and international affairs" (Pew Research Center for the People and the Press 2007, 1). The greater variety in type of news sources, as well as the increased accessibility of political news, has not resulted in a more knowledgeable public.[2]

Although we do not see any increase in political knowledge among the aggregate public, perhaps some changes are evident among those with different levels of education. Of the nine knowledge questions contained on the Pew survey, five used identical wording in 1989 and in 2007.[3] When examining responses to these questions by education, two important conclusions emerge. First, the percentage correctly answering at least four of these five questions declined for *all* levels of education. Second, the percentage point decline was greater for high school graduates compared with college graduates. More specifically, 41% of people with no more than a high school education answered at least four questions correctly in 1989 compared with only 30% in 2007 (a decrease of 11 percentage points). The decrease among college graduates was only six points (80% in 1989 versus 74% in 2007). This smaller decrease among college graduates results in a larger knowledge gap by education level in 2007 compared with 1989.

Markus Prior (2005, 2007) also explores the relationship between education and knowledge in the new media environment. He provides a compelling explanation for why political knowledge has not increased as political information has become more available: Choice is to blame. As political news sources have expanded over past decades, so have entertainment sources. When given the choice between turning to media for political information or nonpolitical information, many citizens choose

---

[2] Reaching even further back in time, Delli Carpini and Keeter (1996) demonstrate that political knowledge levels remained roughly the same between the 1940s and 1989. Many changes in telecommunications occurred over those decades, including the spread of television to nearly all U.S. households and the introduction of cable television. As is the case with recent additions of media sources of political news, these earlier changes to the information environment did not produce significant increases in public knowledge of politics and government.

[3] These five knowledge questions were about the vice president's and state governor's names, whether the United States has a trade deficit, the majority party in the House of Representatives, and the chief justice's ideology.

the latter. Prior argues that these media preferences contribute strongly to political knowledge levels today and explain why knowledge levels have remained largely stagnant despite a more information-rich environment. He also documents that today media preferences are more strongly related to knowledge level than to educational level and that part of the knowledge gap by education can be attributed to differences in media preferences by education level (college graduates are a bit more likely than others to prefer news media over other types of media; see Prior 2007).

As evidence for this conclusion, Prior (2005, 2007) presents survey results that asked respondents which type of television shows they most like to watch. On the basis of their responses, he classified people as preferring entertainment, news, or something in between. Fully 50% of respondents were indifferent toward the news: They did not dislike it, but did not list it as one of their top four preferred television genres. Another 3% plainly disliked television news shows. When comparing people's relative preference for entertainment versus news to their knowledge levels, Prior uncovered a conditional relationship. Specifically, those who showed no interest in television news were less knowledgeable than those who preferred some news, but *only* if they had access to the new media sources of cable television and the Internet. That is, for people without cable television or Internet access, a preference for entertainment or news was not related to political knowledge. However, when people have both cable television and Internet access, knowledge levels were significantly higher (as much as 27% higher) for those people who preferred news rather than entertainment. The current high-choice media environment allows people to "abandon the news for entertainment simply because they like it better" (Prior 2005, 578). One result is lower levels of political knowledge for these entertainment fans.[4]

POLITICAL KNOWLEDGE BY MEDIA SOURCE

So far, it seems that increased news media options have not resulted in increased political knowledge levels among the overall public. However,

---

[4] In their study of news grazers, Jonathan Morris and Richard Forgette reach a similar conclusion. News grazers, people who watch the television with "remote control in hand, flipping to other channels when [they are] not interested in the topic" (Morris and Forgette 2007, 97), are less knowledgeable about political topics than are nonnews grazers. Morris and Forgette attribute this difference to news grazers' preference for sports, entertainment, and weather information over news about politics and government.

Prior's research does indicate that people who choose to consult news rather than entertainment media do have higher levels of political knowledge. In this section, I explore levels of political knowledge among those who are consumers of the news.

In addition to containing a battery of items testing knowledge of political information, the 2007 Pew survey also asked respondents whether they regularly consulted each of 16 different news sources. Both traditional media sources (e.g., local newspapers, broadcast television evening news) and new media sources (such as news websites, cable TV news channels, and *The Daily Show*) were listed. By conducting original analyses of this survey, I address questions beyond those answered by the Pew Research Center in the report referenced in the previous section. In particular, I examine whether a citizen's level of political knowledge is related to the number of news sources consulted, to the use of traditional versus new media sources, and to regularly consulted specific news sources. The new media environment is characterized by a larger number of news sources than ever before as well as by a wider variety of types of news sources. This section considers the relationship between knowledge and these features of the contemporary media universe.

The 2007 Pew survey contained 23 knowledge items – the 9 knowledge questions presented in Table 1.1 and 14 others. These additional questions covered the identification of politicians (e.g., Hillary Clinton, Barack Obama, and Harry Reid), awareness of political facts (that Rudy Giuliani ran for president in 2008, for example), and knowledge of contemporary policy debates (the minimum wage, troop surge in Iraq, etc.). According to how many questions they answered correctly, respondents were divided into high (15–23 correct), medium (10–14), and low (fewer than 10) knowledge groups. Overall, 35% possessed high levels of knowledge, 31% medium, and 34% low.

To examine whether knowledge levels vary by news consumption, I counted the number of news sources each respondent regularly consulted (of the 16 listed in the Pew survey).[5] The relationship between news consumption and level of political knowledge is graphically displayed in Figure 1.1. Individuals who rely on a larger number of news sources are

---

5 Across all respondents, the number of news sources regularly used ranges from 0 to 15; the average is 4.6. The news consumption series of questions began with the following: "Now I'd like to know how often you watch, listen to, or read some different news sources." Then, for each news source, respondents were asked, "Do you [watch/listen to/read]…regularly, or not?" For a list of the 16 sources contained in this series, refer to Table 1.2.

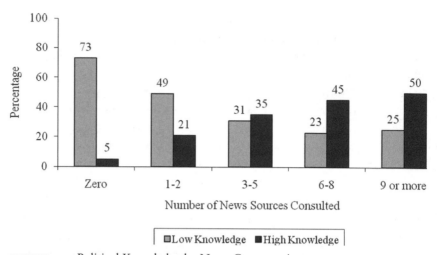

FIGURE 1.1. Political Knowledge by News Consumption.
Note: Bars represent the percentage of people consulting the specified number of news sources who possess low (high) levels of knowledge.

less likely to be in the low-knowledge group and more likely to possess high levels of knowledge. More specifically, 50% of people who regularly consume news from nine or more sources have high levels of knowledge, and only 25% have low knowledge levels. In contrast, only 5% of those who do not regularly consult any news sources possess high levels of knowledge, whereas nearly 75% have low levels of knowledge.

Among those who choose to follow the news, consulting more sources is related to higher levels of knowledge. This finding appears to bear out one potential benefit of the new media environment: More sources for news will lead to a more informed public. This relationship holds, at least, for those people who tune into the news. Yet does it matter which news sources are consulted? Does following the news in new media sources confer any knowledge acquisition advantages over consuming the news in traditional formats?

As a first foray into this new versus traditional comparison, Table 1.2 presents knowledge levels among audience members for each of the seven traditional and nine new media sources queried on the Pew survey. The first column indicates the percentage of each source's audience that possesses a high level of knowledge. The results clearly demonstrate that knowledge levels vary across news outlets and that, within both traditional and new media formats, there are audiences with high knowledge levels and those with low knowledge levels. The news outlets with a majority of their audiences categorized as high knowledge include

TABLE 1.2. *Political Knowledge and Education Level by News Source*

Regular Users of News Source	Percentage of Audience with a High Level of Knowledge	Percentage of Audience Who Are College Graduates	Percentage of Audience Who Regularly Use the Source
Traditional Media Sources:			
The NewsHour with Jim Lehrer (PBS)	53	32	14
National Public Radio	51	40	28
News magazines	48	36	23
Local daily newspaper	43	30	55
Network television evening news	38	26	46
Local television news	35	26	71
Network television morning shows	34	25	34
New Media Sources:			
The Daily Show/The Colbert Report	54	31	16
Websites of major newspapers	54	43	12
The O'Reilly Factor	51	24	17
Rush Limbaugh's radio show	50	36	8
Websites of television news stations	44	36	22
Internet-only sites (e.g., Google news)	41	36	25
CNN	41	30	39
Online political discussion blogs	37	26	11
Fox News Channel	35	22	43

Note: The total number of respondents for this survey was 3,331.
Source: Pew Research Center for the People and the Press (2007, a, 12) and additional analyses

both traditional (PBS's *The NewsHour with Jim Lehrer*, National Public Radio) and new media (*The Daily Show* and *The Colbert Report*, newspaper websites, *The O'Reilly Factor*, and Rush Limbaugh's radio show). Among those sources whose audiences are least likely to possess high levels of knowledge, traditional network television news shows (evening, local, *and* morning) and the new media sources of online blogs and Fox News appear.

By itself, this analysis cannot establish that knowledge levels are primarily a result of which news sources people use. Put differently, we cannot be sure that the quality and nature of the information contained in each source are the primary determinants of audience knowledge levels.

One complicating factor is that audiences for these specific sources differ in their demographic characteristics. Notably, the educational attainment of audience members is not the same across the news sources, as demonstrated in the second column of Table 1.2. The two sources whose audiences have the highest percentage of college graduates are National

Public Radio (40%) and the websites of major newspapers (43%). These sources also appear near the top of the list for knowledge levels of their audiences. Similarly, five sources with audiences possessing low percentages of college graduates (ranging from 22% to 26%) have audiences that display the lowest levels of political knowledge (evening, local, and morning network television news; online blogs; and the Fox News Channel). Thus, for these sources, it is difficult to know whether the audiences' knowledge levels are a product of individual characteristics, such as education, or of what they learn from these specific news sources. Both likely play a part. Furthermore, most people regularly consume news from more than one source, making it difficult to sort out which source contributes most to the knowledge levels presented in Table 1.2.

To control for these (and other) audience characteristics and to attempt to isolate the influence of media sources on knowledge, I performed two multivariate regression analyses. This procedure can simultaneously demonstrate the influence of many factors (such as education, sex, and media consumption) on a single outcome (in this case, political knowledge). The measure of political knowledge used for these analyses is the number of knowledge items a respondent answered correctly. Across the entire sample, the average number of correct answers was 12.1 (of a possible 23). As predictors of knowledge, I included demographic and political characteristics that others have found to be related to knowledge (e.g., Barabas and Jerit 2009; Moy 2008; Prior 2007). These predictors are education, sex, age, income, race, party identification, and enjoyment with keeping up with the news.[6] I assessed media consumption in two ways: (1) by the number of both traditional and new media sources regularly consulted and (2) whether the respondent is a regular consumer of each of the 16 media sources. The results from these analyses appear in Table 1.3.

These models confirm what others have found: Political knowledge is related to a variety of personal characteristics. Citizens with the following characteristics are more likely to be knowledgeable about politics: higher education, male, older, higher income, white, Republican or Democratic

---

[6] These variables are coded as follows: education in seven categories [ranging from (1) eighth-grade education or less to (7) postgraduate training]; male sex as 1 and female as 0; age as number of years old; income in six categories [1 = less than $20,000 to 6 = $100,000 and over]; white race as 1 and other races as 0; Republican Party identification as 1, all others as 0; Democratic Party identification as 1, all others as 0; and how much enjoy following the news in four levels [1 = not at all, 2 = not much, 3 = some, 4 = a lot].

TABLE 1.3. *Predicting Political Knowledge by Traditional and New Media Sources*

	Number of Traditional and New Media Sources	Specific Traditional and New Media Sources
Education	.96 (.05)***	.84 (.05)***
Male	2.28 (.14)***	2.16 (.14)***
Age	.05 (.00)***	.06 (.00)***
Income	.39 (.05)***	.35 (.05)***
White	1.20 (.18)***	.91 (.18)***
Republican	1.06 (.22)***	.82 (.22)***
Democratic	1.26 (.21)***	.90 (.21)***
Enjoyment of news	1.86 (.09)***	1.92 (.09)***
Traditional media sources	.08 (.05)	
The NewsHour with Jim Lehrer		−.29 (.22)
National Public Radio		.96 (.16)***
News magazines		−.10 (.18)
Local daily newspaper		.30 (.15)*
Network TV evening news		−.07 (.15)
Local TV news		.05 (.17)
Network TV morning shows		−.18 (.15)
New media sources	.23 (.05)***	
The Daily Show/The Colbert Report		1.71 (.20)***
Websites of major papers		1.01 (.24)***
The O'Reilly Factor		1.48 (.21)***
Rush Limbaugh		−.17 (.27)
TV news websites		−.19 (.19)
Internet-only news sites		.47 (.18)**
CNN		−.13 (.16)
Online political blogs		−.67 (.23)**
Fox News channel		−.81 (.16)***
Constant	−5.07 (.37)***	−4.05 (.38)***
Number of cases	2,771	2,680
Adjusted R^2	.51	.55

Note: Entries are ordinary least square (OLS) unstandardized coefficients with standard errors in parentheses. Statistical significance is noted as follows: ***$p < .001$; **$p < .01$; *$p < .05$.

(versus political Independents), or enjoy following the news. When it comes to the influence of traditional and new media consumption on knowledge levels, several interesting patterns emerge. First, when considering the *number* of both traditional and new media sources consulted (presented in the left column of Table 1.3), only the latter is significantly related to knowledge. That is, people who rely on more new media sources have higher levels of knowledge than those who rely on fewer new media sources. In contrast, the number of traditional media sources consulted is not related to one's level of political knowledge.

Not all media sources are alike. To see whether different sources are more (or less) likely to increase knowledge among their audience members, the second model treats each news source separately. Important differences across media sources exist (refer to the second column of Table 1.3). Although regularly consuming news from most traditional media sources is not related to political knowledge, consumers of two sources – National Public Radio (NPR) and the daily newspaper – have significantly higher levels of knowledge than people who do not rely on these news sources. More specifically, NPR listeners, on average, correctly answer one more political knowledge question than do nonlisteners (regression coefficient of .96). The impact of daily newspaper reading on knowledge is smaller (number of correct items is .30 higher than for nonreaders), yet still significant.

Among new media sources, six of the nine are related to knowledge. For four of these ("fake news" shows [*The Daily Show* or *The Colbert Report*], websites of major newspapers, *The O'Reilly Factor*, and Internet-only news sites), consumers have higher knowledge levels than nonaudience members. Furthermore, as coefficients in the table indicate, knowledge gains are substantial (more than one correct answer) for three: The number of correct answers was, on average, 1.7 higher among viewers of Jon Stewart or Stephen Colbert, 1.5 higher among those who tune in to Bill O'Reilly, and 1.0 higher for those who read websites of major newspapers compared with those who did not rely on these sources. Two other new media sources produce a different effect: lower levels of knowledge. That is, people who rely on these sources – Fox News and online political blogs – are less knowledgeable than those who do not consult these sources. Compared with nonviewers, viewers of Fox News answered .81 fewer questions correctly. The number correct among online blog readers was .67 lower than nonreaders.

Although the analyses presented here cannot identify the exact reasons why consuming specific news sources relates to higher (or lower) knowledge, the nature and quality of their content undoubtedly play a role. Newspapers, whether in print or online, are information rich and have long been assumed to contribute to a better informed citizenry. The satire of the two "fake news" shows is probably one reason why viewers of these shows have greater political knowledge than nonviewers. Processing and understanding satire require more effort and engagement with the shows' material than with straight news reports (Caufield 2008).

Differences between *The O'Reilly Factor* and other Fox News shows might also account for the finding that viewing the former increases knowledge, whereas watching the latter decreases knowledge. Although most shows on the Fox News Channel are understood to present politics from a conservative point of view, Fox shows differ in format. Notably, *The O'Reilly Factor* sometimes incorporates a debate format, with invited guests debating the show's host, Bill O'Reilly, and (occasionally) one another. Even though not all views are presented as equally valid or reasonable, the act of presenting multiple political views likely contributes to O'Reilly's viewers' displaying higher levels of knowledge than those who watch other Fox news shows. Finally, a closer look at which types of questions O'Reilly viewers were more likely to answer correctly than Fox viewers is illuminating. Of the 23 knowledge questions contained on the Pew survey, 15 focus on knowledge of people and players, and 8 on the substance of politics. Viewers of *The O'Reilly Factor* were more likely to answer all questions correctly than were those who watch other Fox shows, yet the difference in answering correctly was greater for questions about people than about substance (an average gap of 17.2% versus 8.9%). Although closer examination of the content of *The O'Reilly Factor* versus other Fox shows is needed to explain these differences, these results indicate that *The O'Reilly Factor* is more likely to convey information about key political leaders than are other Fox News Channel shows.

NEW MEDIA AND MISINFORMATION

One feature of the new media environment that merits further attention is the rise in the number of partisan information sources. This increase is, in part, due to changes in the market for news (Baum 2003; Nie et al. 2010). Since producing material for the Internet is cheaper (sometimes substantially so) than for traditional media sources, there is less pressure on Internet media organizations to attract a large audience. Thus, Internet news sources are more likely than traditional media to cater to news consumers of a specific political persuasion (e.g., liberal or conservative) or who are interested in narrowly defined political issues. In contrast, to recoup their production costs, the content of traditional news organizations is more likely to be politically centrist. The increase in partisan-oriented news is also apparent on cable television. As the number of cable news shows increased, competition for audiences also increased. In response, some cable channels attempted to appeal to politically narrower audiences, who might be unhappy with centrist news. The result of these market pressures has been cable channels with more obvious political leanings (such as conservative Fox and liberal MSNBC).

Media and public opinion scholars have begun to explore the influence of partisan news formats. Two hot topics are the fragmentation of the news audience into politically like-minded groups (Lawrence, Sides, and Farrell 2010; Sunstein 2001) and the polarization of attitudes as a result of individuals' selective exposure to news that supports their preexisting attitudes (Nie et al. 2010). However, very little attention has been devoted to knowledge effects. Partisan news sources are more focused on advocacy than on informing the public after all, so we might expect citizens who rely primarily on partisan news to be less informed than other members of the public. Indeed, results from my analyses suggest this might be so, demonstrating that online political blog readers and Fox News Channel viewers (excepting viewers of O'Reilly) are less knowledgeable than consumers of less partisan media sources.

In addition to decreasing levels of accurate knowledge, another possible effect of politically biased news sources is increasing levels of misinformation. When we examine how many people correctly answer factual questions about political topics, we focus on what portion of the public is informed about these topics. What about those who do not correctly answer these questions? They could be either uninformed or misinformed. James Kuklinski and his colleagues (2000, 792–3, emphasis in original) distinguish between these two this way: "If people do not hold factual beliefs at all, they are merely *un*informed. They are, with respect to the particular matter, in the dark. But if they firmly hold beliefs that happen to be wrong, they are *mis*informed – not just in the dark, but wrongheaded." Certainly, it can be difficult to determine whether someone who answers a question incorrectly is uninformed or misinformed. Further, for some types of political knowledge, the distinction between these two is not terribly important. Take rules-of-the-game knowledge, for example. The implications for confidently thinking that Congress can override a presidential veto with a three-fifths majority vote (misinformed) versus having absolutely no idea what it takes for Congress to override a veto (uninformed) are not that consequential. Yet holding incorrect beliefs about the substance of politics, particularly about public policies, can have significant consequences. Notably, these misperceptions can influence people's opinions toward the policy (Kuklinski et al. 2000; see also Jerit and Barabas 2006).

Studies of misinformation have been quite rare, so there is much we do not know about this topic. Two recent analyses, however, not only assessed levels of misinformation among the public but also linked these levels to people's primary news sources. These studies thus provide valuable insight into the role that the news media can play in creating misperceptions. In 2003, Steven Kull, Clay Ramsay, and Evan Lewis (2003–4) designed a survey to measure knowledge of facts related to the Iraq War. Their survey, conducted between June and September of that year, contained these three questions:

> Is it your impression that the US has or has not found clear evidence in Iraq that Saddam Hussein was working closely with the al Qaeda terrorist organization?
>
> Since the war with Iraq ended, is it your impression that the US has or has not found Iraqi weapons of mass destruction?
>
> Thinking about how all the people in the world feel about the US having gone to war with Iraq, do you think: The majority of people favor the US having gone to war; The majority of people oppose the US having gone to war; or Views are evenly balanced.

At the time this survey was conducted, the United States had not found evidence linking Saddam Hussein to al Qaeda, it had not found any weapons of mass destruction in Iraq, and a majority of the world's population opposed its war in Iraq. Any survey respondents who expressed beliefs contrary to these facts were thus misinformed about these matters. Overall, Kull, Ramsay, and Lewis found that 60% of their respondents held at least one of these three misperceptions. Furthermore, misinformation about the war in Iraq had consequences for opinion toward the war. People who held misperceptions were significantly more likely to believe that U.S. military intervention in Iraq had been the right thing to do. For example, 23% of those with none of the three misperceptions supported the war. A slight majority (53%) of those holding one misperception supported the war, whereas fully 80% of people having all three misperceptions supported the war in Iraq.

What role did the news media play in contributing to the public's holding these misperceptions? To address this question, Kull, Ramsay, and Lewis compared levels of misinformation by respondents' primary news source. They uncovered tremendous variation in misperceptions by source (see the gray bars in Figure 1.2). Across the three items, the average rate of misinformation was 45% for people whose primary source of news was the Fox News Channel. However, only 11% of those relying

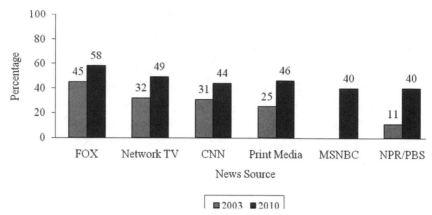

FIGURE 1.2. Misinformation by News Source, 2003 and 2010.
Note: Bars represent the average percentage of misperception-holding by news source. *Sources:* Adapted from Kull, Ramsay, and Lewis (2003–4, 582) and Ramsay et al. (2010, 20–3).

primarily on one of the two public broadcasting outlets (NPR or PBS) were misinformed. Between Fox News and public broadcasters, average levels of misperception-holding were 32% for network news viewers,[7] 31% for CNN viewers, and 25% for users of print media (newspapers or magazines) as their main news source.

Kull, Ramsay, and Lewis (2003–4) also examined whether factors such as party affiliation and support for President George W. Bush were related to misperception-holding surrounding the Iraq War. Many factors were related, especially support for President Bush. Yet one's primary news source also strongly predicted misinformation. Put differently, watching Fox News, *in and of itself*, independently contributed to the likelihood of misperceptions. Kull, Ramsay, and Lewis point to Fox News's coverage of the war in Iraq to explain this finding. Three misperceptions held by the public relate to articulated Bush administration statements as reasons for the United States' invasion of Iraq. Some media outlets were "[r]eluctant to challenge the administration" and thus were a "means of transmission for the administration, rather than a critical filter" (Kull et al. 2003–4, 593).

Clay Ramsay and his colleagues conducted a similar survey the week after the 2010 midterm elections. The 2010 survey contained 11 items that tapped public knowledge of a wide range of topics, all of which were

---

[7] The rate of misperception-holding for each network was 36% for CBS and 30% each for ABC and NBC.

salient during the midterm election. These items assessed knowledge of the impact of the economic stimulus legislation on job creation, likely effects of the health care reform law on the budget deficit, the current state of the economy, recent changes to income tax levels, troop levels in Afghanistan, and President Obama's U.S. citizenship. As demonstrated by the black columns in Figure 1.2, the average level of misperception-holding was higher for all news sources in 2010 compared with 2003; the increase for NPR and PBS is especially notable. In the researchers' words, "Consumers of all sources of media evidenced substantial misinformation, suggesting that false or misleading information is widespread in the general information environment" (Ramsay et al. 2010, 19). Despite this, misinformation continued to vary by news source.[8] As with the prior study, Fox News viewers were most likely to be misinformed in 2010, and along with MSNBC viewers, consumers of NPR and PBS were the least likely to be misinformed. The rate of holding misperceptions did not vary as much between Fox and the public broadcasters as had been the case in 2003, however (a difference of 18 percentage points in 2010 versus 34 in 2003).

What do we make of these findings? They certainly seem to indicate that levels of misinformation are rising. Yet, with only two years' worth of evidence, we need to draw this conclusion cautiously. Perhaps the 2010 election was a period in which public misperceptions were unusually high and future analyses will demonstrate a decline. The degree to which new media sources contribute to misinformation is also not clear. The 2003 and 2010 surveys both demonstrate that traditional and new media sources were both linked to misperception-holding. Furthermore, the 2010 results challenge the initial assumption that relying on media sources that cover political affairs largely from one political perspective would lead to misinformed media consumers. Although Fox viewers were the most likely to be misinformed, viewers of the liberal-leaning MSNBC network were among the least misinformed.

CONCLUSION

One promise of the information revolution was a better informed citizenry. The larger number and wider variety of sources for news, many

---

[8] The 2003 survey asked respondents for their primary news source, whereas the 2010 respondents were asked how often they got news from six different sources. The 2010 results in Figure 1.2 are for those respondents who rely on the source almost every day.

of which are easier to access than in past eras, would seem to lead to the public being better informed about political matters. As the analyses presented in this chapter attest, however, the explosion of new media sources clearly has not resulted in unequivocal increases in knowledge. Some characteristics of the new media universe appear to enhance knowledge acquisition, whereas other characteristics detract from knowledge acquisition. The consequences for democracy, particularly an informed public, are thus mixed.

Among news consumers, those who consult more news sources, which is possible because of the addition of sources in the new media era, are better informed than those who rely on fewer sources. Using new media rather than traditional media sources primarily drives this effect. Furthermore, certain new media sources are especially likely to contribute to increased knowledge. To explain these findings, it seems reasonable to credit increased accessibility as well as diverse news formats and presentation modes. These are all encouraging signs not only for those who tout the promise of new media but also for those who believe that democracy is enhanced when the public is more knowledgeable.

However, when we move beyond those Americans who regularly consume the news to include others, our conclusions are less optimistic. First, across the entire public, levels of political knowledge have not increased as the media environment has changed. At the same time, the gap in knowledge between those with fewer years of formal education versus those with many years of formal education is widening. Enhanced media choice likely influences this trend. Increasingly, it seems that "motivation, not ability, is the main obstacle that stands between an abundance of political information and a well- and evenly informed public" (Prior 2005, 389). People who choose to turn away from the news are less informed, whereas those who choose to spend time with news sources are better informed. A nation comprising knowledge-haves and knowledge-have-nots seems one possible outcome of the new media environment.

To explore fully public knowledge in this environment, new research approaches will be needed. The Pew survey used in this chapter is notable for its rich array of media consumption questions. Most surveys available to public opinion and communications scholars contain fewer questions on media usage and focus on traditional media sources. As a result, tracking the relationship between new media and knowledge over time is difficult. As for assessing public knowledge, more attention to misinformation-holding among the citizenry is clearly warranted. Of all the conclusions in this chapter, the contribution of new media to misperception-holding is the most speculative. Some evidence suggests a connection, but additional research is necessary before concluding definitively that levels of misinformation are rising in the new media environment and that new media sources are primarily to blame. Normatively, we should worry about misinformation, because it can undermine a citizen's ability to fulfill his or her democratic responsibilities. Voting for public officials who most likely represent your concerns is very difficult, for example, if your political beliefs are based on misperceptions. If the quality of information available to the public worsens in the new media environment, then democratic governance could become more challenging.

Although this chapter answers some questions about new media and knowledge, it also raises other questions. Why do some new media sources seem to increase public knowledge, whereas others produce the opposite effect? Are these dissimilar outcomes partly due to the presentation mode of specific media sources? Or are content differences across sources (politically or ideologically driven, satirical versus straight, etc.) more influential? Compared with political information available in the traditional media, is political information available to citizens from new media sources noticeably different, especially in ways that are consequential for knowledge acquisition? Future research should attempt to address such questions. However, doing so will necessitate moving beyond public opinion surveys. As studies of knowledge in the old media environment have demonstrated, multimethodological approaches are well suited to delineating features of media sources that contribute to or impede knowledge acquisition, as well as individual differences in acquisition. Russell Neuman, Marion Just, and Ann Crigler (1992), for instance, relied on experiments, media content analyses, and in-depth interviews (of citizens and journalists) to test their constructionist theory of knowledge gain. Doris Graber (2001) used some of these same methods, along with focus group interviews, to understand how people use political information from television news to make sense of political issues. Employing similarly broad methodological approaches, while incorporating distinct features of specific new media sources, would significantly enhance our knowledge of public knowledge in the new media environment.

References

Barabas, Jason, and Jennifer Jerit. 2009. "Estimating the Causal Effects of Media Coverage on Policy-Specific Knowledge." *American Journal of Political Science* 53 (Jan.): 73–89.

Baum, Matthew A. 2003. *Soft News Goes to War*. Princeton, NJ: Princeton University Press.

Bennett, Stephen Earl. 1989. "Trends in Americans' Political Information, 1967–1987." *American Politics Quarterly* 17 (4): 422–35.

Berelson, Bernard R., Paul F. Lazarsfeld, and William N. McPhee. 1954. *Voting: A Study of Opinion Formation in a Presidential Campaign*. Chicago: University of Chicago Press.

Caufield, Rachel Paine. 2008. "The Influence of 'Infoenterpropagainment': Exploring the Power of Political Satire as a Distinct Form of Political Humor." In *Laughing Matters: Humor and American Politics in the Media Age*, ed. Jody C Baumgartner and Jonathan S. Morris, 3–20. New York: Routledge.

Delli Carpini, Michael X., and Scott Keeter. 1996. *What Americans Know about Politics and Why It Matters*. New Haven, CT: Yale University Press.

Eveland Jr., William P., and Dietram A. Scheufele. 2000. "Connecting News Media Use with Gaps in Knowledge and Participation." *Political Communication* 17 (July–Sept.): 215–37.

Ferejohn, John A., and James Kuklinski, eds. 1990. *Information and Democratic Processes*. Urbana: University of Illinois Press.

Graber, Doris A. 2001. *Processing Politics: Learning from Television in the Internet Age*. Chicago: University of Chicago Press.

Jerit, Jennifer, and Jason Barabas. 2006. "Bankrupt Rhetoric: How Misleading Information Affects Knowledge about Social Security." *Public Opinion Quarterly* 70 (Fall): 278–303.

Jerit, Jennifer, Jason Barabas, and Toby Bolsen. 2006. "Citizens, Knowledge, and the Information Environment." *American Journal of Political Science* 50 (April): 266–82.

Kuklinski, James H., Paul J. Quirk, Jennifer Jerit, David Schwieder, and Robert F. Rich. 2000. "Misinformation and the Currency of Democratic Citizenship." *Journal of Politics* 62 (August): 790–816.

Kull, Steven, Clay Ramsay, and Evan Lewis. 2003–4. "Misperceptions, the Media, and the Iraq War." *Political Science Quarterly* 118 (4): 569–98.

Lawrence, Eric, John Sides, and Henry Farrell. 2010. "Self-Segregation or Deliberation? Blog Readership, Participation, and Polarization in American Politics." *Perspectives on Politics* 8 (March): 141–157.

Morris, Jonathan S., and Richard Forgette. 2007. "News Grazers, Television News, Political Knowledge, and Engagement." *Harvard International Journal of Press/Politics* 12 (1): 91–107.

Moy, Patricia. 2008. "The Political Effects of Late Night Comedy and Talk Shows." In *Laughing Matters: Humor and American Politics in the Media Age*, ed. Jody C Baumgartner and Jonathan S. Morris, 295–313. New York: Routledge.

Neuman, W. Russell. 1976. "Patterns of Recall among Television News Viewers." *Public Opinion Quarterly* 40 (1): 115–23.

Neuman, W. Russell, Marion R. Just, and Ann N. Crigler. 1992. *Common Knowledge: News and the Construction of Political Meaning*. Chicago: University of Chicago Press.

Nie, Norman H., Darwin W. Miller III, Saar Golde, Daniel M. Butler, and Kenneth Winneg. 2010. "The World Wide Web and the U.S. Political News Market." *American Journal of Political Science* 54 (April): 428–39.

Pew Research Center for the People and the Press. 2007. What Americans Know: 1989–2007, Public Knowledge of Current Affairs Little Changed by News and Information Revolutions. Retrieved February 8, 2010, from http://people-press .org/reports/display.php3?ReportID=319.

Pew Research Center for the People and the Press. 2009. Public Evaluations of the News Media: 1985–2009, Press Accuracy Rating Hits Two Decade Low. Retrieved February 27, 2010, from http://people-press.org/reports/pdf/ 543.pdf.

Popkin, Samuel L. 1994. *The Reasoning Voter: Communication and Persuasion in Presidential Campaigns.* Chicago: University of Chicago Press.

Prior, Markus. 2005. "News vs. Entertainment: How Increasing Media Choice Widens Gaps in Political Knowledge and Turnout." *American Journal of Political Science* 49 (July): 577–92.

Prior, Markus. 2007. *Post-Broadcast Democracy: How Media Choice Increases Inequality in Political Involvement and Polarizes Elections.* Cambridge: Cambridge University Press.

Ramsay, Clay, Steven Kull, Evan Lewis, and Stefan Subias. 2010. "Misinformation and the 2010 Election: A Study of the US Electorate." *World Public Opinion.org.* Retrieved January 21, 2011, from http://www.world publicopinion.org/pipa/pdf/dec10/Misinformation_Dec10 rpt.pdf.

Schumpeter, Joseph A. 1976. *Capitalism, Socialism and Democracy*, 5th ed. London: George Allen and Unwin, Ltd.

Sniderman, Paul M., Richard A. Brody, and Philip E. Tetlock. 1991. *Reasoning and Choice: Explorations in Political Psychology.* New York: Cambridge University Press.

Sunstein, Cass R. 2001. *Republic.com.* Princeton, NJ: Princeton University Press.

2

Rethinking Television's Relationship to Politics in the Post-Network Era

Jeffrey Jones

With the new media era upon us, scholars of political communication have turned much of their attention to the Internet's impact on politics. Yet the new media environment also comprises new ways in which the "old medium" of television has been transformed because of technological innovation and industrial reorganization. Television has gone from a stable and predictable medium, dominated by a three-network oligopoly that largely controlled or shaped most aspects of the viewing experience in the network era (1950–80), to an aggressively competitive industry comprised of multiple channels and networks in the cable era (1980–2005), to an industry greatly destabilized by viewer choice and control in the digital, post-postnetwork era (2005 to the present).[1] As a result, practices that traditionally constituted citizens' relationship to politics through the medium have been altered as well. While documenting the decline of television news, the discipline has largely ignored these major transformations. We have numerous books on blogging and politics, for instance, yet such behaviors are not even close to rivaling the continued importance and impact of television in citizens' lives, where it is still the most frequently used medium for information.[2] In short, while the medium has continued relevance to political life, political communication scholars in recent years have paid scant attention to it.

[1] Given the enormous change television has experienced in such a short period, scholars have not settled on the best way to describe the various eras of television's existence. The categorical dates and names used here come from Amanda Lotz (2007), although what I call the "cable era" she labels the "multi-channel transition."

[2] "Internet Gains on Television as Public's Main News Source," *Pew Research Center for the People and the Press*, January 4, 2011. Retrieved from http://people-press.org/report/689.

Amid such transformations, we must be careful that our working ideas and conceptions – and from that, our theories of television in relationship to American democracy – are not outdated as well. The main currents of academic and critical thought about television's role in American democracy have typically posited certain programming forms (e.g., news) as valuable to an informed citizenry and other programming forms (e.g., entertainment shows) as harmful or dangerous, largely because entertainment television is seen as a distraction from the more important business of participation in American civic life, while news is seen as enhancing or encouraging it (Putnam 2000). Because of economic competition and technological innovation, television has changed, including at the level of what constitutes its programming and how it is attended to by viewers. The economics of news production in an intensely competitive environment, for instance, has had enormous consequences for the composition of news and how it appeals to viewers (McManus 1994). The need for inexpensive programming in a vastly increased news hole (twenty-four hours of news) has led to emphasizing program stylistics and the elevation of talk and opinion over traditional reporting. In addition, the competitive environment has led news channels to focus on the creation of niche audience markets, including tailoring news to ideological and partisan concerns. News, then, is about assembling a dedicated viewership (or community) whose loyalties and passions are encouraged by certain performances of public affairs.

Similarly, rampant competition brought on by an array of cable channels has meant an increase in politically themed entertainment programming. Narratives about politics are seemingly everywhere on television, and as a result, such narratives – multiple, varied, and complex stories – increasingly shape citizens' understanding of politics. Therefore, entertainment television may be a greater force in shaping citizens' political views beyond news and information acquisition. Finally, revolutionary technological innovation has increased television viewers' choice and control over the medium. Viewers now possess enhanced abilities to act on or to engage with television texts in multiple ways. Television, in conjunction with digital networks such as the Internet, is increasingly a participatory realm of experience, including in the political field.

In sum, what has been valued and devalued about television in relationship to politics should be reconsidered. News, once seen as centrally important to an informed polity, has been transformed such that it is less valued as an information resource provider. Instead, its value or dangers may lie elsewhere, including articulating ideological passions of viewers and attracting core audiences around its various performances of public affairs, such as at the level of political mobilization. Entertainment programming, once seen as frivolous or even harmful to civic engagement, may have increased value and importance in how citizens relate to and understand public life. The stereotypical, passive receptor of information (e.g., the couch potato viewer) is outfitted with more resources and enticements to become an engaged citizen through interactive capabilities now available with the integration of television and digital networks. Television texts may be the starting point and even instigator of both macro and micro levels of political action.

The focus of this chapter, then, is to examine and evaluate changes in television over the past thirty years in news and in entertainment programming, as well as in viewer engagement with the medium. The chapter concludes with examining several guiding questions posed in the introduction to this volume, namely, how such changes in television affect the broader demands of citizenship, governance, and political culture.

NEWS AS PERFORMANCE OF PUBLIC AFFAIRS

Americans consume approximately four and a half hours of television each day, and in 2008 (the latest statistics available), television watching reached an all-time high of 151 hours of viewing per month for the average American viewer. The expansion of cable channels, the ability to time-shift programming through digital video recorders (DVRs), and the viewing of television online and through cell phones has facilitated greater time spent watching TV.[3] As with the consumption of public affairs information, television news remains the preferred medium of choice. Two of the most authoritative studies regarding news consumption habits – the Pew Project for Excellence in Journalism's "State of the News Media" annual report and the Pew Research Center for People and the Press's biennial report on citizen consumption of news – report that television news remains the dominant source for citizens' news consumption. Television (66%) is the dominant choice for information about national and international news, followed by the Internet (44%), newspapers (31%), and radio (16%).[4] When citizens are asked where they got their news from yesterday, 58% report television, compared with 44% from web

3   Alana Semuels, "Television Viewing at All-Time High," *Los Angeles Times*, February 24, 2009. Retrieved from http://articles.latimes.com/2009/feb/24/business/fi-tvwatching24.
4   "Internet Gains on Television," 2011.

or mobile media, 34% from radio, and 31% from newspapers.[5] What is more, "people spend over an hour – 70 minutes – watching, reading, and listening to the news on a given day. Nearly half of that time (32 minutes) is spent watching television news."[6] An earlier Pew study reports a somewhat surprising statistic: "an overwhelming majority of people (82%) follow the news with some regularity. Just 14% in this survey are classified as Disengaged, as they expressed a general lack of interest in news."[7] Although self-reporting here might suggest we approach the statistic with a dose of skepticism, the number nevertheless suggests that people care enough about public affairs to report attending to the news, and when they do, they prefer television as their source. But what exactly are they watching – network newscasts, cable news channels, or both?

A cursory look at Nielsen viewership ratings paints a misleading picture. The three broadcast network news programs on ABC, CBS, and NBC total 22.3 million viewers a night, while the median viewership for the three cable news channels (Fox News, MSNBC, and CNN) is only 3.88 million viewers in prime time and 2.16 million in daytime.[8] Yet 36% of people report regularly watching cable news, while only 22% report regularly watching nightly network news.[9] Additional statistics demonstrate how the networks are in free fall. According to the Pew Project for Excellence in Journalism study, network news programs have lost an average of 1 million viewers a year since 1980. Their combined ratings – the percentage of all households watching the programs – were 42.5% in 1980, compared with 15% in 2009. One reason for such drastic changes is the availability and convenience of other news sources. For instance, 57% of viewers say they check in on news from time to time, compared with 38% who watch at regular times.[10] Thus, while network news seems to dwarf cable viewership, we must realize that cable news is

---

[5] "Americans Spending More Time Following the News," *Pew Research Center for the People and the Press*, September 12, 2010. Retrieved from http://people-press.org/report/652/.

[6] Ibid.

[7] "Key News Audiences Now Blend Online and Traditional Sources: Audience Segments in a Changing News Environment," *Pew Research Center for the People and the Press*, August 17, 2008. Retrieved from http://people-press.org/report/444/news-media.

[8] "State of the News Media 2010," *Pew Project for Excellence in Journalism*. Retrieved from http://www.stateofthemedia.org/2010/index.php.

[9] "Internet Gains on Television" 2011.

[10] See "Americans Spending More Time," 2010. These statistics do not explain specifically whether viewers are watching cable or network news, only their patterns of temporal viewing. With that said, statistics suggest that these habits will be more conducive to watching twenty-four-hour news networks because of availability.

a twenty-four-hour-a-day enterprise, providing much greater opportunity for people to check in intermittently and watch news at different times throughout the day. In addition, this is not an either/or situation – viewers may watch the nightly evening news *and* cable news. Clearly, though, cable news offers viewers certain features and attractions that have made it a preferred and frequented source of television news. Those attractions are more than simply the convenience in viewing hours cable news offers. In short cable news networks have radically transformed what we call "television news," including how and why viewers now engage politics through it.

For most viewers, the three broadcast network newscasts by ABC, CBS, and NBC define the form. The codes and conventions that compose the formal dimensions of a network newscast (i.e., the anchor and desk, reporters in the field, dispassionate delivery, video evidence, what constitutes relevant issues and events, and so on) represent the normative ideal, or style, of television news (Morse 2004: 210). Yet it is a style that has changed over time, in particular in the 1980s, as network news divisions became more ratings conscious amid increased competition for viewers and corporate demands that news divisions earn a profit (Hallin 1994: 177). While this transformation of network news into a spectacle-centered, entertainment-driven form has been previously documented (Baym 2010; Gunther 1999), less discussed is the more radical and fundamental transformation of the previous normative ideal brought on by the cable news networks.

What has transpired over the past thirty years, beginning with CNN's formation in 1980 and continuing with MSNBC and Fox News's arrival in 1996, is that news has become a *location* or *destination* on the dial, a channel one turns to when seeking access to public affairs. News is now a *brand*, an identifiable corporate commodity with its own value-driven appeal to consumers (not to mention advertisers). Company executives talk openly about their properties as "brands" and "destinations," even their mission of assembling "communities" of viewers around these brands.[11] As each of the three cable networks has carved out a specific brand image for itself – Fox as a destination for conservatives, MSNBC as a place for liberals, CNN as a place for "unbiased reporting" – they implicitly admit that what they are selling is the brand itself, not the

---

[11] CNN notes that its brand's strength is with "casual news viewers" who tune in during big news events, calling the network "a destination channel." See Erin McPike, "Away from Prime Time, CNN Thrives," *National Journal Magazine*, May 22, 2010. Retrieved from http://NationalJournal.com. The head of MSNBC says, "you've got

generic function of delivering news to citizens that was assumed in previous eras. CNN may be losing the prime-time ratings race, yet it argues that the "neutral" brand image it seeks to maintain – that is, how it has decided to perform the news – is the appropriate choice because of its value as currency across the company's numerous brand outlets and platforms, including CNN Headline News, CNN International, CNN.com, CNN Airport Network, CNN Digital, and CNN en Español.[12] It is the brand image – how their version of public affairs will be sold – in viewers' and advertisers' minds, then, that each network seeks to establish and maintain through the product they produce. That is a far stretch from emphasizing quality and integrity of the information they offer or produce for citizens, as was somewhat the rhetoric of earlier eras (see McCarthy 2010).

What, then, constitutes "news" in this environment? "News," as imagined in the normative ideal central to democratic theory, is now radically reconstituted to meet the demands of competition for limited audiences. Cable news channels are engaged in a variety of cost efficient and audience-attracting *performances* around breaking events and politics, broadly construed. What they produce is more aligned with the imperatives and attractions of television as a consumer-centric medium than the normative ideal of reporting derived from newspapers. What has occurred is a fundamental transformation in the basic relationship between those who program and disseminate public affairs television and those who attend to it. Cable news channels construct public affairs performances that will attract niche audiences and do so around three central stylistic and substantive appeals – spectacle, talk, and ideological warfare. Each is used to attract loyal audiences or brand communities to the networks, and each has its own particular appeal.

First, cable news has demonstrated how to craft spectacle performances around major events, as well as how to turn routine "events" (murder, child custody battles, drug overdose) into major ones (e.g., O. J. Simpson, Elian Gonzalez, and Anna Nicole Smith). Perhaps one of the best historical examples of turning news into spectacle – and, in many ways, a defining moment in how cable news would transform news events into spectacle – was CNN's coverage of the first Gulf War (with reporters at the time calling it a "new kind of journalism" and a "new genre of

---

to create community. You've got to have a place where people come. They're like-minded. They share ideas." See Phil Rosenthal, "MSNBC Boss Stands Ready in Ideological Battle with Fox News," *Chicago Tribune*, May 2, 2010. Retrieved from http://www.ChicagoTribune.com.

[12] McPike 2010.

news"; Zelizer 1992: 77). For more than a decade, the fledgling network had struggled economically, precisely because of the fundamental structural features that define its existence. That is, the network had not mastered how to fill twenty-four hours of airtime cheaply (for reporting is enormously expensive) while attracting sizable audiences to specific programming that could be sold to advertisers. The solution presented itself with the first Gulf War. With citizens and military families highly anxious about America's first large-scale military engagement in almost a generation, audiences found comfort in cable news's ability to offer continuous, around-the-clock coverage of the conflict. The war could be made into distinctive programming by packaging it with televisual stylistics – attractive graphics and introductory themes ("War in the Gulf" and "Toward Peace in the Gulf"), transitional music, and promotional narratives (White 1994). Reporters, who were limited in their movement by government-controlled "press pools," learned to rely on visuals of bombing runs and videotape of advanced weaponry provided by the Pentagon and military contractors, while using their own night-vision technology to broadcast spectacle displays of missiles that resembled the popular video game "Missile Command" (Kellner 1992). Although such visual imagery was often context free – the network seldom described exactly what the viewer was witnessing – the content was nevertheless cheap and attractive enough to prove appealing. The network also produced another brand of spectacle by airing live the daily press briefings of generals and military personnel at the U.S. command center. Viewers could watch entire briefings and reporters' questions, not the edited versions that appeared on the broadcast networks. CNN also interspersed interviews with retired U.S. military personnel who constituted a stream of talking head "experts" for the network, few of whom had direct knowledge of the events but could supposedly interpret and mediate the war for the viewing public.

The first Gulf War, then, demonstrated how news could be transformed into something different. Spectacle news is about the instantaneous and continuous transmission of images and information as it occurs. Big news events are to be experienced in real time (e.g., 9/11, Hurricane Katrina, and the Asian tsunami, among others). Spectacle news is also about the constant repetition of dramatic moments and the seemingly endless talk that accompanies such dramatic visuals (e.g., the deaths of Princess Diana and John F. Kennedy, Jr.). Spectacle news is also about access, immediacy, and display. The viewer's role is to engage in surveillance, to monitor the continuous stream of information, and, above all, to keep watching (Caldarola 1994; Englehardt 1994). Ironically, the more viewers watched the war on television, the less they actually knew about the conflict (Morgan, Lewis, and Jhally 1992: 225). As numerous academic studies have also demonstrated, such coverage resulted in cable news serving as a conduit for government propaganda and misinformation (Bennett and Paletz 1994; MacArthur 2004; Mowlana, Gerbner, and Schiller 1992). Reporters and editors were no longer arbiters of truth; that responsibility had been passed to viewers who were now responsible for discerning who was and who was not telling the truth. The network's job was primarily to craft a presentation of these raw materials – a tendency that was repeated across news agencies in the run-up to the Iraq War in 2002–3 (Bennett, Lawrence, and Livingston 2007; Miller 2007; Rich 2006).

The second defining appeal in the transformation of news is the elevation of talk over reporting. By combining anchor-narrated video footage with a heavy dose of in-studio or satellite-beamed guests or experts, the cable networks have demonstrated how to craft endless hours of talk *about* the news more than the reporting *of* it.[13] Such talk happens across all hours of the day, from morning and late afternoon talk shows to weekend roundups and entertainment-oriented talk programming. Indeed, distinguishing between what the networks deem opinion talk shows and what they consider news shows is difficult.[14] Much of the reporting style comprises setting up the issue (for instance, noting that an amendment to proposed health care legislation is set for a vote) and then conducting a discussion with "experts," or political professionals, who espouse their opinion on the matter.

Talk on television is literally cheap. What cable news has discovered is that it is also more popular than reporting. All of the cable networks have filled their prime-time hours with talk and have used strong personalities to craft their network brand image and appeal. From Bill O'Reilly and

---

[13] As one reporter noted about Fox News's and MSNBC's coverage of the Clinton-Lewinsky scandal, "MSNBC and Fox News Channel will keep talking about it, if only because they have to talk about something. Looking for news, as opposed to simply discussing it, would require an investment in reporters neither is willing to make (see Bianco 1999).

[14] Indeed, the Obama administration described Fox as "not really news," but rather an organization "pushing a point of view." Fox responded by saying that the specific shows White House Press Secretary Robert Gibbs pointed to are "opinion shows," not their news programming. It was left up to Jon Stewart to highlight just how fluid the lines between opinion and news reporting really are on Fox. See http://www.politico.com/news/stories/1009/28417.html, http://www.foxnews.com/politics/2009/10/20/white-house-cites-opinion-shows-basis-fox-news-complaints/, and http://www.thedailyshow.com/watch/wed-march-3-2010/anchor-management.

Sean Hannity on Fox News, to Lawrence O'Donnell and Rachel Maddow on MSNBC, to Piers Morgan and Anderson Cooper on CNN, the cable news networks have developed star talkers who will personify each network's approach to news and public affairs. For viewers too, such personalities might serve as public proxy, or a stand-in for the values, beliefs, or feelings that viewers want to have expressed (or experience) in the public sphere. These talkers literally perform an attitude or position or embody a persona that viewers may value (or see in themselves). O'Donnell and Maddow, for instance, may personify liberal viewers' value in intelligence and large vocabularies, their wonkish love of minutiae and knowledge of history, or their outrage at right-wing hypocrisy and mendacity.

This leads to the third defining appeal of cable news – its overt willingness to engage in partisan-ideological warfare. No better example of this is Fox News's talk shows and reporting produced over the past decade. Fox realized early on that its viewers were interested in interpretation and affect more than in straight reporting. The network adopted an overtly conservative and often partisan approach to news/talk but branded it "Fair and Balanced," arguing that such an approach was justified because it served as an antidote to "the liberal media." As Fox News CEO Roger Ailes put it, "I don't understand why being balanced is right of center, unless the other guys are pretty far left.... Most of the American people think the news is left of center" (Kurtz 1999). From an economic perspective, the branding could not have been more ingenious – a way to craft an image that would help it stand out from the competition. The strategy also worked in creating feelings of victimhood by its viewers, feelings that could be remedied by watching with a loyal community of viewers gathered together as much to reaffirm their identity and values as to hear the news.[15]

Fox's ratings began to soar in the late 1990s when it focused on conjuring a series of enemies, including the enemy within, a la the impeachment of President Bill Clinton. After the 9/11 terrorist attacks, Fox became a central ideological rallying point for pro–Bush administration policies of retribution (Kitty 2005). The network engaged in an array of spectacle performances, overtly displaying patriotism and supporting the wars abroad, including sending reporter Geraldo Rivera to the caves of Tora Bora, Afghanistan, with a pistol on his hip to look for Osama bin Laden! The network routinely branded its coverage of the war with declarative

---

[15] Stephen Colbert highlights this tendency in his parody of right-wing talk show hosts but also in his analysis of such hosts in various interviews. See Jones (2010: 185–91).

graphics and slogans, such as "Operation Iraqi Freedom," "War on Terror," "Axis of Evil," "Heart of War," and "Target Iraq," and in the process, completely obscuring any differences between propaganda, journalism, and a television miniseries. But again, Fox was a leading voice in focusing on the enemy *within*, criticizing those who would question the president or the administration's tactics (such as torture) employed during wartime. From the first day of Barack Obama's new administration, the network began an unrelenting narrative that constructed the president as foreigner, socialist threat, and secret Muslim enemy.[16] Writing in *The New York Review of Books*, scholar Mark Lilla captures the dynamics of Fox's rhetorical strategies cum "news" and its popular appeal as such:

> The right-wing demagogues at Fox do what demagogues have always done: they scare the living daylights out of people by identifying a hidden enemy, then flatter them until they believe they have only one champion – the demagogue himself. But unlike demagogues past, who appealed over the heads of individuals to the collective interests of a class, Fox and its wildly popular allies on talk radio and conservative websites have at their disposal technology that is perfectly adapted to a nation of cocksure individualists who want to be addressed and heard directly, without mediation, and without having to leave the comforts of home. The media counterestablishment of the right gives them that. It offers an ersatz system of direct representation in which an increasingly segmented audience absorbs what it wants from its trusted sources, embellishes it in their own voices on blogs and websites and chatrooms, then hears their views echoed back as "news." (Lilla 2010: 56)

Lilla touches on an important point about cable news's use of ideology in its appeals, which is how such performances offer a new means of political representation for viewers. In the new media environment, failures of indirect systems of political representation (such as political parties or traditional news media outlets) are seemingly overcome through more direct forms of representation (Coleman 2005), including representation through political celebrities such as O'Reilly and Maddow. Viewers are invited to embrace these celebrity spokespersons as public proxies of discontent, people whose role as nonelected political rhetors and media populists grants them the ability to "embody the collective in the individual" (Marshall 1997: 241). As P. David Marshall argues, "From this proxy, the celebrity's agency is the humanization of institutions, the simplification of complex meaning structures, and principal site of a public voice of power and influence" (243–4). Through such populist rhetors,

---

[16] See *The Daily Show with Jon Stewart*, January 22, 2008. Episodes can be viewed online at http://thedailyshow.com/videos.

cable news is able to achieve all three audience appeals in one attractive package – spectacle, talk, and ideological warfare. No wonder these are the highest-rated programs on the networks' schedules.

These three features now constitute what is still labeled "news." But scholarly descriptions of such performances as "soft news," "infotainment," or even the "entertainmentization" of news do little to help us understand what exactly is going on here (Baum 2003; Zaller 2003). What has occurred is much more radical and substantial than these labels suggest. In the competitive environment of cable television, news is now about constructing a performance that will assemble a relational community, or communities of like-mindedness (Bishop 2008). Viewers coalesce around the brand because it crafts a meaningful relationship toward public events or politics, depending on their interest in a particular spectacle, talk event, or ideological controversy/mobilization. To be sure, what I am describing is different (or certainly more complex) than the popular myth that simply posits that Republicans watch Fox News, Democrats watch MSNBC, and Independents watch CNN, although, as we have seen, partisanship does constitute one of the appeals. Rather, it is the particular performance of public affairs that each network crafts that attracts viewers for a variety of reasons. Partisanship is one reason, but as we have discussed, performances also include appeals to patriotism, attractions to spectacle imagery, feelings of victimization, enjoyment of technology, likes and dislikes of the news actors themselves, the entertainment value of presentations, and a feeling of representation. What these channels have in common is their understanding that people need or desire such commonness at the tribal level, and that they, the networks, can craft performances around the raw material of public life to please subgroups of the like-minded. Such performances are still labeled "news" because that has been the traditional means through which the public has experienced narratives about politics. Recently, though, that has begun to change, as the next section demonstrates.

ENTERTAINMENT PROGRAMMING AND POLITICAL NARRATIVES

In the network era of television broadcasting, representation of the world of politics was fairly limited. Politics appeared primarily in public affairs programming largely segregated by genre and confined to specific dayparts – network newscasts in the early evening, political talk shows on Sunday mornings, and a brief moment in the early 1960s when networks aired documentaries in early prime time (Curtin 1995). Network prime-time entertainment programming included portrayals of politics, primarily limited to governmental institutions in the form of police procedurals, courtroom dramas, and shows about the FBI and CIA (Greene 2008; Rapping 2003). Entertainment television also had occasional comedic forays with sitcoms occurring in the U.S. military. Generally, though, addressing politics through other forms of hard-edged comedy such as satire and parody was limited (Gray, Jones, and Thompson 2009: 19–28).

The bifurcation of programming into "entertainment" and "news," and the normative valuations of these programming types in relation to citizenship, was born in this era. In this conception of programming, news and similar public affairs programs are valued, but entertainment is deemed insignificant, if not outright dangerous (Putnam 2000). Although entertainment television might portray government institutions, those representations were seen as fictional, and therefore, by definition, "untrue." Thus, with a few exceptions,[17] political communication scholars have typically not explored what these entertaining representations might mean for civic engagement: what messages are conveyed in them, how citizens make sense of politics through them, or how such messages mediate citizens' relationship to the political world.

Perhaps such oversight has also been driven by the dominant scholarly epistemological paradigm in political communication of empiricism and rational reasoning. Stories told by entertainment television are ill-suited for empirical analyses favored by political communication scholars. Yet psychologist Jerome Bruner argues that there are two modes of cognitive functioning – logico-scientific and narrative – both with "distinctive ways of ordering experience [and] constructing reality" (Bruner 1986: 11). The logico-scientific mode "attempts to fulfill the ideal of a formal, mathematical system of description and explanation.... [It] deals in general causes, and in their establishment, and makes use of procedures to assure verifiable reference and to test for empirical truth" (12–13). The narrative mode, however, "leads to good stories, gripping drama, believable (though not necessarily 'true') historical accounts. It deals in human or human-like intention and action and the vicissitudes and consequences that mark their course. It strives to put its timeless miracles into the particulars of experiences, and to locate the experience in time and place" (13). Bruner invokes philosopher Richard Rorty in claiming that these

---

[17] These exceptions have occurred most recently when scholarly interest was piqued by entertainment programming such as *The West Wing* and *The Daily Show*.

alternative modes are related to the central epistemological question that preoccupies Anglo-American philosophy: how to know truth (the quest of scientists) versus how we endow experience with meaning (the preoccupation of poets and storytellers) (12).

While scholars may favor the former, it is entirely possible that citizens are more comfortable in making sense of reality – political or otherwise – using the latter. Furthermore, the narrative mode of cognitive reasoning is significant explicitly because of what it offers that the logico-scientific mode does not: "Narrative displays the goals and intentions of human actors; it makes individuals, cultures, societies, and historical epochs comprehensible as wholes; it humanizes time; and it allows us to contemplate the effects of our actions, and to alter the directions of our lives" (Richardson 1990: 117). As Laurel Richardson concludes, narrative is a mode of representation, but it is also a mode of reasoning – a "rational" way of making meaning (118). Thus, given that television entertainment is first and foremost about stories or narratives, and given the explosion in the variety, amount, and quality of narrative representations of politics on television that now exists, the role that entertainment programming plays in mediating political life cannot be easily dismissed.

In the previous era of television, this compartmentalization of politics had the effect of segregating politics from everyday life. Today, though, television programming reflects the ways in which politics is interwoven into the fabric of everything we do; it is ever present in our lives (Schudson 1998, 2001, 2006). Politics now occurs almost everywhere on television, across genres, dayparts, and channels. The latter two – time and place – means that such programming is now ubiquitous. Contrary to the belief that the public eschews politics on television (as well as in life in general), politics has become almost unavoidable on television. Numerous television genres – dramas, comedy and satire, music, reality, talk, documentary, and vérité – also cover politics. Within and across these genres, politics is narrativized in numerous ways, as well as with varying degrees of complexity. Each programming form allows for different stories to be told, stories about people, institutions, issues, tactics, processes, outcomes, events, and even political culture.

While space will not permit a fuller accounting of each of these, a few examples will suffice. While news crafts narratives about the president, occurring alongside those stories are other narrative interpretations of the man and officeholder. George W. Bush was the subject of numerous comedic and satirical treatments, including late-night talk show hosts' jokes, sketch comedy caricatures on *Saturday Night Live* (1975–present), and satirical fake news and fake talk shows, such as *The Daily Show* (1996–present) and *The Colbert Report* (2005–present). Bush was even the central character in two situation comedies, *That's My Bush!* (2000) and *Lil' Bush* (2007–8), a first for a sitting president (Jones 2009a). While some of these comedic treatments amounted to little more than "Bush is dumb" jokes, other narratives were scathing critiques of the president's policies and his use or abuse of power. At times, these narratives provided important critiques that were difficult to find elsewhere on television, including the news (Baym 2010; Jones 2010).

Outside the comedic realm, one could find narrative interpretations of Bush within music videos (Green Day's "American Idiot," Pink's "Dear Mr. President," and Eminem's "Mosh") and on film channels (*Fahrenheit 9/11* and *Bush's Brain*). Subscription channels such as HBO and Showtime aired documentaries such as *Journeys with George* (2002), casting the candidate as an intellectual lightweight and unserious, and docudramas such as *DC 9/11: Time of Crisis* (2003), casting the president as "action-adventure commander in chief" in the immediate aftermath of the terrorist attacks of September 11, 2001.[18] The president sought to participate in other television narratives, appearing on *Saturday Night Live*, the talk show *Dr. Phil* (2002–present), and the sportsman show *Fishing with Roland Martin*, all during the 2004 election campaign, as well as on *Deal or No Deal* (2005–9) in the waning days of his presidency.[19] In short, how we as citizens might define Bush and understand and evaluate his time in office is mediated through these narratives, some more popular than others, but all contributing to an evaluative, broader, and more wide-ranging discourse than found within the news.

While these are narratives of the real president, the narrativization of fictional presidents occurs as well, in the process, carrying enormous potential for communicating central facets of the political *process*. Take the popular film *The American President* (1995), which is shown repeatedly on various television channels, including subscription channels, such as HBO, and cable movie channels, such as Encore, American Movie Classics, and TBS. Here, the viewer is introduced to numerous aspects of political action and behavior that is helpful in understanding how politics "works." In the first five minutes of the film, we witness a meeting of the president and his advisers and are exposed to concepts that students

[18] Alessandra Stanley, "Sept. 11, Before and After, *New York Times*, September 5, 2003.
[19] For the ways in which popular culture is now central to the narrativization of politicians during election seasons, see Jones (2005, 2009b).

of politics would call political vulnerability, political expediency, timing, agenda setting, political capital, arm-twisting, language choice, presidential decision making, and arguments over contemporary hot-button political issues (see Table 2.1). In short, although fictional, this exposure to the processes of politics has the potential, as Doris Graber has demonstrated, to shape viewers' cognitive schemas about the functioning of politics (Graber 1988, 2001).

Narratives about other facets of political life abound in the post-network era as well. Hot-button political issues like gay marriage are calmly yet earnestly debated by Jon Stewart, a comedian, and Mike Huckabee, the former presidential hopeful, on *The Daily Show* (Jones 2010: 133–6). Government interrogation tactics, or "torture," were central to the plot of the dramatic series about CIA agent Jack Bauer, *24* (2001–10), providing viewers with a sympathetic perspective on such measures, while also demonstrating the horrible toll such actions have on the people our government asks to carry them out.[20] *CSI: Crime Scene Investigation* (2000–present) airs an episode that deals with racial profiling and bias in policing. The HBO drama *Treme* (2010–present) examines the national, state, and local government responses to the flood that followed Hurricane Katrina and the effects of such actions and inactions on the lives of the citizens of New Orleans. A neoliberal philosophy of personal responsibility and self-discipline in the absence of state authority is espoused daily on the lectures delivered by *Judge Judy* (1996–present) (Ouellette 2004). Petty criminality is pathologized in the reality show *COPS* (1988–present) as viewers are invited to embrace repressive policies toward the alien "other" conjured within the narratives (Rapping 2004). Military tribunals are explained on the CBS drama *J.A.G.* (1995–2005), while congressional oversight into everything from the Iran-Contra hearings to hearings on the BP Deepwater Horizon oil spill is available on C-SPAN (Frantzich and Sullivan 1996; Thelen 1996).

The popular Aaron Sorkin–written drama set in the White House, *The West Wing* (1999–2006), subjectively positions the viewer inside the

---

[20] The show has even affected government officials themselves. As *Newsweek* put it in assessing the show's impact, "The most influential legal thinker in the development of modern American interrogation policy is not a behavioral psychologist, international lawyer or counterinsurgency expert.... the prime mover of American interrogation doctrine is none other than the star of Fox television's *24*, Jack Bauer.... The lawyers designing interrogation techniques cited Bauer more frequently than the Constitution." See Dahlia Lithwick, "The Fiction behind Torture Policy," *Newsweek*, July 26, 2008. Retrieved from http://www.newsweek.com.

TABLE 2.1. *Lessons about Political Life from the Film* The American President

Political Science Terms	Film Dialogue	Schemas about Political Life
Political Vulnerability	"If we try to push this through and lose, there will be a very loud thud when we hit the ground, and that is not what you want in an election year."	Importance of election year politics, including the timing and success of a legislative agenda; legislative losses suggest weakness and overall loss of support.
Political Expediency	"We can't take it [the approval rating] out for a spin; we need it to get re-elected." "We have to fight the fights we can win, Louis."	Not wasting political capital on political principles in an election year; pragmatism over ideals; introducing bills with the proper formula for success.
Political Capital	"With a 63% approval rating, I don't need their help [the environmental lobby] to get a bill passed."	Importance of approval ratings to perception of power, allowing the president to set the terms of political deals with both opponents and allies.
Language	"'Crime control,' Robin. 'Gun control' means we're wimps and soft on crime."	Significations have different connotations and therefore different effects on public opinion and perceptions.
Agenda Setting	"You can brief the press this afternoon. The Crime Bill is priority number one on the President's domestic agenda."	Prioritization of specific bills over others; centrality of the press in disseminating that agenda.
Timing	"We want to announce the Crime Bill at the State of the Union, which is 72 days from today. The last nose count put us 18 votes short. Eighteen votes in 72 days."	Announcing major legislation at the State of the Union address; obtaining votes in a limited time frame.
Political Arm-Twisting	"Don't be the nice guy from Brooklyn on this one. Do what the NRA does." "What, scare the shit out of 'em? I can do that."	Playing tough; threatening opponents.
Issues	"People do not relate guns to gun-related crime."	Relationship between gun control and the War on Drugs; relationship between global warming and fossil fuels.
Decision-Making	[reflected by all of the above discussion].	Competing voices of advisers – the young idealist, the experienced realist, the objective statistician, the dutiful mouthpiece.

Source: Compiled by author.

White House, offering a perspective into how the sausage is made (vote counting, deal cutting, crisis management, press relations, etc.), as well as insight into the motivations, desires, and struggles of the political players as they wrestle with difficult decisions (Rollins and O'Conner 2003). Finally, the failure of government institutions – police, courts, schools, and city hall – to address poverty, drug use, apathy, and corruption in America's inner cities is meticulously played out in the HBO drama, *The Wire* (2002–8), the antipolice procedural written by former *Baltimore Sun* reporter David Simon and former Baltimore police detective Ed Burns. Through an expansive cast of sympathetic characters, none of whom fit the easy stereotypes and binaries of good/evil that typify both news and entertainment programming, viewers are invited to explore the failings of government and the human wreckage that survives despite the breakdown of civil society. A show like *The Wire* casts an unblinking eye on characters and facets of American life rarely treated with honesty or respect (Jones 2007). It contributes much-needed pluralism to stories that permeate public life.

The proliferation of all things political within and throughout contemporary entertainment programming has resulted in an *expansion of meaning* in our understanding of politics. Viewers who attend to political narratives are offered additional perspectives from which not only to know politics but also to feel it as something real or familiar. As Bruner contends in his contrasts between analytical and expressive modes of rational thinking, "arguments convince one of their truth, stories of their lifelikeness. The one verifies by eventual appeal to procedures for establishing formal and empirical proof. The other establishes not truth but verisimilitude" (Bruner 1986: 11). Barry Richards argues that this emotional extension associated with the integration of politics and popular culture is no small thing for democracy. For him, the entertainment narrativization of politics, for instance, can begin to address the "democratic deficit" in contemporary political culture, which he defines as "the growing disinterest in or distaste for politics" (Richards 2004: 340). Political communication suffers from an emotional deficit, he argues, "the failure of . . . communications to satisfy the contemporary taste for certain kinds of affective experience." He contends that the "revitalization of democracy" requires that "presentations of politics to the public" be "something [akin to] the emotionally compelling narratives offered by, for example, television soap operas" (Richards 2004: 340; see also Marcus 2002 for the call for scholarly attention to emotion in political reasoning). While the particular genre he uses here as an example is distracting, his larger point is that the compelling nature of melodrama (whether in *24*, *The West Wing*, or Jon Stewart's confrontation with CNBC host Jim Cramer) can invigorate interest in and engagement with politics.

In short, we must reconceptualize entertainment as something deemed frivolous and separate from politics to something central to enunciating what politics means for citizens as they encounter political representations in everyday life. We make a mistake to consider all of entertainment as fiction, and all of fiction as incapable of accessing truth. Entertainment is not an escape from political life, but a familiar avenue through which to transport us back into it. As Liesbet van Zoonen argues, "popular culture . . . needs to be acknowledged as a relevant resource for political citizenship: a resource that produces comprehension and respect for popular political voices and that allows for more people to perform as citizens; a resource that can make citizenship more pleasurable, more engaging, and more inclusive" (van Zoonen 2005: 151). The failure to do so, she notes, can produce dire consequences: "politics has to be connected to the everyday culture of its citizens; otherwise it becomes an alien sphere, occupied by strangers no one cares and bothers about" (3).

FROM AUDIENCES TO USERS

The conception of television audiences as "couch potatoes" has wide and historical cultural currency, accompanied, as it is, with other pejorative formulations of the medium as a "vast wasteland" and the "boob tube." Television audiences are typically seen as "passive" receptors of messages, as opposed to the supposedly more engaged consumptive behaviors of newspaper readers (Livingstone 2004). Harvard political scientist Robert Putnam, in particular, has offered one of the most aggressive critiques of television viewers, construing their behavior as an "affliction" and part of an "epidemic" that produces "physical and psychological ills," and contributing to a general "collapse" of an engaged citizenry (Putnam 2000: 216–46). This conception is part of a much older and wider attack by elites on the "masses" who attend to popular cultural activities (Bottomore 2003). Even the more fair-minded evaluation of the relationship between media consumption and citizenship in Michael Schudson's "Informed Citizen" model of normative democratic behavior is somewhat unitary and one dimensional (Schudson 1998). The Informed Citizen, in his or her consumption of media, seems the equivalent of a potted plant with input needs of sun, water, and occasional food (in this case, only needing information, analysis, and debate from media) for democracy to be sustained or to grow. Yet people are psychological beings with a variety of needs, wants, desires, and interests who operate from a range of competencies, emotions, and cognitive frameworks. As argued above, the more that television offers a broader selection of narratives and performances of politics, the more that viewers avail themselves to using the medium to address and fulfill these needs, desires, and so forth. In the process, television viewership has been transformed.

In the past thirty years, beginning with the increased options offered by cable and the use of remote control and taped/disk recording devices to an array of internal and external TV set technologies that allow for choice and options, viewers have realized a remarkable degree of control over the medium. Viewers are much less subject to the networks' management of the viewing experience. As Jeff Gaspin, president of NBC Universal Television Group, describes it, "The shift from programmer to consumer controlling program choices is the biggest change in the media business in the past 25 or 30 years."[21] This has partly occurred because of cable and set-top digital technologies that allow for on-demand viewing, multiplexed channels (such as the multiple channels for HBO), compressed viewing options (numerous episodes that run back to back), and time-shifted and appointment viewing (from DVRs such as Tivo to DVDs of entire seasons). However, part of this is also associated with other digital technologies and networks, primarily the Internet, streaming technology, and mobile platforms. We can now watch television on a computer screen or a mobile phone, streamed by individual episodes or by clips of show segments. Television was once a "push medium," in which content was placed before the viewer to either consume or not consume. Today, though, digital technologies have transformed television into a "pull medium," where users are in control of what, when, and how they want to watch. In addition to DVRs, DVDs, and mobile phones are popular video aggregation websites, such as YouTube, Google Video, iFilm, TV.com, and Hulu, and free and accessible video archives, such as C-SPAN or the entire catalog of *The Daily Show*, with each episode available for online viewing. Thus, television can be watched on-demand and outside the traditional TV console, with the limitations of time and place somewhat overcome.

The results of these transformations are several, and seemingly contradictory. Such choice and control means that viewership is much more

---

[21] Bill Carter, "NBC Will Offer Its Shows Free for Download," *New York Times*, September 20, 2007, A1.

fragmented, with less in the way of commonality in viewing experiences. Only rarely do networks achieve the enormous numbers of viewers watching the same things at the same times as they did in the past. Viewers have broken off into niches and formulate their own distinctive viewing patterns, driven largely by taste (as discussed previously with news). Yet television has become a much more participatory realm, as viewers express their desire to be involved beyond simple viewing. Control is more than just the choice we exert when watching but also what we do with these materials during or after the fact. In particular, web pages, social networking sites (such as Facebook and Twitter), and blogs allow viewers to circulate, share, comment on, and discuss television materials. Thus, the act of watching becomes a different variety of communal experience within communities of like-minded people and friends. Citizens are able to integrate television into their other actions such as work or leisure away from home. Television still produces the "event" (the blockbuster or lackluster programming), but the web and other digital networks serve as a location for what viewers do with that programming. In this "replay and relay" aspect of the TV experience, viewers can watch or rewatch clips or shows and then relay them to others for their own purposes (Christensen 2009). Geoffrey Baym, for instance, has charted the use and circulation of clips from *The Daily Show* and *The Colbert Report* by political activists, demonstrating how television can serve as a discursive resource within broader political struggles (Baym 2010: 145–64).

The "audience" might more usefully be altered to that of "users." Users are, of course, limited by technological capabilities, access to resources, their own technological competencies, and so on. Nevertheless, users are more empowered to engage in actions of their choosing. Moreover, such actions are encouraged by media producers as part of the experience of viewing. Television networks are acutely aware of splintering and fragmenting audiences. They therefore work to craft new relationships with viewers that allow for more viewer engagement with the text and are focused on creating communities (Jones 2009c). This relates to earlier discussions about cable news and communities of like-minded viewers. Beth Comstock, former NBC Universal's president of digital media and market development, notes that in the digital age, "community is all about gathering people with shared interests and giving them a platform to interact with each other, to engage in relevant content, and to create something new" (Comstock 2006: 9). The web becomes a natural interactive place for this to occur, but television programming is still central to the appeal. One example of this in political programming is

The Colbert Report's ardent fans known as Colbert Nation. The show
not only explicitly works to create a community within the text itself, but
actively cultivates opportunities for fan engagement on its website and
elsewhere by inviting creative forms of political participation through
"play" (Jones 2010: 224–32). Van Zoonen's study of how fans of *The
West Wing* use the Internet to "perform as citizens" is another significant
example (van Zoonen 2005: 123–41).

Television news, in particular, serves as a reservoir of raw material that
citizens can actively draw from for political commentary and criticism.
In the 2008 election, for instance, after Republican vice presidential candidate Sarah Palin's disastrous interview with ABC news anchor Charlie
Gibson, several citizens created what are called "mash-up videos" (a mon-
tage from several sources), blending Palin's largely nonsensical answers
with similar such overrehearsed answers given by Miss Teen South Carolina in a separate viral video popular at that time.[22] In another citizen generated mash-up, Democratic primary candidate Hillary Clinton's
campaign trail performances were spliced together with scenes of the
character Veruca Salt from *Willy Wonka and the Chocolate Factory*,
with Clinton/Salt singing "I Want It Now" (invoking Clinton's perceived
"entitlement" to the Democratic nomination).[23] Rap artist Soulja Boy
employed video footage of the ABC News–moderated debate between
candidates Barack Obama and Hillary Clinton in a music video, slam-
ming the irrelevant line of questioning offered by moderators Charlie
Gibson and George Stephanopoulos in a presidential debate remix called
"Yahh, Gibson, Yahh."[24] And as citizens circulate such materials across
digital networks via YouTube, blogs, e-mail, and social networking sites
such as Facebook and Twitter, we see how television broadcasts are now
just the *starting* point of the trajectory that such programming might take
as it careens through society's various channels of discourse.

What this empowerment of viewers allows, then, is for users to act
with or on television resources in pursuing their needs, wants, desires,
and interests as citizens. Television not only provides a broader range of
narrative appeals and a more expansive set of meanings about public life
but also supplies the materials that viewers use or even "perform" as citizens. Although there is a vast body of research into how the circulation
of information across digital networks transforms politics (Boler 2008;

[22] http://www.youtube.com/watch?v=DzJ9JixTrIs.
[23] http://www.youtube.com/watch?v=Sz9VdoHZshA.
[24] http://www.youtube.com/watch?v=wdnljEV7MP4.

Loader 2007; McCaughey and Ayers 2003; Yang and Bergrud 2008), what is needed is further research into contemporary practices of the viewing culture regarding political information and behavioral practices (such as the ones described here). Digital networks are not distinct but are fully integrated. Thus, researchers must begin to explore how social networking technologies, new media use, and old media forms are connected, not only in the pursuit of political objectives but also through the cultural practices of citizenship within everyday living.

CONCLUSIONS

This chapter has described the ways in which television news and entertainment programming and television viewership have changed over the past thirty years and has argued that normative conceptions within political communication should be reconsidered as a result. What was once valued and devalued should be reexamined in light of the new realities that television presents in mediating and facilitating citizenship.

At this juncture, it would be helpful to address guiding questions posed in the introduction to this volume because of the arguments and data presented here. In many instances, what we have discussed thus far may make these questions more complicated than they at first seem. Does television make for a more informed and active citizenry? Has the quality of news and information improved? With at least three cable news channels presenting reports twenty-four hours a day, one would think that citizens would be flush with quality information that would serve their citizenship needs. But former Fox News host Glenn Beck standing in front of a blackboard wearing a Viking helmet and drawing out complex conspiracy theories that obliterate any intelligible relationship to historical facts, such as national socialism, should not make us confident about viewer acquisition of knowledge from these sources. It is difficult to read the "news as performance" section and believe that the *quality* of news and information is cable news's primary (or even secondary) concern. Indeed, the arguments mounted here suggest the need to rethink the role and function of cable news, away from its utility as provider of quality information and toward other potential roles it may serve. That might include an activation of audiences toward political mobilization, as is perhaps the case with Glenn Beck, his 9/12 Project, and the formation of the Tea Party movement (Zaitchik 2010). Or it may include Fox News's role as the rhetorical center of a Republican Party in slight disarray. As cable news has become almost singularly focused on attracting audiences to the corporate brand, it has, in the process, reassembled American citizens into like-minded communities around its performances. What democratic ideals, then, are and are not being met under such circumstances? Are viewers becoming more partisan or ideologically polarized as a result? These are all points or questions that should undergo empirical inquiry (some of which are addressed in Chapter 1), but they are questions that only arise from recognizing that television news is now a different sort, one that requires we move beyond the journalistic framework or paradigm for understanding its role in society.

If the quality of news as information resource is questionable, certainly the discussions here have pointed to an opening up of entertainment television as a space where alternative political information can be found. From political critiques on *Real Time with Bill Maher* (2003–present) to the revival of political documentaries on HBO and film channels, the array of differing narratives about politics increases the likelihood that television, as a competitive medium, will offer quality programming that was much less available in previous eras. But the guiding questions themselves may need to be rethought.

What does "being informed" mean in contemporary political culture, awash as it is in media that seemingly presents a flood of "information" at every turn? What role for citizen awareness of people or issues, or citizens' abilities to access information on-demand and monitor political behaviors (as described in the "audience as users" section)? And what does being "active" citizens mean in such an environment? Are citizens politically "engaged" when watching the entertainment narratives described earlier? Are they engaged when circulating viral videos of political satire? As I have argued elsewhere, routinely posting political commentary and critiques to 500 Facebook friends or writing a blog read by 3,000 people "is arguably just as important as handing out campaign literature to people with an enormously low percentage chance of being registered to vote, much less voting," yet we tend to value one over the other in our assessments of citizen engagement (Jones 2010: 25).

What about the tone and substance of political discourse amid these changes? There is little doubt that the reproduction of the bombastic style of talk radio into television discourse has encouraged a more aggressive approach to political debate, dialogue, and discussion. And as noted here, cable news is where the bulk of such agonistic performances occur. They make for spectacular (and inexpensive) television and have had the effect of attracting communities of like-minded individuals who have embraced these ideologically driven performances. Some commentators have argued that cable news has also played a leading role in crafting a polarized and bifurcated polity. In attracting such communities, cable news pushes for a diametrically opposed, left and right positioning on issues, even though such rigid thinking may not represent the thinking of a majority of citizens.[25] However, entertainment television may not be much better. Brutally satirical treatments of President Bush and his family (referencing the vaginas of both his wife and mother) on shows like *Lil'Bush* and *That's My Bush!* attest to the overall coarsening of discourse and lack of substance that often occurs within political communication these days. Yet programming such as 24 and *The Wire* also demonstrates how entertainment television can draw out and develop the complexities of politics for viewers, refusing to advance rigid thinking or polarizing positions on issues, and allowing viewers to weigh a plethora of choices, none of which seem particularly appealing, but all of which capture the reality of living within a complicated world.

Finally, what are the effects on governance and the effects on political norms and practices resulting from such changes in television? Here again the glass may be half full *and* half empty, and here again, questions more than answers are easier to come by. In terms of governance, does news's obsession with certain forms of political celebrity – promoting, as Fox News does, such politicians as Sarah Palin and Michelle Bachmann – alter the style and substance of how politicians must conduct themselves to receive media attention in this altered landscape of spectacle and ideologically driven "news"? Do legislators feel the need to emulate or mimic the style and substance of political discourse they see on television talk shows? Does Fox News's persistent narrative formulation, repeated across programs and dayparts, of President Obama as a "socialist" have an effect on voters' opinions (Riehl 2010)? Again, these are empirical questions, but emanating from the recognition that cable news's performance of politics may be producing new or different political effects. Entertainment television may affect governance positively when narratives of political life such as those found in *The West Wing* or even on C-SPAN lead citizens to be more understanding and patient with political decision making. And perhaps the case can be made that an increase in

---

[25] As a participant on these shows, Smerconish provides numerous anecdotes of how the producers of CNN and Fox News essentially rehearsed what they wanted him to say to craft such ideological positioning. If he disagreed and said he wouldn't take that position, they booked someone else who would. See Michael Smerconish, "On Cable TV and Talk Radio, a Push toward Polarization," *Washington Post*, June 11, 2010, A17.

the number and variety of narratives about politics might highlight the failings of politicians – for instance, comedy treatments of Sarah Palin in 2008 – in ways that encourage democratic deliberation and judgment beyond what was offered solely through news in previous eras.

In terms of effects on political norms and practices, cable news junkies may, in the end, know very little about politics, choosing to follow the rantings of their favorite cable talk show demagogue or choosing to seek solace in their commonality with like-minded partisans over the effort it takes to seek common values with fellow citizens. Yet seeing television viewers as users suggests enormous possibilities for transforming political culture. Monitorial citizens can use news footage not only to follow and critique government and politicians but also to mobilize information to hold government *and* the news media – traditional representative figures in a democracy – accountable to publics.

Ultimately, there are few definitive answers to such broad questions, although the analysis here will hopefully encourage examinations of an array of new questions that should be posed in light of changes in the relationship between television and politics that have occurred. Changes in media usually present new opportunities *and* constraints, things that, in this instance, might embolden and improve democratic practice, just as they might restrain or even pollute previous democratic processes. Television, like politics or political institutions, is not something that is *done* to citizens but is an arena of action – a powerful force for conducting social conversation and struggle. The multiple and competing forces that operate within, through, and from the medium, as with democracy itself, will determine how well it serves the broader and more noble cause of self-governance. The discussion here has highlighted how such forces have shifted in power and significance over the past thirty years. The result of such struggles will, perhaps, be broadcast at a later date.

References

Baum, Matthew. 2003. *Soft News Goes to War: Public Opinion and American Foreign Policy in the New Media Age*. Princeton, NJ: Princeton University Press.

Baym, Geoffrey. 2010. *From Cronkite to Colbert: The Evolution of Broadcast News*. Boulder, CO: Paradigm Publishers.

Bennett, W. Lance, Regina G. Lawrence, and Steven Livingston. 2007. *When the Press Fails: Political Power and the News Media from Iraq to Katrina*. Chicago: University of Chicago Press.

Bennett, W. Lance, and David Paletz. 1994. *Taken by Storm: The Media, Public Opinion, and U.S. Foreign Policy in the Gulf War*. Chicago: University of Chicago Press.

Bianco, Robert. 1999. "Airing Our National Laundry: In the Wake of Scandal, Only a Few Came Up Smelling Like a Rose." *USA Today*, February 15, D3.

Bishop, Bill. 2008. *The Big Sort: Why the Clustering of Like-Minded America Is Tearing Us Apart*. New York: Houghton Mifflin.

Boler, Megan. 2008. *Digital Media and Democracy: Tactics in Hard Times*. Cambridge, MA: MIT Press.

Bottomore, Tom. 2003. *The Frankfurt School and Its Critics*. New York: Routledge.

Bruner, Jerome. 1986. *Actual Minds, Possible Worlds*. Cambridge, MA: Harvard University Press.

Caldarola, Victor J. 1994. "Time and the Television War." In *Seeing through the Media: The Persian Gulf War*, eds. Susan Jeffords and Laura Robinovitz (97–105). New Brunswick, NJ: Rutgers University Press.

Christensen, Christian. 2009. "Jesters and Journalists." *British Journalism Review* 20 (2): 9–10.

Coleman, Stephen. 2005. "The Lonely Citizen: Indirect Representation in an Age of Networks." *Political Communication* 22: 197–214.

Comstock, Beth. 2006. "The 3 C's of Success in the New Digital Age." *Television Week*, 24 (April): 9.

Curtin, Michael. 1995. *Redeeming the Wasteland: Television Documentary and Cold War Politics*. New Brunswick, NJ: Rutgers University Press.

Englehardt, Tom. 1994. "The Gulf War as Total Television." In *Seeing through the Media: The Persian Gulf War*, eds. Susan Jeffords and Laura Robinovitz (81–95). New Brunswick, NJ: Rutgers University Press.

Frantzich, Stephen E., and John Sullivan. 1996. *The C-SPAN Revolution*. Norman: University of Oklahoma Press.

Graber, Doris. 1988. *Processing the News: How People Tame the Information Tide*. New York: Longman.

Graber, Doris. 2001. *Processing Politics: Learning from Television in the Internet Age*. Chicago: University of Chicago Press.

Gray, Jonathan, Jeffrey P. Jones, and Ethan Thompson. 2009. *Satire TV: Politics and Comedy in the Post-Network Era*. New York: New York University Press.

Greene, Doyle. 2008. *Politics and the American Television Comedy: A Critical Survey from* I Love Lucy *to* South Park. Jefferson, NC: McFarland and Company.

Gunther, Marc. 1999. "The Transformation of Network News: How Profitability Has Moved Networks out of Hard News." *Nieman Reports* (Special Issue). Retrieved from http://www.nieman.harvard.edu/reportsitem.aspx?id= 102153.

Hallin, Dan. 1994. *We Keep America on Top of the World: Television Journalism and the Public Sphere*. New York: Routledge.

Jones, Jeffrey P. 2005. "The Shadow Campaign in Popular Culture." In *The 2004 Presidential Campaign: A Communication Perspective*, ed. Robert E. Denton, Jr. (195–216). Lanham, MD: Rowman and Littlefield.

Jones, Jeffrey P. 2007. "Institutions That Fail, Narratives That Succeed: Television's Community Realism versus Cinema's Neo-Liberal Hope." *FlowTV* 6(9). Retrieved from http://flowtv.org/2007/10/institutions-that-fail-narratives-that-succeed-television's-community-realism-versus-cinema's-neo-liberal-hope/.

Jones, Jeffrey P. 2009a. "With All Due Respect: Satirizing Presidents from *Saturday Night Live* to *Lil' Bush*." In *Satire TV: Politics and Comedy in the*

Post-Network Era, eds. Jonathan Gray, Jeffrey P. Jones, and Ethan Thompson (37–63). New York: New York University Press.

Jones, Jeffrey P. 2009b. "Pop Goes the Campaign: The Repopularization of Politics in Election 2008." In *The 2008 Presidential Campaign: A Communication Perspective*, ed. Robert E. Denton, Jr. (170–90). Lanham, MD: Rowman and Littlefield Publishers.

Jones, Jeffrey P. 2009c. "I Want My Talk TV: Network Talk Shows in a Digital Universe." In *Beyond Prime Time: Television Programming in the Post-Network Era*, ed. Amanda Lotz (14–35). New York: Routledge.

Jones, Jeffrey P. 2010. *Entertaining Politics: Satiric Television and Political Engagement*, 2nd ed. Lanham, MD: Rowman and Littlefield.

Kellner, Douglas. 1992. *The Persian Gulf TV War*. Boulder, CO: Westview Press.

Kitty, Alexandra. 2005. *Outfoxed: Rupert Murdoch's War on Journalism*. New York: Disinformation.

Kurtz, Howard. 1999. "Crazy Like a Fox: Question His News Judgment, Perhaps, but Never Underestimate Roger Ailes." *Washington Post*, March 26, C1.

Lilla, Mark. 2010. "The Tea Party Jacobins." *New York Review of Books* 57 (9): 53–6.

Livingstone, Sonia. 2004. "On the Relationship between Audiences and Publics." In *Audiences and Publics: When Cultural Engagement Matters for the Public Sphere*, ed. Sonia Livingstone (17–41). Bristol, UK: Intellect Books.

Loader, Brian D. (ed.). 2007. *Young Citizens in the Digital Age: Political Engagement, Young People and New Media*. New York: Routledge.

Lotz, Amanda. 2007. *The Television Will Be Revolutionized*. New York: New York University Press.

MacArthur, John R. 2004. *Second Front: Censorship and Propaganda in the 1991 Gulf War*. Berkeley: University of California Press.

Marcus, George E. 2002. *The Sentimental Citizen: Emotion in Democratic Politics*. University Park: Pennsylvania State University Press.

Marshall, P. David. 1997. *Celebrity and Power*. Minneapolis: University of Minnesota Press.

McCarthy, Anna. 2010. *The Citizen Machine: Governing by Television in 1950s America*. New York: The New Press.

McCaughey, Martha, and Michael Ayers. 2003. *Cyberactivism: Online Activism in Theory and Practice*. New York: Routledge.

McManus, John H. 1994. *Market-Driven Journalism: Let the Citizen Beware?* Thousand Oaks, CA: Sage.

Miller, Toby. 2007. "Bank Tellers and Flag Wavers: Cable News in the United States." In *Cable Visions: Television Beyond Broadcasting*, eds. Sarah Banet-Weiser, Cynthia Cris, and Anthony Freitas (284–301). New York: New York University Press.

Morgan, Michael, Justin Lewis, and Sut Jhally. 1992. "More Viewing, Less Knowledge." In *Triumph of the Image: The Media's War in the Persian Gulf: A Global Perspective*, eds. Hamid Mowlana, George Gerbner, and Herbert I. Schiller (216–33). Boulder, CO: Westview Press.

Morse, Margaret. 2004. "News as Performance: The Image as Event." In *The Television Studies Reader*, eds. Robert C. Allen and Annette Hill (209–25). New York: Routledge.

Mowlana, Hamid, George Gerbner, and Herbert I. Schiller (eds.). 1992. *Triumph of the Image: The Media's War in the Persian Gulf: A Global Perspective.* Boulder, CO: Westview Press.

Ouellette, Laurie. 2004. "'Take Responsibility for Yourself': Judge Judy and the Neoliberal Citizen." In *Reality TV: Remaking Television Culture*, eds. Laurie Ouellette and Susan Murray (231–50). New York: New York University Press.

Putnam, Robert D. 2000. *Bowling Alone: The Collapse and Revival of American Community.* New York: Simon & Schuster.

Rapping, Elayne. 2003. *Law and Justice as Seen on TV.* New York: New York University Press.

Rapping, Elayne. 2004. "Aliens, Nomads, Mad Dogs, and Road Warriors: The Changing Face of Criminal Violence on TV." In *Reality TV: Remaking Television Culture*, eds. Laurie Ouellette and Susan Murray (214–30). New York: New York University Press.

Rich, Frank. 2006. *The Greatest Story Ever Sold: The Decline and Fall of Truth in Bush's America.* New York: Penguin Press.

Richards, Barry. 2004. "The Emotional Deficit in Political Communication." *Political Communication* 21 (3): 339–52.

Richardson, Laurel. 1990. "Narrative and Sociology." *Journal of Contemporary Ethnography* 19 (1): 116–35.

Riehl, Thomas. 2010. "Poll: 55% of Likely Voters Think Obama's a Socialist." *Talking Points Memo*, July 9. Retrieved from http://tpmdc.talkingpointsmemo .com/2010/07/shocking-poll-55-percent-of-voters-think-obamas-a-socialist .php?ref=fpb.

Rollins, Peter C., and John E. O'Conner. 2003. *The West Wing: The American Presidency as Television Drama.* Syracuse, NY: Syracuse University Press.

Schudson, Michael. 1998. *The Good Citizen: A History of American Civic Life.* New York: Free Press.

Schudson, Michael. 2001. "Politics as Cultural Practice." *Political Communication* 18 (4): 421–31.

Schudson, Michael. 2006. "The Varieties of Civic Experience." *Citizenship Studies* 10 (5): 591–606.

Thelen, David. 1996. *Becoming Citizens in the Age of Television.* Chicago: University of Chicago Press.

van Zoonen, Liesbet. 2005. *Entertaining the Citizen: When Politics and Popular Culture Converge.* Lanham, MD: Rowman and Littlefield.

White, Mimi. 1994. "Site Unseen: An Analysis of CNN's *War in the Gulf*." In *Seeing through the Media: The Persian Gulf War*, eds. Susan Jeffords and Laura Robinovitz (121–41). New Brunswick, NJ: Rutgers University Press.

Yang, Kaifeng, and Erik Bergrud (eds.). 2008. *Civic Engagement in a Network Society.* Charlotte, NC: Information Age Publishing.

Zaitchik, Alexander. 2010. *Common Nonsense: Glenn Beck and the Triumph of Ignorance.* New York: Wiley.

Zaller, John. 2003. "A New Standard of News Quality: Burglar Alarms for the Monitorial Citizen." *Political Communication* 20: 109–30.

Zelizer, Barbie. 1992. "CNN, the Gulf War, and Journalistic Practice." *Journal of Communication* 42 (1): 66–81.

3

Interplay

Political Blogging and Journalism

Richard Davis

State Representative Nikki Haley had vaulted into the front-runner position in the 2010 Republican South Carolina gubernatorial primary with
the endorsement of former Alaska governor Sarah Palin when a prominent South Carolina blogger announced on his blog that he had had "an
inappropriate physical relationship" with Haley while she was married.
Immediately, the candidate denied the charge by the blogger, who actually
was a supporter of Haley. She asserted she had been "100% faithful to
my husband" and accused the blogger of making the accusation merely
to attract attention to his blog. The following week, a South Carolina
political consultant who worked for an opposing candidate claimed that
he also had had a sexual encounter with Haley when they were both
attending an out-of-state convention.[1]

Traditional media picked up the blogger's accusation about Haley and
quickly published it. The fact that Haley had already issued a statement
responding to the blogger made the decision to publish easier. By comparison, in 1996 a similar rumor circulated about an affair of South
Carolina's then-governor with his communications director. Reporters
investigated the allegation for several months and ultimately published it
a year later when a gubernatorial candidate raised the charges in an election campaign.[2] Whereas the governor in 1996 could ignore the rumor

---

[1] Shaila Dewan, "Scandal Rattles Politics in Palmetto State, *New York Times*, May
25, 2010, at http://www.nytimes.com/2010/05/26/us/politics/26haley.html/scp=1&sq=
haley&st=cse; Jim Davenport, "Blogger's Relationship Claims Titillate, Frustrate,"
The State, May 28, 2010, at http://www.thestate.com/2010/05/28/1307999/bloggers-
relationship-claims-titillate.html .

[2] Cindi Ross Scoppe, "Scoppe: When Rumor Becomes Allegation," *The State*, June 2,
2010, at http://www.thestate.com/2010/06/02/1312787/scoppe-when-rumor-becomes-
allegation.html.

for a time, Haley assumed the story would move quickly beyond a single blog and addressed it immediately.

This incident demonstrates that political blogs have carved a new niche in politics. They have altered the way political discourse operates by changing how traditional journalists gather and report the news and by requiring politicians to respond to blogs. This change is reflected not only in this particular case, in which there was immediate coverage of an allegation regarding a candidate's personal life rather than concerted efforts to confirm its reliability before publication. It is also reflected in the reliance of news media professionals on political blogs for news, despite their concerns about the veracity of such sources. A recent survey found that 89% of journalists have used blogs for story research, even though half of those news professionals expressed concern that these blogs were less reliable than other news sources.[3] Another survey found that nearly one-third of journalists said they find news sources through political blogs, and 28% said they use political blogs to get ideas for stories (see Table 3.1).

TABLE 3.1. *Frequency of the Use of Blogs in Elements of the News-Gathering Process*

	Find News News	Find Sources	Get Story Ideas
Frequency of Use			
Regularly	13%	6%	3%
Sometimes	46	25	25
Rarely	24	42	44
Never	16	28	28

Source: Davis (2009).

Not surprisingly, journalists who consider blogs more reliable are more likely to use them in the news-gathering process. These journalists tend to be younger, and this fact alone may predict increasing reliance on blogs by the journalistic profession in the future (Sweetser, Port, Chung, and Kim 2008).

The thesis of this chapter is that journalists and bloggers have formed a relationship based not just on conflict and competition but also on

[3] "National Survey Finds Majority of Journalists Now Depend on Social Media for Story Research," *PR Newswire*, January 20, 2010, at http://www.prnewswire.com/news-releases/national-survey-finds-majority-of-journalists-now-depend-on-social-media-for-story-research-82154642.html.

codependency. They clearly battle one another, yet they also significantly influence each other's approaches to their shared task of news and information dissemination. In that sense, they have adopted a symbiotic relationship that shapes and defines each partner as well as affecting political discourse generally. In this chapter the focus is on how bloggers are transforming the news and information environment, a central topic of this volume. In Chapter 9 Matthew Kerbel focuses on how bloggers are influencing policy outcomes by examining the U.S. health care debate of 2010.

WAGING RHETORICAL WAR

Each new form of news dissemination – radio, television, the Internet – has trumpeted itself as superior to existing media. Radio brought listeners a human voice rather than the dry printed text. Television added visual images. Similarly, many bloggers portray themselves as part of a new medium that is more advanced than traditional media.

Blog boasting is at least partly driven by a strategy of self-protection. As each new medium arrives, it must elbow its way into the universe of existing media to survive. This strategy requires not only advertising its own virtues but also disparaging the existing order – the competition. That means bloggers must engage in continual comparison with traditional media to acquire their own audience niche.

In such a competitive environment, it should be no surprise that, despite their differences on ideology, blogs almost uniformly disparage existing media. One survey of bloggers found that the vast majority use their blogs to criticize traditional media (Pole 2007). That denigration usually centers on accusations of media bias. Conservative bloggers fault journalists for catering to the left, whereas liberal bloggers often write that the news media are cowed into serving the interests of the right wing.

At the same time, bloggers heavily rely on traditional media. One survey of blog content found that 69% of blog posts included as a source a traditional media outlet such as the *New York Times*, the Associated Press, or the *Washington Post*. In fact, bloggers rely on the traditional media more than they do on each other: This study found that 64% of the posts contained sources coming from other bloggers (Vaina 2007).

Competition between journalists and bloggers is odd because the two groups somewhat overlap. Many A-list bloggers come from traditional journalism. One survey of 30 political bloggers found that 12 had journalism experience, including some of the best-known bloggers, such as Ana Marie Cox, Hugh Hewitt, and Andrew Sullivan (Perlmutter 2007).

Nevertheless bloggers' comparisons of themselves with traditional media stress their superiority in several areas. They emphasize the accuracy of their reporting over that of traditional media. One blogger wrote, "So far, the blogosphere has a far better record of honesty and accuracy than mainstream organs like the *New York Times* and CBS."[4] Bloggers also point out that they can fix errors more easily because they do not have to wait for the next day's paper to publish the corrections (Smolkin 2004). One blogger claimed that checks and balances in the blogosphere "are far stronger and more effective than the alleged 'checks and balances' of the mainstream media, which, in the absence of political and intellectual diversity, may not operate at all."[5]

Some bloggers consider themselves superior in terms of transparency. When the standard of objectivity is held up as distinguishing the traditional media from bloggers, bloggers counter that journalists are fundamentally dishonest: Bloggers are biased, but they do not lie about it. Josh Marshall asserted that his blog's reporting "is more honest, more straight than a lot of things you see even on the front pages of great papers like the *Times* and the *Post*."[6] According to blogger Hugh Hewitt, journalists' failure to tell the audience their own views makes their news product fundamentally flawed: "I am unwilling to trust the conclusions of somebody who won't tell me their opinions and background."[7]

Bloggers also become condescending when they portray themselves as the future and traditional journalism as the past, decrying the media as outdated relics. One conservative blogger labeled news organizations "obstinate, lumbering, big-media dinosaurs" (Reider 2005: 6). In contrast, bloggers are the future of information gathering. According to one blogger, "weblogging will drive a powerful new form of amateur journalism as millions of Net users – young people especially – take on the role of columnist, reporter, analyst, and publisher while fashioning their own personal broadcasting networks" (Lasica 2001a). Some bloggers have suggested that the blogosphere will replace traditional media. They envision a future in which traditional media no longer serve a useful function.

---

4 Quoted in Paul Burka, "That Blog Won't Hunt," *Texas Monthly*, March 2005, p. 12.
5 Ibid.
6 Interview with Josh Marshall, *Frontline*, PBS, April 24, 2006, at http://www.pbs.org/wgbh/pages/frontline/newswar.
7 Nicholas Lemann, "Right Hook: The Wayward Press," *The New Yorker*, August 29, 2005, p. 34.

As blogs bypass traditional media filters and provide information directly to news consumers, there will no longer be a need for traditional news media sources (Lasica 2001a).

The battle between journalists and bloggers is not necessarily joined, however, because some journalists still debate whether to respond to blogs. Many likely agree with one former CNN executive who argued that journalists should not respond to bloggers "until they are held to the same standard that we are" (Dorroh 2004/5). Journalists often criticize bloggers as "wannabe" journalists who lack the professionalism requisite for the title. Even when journalists do respond to blogs, they do so in a dismissive manner. One news story about blog theories of a jihadist suicide bomber at the University of Oklahoma pointed out that a host of blog "facts" about the student who committed suicide by blowing himself up was inaccuracies. The story quoted the student's father, who said his son was depressed, that "this blog stuff is just smoke. It's bilge."[8]

However, other journalists argue that blogs, particularly the A-list ones, should be responded to. They contend that these blogs should be held to a higher standard than other blogs with small or non-existent audiences because they reach so many readers (Dorroh 2004/5: 48). That argument assumes that a medium attracting large audiences should adhere to journalistic standards in serving its readers. In essence, this claim assumes equivalency with traditional media, thus making blogs, at least in the minds of these journalists, true competitors with traditional journalism.

Certainly competitive elements exist in the relationship. Journalists and bloggers compete because they are alike in many ways. They both gather and disseminate news. They both want to be first with the story. And they overlap in the nature of their content: Both deal with straight news reporting and commentary. A-list political blogs often report current events as well as comment on them, although the degree to which they do so varies significantly. For example, *The Huffington Post* features hard news coverage with lengthy late-breaking wire service news, whereas other blogs such as Hugh Hewitt and *Eschaton* typically ignore the latest breaking news. Similarly, traditional media include commentary and analysis in their news presentation. Newspapers editorialize on their editorial pages and allow others – both columnists and readers – to express opinion on the same pages. In addition, broadcast news programs

---

[8] Ryan Chittum and Joe Hagain, "Student's Suicide Sets off Explosion of Theories by Blogs," *Wall Street Journal*, October 13, 2005, p. B1.

include commentary in segregated segments, either during the news hour or at other times.

Yet the overlap between the two media is hardly complete. Bloggers and journalists tussle over the media's agenda, with bloggers wanting media coverage to reflect more of their priorities and journalists naturally seeking to maintain control over that agenda.

That journalists and bloggers have different agendas is common sense. If blogs completely mimicked journalism, they would have no distinctive appeal. It is precisely because they do not completely duplicate the existing news product that they have acquired an audience. Instead they offer a component of news that is underplayed in news reporting by journalists. Blogs generally emphasize commentary with some hard news, whereas news organizations offer hard news with some commentary.

A SYMBIOTIC RELATIONSHIP

Competition is too narrow a characterization of the relationship between journalists and bloggers. What has developed is a symbiotic relationship in which bloggers and journalists have developed a dependency on one another and blogs have become integrated into the news-reporting process. Journalists read blogs and use blogs as news sources. In turn, bloggers depend on the traditional news product for hard news that they then repeat and use as the basis for blog commentary and analysis.

Journalists and bloggers may benefit from this relationship by relying on each other to provide a facet of news each has difficulty offering. Opinion and commentary occupy an uneasy place in the journalistic profession. Moreover, the type of commentary some blogs engage in – insider political gossip – traditionally has been outside the bounds of respectable journalism and does not interest most of the traditional news audience. In contrast, bloggers have no difficulty with commentary; in fact, they revel in it. Their problem is an inability to match the news media's surveillance capability. Therefore, bloggers, like everyone else, must rely on the news media for news. For national political bloggers, that means particular dependence on national media such as the *New York Times*, the *Washington Post*, and CNN.[9] They read media stories every day and use them as springboards for blog posts.

---

[9] Sue MacDonald, "Drudge Report, DailyKos, and Instapundit Grab Most 'Buzz' among Political Blogs, Says Intelliseek," *Business Wire*, October 27, 2004, p. 1.

Although critical of traditional media, some bloggers admit their dependence on traditional media. Markos Moulitsas, founder of *Daily Kos*, commented that the media are allies in helping him do his job as a blogger: "I don't want to do the reporting. . . . I need the media to do its job and provide the raw data, the raw information that then we can use to decide what's the best course for our country."[10] Josh Marshall also noted that his ideas come from the media: "In general, I'll read an article, then I'll start thinking about it, and I'll have this reflex to write about it."[11]

As players in a symbiotic relationship that both have created, bloggers and journalists have an impact on each other's spheres of activity. Bloggers have affected how journalists function in a new media environment, and journalists have been influential in the development of the blogosphere. The next section discusses how blogging has affected journalism.

The Impact of Bloggers on Journalists

The presence of the blogosphere has had an impact on a variety of aspects of traditional journalism. Effects addressed in this chapter include defining journalism, accelerating the news-reporting process, changing standards for journalistic professionals, carrying out the watchdog role, reshaping the writing and editing processes, and setting the media agenda. Each is discussed in turn.

Defining Journalism. The symbiotic relationship between journalists and bloggers has sharpened the debate over the nature of journalism and just who is a journalist. Are bloggers journalists? If bloggers are not "by nature" journalists, just as not all writers would be considered journalists, then are there certain types of bloggers who fit in the journalistic definition? Are these the A-list bloggers, those who report news more than they comment, or does the term only apply to those who claim to be journalists?

Traditional news professionals have some ambivalence about whether to consider blogs as part of the journalistic community. After all, paying attention to them means acknowledging a potential competitor and perhaps giving a measure of legitimacy to a perpetual critic. Yet how can journalists ignore blogs like *Instapundit*, *The Huffington Post*, and *Daily Kos* that have larger readerships than most daily newspapers? How do

---

[10] Interview with Josh Marshall, op cit.
[11] "Blogger; Joshua Micah Marshall, 34, Editor, Talking Points Memo," *Washington Post*, December 21, 2003, p. M3.

they disregard the work of people whom national political leaders meet with and include in their communication strategies? Not to mention the millions of Americans, many highly politically interested, who read political blogs.

The issue is hardly abstract. It becomes concrete, for example, when determining who should receive press credentials needed to gain special access to places such as the White House Press Room or the Congressional press galleries. These credentials allow entrance into areas not available to non-journalists and grant space within those areas – a warren of cubbyholes where journalists write and submit stories. Should bloggers be accorded the same privileges as reporters for traditional media such as the Associated Press or the *Los Angeles Times*?

The White House does give credentials to bloggers; it first did so in 2005. (In fact, the Obama administration was even accused of using a blogger at a press conference as a set-up to pose a question the president wanted to answer.)[12] In addition, the Congressional press galleries give access to bloggers who are full-time journalists and are not connected to advocacy organizations. During presidential election years, the national party committees invite bloggers to cover the party nominating conventions as part of the official press section.

News professionals are still wrestling with the question of whether the definition of a journalist should be stretched to include bloggers who blend advocacy and journalism. The solution may well be a distinction between bloggers who look much like journalists – have large readerships, work for an organization rather than on their own, and are primarily in the business of news gathering and reporting – and those who lack those characteristics. However, a blogger who independently reports news but has a small audience may object to these distinctions. The introduction of bloggers has complicated the issue of what constitutes a journalist.

Accelerating the News-Reporting Process. Another effect on journalism is the acceleration of the news-gathering and news-reporting processes. The pressure to get news out fast has long characterized the news business. Before radio, newspapers printed several editions throughout the day to deliver the latest news (Emery 1984; Mott 1962). The advent of 24-hour television news channels in the 1980s challenged the major network

---

[12] "Did Obama's White House Set up the Huffington Post Iran Question?" *Los Angeles Times*, June 25, 2009, at http://latimesblogs.latimes.com/washington/2009/06/barack-obama-news-conf-nico-pitney-huffington-post.html.

news divisions to broadcast news more frequently than they had in the 1960s and 1970s. In the mid-1990s, the Internet offered a new venue for constant news transmission, which required a steady dose of news content by media websites. Therefore, journalists have been driven by a deadline pressure imposed by their own news organizations' embrace of new technology.

The latest source of pressure is the blogosphere. As a medium that is defined by time and is capable of instantaneous updating, the blogosphere offers a near-constant content feed. Bloggers can broadcast a news story far more rapidly than can traditional journalists.

One reason bloggers can act so quickly is they do not need to take the time that journalists do to produce a news story. Typically a reporter gets an assignment, physically goes to the event (if necessary), writes the story – including collecting contextual information and material from sources – and then submits it for the editing process. Editing can go through several bureaucratic layers before the story is published. Then, there is the time needed to physically publish the newspaper. News for a newspaper's website skips the production stage, but still must go through the rest of the cycle. For television, the process usually is more complex because of the constraints of film crew allocation and placement, as well as production requirements.

By contrast, a blogger can post in minutes. There is no prior assignment, no need to physically attend the event, no organizational layers, and no production time. In less time than a journalist can be assigned a story, go to the scene and cover it, come back to the office and write it, and then have it edited (even for the Web edition), a story can go through various iterations in the blogosphere and become old news.

This advantage provides blogs with an important niche in delivering breaking news. In an era of 24-hour news cycles and audience expectation of near-instantaneous delivery of news of an event as it occurs, traditional news media organizations face enormous pressures to be fast and first in delivering the latest news. Blogs often exceed the traditional media's ability to inform an audience quickly. The speed of the blogosphere presents a challenge to media accustomed to being the first to report a story to the audience. Has the traditional media, then, lost its ability to be the first to publicize a story? If so, much like how newspapers adjusted to radio, will they have to find a niche of more in-depth reporting or more informed news reporting to replace their lost position of being first out with the story?

Yet the media's demise may be exaggerated, to paraphrase Mark Twain. The blogosphere's jump on news stories is likely to occur only rarely because blogs lack the surveillance and news-gathering capabilities of traditional media. The kind of story that blogs can scoop are those that news media are aware of but do not pick up (because they discount their newsworthiness), or those that emanate from a source in the blogosphere. This story could be information provided by some individual or group with unique access to information. Moreover, that group or individual would have to prefer to pass the information through the blogosphere rather than through traditional media. Although either scenario is possible, the odds of such scooping occurring on a regular basis are low.

There is another impact on journalism related to speed that goes beyond the opportunity to scoop others: the ability to frame a story in a certain way that constitutes the "first impression" for the news audience. Daniel W. Drezner and Henry Farrell have called this a "first-mover advantage in socially constructing interpretive frames for understanding current events" (Drezner and Farrell 2004: 4). The coverage of the 2005 nomination of Harriet Miers to the Supreme Court is a classic example of the "first-mover advantage." Blogs disseminated negative information about Miers faster than the White House could initiate its own image-making effort (Davis 2009: 23–5).

The blogosphere's ability to frame a story is contingent on one major condition – the presence of a universally accepted frame. Without it, there are only conflicting messages. Because the blogosphere is made up of disparate voices, such a frame consensus is difficult to achieve. In the case of Miers, both liberal and conservative blogs accepted the frame of her shortcomings. On most issues, however, there is no such consensus.

Changing Professional Standards. Part of what makes the speed of blog coverage possible is the absence of professional standards for bloggers. Whereas journalists are trained to follow certain norms and codes of professional ethics in the construction of a story, bloggers have no such guidelines. They are also free from journalistic standards of reporting. Bloggers are not required to get confirmation of a tip or check the authority of the source. Some may choose to do so to maintain their own credibility, but they are not required to do so. Andrew Sullivan said blogging is "a way you can throw ideas around without having to fully back them up, just to see what response you get."[13]

Bloggers even brag about their failure to check rumors they broadcast. The owner of a network of blogs explained that "it's implicit in the way

[13] Howard Kurtz, "The Comeback Columnist: Andrew Sullivan Continues to Defy All Expectations," *Washington Post*, April 19, 2001, p. C1.

that a web site is produced that our standards of accuracy are lower. In addition, immediacy is more important than accuracy, and humor is more important than accuracy."[14] While blogging as "Wonkette," Ana Marie Cox saw herself as competing against gossip journalists in print media. But she said the best known print gossip columnist in Washington could not compete with her because "he reports, that's the problem. He, like, checks facts."[15]

Of course, such freedom from journalistic standards is a potential disadvantage. When bloggers get it wrong – spreading rumor as fact – it should affect their credibility. And blogs often get it wrong. One example occurred on Election Night in 2004. As the broadcast networks were reporting election results from state to state, the blogosphere was distributing early exit poll results, which are incomplete, and concluding that John Kerry had won key swing states he had actually lost(Smolkin 2004/5: 44). Some bloggers do admit that blogs can be emotionally raw and they should be tempered with more deliberation. Markos Moulitsas said that there are times "I'll write something that later on I'm thinking, yeah, maybe I should have waited 10 minutes to post that."[16]

Bloggers and journalists operate under fundamentally different rules: Today journalists see themselves as engaging in a form of competition with bloggers, and bloggers see things similarly. And that competition places new pressures on traditional journalists who are accustomed to playing by a certain set of rules. Yet, those same rules are eschewed by their new competitor. Whereas one operates under journalistic rules of obtaining confirmation, which typically takes time, the blogosphere is able to ignore such norms. In the rush to be first or even merely to retain a measure of relevance in a fast-moving Internet environment, journalists may feel pressure to cast aside their training, as evidenced by the story at the beginning of this chapter.

Carrying Out the Watchdog Role. Journalists have long viewed themselves as media watchdogs who reveal politicians' mistakes and government errors. The role has become idealized, particularly in the wake of the Watergate scandal and the role of Woodward and Bernstein

---

[14] Julie Bosman, "First with the Scoop, If Not the Truth," *New York Times*, April 18, 2004, section 9, p. 10.
[15] "Wonkette in the Flesh: An Evening with Ana Marie Cox," Society of Professional Journalists, Columbia University Graduate School of Journalism, at http://spj.jrn.columbia .edu/wonkette.html.
[16] Interview with Josh Marshall, op cit.

in the fall of Richard Nixon. Bloggers are now challenging journalists' watchdog role, claiming that they, not traditional journalists, are the real watchdogs because they are watching the watchdog as well. In addition to political players, the news media themselves have become the object of blog scrutiny. Indeed bloggers relish publicizing media mistakes. One blogger warned the press that he would scrutinize every aspect of media content and "the level of scrutiny will make your editors blush" (Loyalka 2005: 19).

Of course, media watchdog groups are not new. Groups on the left (such as Fairness & Accuracy in Reporting [FAIR]) and those on the right (such as Accuracy in Media [AIM]) have critiqued the media for years. Yet bloggers operate differently. To reach an audience beyond their own mailing lists, organizations such as FAIR and AIM are compelled to work through the very media they are criticizing. In contrast, bloggers – particularly A-list ones – can avoid media and communicate directly with hundreds of thousands and, through linking, potentially millions of readers. Moreover, as mentioned earlier, the tone of blog content typically is highly critical of media content, thus making the watchdog role a natural development for political blogs. In addition, the blog audience would seem to be a highly sympathetic one for such media critique.

For conservatives, the blogosphere is not only an alternative source of information but also a forum for uncovering liberal bias in the traditional media. For example, some bloggers questioned the accuracy of an Associated Press story about a Bush campaign event in 2004, which stated that the crowd had booed when Bush announced that former president Bill Clinton would be undergoing heart surgery. The bloggers placed audio and video of the event on their sites as evidence that the crowd did not boo, which prompted an AP retraction.[17]

In another example, conservative bloggers questioned the accuracy of blog postings by a U.S. soldier in Iraq writing under a pseudonym, which were published in the *New Republic*. The soldier related atrocities committed against Iraqis by U.S. troops, including an incident in which a soldier had mocked a disfigured Iraqi woman.[18] Conservative bloggers claimed the accounts were false and criticized *The New Republic* for publishing them without verification and under a pseudonym.

[17] Stephen Humphries, "Blogs Look Burly after Kicking Sand on CBS," *Christian Science Monitor*, September 22, 2004, p. 1.
[18] John Milburn and Ellen Simon, "Army Denounces Articles Written by GI," *USA Today*, August 9, 2007, at http://www.usatoday.com/tech/news/2007-08-09-soldier-blogger-denounced_N.htm.

A private claimed responsibility for the stories, and the U.S. Army ultimately issued a report concluding the stories had been faked. However, *The New Republic* initially stood by the stories and only later disavowed them.[19] An array of conservative bloggers used the incident to support their charges of media bias. One wrote that the entire incident is "another chapter in the sad history of 'fake, and not accurate, either' news stories."[20] Another pointed to "editorial failures and ethical breaches of the magazine's senior editors."[21]

Liberal bloggers have attacked conservative media as well. The blogosphere played a role in uncovering the identity of a man accredited to the White House press corps from a supposedly independent news service, but who actually was affiliated with a Republican website. Even worse, liberal blogs discovered that the would-be reporter had set up pornographic websites and had even advertised himself, in the nude, as an escort.[22]

From the left, right, or middle, bloggers enjoy pointing out mistakes made by traditional media and forcing corrections and apologies from what they call "big media." For example, a blogger accused a *New York Times* arts reporter of a conflict of interest because she served simultaneously as a member of the board of directors of an art institute. The blogger claimed the reporter was giving the art institute more press than it deserved. The reporter denied the accusations, but also resigned from the board.[23]

Another element of the watchdog role is covering stories that traditional media do not. One blog even has as its slogan "All the News the MSM [Mainstream Media] Forgot to Print."[24] Blogs are most interested in missed stories about journalists themselves and fulfilling the important role of checking journalists' tendency not to criticize their own profession. Indeed, journalists are reluctant to cover their own organizations critically. Nor are journalists quick to criticize one another – whether

[19] Howard Kurtz, "New Republic Disavows Iraq Diarist Reports," *Washington Post*, December 4, 2007, p. C1.
[20] "The Short Happy Life of Scott Beauchamp, Fabulist," August 6, 2007, at http://www .powerlineblog.com/archives/2007/08/018142.php.
[21] Bob Owens, "The Never-Ending Story," *Media Mythbusters*, October 26, 2007, at http://mediamythbusters.com/blog//p=127.
[22] Greg Mitchell, "The 'Gannon' Case: Blogs Roll Again," *Editor & Publisher*, March 2005, p. 26.
[23] Jennifer Huberdeau, "Clark Trustee Resigns after Blogger Criticism," *North Adams Transcript* (Mass), June 15, 2006.
[24] See Pajamasmedia.com.

it is each other's work or the non-journalistic activities of journalistic peers.

One example is the case of CNN executive Eason Jordan. At a panel of the World Economic Forum in Davos, Switzerland, in 2005, Jordan accused the U.S. military of purposely shooting at journalists. When challenged by others, Jordan backed away from the allegation. However, a blogger at the summit decided to write about the incident on a public blog set up by the World Economic Forum after he noticed traditional media were not doing so (Reisner 2005: 10). Two controversies arose. One was over the content of Jordan's assertion; the other was about whether the news media had ignored Jordan's comment because he was a fellow news professional. Bloggers accused the media of ignoring the incident because it involved one of their own, whereas traditional media responded that the accounts of what Jordan had said varied and there was no transcript because the event was officially "off the record." After these controversies led to Jordan's resignation,[25] bloggers gloated over their victory. One called it "Blogs 1 CNN 0." Another claimed that "the Blog is turning into a great equalizer."[26]

Political bloggers also view themselves as watching the watchdog by including those elements of a story that traditional media ignore. Bloggers sometimes see themselves as completing the story – offering perspectives that traditional media do not. This is particularly true of conservative bloggers who view traditional media as one-sided. For example, regarding media coverage of the Iraq war, some conservative bloggers complained that the traditional media only covered the violence and failed to tell their audiences about the successes of the U.S. military or the Iraqi government. "What's important," according to one conservative blogger, "is to fill in both sides of the story or multiple sides of the story."[27]

Although the watchdog role is critical of the media, bloggers often suggest their goal is not to destroy the traditional media, but to reform it (Palser 2005: 70). According to Josh Marshall, the critique that comes from blogs like his is intended to "get people to practice better

---

[25] Reisner (2005); Howard Kurtz, "Eason Jordan, Quote, Unquote," *Washington Post*, February 8, 2005, p. C1; and "CNN Executive Resigns after Controversial Remarks," CNN.com, February 11, 2005, at http://www.cnn.com/2005/SHOWBIZ/TV/02/11/easonjordan.cnn/index.html.

[26] Michelle Malkin, michellemalkin.com, February 11, 2005, at http://michellemalkin.com/2005/02/11/breaking-news-eason-jordan-resigns.

[27] Interview with John Hinderaker, PBS, August 26, 2006, at http://www.pbs.org/wgbh/pages/frontline/newswar.

journalism."[28] Similarly, Markos Moulitsas argued the country needs a press that "acts like a check on government, that acts like it's working in the public interest, as opposed to just trying to ingratiate themselves with the people in power and get invited to the right cocktail parties."[29]

Reshaping the Writing and Editing Processes. Blogging began as a public personal expression, much like writing a personal diary that is photocopied and handed out to perfect strangers. One survey of bloggers found that the most common reason for blogging was to "document their personal experiences and share them with others," and the most common topic of blog writing was "my life and experiences."[30] That style carries over into political blogs: A-list political bloggers take personal thoughts and broadcast them to hundreds of thousands of people. Josh Marshall lamented, "In a way I've lost my ability to have my own private reflections. I've gotten in the habit of just putting everything out there."[31]

Through most of the last century, the professional norms of journalism were diametrically opposite to this personalized approach in news writing. In vehement reaction to the partisan press of an earlier age, journalists were instructed to hide their true feelings behind the mask of objectivity. It was important that the reader be unaware of personal views the reporter held about the subject. Professional norms discouraged personal expression.

Over the past several decades, the pre-eminence of objectivity has been eroded by successive challenges from the "new journalism" movement, advocacy journalism, and public journalism. Moreover, public opinion about the news media has become more critical of journalists' assertions that they are able to maintain objectivity. Most Americans today perceive at least a fair amount of political bias in the news they get.[32]

Blogs are the most recent addition to these anti-objectivity trends of the past half-century. However, blogs are different from these previous

---

[28] Interview with Josh Marshall, op cit.

[29] Interview with Josh Marshall, op cit.

[30] Amanda Lenhart and Susannah Fox, "Bloggers: A Portrait of the Internet's New Storytellers," Pew Internet and American Life Project, July 19, 2006, at http://www .pewinternet.org/PPF/r/186/report_display.asp.

[31] "Blogger; Joshua Micah Marshall, 34, Editor, Talking Points Memo," *Washington Post*, December 21, 2003, p. M3.

[32] Pew Research Center for the People and the Press, "Internet's Broader Role in Campaign 2008: Social Networking and Online Videos Take Off," January 11, 2008, at http:// people-press.org/reports/pdf/384.pdf; and Pew Research Center for the People and the Press, "Internet News Audience Highly Critical of News Organizations," August 9, 2007, at http://people-press.org/reports/pdf/348.pdf.

movements because they come from outside journalism. They offer journalists an alternative method of writing that not only combines the elements of previous movements such as critical analysis and advocacy journalism but also emphasizes the human nature of the reporter over the model of the journalist as an emotion-free professional. One blogger explained that blogs "tend to be impressionistic, telegraphic, raw, honest, individualistic, highly opinionated and passionate, often striking an emotional chord" (Lasica 2001b).

When they adopt blog writing, journalists are freed from the constraints of objective journalism. They are more likely to express personal views, make unsubstantiated assertions, and abandon the reliance on sources to make their points. The blog world's norms are beginning to carry over into and reshape the norms of journalism, allowing journalists to be freer to act more like other bloggers and less like objective journalists. The question remains as to how far these blog norms will extend into journalism. Will the blog writing style become the style incorporated outside the blogosphere; that is, in journalists' traditional formats of news presentation? The answer probably is no. Objective journalism took some time to establish itself as the paradigm for news presentation and has become well-established in the psyche of news (Schudson 1981). The vast majority of the traditional audience still expects and wants a press that is largely free of a particular point of view.[33]

The different norms of blogging and journalism create a conflict for individual journalists who both blog and continue to work as daily reporters covering beats. Perhaps blogging can be viewed as a release – the liberation discussed earlier. For a brief time in their daily routine, they can break out of their set patterns and express personal opinions and, frankly, be themselves. Yet will that type of writing come to affect their traditional writing?

An even more important question is whether journalists will be trusted as neutral descriptors of events after they express their personal views about those same events on blogs. Does that "liberation" ultimately undermine journalists' credibility? The question is particularly important given the decline in credibility already suffered by the press.[34] Will blog expression – as attractive as it may be as a release – harm journalists' ability to perform their main function as news gatherers and reporters?

---

[33] Pew Research Center for the People and the Press, "Internet's Broader Role in Campaign 2008."

[34] Pew Research Center for the People and the Press, "Public More Critical of Press, But Goodwill Persists," June 26, 2005, at http://people-press.org/reports/pdf/248.pdf.

With its roots in personal journals, the blogosphere still values individualistic writing characterized by the absence of editing. When they compare themselves with traditional news media, bloggers point to the absence of a news hierarchy as a distinct advantage in the quality of their writing. They argue they do a better job of writing because they do not have the bureaucracy of traditional news media that "turns even the best prose limp, lifeless, sterile, and homogenized" (Lasica 2001b).

In response to the blogosphere's perceived freshness, individual journalists have started their own blogs, sometimes separate from news organizations. In addition, news media organizations have created blogs to capture the interests of their readers and meet the imperatives of a new medium. On these blogs, staff journalists write in a style that is much more real time, informal, and opinion-laced – much like the blogosphere generally – than the style they use in their jobs. One editor for the *New York Times*' website explained the role of the newspaper's blog as a vehicle for "insights that might not rise to a full article but are worthy of reporting" (Lawson-Borders and Kirk 2005: 49).

News organization blogs also offer more space for news, enabling the dissemination of news that does not fit in the hard copy.[35] Short pieces – news notes that do not justify article-length treatment – are particularly likely to appear on blogs. Because of the looser space constraints, stories or short news notes can go into a blog when they would not meet the threshold for the print edition. One reporter for *The Washington Post* noted "the bar is lower than getting something in a newspaper."[36]

Therefore, one might assume that blogs would provide an opportunity for news media to spend more time on substantive issues. For example, during a presidential campaign a newspaper could add depth to stories about issues and candidates instead of focusing on the horse- race that dominates media coverage (Lawson-Borders and Kirk 2005: 49). Yet blog content is more likely to be shorter versions of what already appears or perhaps even more "inside gossip" than extensive policy discussion.

The blogosphere is creating new dilemmas for news professionals on their own websites. One is the transparency of the newsgathering process. Journalistic blogs potentially make the news-gathering process public because reporters can post story pieces online as they gather news.

[35] Joe Strupp, "Voting for the Web," *Editor & Publisher*, October 2006, p. 62.
[36] Howard Kurtz, "Mainstream Blogs Open Floodgates for Political Coverage," *Washington Post*, October 26, 2007, p. C1.

They need not wait to distribute a final product in the form of a printed newspaper article or a television news story. One reporter-blogger said he will inform his readers of what he is working on and what information he has before he even writes the story. Doing so illuminates the news-gathering process and even invites reader reaction in the formation of the story (Lasica 2001b).

However, does this transparency also lead to confusion and misinformation? The release of information from one source may be contradicted by later sources, yet the reporter has distributed the information as if it were confirmed fact. Or could reading only part of the story lead to inaccurate conclusions, particularly when the reader does not return to read the full product?

Blogs also raise the question of the role of editing. Should journalists' blogs be edited? Is it a violation of the norms of the blogosphere when an individual's writing is edited by someone else? Or are those norms changeable as the blogosphere acquires new members who seek to adapt the medium to their uses?

Editing is fundamental to the journalistic process and antithetical to the original blog culture. This dilemma is exemplified in the case of a reporter for a California newspaper who wanted to post in the newspaper's blog a strongly critical statement about a gubernatorial candidate, but was forced to run the copy through the editor first. Bloggers complained about the news organization's decision to edit the journalist, and the newspaper eventually overturned its decision.[37] However, then some of the reporter's colleagues complained about the new double standard of editing – print stories got edited but blog posts did not (Smolkin 2004). The dilemma for the news organization is that, regardless of who the blog writer is, the news organization still holds responsibility for what is written by a journalist on its blog.

Media Agenda Setting. Another dilemma relating to the political blogosphere is what news professionals should do with blog stories. Bloggers view themselves as a vital component of the news-gathering process. One of the predictions they make is that increasingly they will be viewed as the first source of information, which journalists will then follow. One common mantra is, "If journalism is the first draft of history, blogs might

---

[37] Michael Falcone, "Does an Editors Pencil Ruin a Web Log?" *New York Times*, September 29, 2003, p. C9; Daniel Weintraub, "Scuttlebutt and Speculation Fill a Political Weblog," *Nieman Reports*, Winter 2003, pp. 58–9.

just be the first draft of journalism" (Bloom 2003). Yet journalists are not likely to stand aside to let bloggers write the first drafts of their stories. Following the blogs' agenda places journalists in a secondary position in terms of news dissemination.

Journalistic culture thrives on the notion that journalists are first with information: They have the news before anyone else, and they get to decide what the public will get to know. As discussed earlier, that gate-keeping function is under attack now. Nevertheless, journalists are reluctant to relinquish their primacy as the source of information disseminated to the public.

In addition to pride, other factors slow any journalistic rush to adopt the blogs' agenda. As mentioned earlier, blogs have a reputation for getting things wrong. Many spread rumors and gossip without any compunctions about reliable sourcing or effects on their reputation, although bloggers respond that stories in the making, like sausage, are not pretty. However, journalists may not be able to afford the luxury of an eventual "sorting out." The public likely will not tolerate unsubstantiated stories when it has become accustomed to reliable news.

Moreover, blog stories may not fit news values held by the average consumer of news media. For example, political bloggers typically focus on stories that would be considered "inside baseball" by the vast majority of the public. News media serve that larger, less political audience that political bloggers do not.

Nevertheless, blog stories are out there, and some possess elements of newsworthiness. Some other news outlet may use the blog story and scoop everyone else as a result. Thus blog stories cannot be completely ignored, but neither can they be incorporated into the news product without concern over whether they adhere to professional standards of news judgment and reporting.

JOURNALISM'S EFFECTS ON BLOGS

Bloggers suggest they are changing journalism or at least reforming it. Yet, the effects of the symbiotic relationship are hardly one-way: Journalism is shaping the evolution of blogging as well. As a practice in its infancy, blogging is creating its own traditions to shape the approach of participants to the formation and dissemination of blog content. Hence, the development of blogging can be heavily influenced by more entrenched forces. In addition, as bloggers go mainstream, other forces have strong incentives to influence blogging in certain directions. For example, politicians, party organizations, or interest groups may seek to co-opt blogs to serve particular individual or group goals.

The most powerful outside influence over blogs is likely to be journalism. Journalism shares the same objectives as blogging – to disseminate news and information to a particular audience. Journalists have been integrated into blogging, which increases the opportunities for influence on this evolving activity. That integration has been more pronounced by the fact that blogging has emerged at the same time as newsrooms are downsizing. Many journalists who still want to practice their craft find blogs attractive as an alternative. Journalism may provide a governing model for blogs, help establish blogosphere standards, and help define the niche that blogs hold in the journalism community.

Providing a Governing Model

The current approach to news writing has a long historical tradition. The evolution from the publisher to the partisan editor to the reporter as the author of news occurred primarily in the 19th century, but still heavily influences the current journalistic model. Journalism based on accuracy, rapid delivery, and descriptiveness has become the governing model for the reporting of news. Even the mixing of analysis and commentary within reporting is not a combination invented by blogs. Teddy White, who covered presidential elections as a reporter/analyst rather than just a standard reporter, created a new style of journalism that preceded bloggers by 40 years. That model then becomes one for bloggers to emulate.

Many bloggers cringe at that thought of journalism. They would argue that the news media – with their bureaucracy, biases, and overall bigness – are the epitome of what blogging is replacing. Bloggers, they would argue, have no business imitating a failed model. Moreover, they might add, is not the very presence of blogs evidence of the failure of that model?

Regardless of the antipathy toward journalism held by many bloggers, many are finding it difficult to discard that model of news reporting. It is the most commonly accepted model, and even their audiences have come to expect bloggers to accept much of the journalistic model. Readers accustomed to professional standards of journalism do not easily abandon those expectations in the face of a new medium. They anticipate that blogs will match their expectations of content.

In fact, A-list blogs are increasingly adopting the organizational style of traditional media: They have structural layers, and editors who determine the content that appears on the blog. Blog owners are responsible for the credibility of their blogs and assume editorial functions to assure that a blog writer does not diminish the status of the blog.

Establishing Blogger Standards

More specifically, journalism is affecting bloggers' approaches to their tasks. Bloggers are being held to standards of professionalism that journalists created: They are expected to be accurate, to tell the truth, to use sourcing, and to ensure that those sources are reliable.

The blogosphere is divided over whether to accept these standards. Some bloggers want to be treated as journalists. Others prefer a different model – one that bloggers themselves will create on their own. Yet the very existence of this debate indicates that journalism's standards are being employed as a yardstick for judging bloggers.

The bloggers who likely will gain the greatest audience and have the most impact both in and out of the blogosphere will be those who adhere to standards of journalism. Those bloggers who want to be like journalists have even created an organization, the Media Bloggers Association. The association seeks journalistic credentialing for bloggers, equal access to sources, coverage under shield laws, and the same respect accorded journalists. The association essentially will create a two-tiered blogging world. One part of that world will be bloggers who subscribe to a code of ethics and become journalist-like. The other tier will be everyone else – bloggers who wish to retain blogging's unique characteristics.

That division may become the equivalent of the difference between large corporate-based newspapers and the single-person, small-town newspaper run on a shoestring budget. It is important to remember that the latter model eventually disappeared. Similarly the "Wild West" atmosphere of the blog – the libertarian dream of no external constraints – is fast evaporating for those blogs who seek to be treated seriously as mainstream players.

Defining the Role of Blogs in Journalism

Political bloggers willingly (although not consciously) tamed the "Wild West" when they forged a relationship with journalists. By adopting the role of commentator on traditional media content, they became dependent on the very news organizations they often inveighed against. As journalists began to pay attention to that commentary and bloggers became conscious of that fact, the dependency relationship deepened. Journalists' use of blogs and of bloggers as occasional news sources (much as they do politicians or interest group representatives), as well as news coverage of the blogosphere, all contributed to the dependency. Bloggers felt recognized, appreciated, and useful for their influence in traditional politics. Even for an established journalist like Andrew Sullivan, the attention had to be surprising and gratifying. For those who were unknown such as Markos Moulitsas (*Daily Kos*), Duncan Black (*Eschaton*), or Glenn Reynolds (*Instapundit*), it had to be a truly heady experience.

Once the adulation or, at least, acknowledgment occurred for bloggers, it was impossible not to want it to continue. Yet maintaining the relationship required adapting to it. To continue to be read and quoted and courted, bloggers had to adjust to the needs of the audience – journalists.

CONCLUSION

This description of a symbiotic relationship may ring hollow to many journalists and perhaps even to bloggers, and they may be correct. This symbiotic relationship may not apply to every individual journalist or blogger. Indeed, there are journalists who do not use blogs or pay attention to them, and there are political bloggers who rely on the media for news only very rarely. However, even though as individuals they do not participate in the relationship, they may still be affected by its existence. The symbiotic relationship is likely to be strongest among those bloggers – the A-list bloggers – who act more like journalists in a number of ways.

Again, the existence of a symbiotic relationship does not mean that journalists and blogs do not compete at times. The competition may well be an important component of the symbiosis. It helps establish the independence of the two entities, thus preventing the absorption of one by the other. Blogs especially emphasize that independence. Bloggers relish asserting their autonomy by embarrassing the press in cases in which news organizations committed a public mistake or an individual journalist missed a story.

Nevertheless, these two groups have much in common. First, they share basic personal and professional interests. As one blogger put it, "We may have problems with media coverage and the media may have problems with blog coverage, but we're all at the root political junkies and nerds" (Perlmutter 2008: 166). Second, they both need to gather information and produce a political information product that maintains an audience. A third common element is their desire to create or preserve a niche in a rapidly changing media environment that continually challenges the very definition of themselves and their roles.

The commonality between journalists and bloggers has led to the formation of this symbiotic relationship, one that exists despite the hostility expressed by many bloggers and the public disdain or seeming neglect on the part of some journalists. As long as journalists see bloggers as potential news sources, and bloggers rely on the traditional media for news, their work will continue to be intertwined.

References

Bloom, Joel David. 2003. "The Blogosphere: How a Once-Humble Medium Came to Drive Elite Media Discourse and Influence Public Policy and Elections." Paper presented at the second annual pre-APSA Conference on Political Communication, Philadelphia, August 31.

Davis, Richard. 2009. *Typing Politics: The Role of Blogs in American Politics*. New York: Oxford University Press.

Dorroh, Jennifer. 2004/5. "Knocking Down the Stonewall." *American Journalism Review* (December). Retrieved from http://ajr.org/Article.asp?id=3787.

Drezner, Daniel W., and Henry Farrell. 2004. "The Power and Politics of Blogs." Paper presented at the annual meeting of the American Political Science Association, Chicago, September 2–5.

Emery, Edwin. 1984. *The Press and America: An Interpretive History of the Mass Media*, 5th ed. Englewood Cliffs, NJ: Prentice-Hall.

Lasica, J. D. 2001a, April 29. "Blogging as a Form of Journalism." *USC Annenberg Online Journalism Review*. Retrieved from http://www.ojr.org/ojr/lasica/1019166956.php.

Lasica, J. D. 2001b, May 24. "Weblogs: A New Source of News." *USC Annenberg Online Journalism Review*. Retrieved from http://www.ojr.org/ojr/workplace/1017958782.php.

Lawson-Borders, Gracie, and Rita Kirk. 2005. "Blogs in Campaign Communication." *American Behavioral Scientist* 49: 1–12.

Loyalka, Michelle Dammon. 2005. "Blog Alert: Battalion of Citizen Investigative Reporters Cannot be Ignored by Mainstream Media." *IRE Journal* (July/August): 19.

Mott, Frank Luther. 1962. *American Journalism: A History, 1690–1960*. New York: Macmillan.

Palser, Barb. 2005. "No More Name-Calling." *American Journalism Review* (April/May 2005). Retrieved from http://www.ajr.org/Article.asp?id=3861.

Perlmutter, David D. 2007. "'If I Break a Rule, What Do I Do, Fire Myself?' Ethics Codes of Independent Blogs." *Journal of Mass Media Ethics* 22 (April): 37–48.

Perlmutter, David D. 2008. "Political Blogging and Campaign 2008: A Roundtable." *The International Journal of Press/Politics* 13 (April): 160–70.

Pole, Antoinette. 2007. "Hispanic Bloggers in the Blogosphere: Politics and Participation." Paper presented at the annual meeting of the American Political Science Association, Chicago, August 30–September 2.

Reider, Rem. 2005. "Hold that Obit." *American Journalism Review* 27 (2): 6.

Reisner, Neil. 2005. "The Accidental Blogger." *American Journalism Review* (April/May). Retrieved from http://www.ajr.org/article.asp/id=3841.

Schudson, Michael. 1981. *Discovering the News: A Social History of American Newspapers*. New York: Basic Books.

Smolkin, Rachel. 2004. "The Expanding Blogosphere." *American Journalism Review*. Retrieved from http://www.ajr.org/archive.asp/issue=66.

Smolkin, Rachel. 2004/5. "Lessons Learned." *American Journalism Review* (December/January). Retrieved from http://www.ajr.org/article.asp/id=3783.

Sweetser, Kaye D., Lance V. Porter, Deborah Soun Chung, and Eunseong Kim. 2008. "Credibility and the Use of Blogs Among Professionals in the Communication Industry." *Journalism & Mass Communication Quarterly* 85 (Spring): 169–85.

"The Short Happy Life of Scott Beauchamp, Fabulist." 2007. *Powerline* (August 6). Retrieved August 6, from http://www.powerlineblog.com/archives/2007/08/018142.php.

Vaina, David. 2007. "Newspapers and Blogs: Closer Than We Think." *USC Annenberg Online Journalism Review*. Retrieved April 23, from http://www.ojr.org/ojr/stories/070423_vaina/.

CAMPAIGNS AND ELECTIONS IN THE NEW MEDIA ENVIRONMENT

4

YouTube and TV Advertising Campaigns

Obama versus McCain in 2008

Ann Crigler, Marion Just, Lauren Hume, Jesse Mills, and Parker Hevron

The 2008 campaign marked the first time that a candidate's speech was set to music performed by popular musicians. Will.i.am, lead singer of the Black Eyed Peas, produced a YouTube music video of Barack Obama's "Yes We Can" speech. The "Yes We Can" video received more than 7 million views (January 2011), and Obama's words reached American youth in a way that had never been done. In short order, all of the candidates adopted the Internet as a platform for advertising, making 2008 the first YouTube presidential campaign. Candidates posted their television ads to YouTube as well as ads produced just for the new platform.

This is not the first time that candidates have adopted new technologies to reach voters. Historically, candidates have quickly embraced tools that expanded their access to voters – from Al Smith's first use of television to air an acceptance speech (1928), to Dwight Eisenhower's television ad campaign (1952), to Howard Dean's web-based credit card donation (2004). Now, YouTube, launched on February 14, 2005, has become one of the top three most-visited websites since at least 2008 (Alexa 2011). YouTube's popularity and its potential to reach voters were not lost on candidates.[1]

In 2008, the Obama campaign posted not only ads to YouTube but approximately 1,800 videos, including speeches, Get Out the Vote (GOTV) messages, and supporter videos. The McCain campaign posted

---

[1] In October 2008 (the month before the presidential election), YouTube received more than 80 million unique visitors in the United States, out of 344 million worldwide (Gannes 2008). In other words, more than *a quarter* of the U.S. population watched a video on YouTube during the month before the election.

almost 300 additional videos on its dedicated YouTube channel.[2] Clearly, YouTube had become a major communication avenue for presidential campaign messages. YouTube ads represented a significant integration of a new media tool into electoral politics. Did this new venue affect what candidates communicate to voters? This chapter examines how the Internet has changed political advertising in presidential campaigns.

Scholars have extensively studied political advertising on television. Researchers have explored the function and effects of TV ads, from their impact on political learning (Goldstein and Ridout 2004) to the democratic consequences of negative messages (Brader 2005; Jamieson 1993; Kern 1995; West 2009). There is no consensus on exactly *how* advertising affects campaigns (Kinder 1998), but most agree that advertising influences election outcomes (Bartels 1993; Goldstein and Ridout 2004; Zaller 1992). Whatever the mechanism, candidates believe that advertising serves a vital strategic purpose.

In the 2008 presidential campaign, the candidates spent more money on advertising than in any previous election. The Obama campaign spent $235.9 million on TV advertisements, while the McCain campaign devoted $125.5 million (CMAG 2008). In addition, both major presidential campaigns spent an additional $26 million on Internet advertising (CMAG 2008). Although the Internet is a relatively new campaign medium, scholars document an increasing role for the Internet in political campaigns. Studies have shown a variety of Internet effects, including political information acquisition (Druckman 2005), campaign fund-raising (Bimber and Davis 2003; Sabato 2010), social networking (Haynes and Pitts 2009; Johnson and Perlmutter 2009), and political discourse (Baum and Groeling 2008; Denton 2009). In 2008, 55% of adults received campaign news from the Internet (up from 10% in 1996) and 35% of adults watched some kind of online political video during the campaign (Smith 2009). Broadband access is a prerequisite for access to YouTube, and by 2008, more than half of all Americans had broadband Internet access at home (Smith 2009).

So far, there have not been comprehensive comparisons of TV and Internet political advertising. We address a critical gap in the literature and demonstrate that candidates can use the Internet to deliver political messages different from those aired on television. This chapter

---

[2] Although McCain and the Republican National Committee created and posted more ads on YouTube – more than twice as many as the Obama campaign did – Obama had a much stronger presence on YouTube because of his campaign's use of videos sponsored by both the campaign and his supporters.

analyzes the TV and Internet-exclusive advertisements of the two major U.S. presidential candidates, John McCain and Barack Obama, from July to November 2008. We expect some differences between Internet and television ads because these media target different audiences. Our analysis compares the tone of ads, emotional appeals, the use of deception, and the representation of diverse people in these ads. Ultimately, this chapter addresses a central question of this volume by examining how the addition of YouTube alters the tone and substance of electoral politics. We also consider the potential for YouTube to enhance democratic practices by engaging new groups of citizens.

We first review previous research on ad-targeting to demonstrate why we expect TV and Internet advertisements to differ. On the basis of that literature, we generate hypotheses about how we expect the candidates to alter their advertising strategies for the new medium, and, finally, we report our findings and discuss the implications of our results for the future of Internet campaigns.

TV VERSUS INTERNET ADS

Candidates can advertise in different venues. Darrell West argues that presidential campaigns have to decide on *the frequency* of airing particular messages and the *proper mix* of national and local TV buys (2009). Both the frequency and "mix" choices have been superseded by the Internet. On the web, ads are accessible to a national and even international audience. Rather than grappling with the national versus local television ad buys, the Internet and TV offer candidates a choice between a "proper mix" of appeals to supporters and the general public. Candidates can expect the audience for their TV advertisements to include supporters, opponents, and uncommitted citizens (West 2009). The goals of TV advertising are to reinforce the views of supporters, persuade potential voters, and discourage opponents' supporters from voting. Because of the great expense of TV advertising, most presidential ad-buys since 1988 have not been national, but rather targeted to the media markets in contested "battleground" states. Viewers in these battleground states are likely to have a wide range of views and allegiances (West 2009). The goal of televised ads in contested states is to persuade the "persuadables" (Schnur 2010) and discourage the opposition. Because candidates follow the same strategy of concentrating their ads in hotly contested states, the vast majority of voters around the country never see candidate advertising on television. The Internet has the power to transform that equation. Anyone, around the country or around the world, can click on a candidate's YouTube ad.

This does not mean, of course, that the Internet guarantees widespread viewing of candidate ads. In fact, the reverse is true (CCAP 2008; Smith 2009). The Internet is a motivated medium, meaning that users must seek out content; it does not come to them unbidden. Although Internet ads can be intrusive (pop-up and banner ads), the user generally engages in a positive action (clicking) in order to see an ad. This experience differs from television advertising, in which audiences choose non-ad content and the ads come to them in the same package.

To see candidate ads on the Internet, a user must be motivated to visit either the candidate's site or YouTube channel. Because viewing Internet ads is volitional, people who watch candidate ads are much more likely to be supporters than opponents. As Republican consultant Dan Schnur mentioned, Internet ads are used primarily to motivate and to organize supporters rather than to persuade or discourage potential voters, which is the goal of TV ads (Martin 2008; Schnur 2010).

The 2008 YouTube election illustrated the supporter-based ad-viewing pattern. In October 2008, 77% of Democratic and Democratic-leaning voters reported watching an Obama video on the Internet (CCAP 2008). (See Figure 4.1.) Only 47% of Republican and Republican-leaning voters said they saw an Obama video. Meanwhile, 61% of Republicans reported viewing a McCain video on the Internet, while only 37% of Democrats did the same. Clearly, online videos are more often viewed by the party's

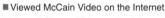

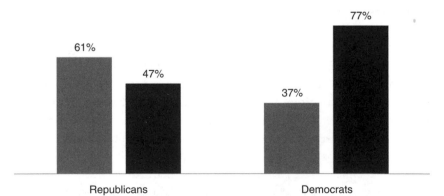

FIGURE 4.1. Percentage of Internet Video Viewership by Party Affiliation.
Source: Cooperative Campaign Analysis Project, 2008.

base than by opposing partisans. In 2008, Democrats were also more likely than Republicans to view ads of their candidate.

Advertising Strategies

In their television ads, candidates appeal to a "general population." The goal is to persuade potential voters to support the ad sponsor. Therefore, we anticipate that in their TV ads candidates will picture people who look like the general population they are targeting. In addition, television ads will use negative or attack messages to demobilize the opponent's supporters in the TV audience. Internet advertising – directed to the base – may not.

Given the novelty of YouTube in the 2008 campaign, it was unclear whether the McCain and Obama campaigns had the time or expertise to adapt to the Internet platform. For example, candidates could have simply taken advantage of the economy of Internet production by uploading their TV advertisements to the web, without adjusting the content. Because both candidates produced a number of Internet-exclusive ads, it suggests they recognized the unique aspects of the new medium and decided to adapt their messages.

Further evidence came from the consultants themselves. A postelection wrap-up at the Unruh Institute of Politics at the University of Southern California revealed that Obama's consultants recognized the volitional nature of Internet access and decided that the majority of their online content should focus on supporters rather than on the general audience. Consultants reported that they directed their efforts to motivating their base to engage in off-line activity (Rospars 2008). That is, the Obama Internet ads were intended to pursue a "base-targeting strategy" rather than a "general population strategy" (Brader 2005).

We propose that, if candidates understand the differences in target audience between Internet and TV ads, their ads for the two platforms will show a different mix of people. In addition, they will craft positive messages for the Internet (speaking primarily to supporters) but use attack ads on television (speaking to a population that includes independents and opponents as well). We found ample evidence of this difference. In the Internet ad "Signs of Hope and Change," the Obama campaign pictured people of all ages and ethnicities engaged in campaign activities explaining why they supported their candidate.[3] The video climaxed with a string of supporters across the country holding up handwritten signs printed

---

[3] Source: http://www.youtube.com/watch?v=EcRA2AZsR2Q.

with the words "hope" and "change." By using particular individuals talking about how they felt about working for Obama, the video targeted supporters who shared their enthusiasm for Obama and his message of empowerment. The McCain campaign made a similar pitch in an Internet ad entitled "I Am Joe."[4] In his ad, people in various jobs – including a truck driver, a store owner, and a schoolteacher – explain that they are voting for John McCain because they "should not be punished" for working hard and making money. The McCain ad was meant to resonate with supporters who opposed Obama's tax plan.

In contrast, many of Obama's TV ads were negative. For example, in the ad titled "Original,"[5] a narrator says of McCain, "He's the original maverick," at which point the ad cuts to a clip of McCain asserting his policy agreements with President Bush. After reciting a list of supposedly Bush policies, the narrator asks, "The original maverick? Or just more of the same?" Likewise, McCain's "Celeb"[6] and its many variations (including "Special," "Family," and "Taxman") all focused on Obama's popularity around the world by showing cheering throngs in Paris and Berlin but asserting that Obama's "quick rise" made him "not ready to lead."

In the following section, we compare how the "base" strategy associated with Internet ads versus the general appeal strategy of television leads to further content differences between Internet and TV ads, especially with regard to emotions, deception, and diversity in the ad content.

Emotions in Advertisements

Political advertising has been described primarily as a vehicle for emotional messages, especially negative emotions (Brader 2005). Candidates using the Internet are communicating primarily with supporters; therefore, we expect Internet ads to appeal to emotions such as enthusiasm for the candidate and anger toward the opponent that will motivate their base. However, on TV, we expect to see a wider range of emotions because the audience is more varied. In addition to enthusiasm and anger appeals, TV ads should also arouse fear or anxiety to encourage independent voters to seek information and to discourage support for the opposition (Brader 2005).

---

[4] Source: http://www.youtube.com/watch?v=ZSoOYjMKCdc.
[5] Source: http://www.youtube.com/watch?v=39WyqGySCPg.
[6] Source: http://www.youtube.com/watch?v=FiPAz8494Vs.

We expected McCain ads to be more negative than Obama ads, first because trailing candidates tend to "go negative" more often than front-runners do (Brader 2005, 2006; Jamieson 1993; West 2009). Trailing candidates may be inclined to use negative ads even when communicating primarily to supporters. Second, past research has found distinct psychological differences between Republicans and Democrats or conservatives and liberals (Hibbing 2010; Jost et al. 2003; Lakoff 1996). Recent research on the 2008 election found that Republicans relied heavily on anger-invoking attacks (Crigler and Mills 2009; Mason and Huddy 2008). Thus, we expect Republicans to use more anger and fear in their Internet ads than Democrats. Republican consultant Dan Schnur, in discussing expectations about partisan audiences, made this point: "Because online messaging is more motivational you will see more purely positive or negative ads on the Internet. They [advertisements] tend to be harsher online because you're preaching to the choir" (2010). Schnur's account dovetails with our assertion that candidates tailor their Internet ads to supporters' emotions. "Your supporters know the other candidate is Satan. They just need to know why. This gets them out volunteering or voting," Schnur added (2010). Given that McCain was trailing and that he was communicating to a predominantly Republican audience on the web, we expect him to "go negative" more often than Obama. We think he would make more anger appeals to his supporters on the Internet than Obama would. Since fear appeals are directed primarily at independents, we expect both candidates to use fewer fear appeals in their Internet ads than in their TV ads.

Deception in Advertisements

Political ads try to portray the candidates in the most favorable light and, in the case of attack ads, to picture the opposition in unflattering ways. To accomplish these ends, ads draw not only on emotions but also on shades of truth and deception (Kamber 1997; Merritt 1984). Ansolabehere and Iyengar (1997) state that because of First Amendment protection, the "potential for distortion and deception [in political speech] is limited only by the marketplace. . . . It is thought to be rampant" (7). Advertising about issues informs potential voters about the candidates' positions (Ansolabehere and Iyengar1997) but can equally misinform voters if the messages are false or deceptive (Neuman, Just, and Crigler 1992). Past research has found that negative ads are more likely to distort facts than positive ads (Kamber 1997: 223).

Ad watches, instituted in the 1990s by many major news outlets (Just et al. 1996), as well as independent watchdog groups, such as FactCheck.org, and media critics, such as the Media Research Center (MRC), the Center for Media and Public Affairs (CMPA), and Fairness and Accuracy in Reporting (FAIR), use fact-checking techniques to draw people's attention to inaccurate claims. Although the goal of fact-checkers is to rectify misleading information in political advertisements, research indicates that they may end up magnifying the effects when they repeat the false claims (Baum and Groeling 2008; Just et al. 1996). If candidates are concerned about ad watches and fact-checkers, they may be more careful about what they claim in the TV ads than on the Internet, which is less visible. If Internet ads get less scrutiny, we might predict that Internet ads could be more deceptive than TV ads. However, because Internet ads contain more positive messages directed to supporters, candidates may feel little need to distort the truth, leading to a prediction that TV ads would be more deceptive than Internet ads. We will show which of these competing forces is at work in Internet and TV ads.

Representation of Diversity in Advertisements

If candidates knowingly used Internet advertisements to appeal to their bases, the ethnic composition of their ads may differ if their bases are more or less diverse. It was the case in the 2008 presidential campaign that McCain's base of support was predominantly white, while Obama's supporters included the majority of Latinos and blacks. Both candidates had incentives to be inclusive in TV ads in battleground states, where the voting population is diverse, but their Internet ads may portray a different a picture (Valentino et al. 2002).

METHODS

To test the "base targeting" versus "general population" strategies, we analyzed McCain and Obama advertisements broadcast on TV or posted on YouTube between July 1 and November 4, 2008. The sample of TV advertisements includes all of the ads that were posted on nationaljournal.com during this period. The Internet advertisements included all candidate or party sponsored ads that were posted on the candidates' or their respective parties' YouTube channels. If advertisements appeared on both TV and the Internet, they were coded as TV ads. Ads coded as "Internet" appeared exclusively on the web.

The sample consisted of ninety-two advertisements for Obama (77 TV ads and 15 YouTube ads) and ninety-four ads for McCain (60 TV ads and 34 YouTube ads).[7] We conducted a systematic, quantitative content analysis of the ads drawing on the work of Ted Brader (2005, 2006). We coded for the presence or absence of negative tone of the ads, criticisms based on issues or character, appeals to emotion or logic, and specific emotions of anger, fear, and enthusiasm. A list of issues was developed from the ads and then used to code the first, second, and third issues mentioned in each ad.[8] In addition, we employed variables that measured the absence, presence, or strong presence of the following characteristics in ads: Focus on Issues, and Focus on Personal Qualities/Character. We also coded the number of people in the visuals – differentiating gender (men vs. women), ethnicity (whites/blacks/Hispanics/Asians), and age (youth/middle aged/elderly). In addition, we included a second tone variable to describe the type of ad (promotional, comparative, or strictly attack). The critical Deception variable was coded on a three-point scale, following a modified version of FactCheck.org criteria (0 = True/Mostly True, 1 = Half True, 2 = Barely True/False).

To test intercoder reliability, two coders coded a randomly selected subsample of nineteen advertisements that included TV and Internet ads from both candidates. Overall agreement between both coders was 94.6%, which indicates a very high level of reliability between coders. They achieved 100% agreement for the following variables: Tone 1 (Promotional, Comparative, Attack); Tone 2 (Negative, Not Negative); Enthusiasm (Present, Not Present); Issues; and Character/Personal Qualities. Coders achieved more than 90% reliability for Emotional Appeal (Present, Not Present) and Deception (True/Mostly True, Half True, and Barely True/False). The values for each were 94.7% and 91.3%, respectively. Coders achieved 85.5% agreement for the Logical Appeal variable, 89.4% for the Fear Appeal variable, and 85.5% agreement for the Anger Appeal variable, all of which demonstrate sufficient intercoder reliability.[9]

---

[7] Because our analysis is concerned with the campaigns' strategic use of TV versus Internet advertising, we did not include any YouTube ads posted by supporters or other groups or campaign videos that were not advertisements.

[8] Contact authors for a complete list of coded variables.

[9] We were able to increase the intercoder reliability for several of the variables by collapsing multiple values and creating dichotomous variables. These variables include Enthusiasm Appeal, Fear Appeal, and Anger Appeal. In addition, the Deception variable was collapsed from five values to three.

RESULTS

We know that the candidates did not simply post their TV ads to the Internet. They spent millions of dollars producing Internet-only ads. Comparing our samples of McCain's and Obama's TV and Internet ads reveals that both campaigns treated Internet ads differently from television messages. At the most basic level, the campaigns acknowledged the low cost of producing Internet ads by producing web ads that were typically twice as long as ads on TV – where additional seconds cost more money. For example, Obama's "Signs of Hope and Change" Internet ad ran two minutes forty-one seconds. McCain's Internet ad "I Am Joe" ran one minute thirty-one seconds on the Internet, but a thirty-second version, "Sweat Equity," aired on TV. Both candidates' Internet ads were longer than their TV ads, but they approached ad content differently on the two platforms.

Promotional Appeals versus Attack Advertising

While both candidates used attack ads on TV in the battleground states, their Internet strategies differed. McCain employed about the same level of attacks in his Internet ads (65%) as on TV (55%), while Obama used significantly fewer attack ads on the web (27%) than on TV (58%), and many fewer than McCain employed in either medium. McCain's campaign may have used attacks on Obama to appeal to their supporters. In the face of their weak position in the national polls, encouraging anger toward the opposing candidate might encourage the base, as Republican consultants have suggested (Donatelli 2008; Schnur 2010). Obama's Internet ads did not lack substance. Rather, Obama's relied on comparative ads to contrast his candidacy and policy positions with McCain's.

The candidates' use of comparative and attack ads on the web led us to investigate how the content of negative ads differed from their more positive counterparts. To answer this question, we conducted an ordinal logistic regression that measured the relationship between negativity and a variety of variables, including deceptive messages, appeals to emotion and logic, focus on personal qualities, issue focus, emotional appeals (and particular emotions such as fear, anger, and enthusiasm), ad medium, and which party sponsored the ad.

We found that attack ads are different from both comparative and positive ads. While some scholars have argued that negative ads have more issue coverage than positive ads (Geer 2006; Kamber 1997), the 2008 negative ads were actually less likely to address issues than positive ads. The more ads focused on issues, the less likely they were to be negative.

As expected, however, negative ads were highly emotional. Negative ads stoked anger at the opposition, while appeals to enthusiasm for the sponsoring candidate were rarely associated with negativity in an ad. Appeals to fear, while present, were not always associated with negativity in the 2008 ads (see Table 4.1).

TABLE 4.1. *Predicting Negativity in Ads (3 Pt. Scale)*

	Ordinal Logistic Regression	
Deception	.887	(.603)
Emotion Appeal	−.486	(1.39)
Logic Appeal	.416	(.472)
Personal Qualities Focus	−.249	(2.49)
Issue Focus	−2.37**	(.842)
Enthusiasm Appeal	−4.92***	(.667)
Fear Appeal	.553	(.550)
Anger Appeal	2.51***	(.569)
Internet Ad	.200	(.540)
Republican Sponsor	.242	(.495)
Pseudo R^2	.662	
N	186	

Notes: All variables coded 0–1 except "Issue Focus" and "Personal Qualities Focus," which are coded 1–3. Significance levels: $*P < .05$, $**P < .01$, $***P < .001$

Emotions in Advertisements

Emotional appeals are the main currency of political advertising. We found that regardless of medium, Obama and McCain ads relied more heavily on emotional appeals than appeals to logic (see Figure 4.2).[10] McCain used more of a mix on the web, but the mean difference between his TV and Internet ads was not significant. Obama, however, struck a different note in his TV and Internet ads. Obama's TV ads appealed to emotion almost twice as often as they appealed to logic (99% to 52%, respectively), while his Internet ads employed substantially more logic appeals (80% appealed to emotion and 72% appealed to logic). The difference in logic appeals between Obama's TV and Internet ads was highly significant.

---

[10] For additional information regarding other statistical significance comparisons in Figures 4.2, 4.3, 4.4, 4.5, and 4.6, please contact the authors.

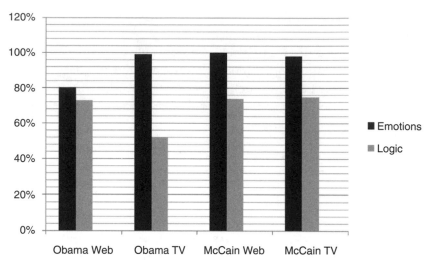

FIGURE 4.2. Percentage of Ads Appealing to Emotion and Logic by Candidate/
Medium.
Notes: Chi-Square significant at $p = .011$, $N = 186$.

Delving more deeply into the candidates' appeals to particular emotions is revealing. The dominant emotion in the candidates' TV ads was
anger. More than two-thirds of McCain's ads and 81% of Obama's ads
stirred up anger. Both candidates' TV ads appealed to fear about equally
(44% compared with 41%). The extensive use of appeals to anger and
fear reinforces the view that the goal of TV ads is to mobilize supporters
while discouraging opponents. McCain's anger appeals were consistent
across ads in the two media. He projected anger in 74% of his Internet ads but used fewer fear appeals on the Internet than on TV (18%
and 44%, respectively). Presumably, McCain sought to rouse his supporters on the Internet by appealing to their anger but soft-pedaled fear.
Notably, McCain's ads expressed enthusiasm/hope/joy only 38% of the
time in either medium.

Obama's media strategy illustrated a stronger contrast between his
television and Internet ads than did McCain's (see Figure 4.3). His TV
ads appealed to the anger that many Americans were feeling about the
Bush administration. Obama coupled his televised anger appeals with
appeals both to fear and to enthusiasm, which prior research suggests
would benefit his messages about change and hope, respectively. Fear
appeals awaken the potential electorate to new options and motivate
people to seek further information. Enthusiasm appeals reassure voters of
their decisions (Just, Crigler, Belt 2007; Marcus, Neuman, and MacKuen
2000; Neuman et al. 2007).

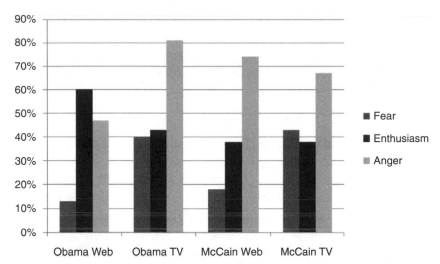

FIGURE 4.3. Percentage of Ads with Emotions Present by Candidate/Medium.
Notes: Chi-Square significant for "Fear" at $p = .016$; Chi-Square not significant for "Enthusiasm" at $p = .46$; Chi-Square significant for "Anger" at $p = .038$, $N = 186$.

On the web, however, Obama appealed mainly to enthusiasm. Sixty percent of Obama's Internet ads contained at least some appeal to the positive emotions of enthusiasm, hope, or joy – a figure almost the inverse of McCain's positive emotional appeals. Obama employed anger in less than half of his Internet ads and fear was largely absent. The Obama campaign recognized that his supporters constituted most of the viewers of his Internet ads. He did not need to make them fearful, because they were already supporting him. He could appeal to their anger to help motivate them to participate and volunteer, but enthusiasm was the most important emotion to convey on the web to consolidate his base.

Because hope and change formed the foundation of Obama's message, it is not surprising that these same tropes figured so strongly in Internet ads directed at his supporters. It is surprising, though, that McCain did not make a stronger attempt to excite the enthusiasm of his supporters on the web. His campaign was clearly aware of the difference between the two media, as evidenced by their downplaying fear appeals on the web compared with TV. The McCain camp, however, may have correctly identified the primary emotion of their supporters as anger rather than hope. Social conservatives tend to be angry about the threat of change and loss of power and status in a changing social environment (Jost et al. 2003; Lakoff 2009). As previous research has shown, anger appeals arouse Republican voters more so than Democrats. The McCain campaign encouraged anger and contempt for Obama by employing mocking humor. One ad posted on YouTube after Obama's trip to Europe jokingly referred to his reception as comparable to that of Moses or Jesus.[11]

Deception in Advertisements

On the basis of data from FactCheck.org, we assessed each ad's truthfulness on a deception scale, which was scored 0 (True/Mostly True), 1 (Half True), and 2 (Barely True/False). Comparing the means of the scale shows that both candidates were more truthful in their Internet ads than in their TV ads. A majority (60%) of McCain's Internet ads scored True or Mostly True, while 100% of Obama's Internet ads were True or Mostly True. In contrast, almost half (48%) of Obama's TV ads were True or Mostly True, compared with 31% for McCain.

There seems to be more temptation to deceive on TV, where the goal is to persuade a mixed audience of supporters, independents, and opponents, than on the Internet, where the audience is mostly made up of supporters. McCain, however, was significantly less truthful in his ads than Obama (see Figure 4.4). More than half (52%) of McCain's TV ads were rated "Barely True/False" compared with only 30% of Obama's TV ads. In addition to a lack of truthfulness, McCain's TV ads exhibited other forms of deception and distortion. A notable example was his TV ad "Ladies and Gentlemen," which used an ominously grayed palette to show Joe Biden speaking about Barack Obama in a slowed and distorted voice, while showing a series of frightening visuals of war and threats (including Iran's President Ahmadinejad).

A comparison of means test demonstrates that Obama's web ads were significantly more truthful than his TV ads (see Figure 4.5). This was not the case for McCain. The average values for truthfulness in McCain's TV and Internet ads were not significantly different.

We questioned whether candidates were more likely to use deception in certain kinds of ads. For example, we considered whether attack ads were more deceptive than promotional ads. An ordinal-logistic regression examined the relationships between deception in ads and a variety of variables, including platform (Internet vs. TV), Tone, Ad Sponsor, Issues, Character/Personal qualities, the use of Emotional Appeals, the use of Logical Appeals, and the use of Fear and Anger. Attack ads and ads appealing to anger were significantly more likely

[11] Source: http://www.youtube.com/watch?v=mopknolPzM8.

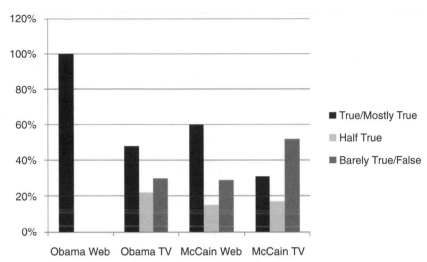

FIGURE 4.4. Percentage of Deception in Ads by Candidate/Medium.
Notes: Chi-Square significant at $p = .000$, $N = 186$.

to be deceptive than other kinds of ads. Internet ads were significantly less deceptive than other ads. The results confirm our hypothesis that ads targeting supporters have less need for deception. The results also show that Republican ads were more likely to be deceptive than Democratic ads in 2008 because they attacked more (see Table 4.2).

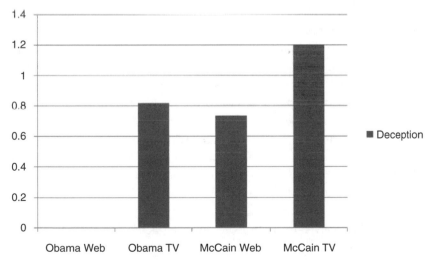

FIGURE 4.5. Means of Deception in Ads by Candidate/Medium.
Notes: Chi-Square significant at $p = .000$; $N = 186$. Coded: True/Mostly True $= 0$, Half True $= 1$, False/Barely True $= 2$.

TABLE 4.2. *Predicting Candidate Deception in Ads*
(3 pt. Scale)

	Ordinal Logistic Regression	
Tone	3.14**	(.952)
Issue Focus	1.83*	(.823)
Personal Qualities Focus	−21.6	(.000)
Emotion Appeal	20.0	(.469)
Logic Appeal	−.007	(.384)
Fear Appeal	.208	(.387)
Anger Appeal	1.76**	(.608)
Internet Ad	−1.94***	(.476)
Republican Sponsor	2.35***	(.479)
Pseudo R^2	.424	
N	186	

Notes: All variables coded 0–1 except "Tone," Issue Focus," and "Personal Qualities Focus," which are coded 1–3. Significance levels: $*P < .05$, $**P < .01$, $***P < 0.001$

Deception in ads was also associated with different topics. As Table 4.3 shows, both candidates were less truthful when talking about taxes than when talking about other subjects. Each of the four Obama television ads that mentioned taxes were coded Barely True or False. McCain's tax ads were Barely True or False in 71% of his seven television ads and in 57% of his Internet ads. For example, FactCheck.org called out McCain for his ad "Painful," which claimed that Obama would raise taxes on people making as little as $42,000 a year. The accompanying graphic showed two children huddled around a woman. In fact, Obama's plan would raise taxes only on single persons making $42,000 a year and the amount of the increase would have been $15. The thrust of Obama's tax plan was to raise taxes on those making more than $250,000. Obama's TV ads also used deception in discussing health care (75% of his TV ads about health care were coded as Barely True or False). One theme in Obama's Medicare ads was that McCain would cut benefits or eligibility for Medicare – a claim that the McCain campaign flatly denied. Instead, McCain promised to reduce Medicare spending by reducing fraud and introducing digital records.

One difference between Obama's and McCain's use of deception was that McCain deceived on both issues and character. Notably, McCain's ads were rated barely truthful or false when attacking Obama's honesty and values as well as Obama's corporate and interest-group support. According to FactCheck.org, one of the more dubious claims that McCain

TABLE 4.3. *Most Deceptive Ad Topics by Candidate and Medium*

	N	True/Mostly True	Half True	Barely True/False
Obama Web				
NONE	15	15 (100%)	0 (0%)	0 (0%)
McCain Web				
Taxes	7	1 (14%)	2 (29%)	4 (57%)
Candidate Honesty	3	1 (33%)	0 (0%)	2 (67%)
Obama TV				
Taxes	4	0 (0%)	0 (0%)	4 (100%)
Healthcare	8	1 (12.5%)	1 (12.5%)	6 (75%)
Corporations/Special Interests	10	3 (30%)	5 (50%)	2 (20%)
Energy Policy	6	3 (50%)	2 (33%)	1 (17%)
McCain TV				
Corporations/Special Interests	4	0 (0%)	0 (0%)	4 (100%)
Candidate Honesty	4	0 (0%)	1 (25%)	3 (75%)
Banking Crisis, Bailout	4	1 (25%)	2 (50%)	1 (25%)
Taxes	7	2 (29%)	0 (0%)	5 (71%)
Economy	9	4 (45%)	2 (22%)	3 (33%)
Values	17	8 (47%)	2 (12%)	7 (41%)

Notes: Only topics commonly used by the candidates on TV and the web were included. Deception ratings developed from FactCheck.org data.

made about Obama was in the ad "Blind Ambition," which stated that Obama had "blind ambition" and "when convenient, he worked with terrorist Bill Ayers. When discovered, he lied" ("Blind Ambition," a thirty-second TV ad). FactCheck.org reported that Obama never lied about his relationship to Bill Ayers and denounced Ayers's Weather Underground activities. McCain's campaign levied personal attacks against Obama on both television and the Internet but especially on TV (see Table 4.3).

Representation of Diversity in Advertisements

Given that both campaigns appeared to recognize that Internet ads were directed at supporters more than the general population, we expect Internet ads' representations of the population to depend on each candidate's base of support. We note that there was more time to show different groups of people in web ads than on TV, because web ads were much longer than the typical thirty-second TV spot. The Internet ads for both candidates included more people altogether than their TV ads (see Figure 4.6). As expected, the types of people shown in ads varied between

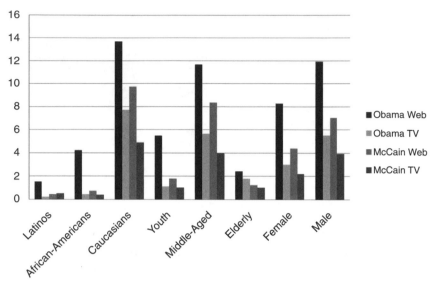

FIGURE 4.6. Mean Numbers of Groups in Ads.
Notes: Chi-Square significant at $p = .000$; $N = 186$.

the Democratic and Republican candidates. While there were no significant differences between the candidates' ads in depicting Caucasians, Asians, middle-aged and elderly people, or men, Obama and McCain ads diverged significantly on other groups pictured with the candidates. A few of Obama's Internet ads highlighted blacks, Latinos, and youth, as well as women, but his television ads did not emphasize these groups. None of McCain's ads featured these groups.

Like Reagan's "Morning in America" ad, Obama's "Signs of Hope and Change" ad, begins with reassuring music accompanying iconic American symbols "from sea to shining sea," followed by a sequence of people – starting off with a middle-aged Latina, two African American men, and a white working man. Diversity was represented throughout the ad by individuals of different classes, ages, genders, races, disabilities, often working together on the Obama campaign.

The representation of young people in Obama's web ads may also be attributable to Obama's supporters being younger than McCain's supporters and were therefore more likely to use the Internet (Rospars 2008). While the McCain campaign did not adjust its Internet ads to suit the ethnic makeup of his base, there was one exception: McCain's Internet ads pictured McCain with more young people than his TV ads. For example, his Internet ad "I am Joe" includes a young family, a young schoolteacher, and a young couple, along with middle-aged and older people. This difference suggests that McCain's campaign was making an effort to target likely web users among his supporters.

CONCLUSION

The introduction of YouTube as a message-delivery vehicle altered both the tone and substance of political advertising in the 2008 campaign. Because the Internet is a motivated or volitional medium, ad viewers must have incentives to go to a candidate site or search for ads on YouTube. Therefore, most web ads are viewed by people already interested or committed to the candidates. Candidates have even greater incentive to adapt their ad strategies to the Internet if their supporters are heavy Internet users, as we saw with Obama. As discussed in Chapter 7, Internet ads, like other Internet tools, generally "preach to the choir."

Although both candidates' Internet ads targeted supporters, their ads were substantially different. Being ahead nationally, Obama could afford to be more positive than McCain in his web ads. In addition, Obama's Internet audience included many young voters who embraced his call for change. To reach that audience, Obama relied on promotional and comparative ads rather than attacks, more appeals to logic than to emotion, and fewer anger appeals than his TV ads. In contrast, McCain moderated his TV strategy for the Internet less consistently than Obama did. In addressing his supporters on the web, McCain employed fewer fear appeals than in his TV ads, but he maintained the same level of anger. While McCain made an effort to appeal somewhat more to young people in his web ads, across the two media his ads looked a good deal alike.

In an election postmortem, McCain's web consultants reported that a lack of money and the age demographic worked against McCain campaign's Internet strategy (Donatelli 2008). Possibly, with more time and more money, McCain would have made a greater effort to target supporters on the Internet. The comparative lack of younger supporters may have discouraged McCain's campaign from pursuing a more costly Internet ad strategy.

In 2008, both candidates used less deception on the Internet than they did on TV. One lesson we can draw from our study is that the threat of "ad watches" is not so strong as to suppress deception on TV. Consultants have long agreed that being behind in the race calls for desperate measures. As the trailing candidate, McCain resorted to more deception and ad hominem attacks than Obama did in his ads. Further research is needed to explore whether deception is more associated with trailing candidates, the type of issues being discussed in the ads, the preferences of a particular candidate or party, or the medium.

The Internet is not a platform that inherently benefits one party over the other. In 2010, the election of Scott Brown to the U.S. Senate in Massachusetts saw Republican organizers able to catch up with Obama's success in using the Internet to raise cash from small donors. In the 2010 midterm elections, Tea Party activists, like the Democrats in 2008, organized effectively through the Internet. Going forward, both parties will attempt to exploit the campaign capacities of the Internet.

Our results contain tantalizing suggestions about the future of Internet advertising. Continuing research should examine additional elections at multiple levels to see how campaign strategies adapt to the public's increasing reliance on the Internet. In addition, further research is needed in Internet ad diffusion ("going viral") and social networking, as well as supporter-sponsored ads – such as Will.i.am's "Yes We Can" ad – that enter campaign discourse.

Ultimately, from the evidence that we present, it appears that the Obama campaign's successful use of YouTube provided a new tool to reach out to partisan supporters and to potential voting blocs that traditionally have been less interested in politics. In this regard, YouTube and other Internet tools offer the opportunity for candidates to enhance citizen engagement and improve democratic practices. The study of future election cycles will help to clarify the role that the Internet can play in engaging more diverse citizens in the political process.

References

Alexa: The Web Information Company. 2011. http://www.alexa.com/topsites.

Ansolabehere, Stephen, and Shanto Iyengar. 1997. *Going Negative: How Political Advertisements Shrink and Polarize the Electorate*. New York: Free Press.

Bartels, Larry M. 1993. "Messages Received: The Political Impact of Media Exposure." *American Political Science Review* 87: 267–85.

Baum, Matthew A., and Tim Groeling. 2008. "New Media and the Polarization of American Discourse." *Political Communication* 25: 345–65.

Bimber, Bruce A., and Richard Davis. 2003. *Campaigning Online: The Internet in U.S. Elections*. New York: Oxford University Press.

Brader, Ted. 2005. "Striking a Responsive Chord: How Political Ads Motivate and Persuade Voters by Appealing to Emotions." *American Journal of Political Science* 49 (2): 388–405.

Brader, Ted. 2006. *Campaigning for Hearts and Minds: How Emotional Appeals in Political Ads Work*. Chicago: University of Chicago Press.

CCAP. 2008. *Principal Investigators Simon D. Jackman and Lynn Vavreck*. Data taken from January Wave.

CMAG. 2008. "Elections by the Numbers: 2008 Race for the White House: A Made-for-TV Election." *CMAG EYE*, December 2008.

Crigler, Ann, and Jesse Mills. 2009. "Emotions and Horserace Framing: Studying the Effects of Anxiety and Reassurance on Partisan Identifiers." Paper presented at the 2009 annual meeting of the American Political Science Association, Toronto, Canada.

Denton, Robert E. (ed.). 2009. *The 2008 Presidential Campaign: A Communication Perspective*. Lanham, MD: Rowman and Littlefield.

Donatelli, Becki. 2008. "Technology in Politics: How Campaigns Use the Internet to Talk to Voters." Politico and USC College, Unruh Institute of Politics Conference on *Election 2008 Obama vs. McCain: What Happened and What Happens Next?* November 21–22, 2008.

Druckman, James N. 2005. "Does Political Information Matter?" *Political Communication* 22: 515–19.

Gannes, Liz. 2008. "Just Wow: YouTube Had 344M Global Uniques in Oct." *NewTeeVee*. Retrieved from http://newteevee.com/2008/12/01/just-wow-youtube-had-344m-global-uniques-in-oct/, December 1.

Geer, John. 2006. *In Defense of Negativity: Attack Ads in Presidential Campaigns*. Chicago: University of Chicago Press.

Goldstein, Kenneth, and Travis Ridout. 2004. "Measuring the Effects of Televised Political Advertising in the United States." *Annual Review of Political Science* 7: 205–26.

Haynes, Audrey A., and Brian Pitts. 2009. "Making an Impression: New Media in the 2008 Presidential Nomination Campaigns." *Political Science and Politics* 42: 53–8.

Hibbing, John B. 2010. "Different Slates: Physiological and Cognitive Differences across the Political Spectrum." Presentation to the Neuropolitics Workshop at California Institute of Technology, December 10.

Jamieson, Kathleen Hall. 1993. *Dirty Politics: Deception, Distraction, and Democracy*. New York: Oxford University Press.

Johnson, Tom, and Dave Perlmutter (eds.). 2009. "The Facebook Election: New Media and the 2008 Election Campaign." Special Symposium. *Mass Communication and Society* 12 (3): 375–6.

Jost, John, Jack Glaser, Arie W. Kruglanski, and Frank J. Sulloway. 2003. "Political Conservatism as Motivated Social Cognition." *Psychological Bulletin* 129 (3): 339–75.

Just, Marion, Ann Crigler, Dean Alger, Timothy Cook, Montague Kern, and Darrell West. 1996. *Crosstalk: Citizens, Candidates, and the Media in a Presidential Campaign*. Chicago: University of Chicago Press.

Just, Marion, Ann Crigler, and Todd Belt. 2007. "Don't Give Up Hope: Emotions, Candidate Appraisals, and Votes." In *The Affect Effect: Dynamics of Emotion in Political Thinking*, ed. W. Russell Neuman, George E. Marcus, Michael MacKuen, and Ann Crigler (231–59). Chicago: University of Chicago Press.

Kamber, Victor. 1997. *Poison Politics: Are Negative Campaigns Destroying Democracy?* New York: Insight Books, Plenum Press.

Kern, Montague. 1995. *Thirty-Second Politics: Political Advertising in the '80s.* 1989, Westport, CT: Praeger-Greenwood. Chapter reprinted in Davis, Richard (ed.). 1995. *Politics and the Media* (190–206). Mahweh, NJ: Lawrence Erlbaum.

Kinder, Donald R. 1998. "Communication and Opinion." *Annual Review of Political Science,* 1: 167–97.

Lakoff, George. 1996. *Moral Politics: How Liberals and Conservatives Think.* Chicago: University of Chicago Press.

Lakoff, George. 2009. *The Political Mind.* New York: Penguin Books.

Martin, Jonathan. 2008. "Technology in Politics: How Campaigns Use the Internet to Talk to Voters." Politico and USC College, Unruh Institute of Politics Conference on *Election 2008 Obama vs. McCain: What Happened and What Happens Next?* November 21–22, 2008.

Mason, Lilliana Hall, and Leonie Huddy. 2008. "The Emotional Basis of Political Mobilization." Paper presented at the 2008 annual meeting of the American Political Science Association, Boston, MA.

Merritt, Sharyne. 1984. "Negative Political Advertising: Some Empirical Findings." *Journal of Advertising* 13 (3): 27–38.

Neuman, W. Russell, Marion Just, and Ann Crigler. 1992. *Common Knowledge.* Chicago: University of Chicago Press.

Neuman, W. Russell, George E. Marcus, Ann Crigler, and Michael MacKuen. 2007. *The Affect Effect: Dynamics of Emotion in Political Thinking and Behavior.* Chicago: University of Chicago Press.

Rospars, Joe. 2008. "Technology in Politics: How Campaigns Use the Internet to Talk to Voters." Politico and USC College, Unruh Institute of Politics Conference on *Election 2008 Obama vs. McCain: What Happened and What Happens Next?* November 21–22, 2008.

Sabato, Larry. 2010. *The Year of Obama: How Barack Obama Won the White House.* New York: Pearson Longman.

Schnur, Dan. 2010. Telephone Interview with authors. February 11, 2010.

Smith, Aaron. 2009. "The Internet's Role in Campaign 2008." Pew Internet and American Life Project. April 15.

Valentino, Nicholas A., Vincent L. Hutchings, and Ismail K. White. 2002. "Cues That Matter: How Political Ads Prime Racial Attitudes during Campaigns." *American Political Science Review* 96 (1): 75–90.

West, Darrell. 2009. *Air Wars: Television Advertising in Presidential Election Campaigns, 1952–2008,* 5th ed.. Washington, D.C.: CQ Press.

Zaller, John. 1992. *The Nature and Origins of Mass Opinion.* Cambridge: Cambridge University Press.

5

The Rise of Web Campaigning in Finland

Tom Carlson and Kim Strandberg

In May 2009, about a month before the Finnish elections for the European Parliament, Taru Tujunen, party secretary for the Finnish National Coalition Party, stated, "During each election, I believe that I have proclaimed that *this* is the first Internet election" (Verkkouutiset 2009). Tujunen was certainly being ironic in discussing her party's Web campaigning strategies, but her comment highlighted that the party (a major player in Finnish modern elections) has, for each recent election, gradually advanced in its use of the Internet as a campaign tool. According to Tujunen, campaigns must be present where the voters are today – online. Thus the days of traditional campaign meetings, in which candidates representing the party and voters met locally and interacted directly, were coming to an end: This form of campaigning is – and here she used a Finnish metaphor – "snow from last year's winter" (Verkkouutiset 2009).

Indeed, scholars examining changes in election campaigning practices across time in Europe have usually stressed the role of the advances in communication technology (e.g., Norris 2000a). In the *premodern* era of campaigning, direct interpersonal communications (e.g., campaign meetings) and print media (party press, pamphlets) were central. In the *modern* campaign era, the television developed into the most important forum of campaign events. In the emerging *postmodern* campaign era, the Internet is playing a key role. Interestingly, and in contrast to the Finnish party

The authors have contributed equally to this work. This chapter substantially extends an earlier work (Carlson and Strandberg 2008). We thank Professor Pekka Isotalus for providing the names of the candidates with websites in the 1996 European Parliament elections.

secretary's dismissal of old types of campaigning, scholars have noted that Web campaigning in two respects represents a return to the pre-modern campaign era (Norris 2000a: 149; Ward and Gibson 2003: 189–90). First, the Web has the potential to again decentralize campaigning. Whereas television in many European countries facilitated the development of centralized campaigns organized by strong party organizations, the Web offers a reasonably cheap and functional platform for campaigning that strengthens individual candidates and their campaigns at local levels (Zittel 2009). Second, because new media allow different forms of interactivity, there might be a revival of interpersonal communication between campaigns and voters. In developing various interactive practices that facilitate contact and thereby engage voters, Web campaigns by candidates may play a more important role than online centralized party campaigns (Gibson 2004; Greer and LaPointe 2003; Zittel 2009).

Against that background, this chapter – one of three in this book providing a comparative angle by focusing on contexts outside the United States – analyzes the longitudinal evolution of candidate-driven Web campaigns in Finland from two perspectives that link to the overarching questions of this book. Our first goal is related to the general question about whether the new media environment has enhanced various democratic ideals. Given that the Internet has made it easier for candidates to run personal campaigns at the constituency level, we address the question of whether the new media environment has, over time, enhanced the democratic ideal of equal campaigning opportunities by leveling the playing field for various types of candidates. Specifically, we focus on the adoption of Web campaigning by analyzing longitudinal changes in the profile of the candidates maintaining personal campaign websites: Were there initially "digital gaps" between different types of candidates in adopting websites (e.g. resource-based gaps), and have such gaps remained, narrowed, or widened over time? According to the early equalization thesis, which states that the Internet in the long run provides a leveling effect in the electoral process (Barber 2001; Corrado and Firestone 1997), such gaps should narrow over time.

Our second goal is related to the overarching question of the book about the impact of the new media environment on activating citizens politically. Here, we address the question of whether candidates' campaigns websites across time have moved beyond being primarily "electronic brochures" (Kamarck 2002: 89) to being sites that use media-specific features to activate and engage voters. In so doing, we touch on one of the key questions of the book concerning the impact of the new media environment on political practices: To what extent have candidates running Web campaigns across time adopted a practice of providing a range of different interactive opportunities for voter engagement? Particularly, we empirically address the question of whether certain types of candidates (e.g., well-resourced candidates) have longitudinally adopted this Web campaigning practice more extensively and quickly than other types.

GOING BEYOND THE U.S. CASE

Studies of Web campaigning have become a staple in political communication research. Although the bulk of research focuses on the United States, there is a growing body of Web campaigning studies in other nations (e.g., Gibson 2004; Kalnes 2009; Kluver et al. 2007; Lilleker and Malagón 2010; Schweitzer 2008; Zittel 2009). However, the few studies that have empirically and systematically analyzed trends in candidate Web campaigning across time have solely examined the U.S. electoral context (Druckman, Kifer, and Parkin 2007; Greer and LaPointe 2003; Gulati and Williams 2007; Schneider and Foot 2006; Williams and Gulati 2006).Certainly, the candidate-focused and highly competitive election system in the United States has made it relevant to specifically examine Web campaigns by U.S. candidates (Gibson 2004). Nevertheless, research findings in the context of U.S. campaigns may be a case of "American exceptionalism" (Lipset 1996; Wilson 1998). As Norris (2003) emphasizes in a cross-national study of party websites, it is uncertain how far U.S. findings can be generalized to other nations. Hence, to broaden our understanding of the longitudinal dynamics of candidates' adoption of Web campaigning, it is meaningful to study the topic in a political and electoral context outside the United States. It is especially important to extend the longitudinal study of Web campaigning by candidates to multiparty systems with proportional elections rather than two-party systems with first-past-the-post elections.

As for Western Europe, Gibson (2004) points out that the strong party system in most of the nations has hampered Web campaigning activities among individual candidates in parliamentary elections. However, Finland is a deviant case. In contrast to other Scandinavian countries and most other Western European nations, individual candidates play a crucial role in campaigns in Finland. In the Finnish electoral system, which is based on proportional representation in multimember districts, voters do not cast ballots according to party lists of candidates but instead

vote for unranked individual candidates representing parties or electoral
alliances. As in the United States, this system generates candidate-driven
campaigns: The candidates invest in personal campaigns and have their
own support groups that organize campaign activities, raise money, and
generate publicity (Ruostetsaari and Mattila 2002). These groups operate
relatively independently from the parties; on the constituency level, the
party organization functions as a background resource and coordinator.

Another circumstance making Finland a good case study in terms of the
evolution of Web campaigning by candidates is that the basic prerequisite
for online electioneering – a high level of societal Internet penetration –
was fulfilled early in Finland (Norris 2000b). Like their U.S. counterparts,
Finnish candidates had by the mid-1990s started to use the Web in their
campaigns. This is illustrated in Figure 5.1, which shows the adoption
of personal campaign websites by candidates across time in the United
States and Finland.

The growth in the number of candidates with personal websites in
Finnish campaigns has been rather similar to that in the United States,
although at a somewhat slower pace. The slower adoption of personal websites in Finland can be explained partly by the fact that U.S.

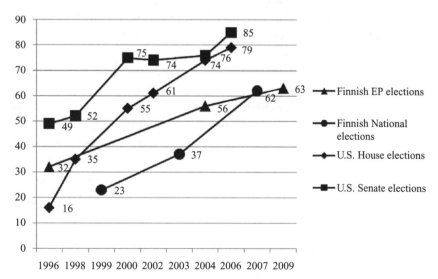

FIGURE 5.1. The Share of Candidates with Campaign Websites in U.S. Congressional Elections 1996–2006, Finnish Elections for European Parliament (EP)
1996–2009, and Finnish National Elections 1999–2007 (%).
Sources: The United States: Gulati and Williams (2007, 448); Finland: see the
data and method section.

campaigns produce innovations that are later adopted elsewhere and partly by the fact that some types of Finnish candidates – above all, fringe- and minor-party candidates – initially relied on their parties' Web presentations of candidates (see Carlson and Djupsund 2001).

The growth pattern in the adoption of personal campaign websites differed between candidates running in the Finnish national elections and those in the Finnish elections for the European Parliament. Therefore, we find it essential to examine various gaps in the Finnish candidates' longitudinal adoption of websites and of practices providing a range of opportunities for voter engagement across both election types.

Next, before turning to the empirical analysis, our areas of inquiry will be put into a theoretical context and related to relevant findings in earlier research. The two following sections deal with this matter on a general level while the third and final section of the framework focuses particularly on the role of the two examined election types (i.e., Finnish national elections and EP elections) to patterns of candidates' Web campaigning.

DIGITAL GAPS IN WEBSITE ADOPTION

Research on the adoption and diffusion of innovations has distinguished certain characteristics of types of early adopters (Rogers 1995). Regarding the diffusion of new communication technologies, Rogers (1986: 132–4) summarizes that early adopters, compared with later adopters, are predominantly male, younger in age, and possess a higher socioeconomic status. Initial studies examining the general public's access to the Internet found similar "digital gaps": The early Internet users were disproportionately young, better educated, male, and socioeconomically better off (Norris 2001: 68–9).

In a longitudinal analysis of the social profile of Internet users, Norris (2001) posits two scenarios of future population trends on the Internet. The *optimistic* perspective predicts that "the social profile of the online population will gradually broaden over time until eventually it comes to mirror the society as a whole" (Norris 2001: 70). In other words, over time, the digital gaps will narrow. Alternatively, the *pessimistic* scenario, based on Rogers' discussion of characteristics of earlier and later adopters, states that the "adoption of successful new technologies often reinforces economic advantages" so that the "rich get richer, and the less well-off . . . fall further behind" (Norris 2001: 71). This interpretation predicts that the digital gaps will widen over time.

However, concerning the use of Web campaigning, the relevant traits of earlier and later adopters among candidates may be different. In examining website use by candidates, scholars have frequently paid attention to two types of candidate traits: demographics (e.g., Gibson and McAllister 2006; Gibson and Römmele 2003; Herrnson and Stokes 2003) and political resources (e.g. Cunha et al. 2003; Davis 1999; Margolis and Resnick 2000; Margolis, Resnick, and Levy 2003).

In the context of the equalization thesis, we find two demographic traits particularly interesting: candidate age and gender. Considering age, it can be assumed that the early adopters of websites among candidates were disproportionately young. At least in nations with proportional multi-member district systems, young candidates usually have less financial and organizational resources for mounting expensive offline campaigns. For them, the Web levels the playing field. Moreover, in the emergent Internet era, the young generation showed greater interest in the Internet, thus making younger candidates more likely to go online. Empirically, it has been demonstrated that youth has an independent and significant impact on having a personal campaign website (Gibson and McAllister 2006; Zittel 2009). Still, an unexplored question is whether the initial advantage of the young candidates in campaigning online has diminished over time.

In relation to gender, the early observed male advantage in the general public's Internet use may not necessarily be reflected in Web campaigning. One reason why female candidates might be early adopters of the new campaign tool may be their need to retain control over their campaign messages, because the news coverage tends to treat them disadvantageously compared with male candidates (e.g. Kahn 1996). Furthermore, as Bystrom et al. (2004: 214) conclude, campaign websites "may be the best venue for female candidates wanting an equal competition with male candidates, especially in situations where resources are limited." In fact, some studies have observed a lack of gender significance in candidates' Web presence (Carlson 2007; Gibson and McAllister 2006; Greer and LaPointe 2003). However, we lack longitudinal empirical observations about the propensity of male and female candidates to go online.

Concerning resources, two aspects are central: the size of the candidate's party and candidate status. With reference to party size, small-party candidates have theoretically been perceived as being more inclined to adopt websites than major-party candidates (e.g. Corrado and Firestone 1997; Davis 1999; Gibson and Ward 1998). Through offering an affordable channel of communication, the Internet seems suitable for minor candidates lacking resources to efficiently campaign through traditional media (Davis 1999; Gibson and Ward 1998). More recently, however, most empirical studies focusing on single elections have demonstrated that major-party candidates are online at a higher rate than candidates running for smaller parties (Gibson et al. 2003; Gibson and Ward 2002; Margolis, Resnick, and Levy 2003).

Still, longitudinal evidence regarding the impact of party size on candidate website adoption is scarce. Kamarck's study (2002) of the 1998 and 2000 U.S. congressional and gubernatorial elections points in the direction of unaltered or even widening digital gaps in favor of major-party candidates. Between 2002 and 2006, the gap in website adoption between major-party candidates and third-party/Independent candidates has narrowed in Senate races but remained in House elections (Gulati and Williams 2007). Obviously, there is a need to study this trend in nations with multiparty systems, such as Finland.

Concerning candidate status, it has been argued that challengers should be more inclined to turn to alternative ways of campaigning than incumbents, because they are lagging behind in name recognition, campaign leverage, and governmental resources (Davis 1999; Gibson 2004; Gibson and McAllister 2006; Margolis and Resnick 2000). Conversely, the same incumbent resources – name recognition, campaign leverage and party/governmental resources – may theoretically be perceived as facilitating website adoption (Davis 1999; Gibson 2004; Margolis and Resnick 2000). Empirically, Kamarck (2002) found that challengers were online at a higher rate than incumbents in the 1998 U.S. elections and that this gap remained in the 2000 elections. In the 2006 House race, that gap was still evident (Gulati and Williams 2007). Outside the United States, systematic longitudinal evidence is lacking on the impact of candidate status. The competitive character of the plurality system with single-member districts, used in the United States, may have a different impact on candidates' need to adopt campaign websites than do proportional systems, based on proportional representation in multimember districts, such as in Finland.

PROVISION OF OPPORTUNITIES FOR ENGAGEMENT

In studying the evolution of party websites, Schweitzer (2008) distinguishes two theoretical paradigms. The innovation hypothesis states that the inherent features of the new media will revolutionize electoral online communication and make it distinct from offline campaigning. Over time,

Web campaigns should encourage interaction, thus providing increased opportunities for communication and voter engagement. Conversely, the normalization hypothesis (Margolis and Resnick 2000) suggests that online campaigns reproduce typical patterns of offline electioneering, thereby negating the innovative qualities of the Internet. This hypothesis posits that interactive elements facilitating two-way communication and voter engagement are disregarded because campaigns fear losing control over the campaign message online (see Stromer-Galley 2000).

On the subject of candidate Web campaigns, U.S. studies seemingly support the innovation hypothesis. Longitudinal evidence shows that candidate websites have slowly adopted site elements that go beyond brochure ware, including various interactive features and opportunities for voter engagement, involvement, and mobilization (Druckman, Kifer, and Parkin 2007; Foot and Schneider 2006; Greer and LaPointe 2003; Kamarck 2002; Schneider and Foot 2006). Yet growth in the use of the most pronounced form of interactivity – two-way communication (e.g., chats and discussion boards) – has been marginal (Druckman, Kifer, and Parkin 2007: 434; Gulati and Williams 2007: 456), reflecting the candidates' need to retain control over their campaign messages. Outside the United States, it is yet uncertain whether these trends apply.

There are little data on the longitudinal trajectory of providing interactive features and opportunities for voter engagement according to the candidate attributes discussed earlier. In terms of gender, feminist scholars have declared the Internet a "woman's medium," emphasizing the interactive, communicative, and community-building aspects of the Web (van Zoonen 2002). An early study of U.S. Senate candidates' Web campaigns showed that female candidates were more likely than male candidates to provide interactive Web features (Puopolo 2001). More recent cross-sectional studies have not found such gender differences (Carlson 2007; Druckman, Kifer, and Parkin 2007; Greer and LaPointe 2003). Still, longitudinal evidence is lacking to further substantiate this relationship.

With respect to age, it can be assumed that young candidates – being part of the Internet generation and appealing particularly to this voter segment – are more inclined than older candidates to test interactive and engaging Web capabilities in their Web campaigns (Zittel 2009). An open question is whether such a generational gap has prevailed across time.

Concerning the impact of candidate status, Druckman, Kifer, and Parkin (2009) have empirically demonstrated that incumbent candidates provide less interactive features and engagement opportunities for voters on their websites than do challengers; they suggest this is because of the risk of losing control over the online campaign. However, an unaddressed question is whether the tendency of challengers to engage in more risky behavior online than incumbents is stable across time and valid beyond the U.S. first-past-the-post-electoral system. In proportional systems, as the Finnish one, many challenger candidates act as supplementary candidates to fill out the party's slate and, consequently, do not campaign wholeheartedly.

The issue of taking or avoiding risks online may theoretically apply also to the question of the Web strategies of major- and minor-party candidates. Candidates running for small parties – many of which are not very competitive – may be more inclined than major-party candidates to test interactive features and engagement opportunities for voters. Again, longitudinal evidence is scarce if not absent outside the United States.

FINNISH WEB CAMPAIGNING IN NATIONAL AND EUROPEAN ELECTIONS

Our empirical analysis includes Web campaigning in both Finnish national parliamentary elections and Finnish elections for the European Parliament (EP) elections. This section discusses the impact of these election types on candidates' Web campaigning efforts.

In both election types, the Finns cast their votes for individual candidates, and therefore, the candidates carry out personal campaigns. However, in Finland, as in most other European Union member states, the EP elections are regarded as second-order elections (Schmitt 2005): They are seen as less important by the parties, and voter turnout is lower as well. Moreover, the EP election campaigns do not attract the attention of the news media to the same extent as do national elections (de Vreese 2003). Arguably, the second-order nature of EP elections strengthens the incentives for individual candidates to campaign online. In addition, in Finland, the EP election is a relatively competitive election: Compared with the national elections, where approximately 10% of the fielded candidates gain a seat in the Finnish parliament, only 5% of the Finnish candidates running for European Parliament win a seat. Consequently, EP candidates might be more compelled to seize every possible vote by every possible means, including Web campaigning, than would candidates running in national elections. In addition, because the whole country is a single constituency in the EP elections, Web campaigning might be considered a cost-efficient way for the candidates to mount a nationwide campaign. Accordingly, we presume that (1) the gaps between different types of candidates in website adoption should be smaller in EP elections than in national elections and (2) the gaps between various kinds of candidates in employing a range of engagement features should, across time, be smaller in the more competitive EP elections than in the national races.

DATA AND METHODS

Our analysis of the longitudinal adoption of Web campaigning by candidates in Finland has two components. In the first part, we longitudinally examine the Web presence of all candidates according to candidate gender, age, party affiliation (major, minor, or fringe party), and status (incumbent or challenger). The party classification is based on a categorization by Norris (2003): *Major* parties have more than 20% of all seats in the national parliament; *minor* parties have more than 3% but less than 20% of the seats; *fringe* parties lack at least 3% of the elected members of the parliament. The age of the candidates is *dichotomized* as a younger generation (18–34 years) and an older generation (more than 34 years of age; cf. Zittel 2009).

In creating a new longitudinal dataset for the first part of our study, we compiled data from previous single-election studies and projects surveying the frequency of Finnish political candidates having websites. To study expressly personal Web campaigns by candidates, we then excluded two types of sites: (1) candidate sites that were set up by party organizations and (2) official sites by incumbents maintained by the Finnish Parliament.[1] In constructing the new longitudinal dataset, we used as the starting point the study by Isotalus (1998) examining the use of websites by candidates in the 1996 Finnish EP elections. For the entire field of candidates, we coded data concerning their Web presence, gender, age, party affiliation, and status. To compare their propensity to campaign individually online in 1996 with later EP elections, we used data from our study of candidates' Web campaigns in the 2004 Finnish EP elections (Carlson and Strandberg 2005, 2007) and gathered data from the recent 2009 elections.

With reference to the national elections, we compiled data from the 1999, 2003, and 2007 elections. For the 1999 and 2003 elections, we used data on the candidates' Web presence collected in our earlier studies (Carlson 2007; Carlson and Djupsund 2001; Strandberg 2006).

---

[1] It is an established practice that Finnish members of parliament do not use their official personal sites maintained by the Parliament for personal election campaigns.

For the most recent national elections, in 2007, we used data that we gathered during the campaign. For all six elections included in this study, every fielded candidate ($N = 6,676$) was surveyed for his or her personal Web presence, using various sources and search techniques, in the final two weeks of the election campaign. Table 5.1 shows the distribution of candidates with personal websites in these elections.

TABLE 5.1. *Web Campaigning in the Six Elections: Data for the Longitudinal Analysis*

Election Type	Year	Number of Candidates	Candidates with Personal Websites		Number of Websites Coded for Content Analysis
			n	%	
EP Elections	1996	207	66	32	–
	2004	227	128	56	61 (48% random sample)
	2009	241	152	63	68 (45% random sample)
National Elections	1999	1,991	452	23	47 (10% random sample)
	2003	2,013	739	37	733 (all sites)
	2007	1,997	1,247	62	281 (23% random sample)

Notes: The random samples of sites for content analysis were drawn from all identified personal websites in the respective campaign. For example, for the 2004 EP elections, the 61 sampled sites amount to 48% of the total 128 identified sites. Content analysis data were not gathered in the 1996 EP elections.

The second part of the analysis concerns change over time in website provision of interactive features and opportunities for voter engagement by the candidates in the EP elections and national elections. Again, in creating a new longitudinal dataset, we compiled data from our earlier studies and projects based on quantitative content analysis of website features (Carlson 2007; Carlson and Djupsund 2001, Carlson and Strandberg 2005, 2007; Strandberg 2006). The right column in Table 5.1 shows the number of websites that we content-analyzed for each examined election (a total of 1,190 sites).

Because the analyses undertaken in these separate projects did not use fully comparable sets of variables, we had to use only those variables that were measured and operationalized in similar fashions. Moreover, to achieve longitudinal comparability, we had to choose those interactive Web features and opportunities for engagement that have been available to candidates throughout the time span (1999–2009). Taking these requirements into account, we focused on the presence or absence of five features that may contribute to the engagement of site visitors. In the following discussion, these devices are labeled "engagement features" (cf. Lusoli and Ward 2005). Two features – (1) live chat functions and (2) online discussion boards – enable two-way communication between a site visitor and the campaign and/or other visitors (cf. Druckman, Kifer, and Parkin 2007; Gulati and Williams 2007). Two other features, which are interactive in a more restricted sense, provide opportunities to become involved in the campaign of the candidate: (3) a volunteer sign-up form that visitors can submit indicating campaign activities in which they might participate and (4) an opportunity for a visitor to sign up online to receive e-mail from the candidate's campaign (cf. Foot and Schneider 2006; Gulati and Williams 2007). The final feature, (5) the online provision of feedback forms, enables site visitors to talk back to the campaign. The content analyses used here coded for the presence or absence of these five features on the examined websites.

To study longitudinal change in the extent of the provision of engagement features, we used Schneider and Foot's (2006: 28) categorization of the level of adoption of different Web campaigning practices. Thus, we coded the level of adoption in the provision of engagement features as "not adopted" (none of the five features provided on the website), "emerging adoption" (one to three features present on the site), or "established adoption" (four to five features supplied on the site).

FINDINGS ON WEBSITE ADOPTION IN FINNISH ELECTIONS

Table 5.2 shows the distribution of candidates with websites in both election types according to the candidate traits discussed in our framework. Clearly, there is a relationship between candidate traits and adoption of campaign websites over time, and this relationship differed to some extent between the national and the EP elections. Female candidates had websites to a slightly higher degree than males in the 1996 EP elections. However, although this gap increased in the 2004 election, the gender difference is no longer evident in the 2009 election. Interestingly, in the national elections, the evolution has been the opposite. Whereas there was no initial gender gap in the 1999 elections, a larger share of female than male candidates were online in 2003, and this female advantage remained in the 2007 election. In terms of age, we note that the young generation was online to a larger extent than older candidates in the 1996 EP elections. In the 2004 elections, this gap narrowed somewhat, but widened again in the 2009 elections. In the national elections, the generational gap narrowed from 1999 to 2003 and remained unaltered in 2007. In both

TABLE 5.2. *The Share of Candidates with Websites in the Six Elections according to Candidate Traits (%)*

	European Elections						National Elections					
	1996		2004		2009		1999		2003		2007	
	%	n	%	n	%	n	%	n	%	n	%	n
Gender												
Male	30	128	52	141	63	139	23	1,260	33	1,215	58	1,199
Female	35	79	64	86	63	102	23	731	42	798	69	798
Age												
18–34	49	41	67	49	77	52	37	379	44	410	70	458
35 and older	28	166	56	171	59	189	19	1,612	35	1,603	60	1,539
Party												
Major	58	48	97	60	100	60	42	674	66	679	90	688
Minor	37	60	79	75	89	70	23	556	34	738	64	841
Fringe	16	99	12	92	27	111	6	761	6	596	19	468
Status												
Incumbent	64	11	100	10	100	8	22	182	47	170	74	169
Challenger	30	196	54	217	62	233	23	1,809	36	1,843	61	1,828

Notes: n represents the total number of observations (e.g., 30% of the 128 male candidates running in the 1996 EP elections had their own websites). Because the universe of candidates is analyzed, tests of statistical significance were not carried out.

election types, a significant generational gap is still evident in the most recent elections.

As for party affiliation, the most striking observation is that fringe-party candidates are increasingly lagging behind minor- and major-party candidates across both election types in adopting campaign websites. However, the gap between major- and minor-party candidates has slightly narrowed over time in the EP elections. In the national elections, that gap widened between 1999 and 2003, but narrowed somewhat between the 2003 and the 2007 elections. A comparison of the two election types shows that, for the most recent elections, a larger party-size gap is found in the national elections than in the EP elections.

Finally, a wide digital gap related to candidate status remains in both election types: Incumbents are online to a larger extent than challengers. The gap in the EP elections is large and has remained nearly the same across all three elections. However, the number of incumbents in the EP elections is too low to draw any conclusions. In the national elections, the digital gap that emerged between the 1999 and 2003 elections remained in the 2007 elections.

To distinguish the independent effects of candidate traits on website adoption in Finnish elections over time, we ran six logistic regression models, one for each election, predicting candidate Web presence. Table 5.3 presents the three models for the EP elections. Because of a lack of variation in Web presence, the two latter models exclude the status variable and collapse the categories minor and major concerning the party-size variable.

Table 5.3 reveals that, controlling for all other variables, being male or female has not been a significant factor in explaining the candidates' online presence in any of the EP elections. The longitudinal generational gap observed in Table 5.2 remains in the regressions as an independent effect of being young on campaigning online in the 1996 and 2004 elections. However, representing the young generation is no longer a significant predictor of Web presence in the 2009 elections. Regarding party affiliation, the longitudinally observed large gap between fringe-party candidates and minor/major-party candidates is strongly supported by the regression models. Running for a minor or major party is the strongest predictor of Web presence in all three EP elections.

The corresponding regression models for the Finnish national elections (see Table 5.4) shows that among the gaps observed earlier, two remain and two disappear.

First, gender itself was not especially influential on the candidates' propensity to go online; the female advantage observed in 2003 and 2007 is not confirmed when controlling for other variables. Potentially, this finding could be explained by the strong male dominance among the candidates running for fringe parties; these candidates seldom had their own websites (see Carlson 2007). Second, the candidate status gap in the 2003 and 2007 elections noted in Table 5.2 is reversed when controlling for other factors. Being a challenger – not an incumbent – has an independent impact on Web presence. Most likely, the party-size variable diminishes the independent impact of incumbency because the overwhelming majority of incumbent candidates run for major or minor parties. Regarding the earlier observed generational gap, belonging to the young generation has remained a significant independent predictor when controlling for other factors, although its power has weakened. Examining the independent impact of party size, finally, the models confirm the patterns observed earlier. Fringe-party candidates increasingly lag behind both minor- and major-party candidates. Strikingly, the independent impact of running for a major party has grown significantly more than the impact of running for a minor party.

TABLE 5.3. *Predicting Candidate Adoption of Websites in the EP Elections (Logistic Regression)*

	1996			2004			2009		
	Coeff.	S.E.	Sig.	Coeff.	S.E.	Sig.	Coeff.	S.E.	Sig.
Gender	.128	.346	.712	.734	.450	.103	.689	.402	.087
Age									
18–34	1.139	.406	.005	1.242	.527	.018	.648	.477	.174
Status	.594	.715	.406	–	–	–	–	–	–
Party Size									
Major Party	1.959	.438	.000	–	–	–	–	–	–
Minor Party	1.237	.400	.002	–	–	–	–	–	–
Major/Minor	–	–	–	4.085	.485	.000	3.734	.443	.000
Constant	–2.049			–2.859			–1.564		

Notes: The dependent variable: 0 = Candidate does not have a website, 1 = Candidate has a website. *Predictors:* Gender: Male (1); Female (0). Age: reference category (0) = 35 years or older. Status: 1 = Incumbent; 0 = Challenger. Party size: reference category (0): fringe party.

1996: Nagelkerke R^2 = .222; % correct = 73.4; N = 207.

2004: Nagelkerke R^2 = .629; % correct = 86.8; N = 220.

2009: Nagelkerke R^2 = .581; % correct = 84.2; N = 247.

TABLE 5.4. *Predicting Candidate Adoption of Websites in the National Elections (Logistic Regression)*

	1999			2003			2007		
	Coeff.	S.E.	Sig.	Coeff.	S.E.	Sig.	Coeff.	S.E.	Sig.
Gender	.278	.123	.024	-.031	.110	.776	-.128	.116	.272
Age									
18–34	.917	.139	.000	.418	.133	.002	.519	.138	.000
Status	-.679	.199	.001	-.464	.177	.009	-.791	.216	.000
Party Size									
Major Party	2.663	.182	.000	3.541	.197	.000	3.927	.190	.000
Minor Party	1.669	.191	.000	2.141	.192	.000	2.070	.1412	.000
Constant	-3.234			-2.839			-1.505		

Notes: The dependent variable: o = Candidate does not have a website, 1 = Candidate has a website. *Predictors:* Gender: Male (1); Female (o). Age: reference category (o) = 35 years or older. Status: 1 = Incumbent; o = Challenger. Party size: reference category (o): fringe party.

1999: Nagelkerke R^2 = .248; % correct = 78.8; N = 1,991
2003: Nagelkerke R^2 = .343; % correct = 74.3; N = 2,013
2007: Nagelkerke R^2 = .399; % correct = 76.6; N = 1,997.

The main findings can now be summed up as follows:

- In both EP and national election types, gender has not been a decisive factor in explaining the adoption of websites by candidates.
- The likelihood of the younger generation candidates using Web campaigns has declined in EP elections, but they are still likely to use Web campaigns in national elections.
- In both EP and national elections, those running for a fringe party are much less likely to have a Web presence.
- In national elections, the likelihood of majority party candidates using websites has increased more relative to those running for a minor party. In EP elections, the likelihood of representing either a minor or major party and engaging in Web campaigns is hard to access, although the digital gap between major- and minor-party candidates has decreased over time.
- Challengers are more likely to run Web campaigns in national elections than are incumbents.

DO WEB CAMPAIGNS MATTER?

Thus far, our findings – the steady growth of candidates with websites and the still remaining digital gaps among the candidates – raise a question that should be addressed before we turn to the website provision of engagement features by candidates: Do candidates who have a personal campaign website win more often than those who do not? We longitudinally examined this question in an admittedly crude way: For each election, we observed whether candidates with websites are disproportionately represented among the elected candidates. In this analysis, we excluded fringe-party candidates who in the Finnish multiparty system are very rarely elected to the national or the European Parliament. Figure 5.2 shows, for each of the six examined elections, the share of elected major/minor-party candidates with websites compared to the corresponding share of *all* fielded candidates representing major or minor parties.

In both election types and at each election year, candidates with websites are disproportionally overrepresented among the elected candidates. Although the figures suggest that candidates with websites are successful, it should be stressed that the differences in proportions in Figure 5.2 are less than dramatic and, moreover, that the success of the elected candidates may not be due to having a website per se. Rather, we suspect that the findings are more a reflection of the type of candidates using websites:

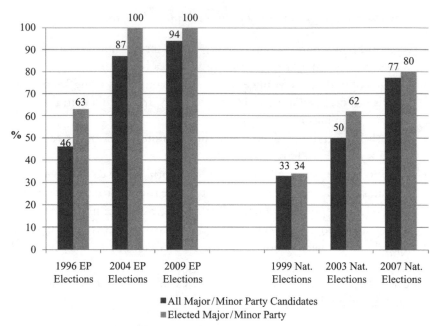

FIGURE 5.2. The Share of Candidates with Websites among All Candidates and Elected Candidates (%)

Note: For the the total number of all major/minor-party candidates per each election, see Table 5.2. The number of all elected major/minor-party candidates is 200 in each national election. In the EP elections, the corresponding number is 16 (1996), 14 (2004), and 13 (2009).

Competitive and serious candidates trying to seize every possible vote incorporate the Web as part of their campaigns' repertoire to a higher degree than candidates who simply fill out the party's list of candidates and lack any chance of being elected themselves (cf. Strandberg 2006: 127–8). If having a website has become an essential part of a successful campaign by a serious contender, then, how has the practice of providing features for voter engagement online by candidates evolved over time?

ADOPTING PRACTICE OF PROVIDING ENGAGEMENT FEATURES

We begin this section by examining the extent to which the candidates' websites in the two types of Finnish elections have provided interactive engagement features over time. To repeat, in Table 5.5, "not adopted" signifies that none of the five measured features was provided, "emerging adoption" indicates that one to three features were present, and "established adoption" denotes that four to five features were supplied.

In terms of the evolution of the provisional engagement features, an increase has occurred in the most recent Finnish national elections, with

TABLE 5.5. *Provision of Engagement Features on Candidate Websites in the National and the EP Elections (% of candidates reaching adoption levels)*

	National Elections			EP Elections	
	1999	2003	2007	2004	2009
Level of adoption					
Not adopted	85	56	27	38	25
Emerging adoption	15	44	71	62	73
Established adoption	0	0	2	0	2
	(n = 47)	(n = 733)	(n = 279)	(n = 61)	(n = 68)

71% of the candidates' sites reaching the emerging level of adoption. The longitudinal change is also statistically significant ($p < .001$; χ^2-test). However, for the Finnish EP elections, there were no statistically significant changes across time. Most likely, the increases for the EP elections occurred earlier than between the 2004 and 2009 elections. Potentially, the more competitive nature of the EP contest spurred candidates to adopt a wider range of interactive Web features earlier than in the national elections. Still, across the election types, hardly any candidate site has yet reached the established level of adoption. In addition, among the candidates on the emergent adoption level, their sites rarely provided opportunities for two-way communications were rarely provided; none offered a live chat and only one-quarter provided a discussion board.

Tables 5.6 and 5.7 address the question whether certain types of Finnish candidates have been forerunners in adopting various engagement features. In the EP elections, Table 5.6 shows that only resources matter in adopting a range of engagement features. A clear gap between fringe-party candidates and minor/major-party candidates is evident at the emerging adoption level. However, the initial gap between major- and minor-party candidates in the emerging adoption level (83% and 46%, respectively; $p < .01$, Fisher's exact test) has closed over time. It should also be noted that a clear majority of all types of candidates, except the fringe-party candidates, have reached the emerging level of adoption.

By and large, the corresponding findings for the national elections (Table 5.7) are consistent with those concerning the EP elections. First, as in the EP elections, there have never been any statistically significant adoption gaps between male and female candidates nor between the young and the old generation of candidates. Second, resources matter in having a site providing an emerging level of engagement features. However, the equalization trend observed between minor- and major-party candidates for the EP elections is not echoed here: A statistically significant gap between

TABLE 5.6. *Provision of Engagement Features on Candidate Websites in the EP Elections according to Candidate Traits (% of candidates reaching adoption levels)*

| | Level of Adoption | | | | | |
| | None | | Emerging | | Established | |
	2004	2009	2004	2009	2004	2009
Gender						
Male	29	33	71	65	0	3
Female	48	14	52	86	0	0
Age						
18–34	43	27	57	73	0	0
35 and older	36	25	64	76	0	2
Status						
Incumbent	17	0	83	83	0	17
Challenger	40	27	60	73	0	0
Party Size						
Major Party	17^a	7^b	83^c	89^d	0	4
Minor Party	54^a	17^b	46^c	83^d	0	0
Fringe Party	75^a	65^b	25^c	35^d	0	0

Notes: Percentages sharing the same superscripted letter differ from each other significantly at $p < .05$ (gender, age, and status: Fisher's exact test; party size: Freeman-Halton extension of Fisher's exact test).
N (2004/2009): Female: 27/28; Male: 34/40; Ages 18–34: 14/15; Ages 35–: 47/53; Major Party: 29/28; Minor Party: 28/23; Fringe Party 4/17; Incumbents: 6/6; Challengers: 55/62.

these two groups, which was not present in the 1999 national elections, has formed over time (2003: $p < .01$; 2007: $p < .001$, Fisher's exact test). Incumbents had an emerging level of adoption to a significantly higher extent than challengers in the 2003 elections. This gap has diminished in the 2007 elections. Separate regression analyses (not reported here) show that in 2003, incumbency, running for a minor party, and running for a major party had independent impacts on reaching the emerging level of adoption. In the 2007 election, running for a major party is the only remaining significant predictor. Finally, similarly to the EP elections, it is noteworthy that a clear majority of all candidate types have reached the emerging adoption level of providing engagement features.

DISCUSSION AND CONCLUSIONS

The first query of this chapter was whether the Web across time has enhanced the democratic ideal of campaigning opportunities by leveling the playing field for different types of candidates. Our analysis of

TABLE 5.7. *Provision of Engagement Features on Candidate Websites in the National Elections according to Candidate Traits (% of candidates reaching adoption levels)*

| | Level of Adoption | | | | | | | | |
| | None | | | Emerging | | | Established | | |
	1999	2003	2007	1999	2003	2007	1999	2003	2007
Gender									
Male	82	54	28	18	46	69	0	1	2
Female	90	58	26	11	42	71	0	0	3
Age									
18–34	84	55	23	16	45	73	0	1	2
35 and older	86	56	28	14	44	69	0	0	2
Status									
Incumbent	85	43^a	29	15	57^b	68	0	0	3
Challenger	86	57^a	27	14	42^b	70	0	1	2
Party Size									
Major Party	85	50^a	17^b	15	49^c	81^d	0	$1^\dagger$	2
Minor Party	80	62^a	35^b	20	38^c	62^d	0	$0^\dagger$	3
Fringe Party	100	78^a	50^b	0	22^c	50^d	0	$0^\dagger$	0

Notes: Percentages sharing the same superscripted letter differ from each other significantly at $p <$ .05 (gender, age, and status: Fisher's exact test; party size: Freeman-Halton extension of Fisher's exact test for year 1999 and 2007, χ^2-test for year 2003).
$\dagger$ = the χ^2 test not conducted as more than 20% of the cells have an expected count less than 5.
N (1999/2003/2007): Female: 19/334/122; Male: 28/399/157; Ages 18–34: 19/179/59; Ages 35–: 28/554/220; Major Party: 34/448/138; Minor Party: 10/244/121; Fringe Party: 3/41/20; Incumbents: 40/81/30; Challengers: 7/652/249.

the Finnish case has provided mixed evidence. On the one hand, some findings point to a leveling trend. In both election types, across time, female candidates are as likely as male candidates to campaign online. Being a challenger significantly influences Web presence in all examined national elections. In national elections, across time, young candidates are more likely than older candidates to campaign online. In the EP elections, minor-party candidates have closed the gap with major-party candidates. On the other hand, some findings suggest that the playing field has not leveled in the Finnish case. Across time, running for a major party strongly predicts candidate Web presence in the national elections. In fact, the advantage of major-party candidates in campaigning online has grown remarkably over time. Fringe-party candidates lag severely behind in both election types. Moreover, in the EP elections, the youth advantage in online presence has diminished over time.

We expected that the gaps between different types of candidates in website adoption would be smaller in EP elections than in national elections. Our findings partly support this expectation. Most important, in contrast to the national elections, the minor-party candidates in the EP elections have closed the digital gap with the major-party candidates. Additionally, the generational gap in online presence, still evident in national elections, has diminished in the EP elections. Arguably, when neither party support nor interest from traditional media is in abundance in the second-order EP elections, the candidates are even more inclined to launch personal websites. In addition, because there is greater competition for seats is in EP elections compared with national elections, and the whole country is one district, compared with 15 districts in national elections, EP candidates try harder to seize every vote by all possible means than candidates do in national elections.

Going beyond the Finnish case, then, what is the significance of these findings, and how do they compare with findings from other countries? Obviously, it is hazardous to generalize and draw conclusions from a single case study. This is especially the case when longitudinal trends in candidate Web campaigning have previously been analyzed solely in the United States. Nevertheless, some tentative conclusions are in order. Interestingly, the U.S. finding that minor-party candidates have closed the gap with major-party candidates in senatorial races (Gulati and Williams 2007) is in Finland echoed only in the EP elections, not in the national elections. This observation yields the general conclusion that election systems and types have an impact on the incentives of candidates to campaign individually online. If we place the three election types on a continuum, the U.S. Senate elections and the Finnish EP elections – having in common competitiveness, district magnitude, and relatively low party control over candidate campaigns – are closer to each other than the Finnish national elections are to the U.S. senatorial races. Concerning the Finnish national elections, conversely, our findings suggest that parties – particularly party size – clearly matter for the candidates' Web campaigning efforts. Although the Finnish election system produces candidate-driven campaigns, it also has traces of the traditional strong role of parties in election campaigning in Western Europe (Gibson 2004). Apparently, in running personal campaigns, major-party candidates in national elections benefit from various resources provided by their party organizations.

The second query of this chapter concerned the extent to which candidates running Web campaigns across time have adopted a practice of providing a range of interactive opportunities for voter engagement.

In the Finnish case, although a clear majority within each of the candidate groups examined (except for fringe-party candidates) has over time reached the level of emergent adoption, hardly any candidate has – over a 10-year period – advanced to the established adoption level, providing rich opportunities for communication and voter engagement. Strikingly, having reached the level of emergent adoption, very few candidates provided more uncontrolled interactive features such as chats and discussion boards. Because U.S. candidates, too, have been reluctant over time to offer unstructured two-way discussion opportunities, a tentative conclusion is that candidates, across time and across systems, avoid losing control over the online campaign message. Obviously, the recent breakthrough of different social media in campaigns (e.g., blogs, Facebook, YouTube, Twitter) may challenge this praxis.

Contrary to what could be expected, our analysis of the Finnish case shows that young candidates – the Internet generation – have not across time done better in providing engagement features than the older generation. Similarly, female candidates have not been more eager than their male counterparts to provide opportunities for engagement. Instead, resources, specifically party size, matter here, too. At all points in time, fringe-party candidates lag behind in both election types. Moreover, in the national elections, major-party candidates still do better than minor-party candidates in providing engagement features. Interestingly, in the EP elections, minor-party candidates have closed the gap with major-party candidates across time. This could be a reflection of both types of candidates trying harder to engage a constituency that is generally uninterested in the EP contests.

In sum, the evolution of website adoption and use by candidates has been less than revolutionary. Across time, resources matter in Web campaigning, mostly reproducing familiar offline patterns, and in providing opportunities for voter engagement, candidates prefer to play it safe.

References

Barber, Benjamin. 2001. "The Uncertainty of Digital Politics." *Harvard International Review* 23 (1): 42–7.

Bystrom, Dianne G., Mary Christine Banwart, Lynda Lee Kaid, and Terry A. Robertson. 2004. *Gender and Candidate Communication*. London: Routledge.

Carlson, Tom. 2007. "It's a Man's World? Male and Female Election Campaigning on the Internet." *Journal of Political Marketing* 6 (1): 41–67.

Carlson, Tom, and Göran Djupsund. 2001. "Old Wine in New Bottles? The 1999 Finnish Election Campaign on the Internet." *Harvard International Journal of Press/Politics* 6 (1): 68–87.

Carlson, Tom, and Kim Strandberg. 2005. "The 2004 European Election on the Web: Finnish Actor Strategies and Voter Responses." *Information Polity* 10 (3–4): 189–204.

Carlson, Tom, and Kim Strandberg. 2007. "Finland: The European Parliament Election in a Candidate-Centered Electoral System." In Randolph Kluver, Nicholas W. Jankowski, Kirsten A. Foot, and Steven M. Schneider (eds.), *The Internet and National Elections: A Comparative Study of Web Campaigning* (pp. 29–42), London: Routledge.

Carlson, Tom, and Kim Strandberg. 2008. "Plus ça change, plus ç'est la même chose? The Evolution of Finnish Web Campaigning 1996–2004." In Jesper Strömbäck, Mark Ørsten, and Toril Aalberg (eds.), *Communicating Politics: Political Communication in the Nordic Countries* (pp. 161–79), Gothenburg, Sweden: Nordicom.

Corrado, Anthony, and Charles M. Firestone, eds. 1997. *Elections in Cyberspace: Toward a New Era in American Politics.* Washington, DC: Aspen Institute.

Cunha, Carlos, Irene Martín, James Newell, and Louis Ramiro. 2003. "Southern European Parties and Party Systems, and the New ICTs." In Rachel Gibson, Paul Nixon, and Stephen Ward (eds.), *Political Parties and the Internet: Net Gain?* (pp. 70–97), London: Routledge.

Davis, Richard. 1999. *The Web of Politics: The Internet's Impact on the American Political System.* New York: Oxford University Press.

De Vreese, Claes H. 2003. "Television Reporting of Second-Order Elections." *Journalism Studies* 4 (2): 183–98.

Druckman, James N., Martin J. Kifer, and Michael Parkin. 2007. "The Technological Development of Congressional Candidate Websites: How and Why Candidates Use Web Innovations." *Social Science Computer Review* 25 (4): 425–42.

Druckman, James N., Martin J. Kifer, and Michael Parkin. 2009. "Campaign Communications in U.S. Congressional Elections." *American Political Science Review* 103 (3): 343–66.

Foot, Kirsten A., and Steven M. Schneider. 2006. *Web Campaigning.* Cambridge, MA: MIT Press.

Gibson, Rachel. 2004. "Web Campaigning from a Global Perspective." *Asia Pacific Review* 11 (1): 95–126.

Gibson, Rachel K., and Ian McAllister. 2006. "Does Cyber Campaigning Win Votes? Online Communication in the 2004 Australian Election." *Journal of Elections, Public Opinion and Parties* 16 (3): 243–63.

Gibson, Rachel, and Andrea Römmele. 2003. "Regional Web Campaigning in the 2002 German Federal Election." Paper presented at the annual meeting of the American Political Science Association, Philadelphia.

Gibson, Rachel K., and Stephen J. Ward. 1998. "UK Political Parties and the Internet: 'Politics as Usual' in the New Media?" *Harvard International Journal of Press/Politics* 3 (3): 14–38.

Gibson, Rachel K., and Stephen Ward. 2002. "Virtual Campaigning: Australian Parties and the Impact of the Internet." *Australian Journal of Political Science* 37 (1): 99–129.

Gibson, Rachel K., Michael Margolis, David Resnick, and Stephen J. Ward. 2003. "Election Campaigning on the WWW in the USA and UK: A Comparative Analysis." *Party Politics* 9 (1): 47–75.

Greer, Jennifer D., and Mark E. LaPointe. 2003. "Cyber-Campaigning Grows Up. A Comparative Content Analysis of Websites for US Senate and Gubernatorial Races, 1998–2000." In Rachel K. Gibson, Andrea Römmele, and Stephen J. Ward (eds.), *Electronic Democracy: Mobilisation, Organisation and Participation via new ICTs* (pp. 116–32), London: Routledge.

Gulati, Girish J., and Christine B. Williams. 2007. "Closing the Gap, Raising the Bar: Candidate Website Communication in the 2006 Campaigns for Congress." *Social Science Computer Review* 25 (4): 443–65.

Herrnson, Paul S., and Atiya Kai Stokes. 2003. "Politics and the Digital Divide: District Characteristics and Candidate Internet Use in State Legislative Campaigns." Paper presented at the Annual Meeting of the Midwest Political Science Association, Chicago.

Isotalus, Pekka. 1998. "Euroehdokkaatkotisivuillaan." In Pekka Isotalus (ed.), *Kaveri vai peluri, Poliitikko mediassa* (pp. 152–71), Jyväskylä, Finland: Atena.

Kahn, Kim F. 1996. *The Political Consequences of Being a Woman: How Stereotypes Influence the Conduct and Consequences of Political Campaigns.* New York: Columbia University Press.

Kalnes, Øyvind. 2009. "Norwegian Parties and Web 2.0." *Journal of Information Technology & Politics* 6 (3/4): 251–66.

Kamarck, Elaine Ciulla. 2002. "Political Campaigning on the Internet: Business as Usual?" In Elaine C. Kamarck and Joseph S. Nye Jr. (eds.), *Governance.com: Democracy in the Information Age* (pp. 81–103), Washington, DC: Brookings Institution Press.

Kluver, Randolph, Nicholas W. Jankowski, Kirsten A. Foot, and Steven M. Schneider, eds. 2007. *The Internet and National Elections: A Comparative Study of Web Campaigning.* London: Routledge.

Lilleker, Darren G., and Casilda Malagón. 2010. "Levels of Interactivity in the 2007 French Presidential Candidates' Websites." *European Journal of Communication* 25 (1): 25–42.

Lipset, Seymour M. 1996. *American Exceptionalism: A Double-Edged Sword.* New York: W. W. Norton.

Lusoli, Wainer, and Janelle Ward. 2005. "'Politics Makes Strange Bedfellows': The Internet and the 2004 European Parliament Election in Britain." *Harvard International Journal of Press/Politics* 10 (4): 71–97.

Margolis, Michael, and David Resnick. 2000. *Politics as Usual: The Cyberspace "Revolution."* Thousand Oaks, CA: Sage.

Margolis, Michael, David Resnick, and Jonathan Levy. 2003. "Major Parties Dominate, Minor Parties Struggle: US Elections and the Internet." In Rachel Gibson, Paul Nixon, and Stephen Ward (eds.), *Political Parties and the Internet: Net Gain?* (pp. 53–69), London: Routledge.

Norris, Pippa. 2000a. *A Virtuous Circle: Political Communications in Postindustrial Societies.* Cambridge: Cambridge University Press.

Norris, Pippa. 2000b. "The Internet in Europe: A New North-South Divide?" *Harvard International Journal of Press/Politics* 5 (1): 1–12.

Norris, Pippa. 2001. *Digital Divide? Civic Engagement, Information Poverty and the Internet Worldwide.* New York: Cambridge University Press.

Norris, Pippa. 2003. "Preaching to the Converted? Pluralism, Participation and Party Websites." *Party Politics* 9 (1): 21–45.

Puopolo, Sonia. 2001. "The Web and U.S. Senatorial Campaigns 2000." *American Behavioral Scientist* 44 (12): 2030–47.

Rogers, Everett M. 1986. *Communication Technology: The New Media in Society*. New York: Free Press.

Rogers, Everett M. 1995. *Diffusion of Innovations*, 4th ed. New York: Free Press.

Ruostetsaari, Ilkka, and Mikko Mattila. 2002. "Candidate-Centred Campaigns and their Effects in an Open List System: The Case of Finland." In David M. Farrell and Rüdiger Schmitt-Beck (eds.), *Do Political Campaigns Matter? Campaign Effects in Elections and Referendums* (pp. 93–107), London: Routledge.

Schmitt, Hermann. 2005. "The European Parliament Elections of June 2004: Still Second Order?" *West European Politics* 28 (3): 650–79.

Schneider, Steven M., and Kirsten A. Foot. 2006. "Web Campaigning by U.S. Presidential Primary Candidates in 2000 and 2004." In Andrew P. Williams and John C. Tedesco (eds.), *The Internet Election: Perspectives on the Web in Campaign 2004* (pp. 21–36), Lanham, MD: Rowman and Littlefield.

Schweitzer, Eva Johanna. 2008. "Innovation or Normalization in E-Campaigning? A Longitudinal Content and Structural Analysis of German Party Websites in the 2002 and 2005 National Elections." *European Journal of Communication* 23 (4): 449–70.

Strandberg, Kim. 2006. *Parties, Candidates and Citizens Online: Studies of Politics on the Internet*. Åbo, Finland: Åbo Akademis Förlag.

Stromer-Galley, Jennifer. 2000. "On-Line Interaction and Why Candidates Avoid It." *Journal of Communication* 50 (4): 111–32.

Van Zoonen, Liesbet. 2002. "Gendering the Internet: Claims, Controversies and Cultures." *European Journal of Communication* 17 (1): 5–23.

Verkkouutiset. 2009. *Ensimmäiset todelliset nettivaalit*. Retrieved January 24, 2011, from http://www.verkkouutiset.fi/index.php?option=com_ontent&view=carticle&id=4125%3Aqensimmaeiset-todelliset-nettivaalitq&Itemid=8.

Ward, Stephen, and Rachel Gibson. 2003. "Online and on Message? Candidate Websites in the 2001 General Election." *British Journal of Politics and International Relations* 5 (2): 188–205.

Williams, Christine B., and Girish J. Gulati. 2006. "The Evolutionary Development of Campaign Websites: The U.S. Senate, 2000–2004." Paper presented at the Annual Meeting of the American Political Science Association, Philadelphia.

Wilson, Graham K. 1998. *Only in America? The Politics of the United States in Comparative Perspective*. Chatham, NJ: Chatham House.

Zittel, Thomas. 2009. "Lost in Technology? Political Parties and the Online Campaigns of Constituency Candidates in Germany's Mixed Member Electoral System." *Journal of Information Technology & Politics* 6 (3): 298–311.

6

E-Campaigns in Old Europe

Observations from Germany, Austria, and Switzerland

Urs Gasser and Jan Gerlach

The Internet has changed the ways in which we create, access, and use information, knowledge, and entertainment. In turn, these tectonic shifts have led to the emergence of a new type of networked public sphere that has the potential to alter the dynamics of political communication in general and election campaigns in particular. When compared with traditional media, Web 2.0 and new media appear to be well-suited tools for use by political candidates to tap into a broad range of voters. Perhaps the most prominent example of these changes in the information environment is the Obama presidential campaign in the United States, in which the Internet played a significant role as a communication, mobilization, and fundraising tool. Examples from other parts of the world, where citizen journalism, participatory news media, and the blogosphere have had a remarkable influence on the outcome of elections, including in the Ukraine and South Korea, have gained much attention from scholars and the public at large.[1] More recently, the so-called Twitter revolution in Iran and the role that social media played in the political turmoil in Egypt in early 2011 are complex cases of online mobilization, in which not only locals but also users from all over the world participated.

The consensus among European scholars is that U.S. campaign communication tactics generally influence those used in other global regions, including Europe. Considering these trends against the backdrop of a

---

[1] See Joshua Goldstein, *The Role of Digital Networked Technologies in the Ukrainian Orange Revolution*, Berkman Center Research Publication No. 2007–14, 2007; and also Mary Joyce, *The Citizen Journalism Web Site 'OhmyNews' and the 2002 South Korean Presidential Election.* Berkman Center Research Publication No. 2007–15, 2007.

largely U.S.-centric body of (qualitative and quantitative) research aimed at investigating the Internet's impact on political communication and campaigning, this chapter explores the role of the Internet in recent campaigns in the German-speaking regions of Europe; in particular, it contrasts developments in these countries to those in the United States.

The tentative result of this exploratory study is quite unexpected and interesting: Despite what is often called an "Americanization" of the campaigning culture in Germany, Austria, and Switzerland with its emphasis on the role of electronic media, the Internet currently plays a relatively unspectacular role in the political realities of these European countries. Online media are only one among many channels that are used for political campaigning, and they actually only play a minor role in the mix. When the Internet is used for campaigns, Web 1.0 approaches (such as static websites of political parties or their candidates) dominate the landscape. Web 2.0 applications such as social network sites like Facebook or video platforms like YouTube are still not commonly used in many European political campaigns.

This chapter approaches the role of the Internet in German-speaking countries by first providing a brief overview of recent trends in political campaigning in the United States and the German-speaking part of Europe. The following sections summarize and describe the e-campaigning efforts used in the 2008 U.S. presidential election for context and then present qualitative evidence that illustrates the use of the Internet in campaigns and other political initiatives in Germany, Austria, and Switzerland. The chapter concludes with a series of observations about the state of e-campaigns in German-speaking Europe and, finally, identifies a number of factors that might account for differences between German, Austrian, and Swiss online campaigns on the one hand and transatlantic differences on the other.

TRENDS IN POLITICAL CAMPAIGNING

Before turning to the specific examples of how the Internet is used in political campaigns in Germany, Austria, and Switzerland, it is helpful to set the stage by looking at some general trends in political campaigning. Although important differences in detail remain between political communication in the United States and Europe, there is broad consensus that the U.S. campaigning culture has affected the political communication in Europe over the past few years. This "Americanization" is perhaps among the most visible changes in European political communication, but is arguably only one part of the modernization process of political campaigning, which is now in a postmodern phase in which campaigning has become permanent (Bosch 2007: 21; Norris 2000).

One trend that has been observed across Germany, Austria, and Switzerland and that is generally perceived to be influenced by U.S. campaign culture is professionalization. The turn to professionalization of campaign management was motivated by the sheer power of mass media, primarily television. In the late 1970s and early 1980s, politicians in Germany started to realize that it was too risky to leave coverage and editing of campaign information to journalists alone (Holtz-Bacha 2002). With mass media facing increased economic pressure and focusing on their own financial goals instead of democratic discourse, a process referred to as commercialization of the media continues to be dominant (Gerth et al. 2009). A strong indicator for the trend of professionalization in political communication in general and campaigning in particular is the introduction of new degree programs of public relations (PR) in politics, even though in 2006 no large market for political PR and advertisement consultants existed in Western Europe (Vowe and Dohle 2007: 341; cf. Jarren and Donges 2006: 228). These phenomena exist in tandem with the externalization (or outsourcing) of campaign communication, in which communication activities are shifted from volunteers and unsalaried party officials to communication professionals (see Hoffmann, Steiner, and Jarren 2007: 54). The shift in traditional social structures and settings toward less rigid ideological groups of society without strong party affiliations has brought a need for a different message strategy, because political parties can no longer reach a traditional constituency through ideology (Holtz-Bacha 2002: 26). Instead of communicating straightforward information on their worldviews or creating a detailed online political profile at websites such as smartvote.ch,[2] parties tend to emphasize a positive image and "good product qualities" (Schulz 1998: 378). In response to the underlying logic of mass media, ideological concepts have given way to isolated issues, which the parties try to link themselves with (Jun 2009: 283).

The ongoing trend toward professionalization and de-ideologization also leads to a need for new content in campaigns, in which personalities and candidates replace ideologies (Holtz-Bacha 2002: 27). Although

---

[2] Smartvote.ch is a website that voters can go to help them choose their representatives based on a set of standardized criteria for each party. This provides a time-saving, efficient way for voters to make informed decisions.

this phenomenon was long believed to only occur in presidential political systems such as in the United States, most of Western Europe has also seen the rise of personalization in political campaigning (Jarren and Donges 2006: 270). In today's information environment, messages need to be associated with a person (or a personality) to be picked up by the media (see Weinmann 2009: 38): Political leaders are mediators of political programs and topics (Jarren and Donges 2006: 271). As Gerth et al. (2009: 76) put it, "personalization is presumed to be an essential method for conveying highly complex political information to laymen audiences, and it therefore establishes a specific kind of relationship between everyday life and politics." However, privately owned TV stations in Germany and Austria tend to focus their political coverage on persons, whereas state-funded TV stations are considered to be more issue oriented (cf. Plasser, Pallaver, and Lengauer 2009: 190).

Personalization of campaigns goes hand in hand with the visualization of campaigns as the media increasingly work with images. Even in today's Web 2.0 media environment, mass media and political actors find themselves in a symbiotic relationship, because politicians need exposure to persist in the new economy of news (Holtz-Bacha 2000: 164) and the media system is in need of political information, which is delivered by political actors (Jun 2009: 272). However, because politics generally does not appeal to the masses – except in moments of crisis – politicians move their communication toward entertainment (Holtz-Bacha 2000: 164). Photographs, symbols, and images convey emotions, which are intensified by the orchestration of politics as events (or scandals), for which the media represent the stage. Because of television's role as the predominant medium of the past few decades, political actors have been forced to accept the entertainment setting of political communication (Jun 2009: 275), and political parties to conduct actual event management (Imhof 2006: 18). Closely connected to this trend of making emotional appeals is a tendency toward negative campaigning (i.e., discrediting an opponent). Often this discrediting occurs by targeting the conduct of the campaign itself, such that one candidate's campaign is portrayed as morally superior over another candidate's campaign (Holtz-Bacha 2002: 27).

These three trends – professionalization, personalization, and emotional appeals – of campaigning are arguably accelerated by the wide use of the Internet. In an environment of fast exchange of information and tendencies toward sound bites and more concise content (e.g., in microblogging like Twitter), the public attention span is becoming shorter and political communication must follow these trends to be effective.

Of course, personalization also drives more and more politicians to use the Internet to communicate via their own channels. This might seem somewhat contradictory to the trend of professionalization. However, as the example of the Obama campaign shows once again, politicians' "personal" communication can also be run by professionals without losing its effectiveness. Furthermore, personalization also brings about a higher level of emotional appeals as politicians express opinions and feelings regarding policies and governmental actions.

RECENT DEVELOPMENTS IN THE UNITED STATES

As several contributors in this volume address, such as Zoe Oxley and Matthew Kerbel in Chapters 1 and 9, respectively, U.S. voter demand for political news and information on the Internet has dramatically increased over the last few years. At the same time, as examined by Crigler et al. in Chapter 4, U.S. political campaigns have increasingly used the Internet as a communication channel, fundraising tool, and advertising medium. Before moving on to analyze the use of the Internet in German, Austrian, and Swiss politics, it is important to review some of the key recent developments in U.S. politics as a basis for comparison.

Although traditional methods of campaign communication still rule Election Day, U.S. political strategists universally regard a robust Internet campaign strategy as a necessary complement to an offline campaign strategy (Graf 2008). The Internet is a relatively new medium in terms of being a central source for U.S. political campaign news and election information. In 1996, a mere 4% of adult Americans went online for information about the presidential election.[3] However, during each presidential election since 1996, the Pew Research Center has observed consecutive increases in the percentage of adult Americans who seek news or information related to campaigns on the Internet – 18% in 2000 and 29% in 2004.[4] During the 2008 presidential campaign, which drew an unprecedented amount of public interest, 44% of the voting-age population went online to get information and news about politics or the election. This figure represents six in ten Internet users in the United States.[5] Moreover, 26% of all U.S. adults selected the Internet as their

---

[3] Pew Internet & American Life Project, "The Internet's Role in Campaign 2008," Pew Research Center, April 2009.
[4] Ibid.
[5] Ibid.

primary source for campaign news and election information compared to 28% for newspapers and 76% for television.[6]

Concurrent with the recent explosion of Internet use by voters during elections, the Internet has also quickly developed into a strategic political communication and advertising medium for candidates. Historically, U.S. candidates have primarily directed their political communication efforts at television, radio, and print media audiences (Graf 2008). Although television continues to be the dominant medium for advertising, candidates are beginning to allocate significant sums to new media advertising through social networks, blogs, and video-sharing sites. During the 2008 presidential election, candidates Barack Obama and John McCain spent approximately $26 million on Internet advertising in contrast to the $235.9 million (Obama) and $125.5 million (McCain) spent on television advertising.[7] These figures sharply contrast to the amounts spent for online advertising by candidates George W. Bush and John Kerry four years earlier in the 2004 presidential election – $1.3 million (Kerry) and $419,000 (Bush).[8]

Since 2005, candidates have created dynamic, interactive digital presences, manifested in blogs, social networking, and new media websites like Facebook, YouTube, Flickr, and Twitter. These interactive presences are made possible by the emergence of popular and interactive online media that had not existed or achieved critical mass during earlier campaigns. Although some campaigns used blogs during the 2004 election, they were then generally regarded as a token novelty; however, the widespread use of blogs by all candidates in 2008 seems to indicate a strategic paradigm shift (Graf 2008). Social network platforms were also strategic focal points during the 2008 election as communal locations, both within and outside the candidate-controlled environments, for the aggregation of campaign information, advertising, and discourse. When combined with new media hosting websites, the interactive nature of these social networks websites facilitated two-way conversations with candidates' base supporters in real time *while* simultaneously providing a distribution channel to respond to opposing candidates through text, image, audio, and video (Graf 2008). For example, both the Obama and McCain campaigns published large numbers of videos on YouTube – 1,800

---

[6] Ibid.
[7] CMAG, "Election by the Numbers: 2008 Race for the White House: A Made–for-TV Election," December 2008.
[8] Pew Internet & American Life Project, "Data Memo – By: Michael Cornfield Re: Presidential Advertising on the Internet," Pew Research Center, October 2004.

videos (Obama) and 2,100 videos (McCain).[9] These "official" campaign videos were well received, but perhaps more interesting is that user-generated videos related to the campaign were nearly equal in viewership.[10]

In the 2008 election, interactive social websites were used as mobilization tools that enabled grassroots activism from base supporters, who then engaged others by sharing official campaign materials as well as user-generated materials. Even before Election Day 2008, some commentators described this new participatory environment as the beginning of a fundamental shift in political campaign strategy. Chapter 4 analyzes this trend by comparing Obama's and McCain's YouTube and TV advertising campaign strategies.[11] Moreover, the Pew Research Center found that approximately 59% of all U.S. Internet users received or shared information related to the 2008 campaigns using e-mail, text messaging, instant messaging, or Twitter, a significant increase from the 2004 election.[12] One in five Internet users acknowledged participatory involvement on a social networking site, online discussion forum, listserv, or other website that allowed comments and discussion. Effectively, a large proportion of Internet users actively engaged in some form of political discourse or activism by sharing political commentary, writing, audio, video, or still images with others online.[13]

The central role of the Internet in the 2008 election has been the subject of empirical study and worldwide scholarly debate for the last several years. Joe Trippi, former campaign manager to 2004 Democratic presidential candidate Howard Dean, attributed Obama's success in key states to his ability "to move thousands of people to organize" using Web 2.0 tools in ways that, in the past, "would have required an army of volunteers and paid organizers on the ground."[14] As such, the campaigns garnered worldwide attention.

---

[9] Barack Obama, YouTube Channel, http://www.youtube.com/user/BarackObama dotcom; John McCain, YouTube channel, http://www.youtube.com/user/JohnMcCain dotcom.

[10] Pew Internet & American Life Project, "The Internet's Role in Campaign 2008."

[11] Adam Nagourney, "The '08 Campaign: Sea Change for Politics as We Know It," *New York Times*, November 3, 2008, p. A1. Retrieved from http://www.nytimes.com/2008/11/04/us/politics/04memo.html?_r=1.

[12] Pew Internet & American Life Project, "The Internet's Role in Campaign 2008."

[13] Ibid.

[14] Claire Cain Miller, "How Obama's Internet Campaign Changed Politics," *New York Times*, November 7, 2008. Retrieved from http://bits.blogs.nytimes.com/2008/11/07/how-obamas-internet-campaign-changed-politics.

E-CAMPAIGNS IN GERMANY, AUSTRIA, AND SWITZERLAND

Has the Internet similarly shaped the political information environment in Germany, Austria, and Switzerland? A comparison of these three countries' use of Internet technology reveals not only differences among them but also suggests that the German-speaking countries in Europe have not followed the same usage patterns as those observed in U.S. campaigns.

Germany and the 2009 "Superwahljahr"

In 2009 Germany experienced a "Superwahljahr" – a year in which an unusually large number of elections take place – when candidates ran for the German presidency, for seats in the national parliament (Bundestag), and for parliaments in the states of Hessia, Saxony, Thuringia, Saarland, Brandenburg, and Schleswig-Holstein. The success of Obama's impressive online campaign in the previous year stimulated great interest in the possibilities of mobilization through the Internet.[15]

German parties began their online campaigns for the 2009 elections by redesigning their websites and bringing them up to speed. Social Democrats (SPD), for instance, decided to make their online campaign at wahlkampf09.de[16] the centerpiece of their election campaign and the motor of voter mobilization.[17] The party implemented a fresh look, moving from the traditional red to a blue background. More importantly, it installed a community site (meinespd.net), a social network in which supporters could go online to share their thoughts, discuss political matters, and add their own views to promote a cause.[18] Anybody can register for this site, not only members of the party, which has led to some conflicts between users and administrators.[19] In addition, a personal website for chancellor candidate Franz Walter Steinmeier was set up. This

---

[15] Marcel Reichart et al., Internet Politics Studie. Eine Analyse der erfolgreichen Online-Wahlkampagne des US-Präsidenten Barack Obama und wie sich die deutschen Parteien im Internet für das Superwahljahr 2009 aufstellen. Retrieved from http://www.dld-conference.com/upload/DLD_Internet_Politics_20_01_09.pdf.

[16] The domain now forwards users to meinespd.net.

[17] Günther Lachmann, "Die SPD setzt im Wahlkampf auf Internet-Kampagnen," *Die Welt*, January 8, 2009. Retrieved from http://www.welt.de/welt_print/article2988992/Die-SPD-setzt-im-Wahlkampf-auf-Internet-Kampagnen.html.

[18] Sebastian Gievert, "SPD-Wahlkampf: Das Herz schlägt online," January 7, 2009. Retrieved from http://politik-digital.de/spd-online-wahlkampf-kampagne.

[19] "No We Can't," *Der Freitag*, September 23, 2009. Retrieved from http://www.freitag.de/wochenthema/0939-wahlkampf-spd-wahlkampfzentrale-insider.

website links to Facebook, Flickr, and YouTube to encourage voters to create their own groups and spread the word about their party. It was meant to be an interface between the organization and its voters who could download information on the party's program and use it in their own supportive endeavors.[20] Kajo Wasserhövel, managing director of the Social Democrats, was quoted in January 2009 as saying that the Internet was on the verge of becoming the dominant medium of all political communication (Lachmann 2009).

In more traditional online territory, but similar to the Social Democrats' efforts, the Christian Democratic Union (CDU) – the party of chancellor and then candidate Angela Merkel – set up a website for online supporters called "teAM Deutschland" at team2009.de, which currently has roughly 28,000 registered users. Similar to the approach taken by the Social Democrats, the conservatives designed their website to be a "launch pad" for the activities of their supporters.[21]

As the journal of the German parliament (Bundestag) pointed out, parties had to learn during the 2009 election campaigns how to manage their social network activities.[22] Therefore it comes as no surprise that social media activities by mainstream parties have been considered to be far from perfect; the digital business association (Bundesverband digitale Wirtschaft) assessed the parties' Web 2.0 usage as "below average,"[23] and political online pundits criticized the SPD's work in this area as being more "Web 1.5" than Web 2.0.[24] In addition, the Greens' Facebook fan page lacked a sense of personalization,[25] whereas the candidates' Facebook fan pages did not address voters directly.[26] According to research conducted by the Institute for Media and Communication Management

---

[20] Gievert, "SPD-Wahlkampf: Das Herz schlägt online."

[21] Laura Weissmueller, "Obama Hilf!," *Sueddeutsche Zeitung*, February 27, 2009.

[22] Hagen Albers, "Onlinewahlkampf 2009," *Aus Politik und Zeitgeschichte* 2009/51, 2009. Retrieved from http://www.das-parlament.de/2009/51/Beilage/006.html.

[23] Cited in "Parteien verschenken Online-Wahlkampf-Potenzial," *Computerwoche*, September 22, 2009. Retrieved from http://www.computerwoche.de/netzwerke/web/19061\68.

[24] Ibid. See also Sebastian Gievert, "'Und alle so Yeaahh' – Die Webwahlkampfbilanz," September 27, 2009. Retrieved from http://www.politik-digital.de/bundestagswahl-onlinewahlkampf-bilanz-2009.

[25] Klaus Eck, "VI. Social-Media-Check Wahl 2009: Die Grünen auf Facebook," September 23, 2009. Retrieved from http://klauseck.typepad.com/prblogger/2009/09/v-socialmediacheck-wahl-2009-die-gr%C3%BCnen-auf-facebook.html.

[26] Klaus Eck, "I. Social-Media-Check Wahl 2009: Die Facebook-Fanpages der Spitzenkandidaten," September 17, 2009. Retrieved from http://klauseck.typepad.com/prblogger/2009/09/socialmediacheck-wahl-2009-die-facebookfanpages-der-spitzenkandidaten-.html.

at the University of St. Gallen, only the recently founded Pirate Party of Germany enjoyed relative "digital acceptance," with more than 27,000 followers on Twitter.[27] On video platforms, the pirates dominated the traditional parties by far in the final phase of the campaigns; their videos were viewed 260,000 times in the first week of September, whereas videos of the runner-up CDU had approximately 103,000 views.[28]

Put in a context of 62 million German voters, 46.3 million Internet users, 14.6 million users of social networking sites, and 1.4 million members of political parties,[29] the parties' efforts to increase their interactive Web presence seemed quite promising, especially given that 83% of first-time voters used the Internet to find political information.[30] However, another study found that 72% of voters do not consult the Internet when forming their political opinion.[31] Because it is mainly young Germans who rely on the Internet for information on politics, the expectations for the impact of the Internet on elections are low. Even with the growth in the number of digitally skilled people, the generation "born digital" still does not determine the outcome of elections.[32]

Yet a look at the German parliamentary elections of 2002 and 2005 shows that the Internet has become more important as a medium for political communication. In 2002, only 42% of candidates had personal websites, in contrast to 59% of candidates in 2005 (Zittel 2007: 11). For the 2009 elections, this rate reached 85%.[33] Of course, these numbers do not show how effectively politicians communicate online or the impact of

---

[27] Cf. Miriam Meckel and Katarina Stanoevska-Slabeva, "Auch Zwitschern muss man üben. Wie Politiker im deutschen Bundestagswahlkampf twitterten," *Neue Zürcher Zeitung*, November 10, 2009. Retrieved from http://www.nzz.ch/nachrichten/kultur/medien/auch_zwitschern_muss_man_ueben_1.3994226.html. On November 10, 2009, the account http://twitter.com/Piratenpartei had about 20.000 followers.

[28] Readers Edition, "Piratenpartei als Nr. 1 im Online-Wahlkampf," September 10, 2009. Retrieved from http://www.readers-edition.de/2009/09/10/piratenpartei-als-nr-1-im-online-wahlkampf/.

[29] Gievert, "'Und alle so Yeaahh' – Die Webwahlkampfbilanz."

[30] T-Online, "Erstwähler informieren sich vor allem über das Internet," May 20, 2009. Retrieved from http://bundestagswahl.t-online.de/bundestagswahl-2009-erstwaehler-informieren-sich-vor-allem-ueber-das-internet/id_18734876/index.

[31] Jörg Lessing, "Das überschätzte Wahlkampfmedium," *Stuttgarter Nachrichten*, September 18, 2009. Retrieved from http://content.stuttgarter-nachrichten.de/stn/page/detail.php/2202570.

[32] Christian Tretbar, "Online ist offline," *Der Tagesspiegel*, September 27, 2009. Retrieved from http://www.tagesspiegel.de/politik/online-ist-offline/1606720.html.

[33] See the press release, "85 Prozent der Kandidaten zur Bundestagswahl 2009 im Netz," by Volz Innovation. Retrieved from http://www.bwcon.de/bwcon_newsdetail.html?&no_cache=1&tx_ttnews[tt_news]=4371&tx_ttnews[backPid]=505.

specific uses of new communication technologies. Still, they are a proxy for how Internet savvy candidates have become.

However, not only the political parties aimed to mobilize voters for the 2009 elections. There were also campaigns without a traditional political agenda that tried to simply motivate citizens to go to the polls. "Geh Nicht Hin" ("Don't Go!"), for instance, was an initiative that sparked discussion through a video on YouTube, in which a couple of German celebrities provocatively express their reasons for not voting.[34] In a follow-up video that was published about a week later, they revoke their original statements and tell the viewers to go vote.[35] The videos were jointly produced by an independent platform, which sought to foster the democratic and digital development of the European information society, and a TV production company that admittedly drew inspiration from a similar American initiative.[36] The videos and copies were viewed approximately 125,000 times by the end of July 2009, two months before the national elections.[37]

Mobilization via the Web often seeks to translate activism from cyberspace into action in the offline world, both during and outside of election campaigns. The Internet is an ideal space and instrument for bottom-up mobilization in nonelection years. Three examples illustrate this point. Radical right extremists have been running a negative campaign against Islam on blogs, social networking sites, and discussion forums. These blogs and forums serve as information platforms that deliver arguments for the renunciation of Islam, and users' comments reaffirm their views (see Busch 2008: 446). In another example, for the global climate summit in Copenhagen in 2009, a coalition of environmental organizations founded an initiative called "climate pirates" that focused on physically bringing their support of a strong climate treaty (which would limit global warming to 2° Centigrade) to the Danish capital on a sailing vessel. To achieve this global goal, they called for a stop to the construction of coal power plants in Germany.[38] The climate pirates used video platforms and their website to distribute information, offered a manual as well as audio files for the choreography of flash mobs, and

---

34 See http://www.youtube.com/watch?v=Wfi_ivppEwI.
35 See http://www.youtube.com/watch?v=KjIunxvD38k.
36 See the "about" section of the initiative's website at http://www.gehnichthin.de/%C3%BCber-uns.
37 See the release from July 28, 2009. Retrieved from http://www.politik-digital.de/sites/politik-digital.de/files/PressemitteilungGehnichthin.pdf.
38 See the website, http://www.klimapiraten.net/site/node/7.

asked for donations on their websites through a "rent-a-pirate" program. A quite different example of grassroots mobilization is Campact, an association that organizes citizens for different political causes. Campact helps civil society organizations mobilize citizens for protests through the use of e-mail newsletters, social networking sites, and online fundraising.[39]

Austrian Elections

Austria held its last national parliamentary elections in September 2008, when Obama's campaign was in full swing. The online campaigns were built on basic elements such as party websites that presented pictures, videos, and election posters.[40] The People's Party offered its supporters educational and advertising materials and a carpooling system for the first campaign event. It also offered two different community websites, one of which included interactive forums for supporters to exchange thoughts.[41] Social Democrats also launched their own community website for registered users called New Politics ("Neue Politik"), but it generated anger after a user uploaded a picture of a young woman making a derogatory gesture.[42] The Greens seemed to be the most confident in the interactive potential of the Web as they asked Internet users to choose from different campaign posters and submit their own suggestions.[43] They were also the only ones to offer all information in German, English, Croatian, and Turkish.[44] However, online pundits criticized the parties' social media activities for their lack of dialogue with the public, because most channels on video platforms and blogs had the comments feature switched off.[45]

One year later, in 2009, the People Party's online endeavors took better advantage of the potential for online communication: Their redesigned

---

[39] Cf. http://www.campact.de/campact/about/home.

[40] See Thomas Frank and Manuela Tomic, "Wahlkampf im Internet ist Nebensache," *Kleine Zeitung*, August 27, 2008. Retrieved from http://www.kleinezeitung.at/nachrichten/politik/regierung/1499612/index.do.

[41] Dominik Leitner, "Die Politik am Irrweg Web 2.0," August 24, 2008. Retrieved from http://neuwal.com/index.php/2008/08/24/die-politik-am-irrweg-web-20/.

[42] Ibid.

[43] Christoph Chorherr, "Grüne Plakate," September 9, 2008. Retrieved from http://chorherr.twoday.net/stories/5049146/.

[44] Frank and Tomic, "Wahlkampf im Internet ist Nebensache."

[45] See, for example, Leitner, "Die Politik am Irrweg Web 2.0," and Dieter Zirnig, "Wahlkampf im Internet, Wahlkampf 2.0 oder 'I like Chopin,'" September 20, 2008. Retrieved from http://neuwal.com/index.php/2008/09/20/neuwal-wahlkampf-im-internet-wahlkampf-20-oder-i-like-chopin/.

website had links to all major social networking sites and an integrated video platform, just in time for elections for the European Parliament.[46] For that same election, Social Democrats sought to reach out to potential voters by engaging 120 so-called ambassadors (including some retirees) in activism on social media sites. The ambassadors received special training for their online campaign, which – according to the Social Democrats' head of communication – was the first of its kind in Europe, although it did not represent the party's main channel of mobilization.[47] In April 2009, Chancellor Werner Faymann (Social Democrats) addressed the nation for the first time exclusively through a video webcast.[48]

In its campaign for the 2009 parliamentary elections in the province of Upper Austria (Oberösterreich), the People's Party explicitly addressed topics that appealed to young voters.[49] The party joined forces with its young chapter to reach out to youth via its Internet community portal, "My Box."[50] This strategy was fitting because Austria had just introduced voting rights for 16-year-olds in 2008. However, newly admitted voters only accounted for 2 to 3 % of the electorate.[51] Governor Pühringer of the People's Party (or rather, his team) was quite active on Twitter during the days before the vote, yet the account was only used as a mobilization tactic, because no dialogue with voters was established. Shortly after the new government coalition was formed, the account went silent.[52] Pühringer's YouTube channel only has had a few new uploads since the election, although many testimonials, speeches, and documentation of the campaign were posted on it in the months before the election.[53] The other parties were also active on YouTube, however, no videos seemed to have exceeded the threshold of 1,000 views.[54] This fact may support

[46] Anita Zielina, "ÖVP gibt sich 'neues Gesicht,'" derStandard.at, April 15, 2009. Retrieved from http://derstandard.at/1237229956942/OeVP-gibt-sich-neues-Gesicht.
[47] Rosa Winkler-Hermaden, "'Coole Großmütter' sollen Wähler mobilisieren," derStandard.at, May 13, 2009. Retrieved from http://derstandard.at/1241622461021/Coole-Grossmuetter-sollen-Waehler-mobilisieren.
[48] Anita Zielina, "Politiker entdecken Youtube. Einmal Obama mit einem Hauch Drama," derStandard.at, April 1, 2009. Retrieved from http://derstandard.at/1237228892322/Politiker-entdecken-Youtube-Einmal-Obama-mit-einem-Hauch-Drama.
[49] Österreichischer Rundfunk, "Premiere: Wählen mit 16 bei Nationalratswahl," September 25, 2008. Retrieved from http://burgenland.orf.at/stories/309948/.
[50] See http://www.mybox.at/.
[51] ÖVP Oberösterreich, "100 Tage bis zur Landtagswahl," June 19, 2009. Retrieved from http://www.ooevp.at/22745/?MP=61–5780.
[52] See http://twitter.com/teampuehringer.
[53] See http://www.youtube.com/user/lhpuehringer.
[54] For a list of YouTube videos by the parties in Upper Austria see http://delicious.com/karlstaudinger/vidwatch?page=1.

the conclusion of an Austrian newspaper's assessment of the 2008 online campaigns: Internet users seem to have little interest in political parties.[55]

However, the Austrian student protests in fall 2009 were primarily organized via the Web – through social networks and via their website www.unsereuni.at, which hosts a Wiki.[56] The protestors used Twitter as they organized seizures of university buildings to make their call for university reforms heard. This very interactive and mobile form of communication allowed students and supporters of educational reform to simultaneously spread information from several hotspots in real time as protests spread from Vienna, where they had started, to other Austrian university towns. Through so-called re-tweets (e.g., the replication of an original message on Twitter), people were mobilized to join others at specified places.[57] The students also used Facebook, posted pictures of protests on Flickr, and uploaded videos on YouTube to document their actions. Judging by this quite impressive cycle of mobilization, one might expect that other stakeholder groups and grassroots movements would also successfully use Web 2.0 to engage people on other important issues. However, experts have expressed disappointment with the lack of presence and activity by nongovernmental organizations in the realm of Facebook, Twitter, and the likes in Austria.[58]

Yet, grassroots activities on the Internet are not completely dead in Austria, as Vienna's Greens demonstrated in summer 2009 when independent supporters of a group called Grüne Vorwahlen ("Green pre-elections")[59] took advantage of a provision in the party's statute, which allows for nonmembers to vote on the party's candidates in pre-elections.[60] The only conditions for doing so are a testimonial of support and no other party affiliation. There were 445 testimonials submitted, which would theoretically allow their authors[61] to take part in the

---

[55] Frank and Tomic, "Wahlkampf im Internet ist Nebensache."

[56] Michael Kremmel and Anita Zielina, " Netzwerk-Protest macht Politiker ratlos," der-Standard.at, November 3, 2009. Retrieved from http://derstandard.at/1256743667434/Netzwerk-Protest-macht-Politiker-ratlos.

[57] Vienna Online, "Studentenproteste 2.0: Besetzer vernetzen sich im Internet," October 29. 2009. Retrieved from http://www.vienna.at/news/wien/artikel/studentenproteste-20-besetzer-vernetzen-sich-im-internet/cn/news-20091029–12334498.

[58] Michael Hartl, "Heißen NGOs bald NSOs?" November 25, 2009. Retrieved from http://michaelhartl.at/heien-ngos-bald-nsos.

[59] See http://www.gruenevorwahlen.at/.

[60] "Internet-Basisbewegung bringt Wiener Grüne ins Schwitzen," heute.at. Retrieved from http://www.heute.at/news/politik/Internet-Basisbewegung-bringt-Wiener-Gruene-ins-Schwitzen;art422,56559.

[61] Two hundred of which were described as "Internet Fuzzis" (which can be translated as "nerds") by one of the initiative's founders; see Teresa Eder, "'Internet

pre-election process for Vienna's municipal elections of 2010.[62] Apparently not all Greens[63] welcomed this shift of power from party officials to nonmembers.[64] However, the Grüne Vorwahlen group still is well connected via Twitter and Facebook.

Swiss Referendums and the Rise of the Pirate Party

In 2006, 68% of Swiss members of parliament were reported to have a personal website.[65] However, a study of the parliamentary elections in Switzerland that were held in the fall of 2007 found that barely more than 50% of the candidates of the six largest parties, which had already been represented in parliament, from the six most populous cantons had their own personal website (Brändli and Leuener 2007: 80). In addition, almost 50% of the candidates included in the survey said they only updated their personal website weekly, in contrast to 8.4% who did so on a daily basis (Brändli and Leuener 2007: 143). Thus this 2007 survey indicated that the candidates had not fully exploited the capabilities of the Internet. Yet 74.2% of the candidates believed that a personal website had been rather important or very important in the election campaign (Brändli and Leuener 2007: 148).[66]

The first professionally produced video clips by or for Swiss politicians started to appear on YouTube in early 2007.[67] That same year the Liberal Democratic Party's cantonal division of Aargau announced that it would hire professionals to produce Web videos in support of its candidates and to address voters who could not otherwise be reached.[68] Although Federal Council Moritz Leuenberger's blog had 2,780 visitors per day in the first 15 months of its existence (from March 2007 to June 2008), the newspaper *Neue Züricher Zeitung* stated – only a few days after the first entry was posted – that blogs only receive attention by the general

    Fuzzis' wollen 'Grünes Haus' stürmen," derStandard.at, June 5, 2009. Retrieved from http://derstandard.at/1244116982836/Internet-Fuzzis-wollen-Gruenes-Haus-stuermen.

[62] Some of the testimonials were rejected by the party, cf. http://www.gruenevorwahlen.at/2009/07/entstand-die-nackten-zahlen/.

[63] Including some former members of the Green party.

[64] Eder, "'Internet Fuzzis' wollen 'Grünes Haus' stürmen."

[65] See, for example, Pierre Kilchenmann and Jean-Loup Chappelet, "Les parlementaires Suisses face à l'Internet en 2006." Retrieved from http://www.gov.ch/idheap.nsf/view/D142C5B6A755780CC1257265002CDAB9/$File/LesParlementairesSuissesFace Internet2006.pdf.

[66] Note that this survey only included candidates with personal websites.

[67] "Die Schweizer Politik entdeckt Youtube," persoenlich.com, March 19, 2007. Retrieved from http://www.persoenlich.com/news/show_news.cfm?newsid=66673.

[68] Ibid.

public when traditional media report on them[69] (Gasser et al. 2010: 79). In contrast, in an interview on September 27, 2007 (approximately one month before the election), political scientist Wolf Linder asserted that the 2007 election campaigns had entered the digital age, referring not only to candidates' and parties' websites but also to blogs and discussion forums set up by newspapers.[70] Yet, there were no indications that social media sites such as Facebook or MySpace had an impact on the election campaigns of 2007.

The use of the Web has increased rapidly since then, but not for all candidates and in all regions. In the municipal elections in fall 2008, for instance, there was a digital divide among candidates as far as social media is concerned: Whereas only 10% of the candidates in Berne even had their own website, observers pointed out the high degree to which young politicians in Basel took advantage of Facebook or MySpace.[71] By 2010, the parties seemed to be very active on the Internet in the elections for the municipal parliament and government of the city of Zurich; for example, Social Democrats dedicated 10% of their campaign spending to online activities.[72] Their website presented the party's candidates and had the latest official video clips embedded from YouTube. It also was linked to a Facebook page, where the Social Democrats asked people to submit suggestions for things or projects that they think "Zurich needs" and that should be promoted by a party representative. Although the Greens of Zurich and the local chapter of the People's Party (SVP) did not link to any social media on their websites, the Christian Democrats (CVP) offered a link to a group on Facebook that supported their candidate for the executive branch. Surprisingly, Twitter was widely neglected by candidates in the 2010 Zurich election.

Yet, it comes as no surprise that the Pirate Party, which was founded in the summer of 2009, was the most Internet savvy. March 7, 2010, marks the first time that the "pirates" ran in political elections in Switzerland

---

[69] "Das Internet spielt nur die Nebenrolle. Die Schweizer Politik ist nicht bereit für Blogs und Videofilmchen," *Neue Zürcher Zeitung*, March 25, 2007. Retrieved from http://www.nzz.ch/2007/03/25/il/articleF1KQK.html.

[70] See the interview with Wolf Linder on news portal Swissinfo. Retrieved from http://www.swissinfo.ch/ger/Unueblich_scharfer_Schweizer_Wahlkampf.html?cid=596644.

[71] Nina Jecker, "Wahlkampf im Web: Viele verpassen ihre Chance," *20 Minuten Bern*, October 24, 2008. Retrieved from http://www.20min.ch/print/story/21705879; Anna Luethi, "Jungparteien setzen beim Wahlkampf aufs Internet," *20 Minuten*, August 27, 2008. Retrieved from http://www.20min.ch/news/basel/story/29503716.

[72] Adi Kälin, "Ein wenig Wahlkampf auch im Internet. Kandidaten für Zürcher Stadtrat sind stärker präsent als vor vier Jahren," *Neue Zürcher Zeitung*, January 13, 2010. Retrieved from http://www.nzz.ch/nachrichten/zuerich/stadtzuercher_wahlen_2010_dossier/hintergrundartikel/wahlkampf_internet_zuerich_1.4498760.html.

as candidates competing for seats in the municipal parliament of the city of Winterthur. Three weeks later, pirate candidates ran for seats in the cantonal parliament of Berne. The party had a Twitter account, which it updated several times a day, but its tweets did not address the election in any special way. There is also a Facebook group for the whole country with 3,600 Pirate Party supporters, although the group that was created for the election in Winterthur has merely 90 members. At the time of this writing, no videos were available on YouTube that addressed the local elections. Interestingly, the pirates seem to be very focused on increasing their visibility on politnetz.ch, which is an independent political platform that allows candidates to express their opinion on a variety of issues.

An important aspect of Swiss democracy is that Swiss citizens not only vote for their political representatives but they also contribute their views in frequently held referendums. Four times a year, citizens are asked to decide on changes to the constitution or to laws on a federal level (most times, cantonal or municipal polls are held on the same dates). These referendum campaigns are run in an increasingly aggressive style by the People's Party, which has celebrated big wins in recent referendums.[73] While (already high) Internet penetration is on the rise and numbers of Facebook users are growing, the Internet is playing an increasingly prominent role in referendum campaigns in Switzerland.[74] A recent survey shows that 22% of citizens used the Internet to gather information concerning the referendums of November 2009.[75] However the Swiss still seem reluctant to donate money to political causes online.[76]

Whereas the People's Party video channel on YouTube contains mainly testimonials and speeches by politicians, the party has caused the biggest stir in the Internet arena with an innovative online game, in which players direct a goat ("Zottel" is the mascot of the People's Party) to kick "criminal" foreigners out of the country. Populist approaches such as this seem to work very well on the Internet, because they are then picked up by traditional media, which amplify their reach. The impression that

---

[73] For example, on a ban on the construction of minarets.

[74] Urs Geiser, "Online politics gains ground despite scepticism," August 3, 2009. Retrieved from http://www.swissinfo.ch/eng/politics/internal_affairs/Online_politics_gains_ground_despite_scepticism.html?cid=126350.

[75] Claude Longchamp, "Politische Internetnutzung erreichte 2009 neue Höchstwerte," February 11, 2010. Retrieved from http://www.zoonpoliticon.ch/blog/8007/internetnutzung-erreichte-2009-in-abstimmungskampfen-neue-hochstwerte/.

[76] Niklaus Nuspliger, "Kampfzone Internet: Abstimmungskampagnen gehen online – mit bescheidenem Erfolg," *Neue Zürcher Zeitung*, January 19, 2009. Retrieved from http://www.nzz.ch/hintergrund/dossiers/abstimmung_zur_personenfreizuegigkeit/hintergrundartikel_personenfreizuegigkeit/kampfzone_internet_1.1724423.html.

the People's Party seems to be the front-runner in Internet political communication is further supported by the fact that the weekly TV show of former Federal Council and figurehead of the party, Christoph Blocher, has been uploaded for streaming on the Web for more than two years. In this interview-based show, Blocher often addresses contemporary debates and issues.

In Switzerland, mobilization of voters via the Internet and Web 2.0 applications also works from the bottom up, but has not been widespread. For instance, a coalition of bloggers was very active in trying to motivate people to go to the polls for a referendum on a treaty on freedom of movement with the European Union in February 2009. However, although a website aggregating their blog entries existed, it did not seem to play an important role in mobilization efforts.[77] Some of the bloggers contributing to "Bloggen für die Bilateralen"[78] – as the website was called – were relatively famous, and others were freedom of movement advocates with clear party affiliations or even members of parliament. Therefore, this effort cannot be considered a truly grassroots initiative.

Another online movement committed to the same cause created the website, dabei-bleiben.ch ("staying with-in"), which was supported by several youth chapters of Swiss political parties and political youth organizations such as the Young Swiss Europeans who advocate Switzerland's membership in the European Union. The initiative's group on Facebook counted (at the time of this writing – about one year after the referendum) almost 4,000 members.[79] Yet, apart from one video on YouTube,[80] no other creative activities seemed to have found their way onto the Web to support this effort.

As in other European countries, real bottom-up mobilization has been found among educated youth; following the example of other European countries, students in Zurich,[81] Basel,[82] Berne,[83] and elsewhere began

---

[77] Unfortunately, the website is no longer active.
[78] German for "blogging for the bilateral treaties."
[79] See http://www.facebook.com/n/?group.php&gid=20269608827.
[80] See http://www.youtube.com/user/dabeibleiben.
[81] Alois Feusi, "Studentenprotestchen in Zürich. Gegen, Verschulung des Lehrplans' und Missstände der Bolognareform," *Neue Zürcher Zeitung*, November 17, 2009. Retrieved from http://www.nzz.ch/nachrichten/zuerich/studenten_proteste_zuerich_1.4029520.html.
[82] Simone Rau, "Wir bleiben in der Aula," *Der Bund*, November 18, 2009. Retrieved from http://www.derbund.ch/schweiz/dossier/studentenproteste/Wir-bleiben-in-der-Aula/story/27266066.
[83] "1200 Studierende ohne Vorlesung," *Der Bund*, November 18, 2009. Retrieved from http://www.derbund.ch/schweiz/dossier/studentenproteste/1200-Studierende-ohne-Vorlesung/story/13308161.

to protest against education politics at their universities in November 2009.[84] The protesters' website, www.unsereunizh.ch, was used to spread information and mobilize supporters, as were a Facebook group with (currently) approximately 1,200 members and a Twitter account. The latter apparently had a very limited reach with only 150 followers at the time of this writing.

General Observations

Comparing international politics in general and political communication in particular among countries is always difficult, because they differ by area, population, history, and culture. Comparing the use of the Internet in e-campaigns across German-speaking countries on the one hand and between these countries and the United States on the other hand is further complicated by the fact that in the European countries we surveyed no reliable quantitative studies were available to provide the foundation for such an analysis. That being said, we can make two general observations based on these case studies.

First, it seems safe to conclude that by virtually any measure – from audience to diversity of content, from campaign spending to using Web 2.0 strategies – the Internet currently plays a much less prominent role in political communication and e-campaigns in German-speaking countries than in the United States. For observers who spend time on both sides of the Atlantic, this finding comes as no surprise. However, the finding is interesting because German-speaking countries have been influenced by other significant trends in U.S. political campaigning over the past decades. Later in this chapter, we identify factors that may aid in explaining such differences between adoption of Internet strategies versus other American influences and whether these differences are temporary or structural in nature.

Second, there seem to be differences in Internet usage in the context of political communication and e-campaigns across the three countries we surveyed. The observations presented in this study suggest that German politicians and parties have embraced the Internet more than their colleagues in Austria or Switzerland and, at the very least, have taken the lead in using information technology. The percentage of German candidates

---

[84] Protesters in Zurich also offered an audio feed from an occupied auditorium. See Christoph Landolt, "Uni-Besetzer schalten sich selbst stumm," *Tagesanzeiger*, November 20, 2009. Retrieved from http://www.tagesanzeiger.ch/zuerich/stadt/UniBesetzer-schalten-sich-selbst-stumm/story/30290547.

who have a personal website exceeds by far the percentage of Swiss candidates online. Twitter usage among politicians is still very rudimentary in Switzerland, and the German Pirate Party's 27,000 followers seem almost utopian by Swiss standards. The Swiss apparently are slow adopters in this field. Some general characteristics of online political communication in German-speaking Europe and possible reasons for the differences in the three countries in this study are discussed in the following sections.

CHARACTERISTICS OF POLITICAL COMMUNICATION
IN GERMAN-SPEAKING EUROPE

Despite the differences among German-speaking countries, several common characteristics of political communication can be distilled from our anecdotal review of Germany, Austria, and Switzerland, which may provide the basis for a more granular comparison between these three countries and the practices in other countries, including the United States.

An extensive literature review, a systematic search of news reports, and a small number of interviews with local party leaders indicate that the Internet has not taken center stage in political communication, mobilization, and fundraising for elections and other political initiatives. Even as a medium for communicating political information, it remains only one of many channels. For instance, General Secretary Guido Schrommer of the Swiss Liberal Party expressed skepticism about the reach of political messages on the Internet, saying that his party probably would not gain new voters on the Web.[85] In similar ways, politicians like the head of communications of the Austrian Socialists openly admitted that the Web is not their most decisive channel in election campaigning.[86] As political communication expert and researcher Kathrin Wimmer confirms for German political parties, the Internet remains one of many media used for political communication.[87] Voter demographics simply do not yet require that political actors reconsider their online strategies and make any significant changes in their approaches.[88]

---

[85] "Das Internet spielt nur die Nebenrolle. Die Schweizer Politik ist nicht bereit für Blogs und Videofilmchen," *Neue Zürcher Zeitung*, March 25, 2007. Retrieved from http://www.nzz.ch/2007/03/25/il/articleF1KQK.html.

[86] Rosa Winkler-Hermaden, "'Coole Großmütter' sollen Wähler mobilisieren," derStandard.at, May 13, 2009. Retrieved from http://derstandard.at/1241622461021/Coole-Grossmuetter-sollen-Waehler-mobilisieren.

[87] Kathrin Wimmer, "Die Internetkampagnen im Bundestagswahlkampf 2009." Retrieved from http://www.cap-lmu.de/publikationen/2009/wimmer.php.

[88] Tretbar, "Online ist offline."

Compared to the United States, German-speaking Europe so far has not experienced a large-scale adoption of social media (Web 2.0) applications such as social networks or interactive video platforms by political actors, including political parties and individual candidates. Instead of engaging interactively with voters, they often simply display their programs and campaign posters on their respective websites. For example, in the March 2010 municipal elections in Zurich, Twitter was widely neglected by candidates. Interestingly, several observers expressed disappointment with these backward-oriented practices and criticized the big parties for not accepting the power shift from senders to users and being unwilling to engage with them in an honest dialogue.[89] However, others held that the parties just lacked a clear message that could serve as the basis for an advanced online strategy.[90]

Many politicians lack extensive experience with social media, and have only adopted such tools, if at all, in more recent campaigns. For example, German Social Democrats' overall activities on Twitter have been described as "barely responsive" by a prominent PR blog.[91] In addition, more than three-quarters of German politicians' Twitter accounts were registered only in 2009, just a few months before the elections.[92] It is also not uncommon for politicians' social media accounts to go silent after a campaign has ended, as did the Twitter account of Governor Pühringer from Upper Austria. The mere fact that many YouTube channels and blogs had the comments feature switched off also gives a hint as to politicians' uneasiness with social media usage and the lack of control associated with it.

Youth chapters of political parties use social media for at least two reasons. First, the lack of extensive financial resources requires them to find other ways of campaigning than running expensive ads in newspapers or posters on billboards. The use of Web 2.0 applications is a cheaper alternative. Second, both the people who run such campaigns and their targeted audience are "born digital," having grown up within the

---

[89] Gievert, "'Und alle so Yeaahh' – Die Webwahlkampfbilanz."

[90] See Laura Weissmueller, "Obama Hilf!," *Sueddeutsche Zeitung*, February 27, 2009 quoting CDU General Secretary Ronald Pofalla.

[91] Klaus Eck, "VIII. Social-Media-Check Wahl 2009: SPD und Twitter," September 25, 2009. Retrieved from http://klauseck.typepad.com/prblogger/2009/09/viii-socialmediacheck-wahl-2009-spd-und-twitter-.html.

[92] Miriam Meckel and Katarina Stanoevska-Slabeva, "Auch Zwitschern muss man üben. Wie Politiker im deutschen Bundestagswahlkampf twitterten,'" *Neue Zürcher Zeitung*, November 10, 2009. Retrieved from http://www.nzz.ch/nachrichten/kultur/medien/auch_zwitschern_muss_man_ueben_1.3994226.html.

knowledge economy of the Internet. For these digital natives, communicating online does not pose a great challenge because they already are acquainted with it. Many of the Swiss parties' youth chapters have used Facebook and similar platforms to conduct their campaigns regarding issues such as freedom of movement with the European Union.[93]

Grassroots movements also use social media to mobilize supporters where civic and political engagement overlap. Perhaps the most impressive examples are the recent student protests and the online campaign by advocates of a strong environmental treaty in the Copenhagen summit. In addition, Austrian university students used Twitter extensively to mobilize support for their protests against what they consider to be a failed educational system. The hashtag "unibrennt" (German for "university is burning") was used an astonishing 50 times per second at peak times.[94] The anger about failed reforms of the so-called Bologna process, which aimed to harmonize university education across Europe,[95] quickly spread to other countries.

Apart from a few exceptions, political parties use video platforms such as YouTube mostly to upload speeches or documentation of campaign rallies. Creative or even entertaining videos are rare; even the German Pirate Party's uploads, which gained a lot of public attention, do not stand out much. Videos of testimonials and speeches make up nearly all the material on the Swiss People's Party's YouTube channel, and Governor Pühringer of Upper Austria also had videos of the campaign on his YouTube channel. The music videos of (controversial) Austrian right-wing politician H. C. Strache, such as the one for a song called "Österreich zuerst" ("Austria first"), were a little more creative, although rather nationalist in their tone.[96]

In all three countries, online platforms have been used increasingly by voters to gain a clearer picture of the parties' programs and candidates' views. They even allow users to fill out a survey to match their own

[93] Nuspliger, "Kampfzone Internet: Abstimmungskampagnen gehen online – mit bescheidenem Erfolg."

[94] "Studentenproteste 2.0: The revolution is twittered," derStandard.at, October 28, 2009. Retrieved from http://derstandard.at/1256743585736/Studentenproteste-20-The-revolution-is-twittered.

[95] The so-called Bologna reforms, in the course of which bachelor and master degrees were introduced in many European countries, have often been criticized for allegedly producing employees rather than free thinkers. See, for example, an interview with theology professor Marius Reiser, who left his chair in protest against the reforms, at http://www.goethe.de/wis/fut/uhs/en4681040.htm.

[96] See http://www.youtube.com/watch?v=pVnzYs4HYBQ.

views with candidates' profiles to ease the information-gathering burden for voters. Wahl-o-mat[97] in Germany, Wahlkabine.at in Austria, and Smartvote.ch in Switzerland are ambitious projects that bring some clarity into the choice among candidates while leaving out any emotional aspects or campaign strategies. In the 2007 national elections, 84% of Swiss candidates had their own profile on smartvote.ch.[98] The platform, which allows users to match their views to those of individual candidates, is very popular with users, as more than 900,000 voting suggestions were issued.

In Switzerland, centralized platforms run by third parties are popular places for political discussions. Prominent examples include politnetz.ch or NZZ Votum, on which all sides of the political spectrum can have their say. NZZ Votum – run by one of the biggest newspapers in the country – is more or less a blog that contrasts different political opinions by letting selected personalities from different parties or stakeholder groups write entries on certain topics. In contrast, Politnetz.ch is community based and allows politicians to easily set up profiles. According to its executive manager, one of the advantages of Politnetz over Facebook is its community-management feature, which ensures that discussions are kept within the limits of the law.[99] Because of their relative independence from political parties, these platforms seem to be trusted by users and have gained popularity over the past few years. As a result, political discussion seems to be less centralized and more fragmented in Germany and Austria, when compared to Switzerland.

It is important to reiterate that these characteristics are mostly based on anecdotal evidence and are therefore tentative in nature. In addition, the state of play regarding e-campaigns in German-speaking Europe, as in other countries, is likely to change over time as information and communication technology advances and user practices and media usage habits evolve. Nonetheless, the initial comparison of e-campaigning in German-speaking countries with that in other countries, particularly the United States, reveals significant differences in the role played by the Internet. In the next section, we outline a few factors that might explain some of these

---

97 See http://www.bpb.de/methodik/XQJYR3,0,0,Willkommen_beim_WahlOMat.html.
98 See http://www.smartvote.ch. For more on Smartvote, its impact and criticism, see Gasser et al. 2010.
99 Simon Wüthrich, "Eine Online-Plattform für Schweizer Politik 2009," August 4, 2009. Retrieved from http://startwerk.ch/2009/08/04/politnetz-online-plattform-fuer-schweizer-politik/.

differences. However, future research efforts in the field are necessary to confirm which of these factors, if any, might explain the differences.

FACTORS INFLUENCING THE POLITICAL ROLE OF THE INTERNET

The effect of the Internet on the information environment of a given society depends on various context-specific factors, including technological, economic, social, and cultural parameters. The same holds true with regard to its impact on political communication in general and the ways in which campaigns are run in particular. The current state of research does not allow for a reliable answer to the question of why the Internet plays different roles in the political realities of German-speaking countries when compared to the United States. However, we suggest several influential factors that may be of particular interest when analyzing the current state of play in Germany, Austria, and Switzerland.[100]

One important variable is time. Different societies adopt new technologies or use new technologies for particular purposes at different speeds. For instance, Europe has had a slower uptake of e-commerce services than the United States. This may suggest that the relatively limited role that the Internet currently plays in political campaigns is essentially a question of time, especially in light of the overall communication trends outlined at the beginning of this chapter. According to this argument, countries such as Germany, Austria, and Switzerland are likely to catch up over time with countries such as the United States in which digital technologies already play a prominent role in political campaigns. Of course, such a view builds on the methodologically problematic assumption that a particular level of adoption will prevail.

Another possible factor that shapes the stages of evolution across nations with respect to e-campaigns has to do with the number of people living in a country and building the pool of individuals who potentially engage in Internet-enabled political communication. In a small country such as Switzerland, which has four official languages, it might be more difficult to create a critical mass of users who would use, for example, a Facebook campaign site provided by a political party than in a larger

---

[100] A serious attempt at answering this question would require a thorough analysis of the factors that are responsible for the more extensive usage of the Internet in campaigns in countries outside Germany, Austria, and Switzerland, which would then open the door for a careful comparison of factors and the formulation of working hypotheses. In the light of this knowledge gap, one can only provide a series of possible factors of influence and speculate about their relative importance.

country such as Germany or even the United States – a factor that might be significant given the strong network effects that are at play. In addition, at the national level, size might be a factor that could result in the need for a centrally organized online campaign when the population of rural areas cannot be reached otherwise. In the three countries covered here, this is quite unlikely to be the case, however.

Differences in the structure and processes of the respective political systems also help explain the varying role that the Internet plays in political campaigns. Switzerland, with a political system that largely consists of nonprofessional politicians, is illustrative in this respect, because the system fosters a close relationship between citizens and politicians, which may decrease the need for extensive, professionally orchestrated and mediated campaigns. The structure of the respective party system is another important factor that needs to be considered; campaigns might look very different in systems with 10 or more political parties versus a system with 2 parties. Moreover, the Swiss political system of "Konkordanz" (in which all relevant parties are included in the executive branch of government and unanimously support joint decisions once they are made) may decrease the need for aggressive campaigning because it would have little impact on the composition of the government.

Further, the culture of political communication as it has emerged over time is also likely to shape the ways in which a new information and communication technology such as the Internet is adopted and used by the relevant actors. Consider, for instance, the lack of experience with the use of video in some European countries as a consequence of the prohibition of political advertisements on TV (as is the case in Switzerland) or strict regulation (as in Germany) and its implications for the introduction of YouTube-like campaigns. Cultural factors might also be responsible for national differences regarding the preferred online platforms over which political information is exchanged in the runup to an election or referendum.

In addition, a number of variables may have some impact on Internet usage in political communication, but are likely to have less weight with regard to the explanation of the phenomena described in this chapter. The different rates of adoption of the Internet in political campaigns across countries might be influenced by demand-side factors such as income inequality or varying levels of media literacy. In this study, however, it seems rather unlikely that these factors play a key role in explaining national differences, as the case of Switzerland with its relatively high income per capita and high levels of education illustrates. Such an argument would also be inconsistent with the exponential growth and popularity of e-commerce services in Switzerland, which obviously also require access and skills.

Among the supply-side factors, in contrast, are the availability of easy-to-use online platforms for political campaigns as well as the creation of rich content that attracts users. The design of such tools needs to take into account user preferences, which in turn can vary significantly across countries. In some instance, users might have a preference for relatively straightforward applications and services, as the experience with e-government platforms illustrate. In other situations, providers of advanced and "fancy" applications and content will be more attractive and successful.

Another variable that might help explain different characteristics and stages of evolution when it comes to e-campaigns is the financial resources available to create such programs. Especially where the institutional framework provides for high numbers of elections at various levels (e.g. national, regional, municipal) within a certain period of time, the cost factor might become relevant. This line of reasoning also leads to the broader question of how political campaigns are financed and on what scale.

Finally, all the factors we have identified so far interact with the legal and institutional framework of a given country. Financial factors, for instance, are shaped by legislation concerning donations such as provisions on disclosure of donations to parties and tax laws, which may or may not allow deduction of donations from income. Another illustrative example of legislation that may have an impact on the adoption of online campaigns are voting laws: When Austria lowered the minimum age for voting rights to 16, many digital natives were admitted to the polls, dramatically increasing the number of users who could be reached through online campaigns.

Although more contextual factors could be added to this list, this brief overview of some of the parameters that are likely to shape the adoption of the Internet for political campaigns illustrates the complexity of the environment in which the Internet is used as a tool of political communication, mobilization, and fundraising. This complexity, in turn, makes it challenging to study the various variables in a systematic way, especially from a comparative perspective, and to reach reliable explanations of cross-cultural differences regarding the use of the Internet in e-campaigns and related political activities.

CONCLUSION

Because there are few empirical data on the use of the Internet in political campaigns in Germany, Austria, and Switzerland that would allow for a reliable comparison across these countries, and between them and the United States, this exploratory study mostly relies on anecdotal evidence to describe the development of online political communication in the German-speaking part of Europe and to contrast it with recent experiences from the United States. Interesting examples from previous election campaigns include the community websites set up by the Social Democrats and the Christian Democrats for the 2009 parliamentary elections in Germany, a YouTube national campaign that crossed party lines with different celebrities asking people to vote called "Geh Nicht Hin!" (Don't Go!), a provocative online game with an aggressive goat kicking foreigners out of Switzerland, and Twitter communication among student protesters in Austria.

Even though data are scarce, the materials collected are arguably rich enough to describe a number of characteristics of online politics in these German speaking countries, especially when contrasted against observations from the United States. These findings include the relatively modest role that the Internet plays in campaigns, in which Web 1.0 applications such as personal websites of politicians or parties dominate over the use of more advanced interactive social media applications like Twitter or Facebook. Candidates and politicians have only adopted social media for recent elections and are still learning how take advantage of these new tools, whereas the parties' youth chapters use Web 2.0 more naturally. Grassroots movements use social media quite successfully to mobilize supporters, yet video uploads by the parties in general are rarely creative, mostly containing speeches and campaign documentation. Finally, it is interesting that online voting aids that help citizens choose candidates or parties that match their views have become quite popular in all three countries.

This chapter reveals differences among the stages of evolution of online campaigns in Germany, Austria, and Switzerland. However, and even more significantly, it shows that these differences are more pronounced between the United States and the German-speaking part of Europe. The question of why these differences exist cannot be answered in a definitive way given the current state of research. Instead, this chapter offered some potential explanations that likely shape the state of play in e-campaigns.

There is a clear need for further research to analyze the developments of online campaigns on both sides of the Atlantic and to gain a deeper understanding of how online politics in "old Europe" is influenced by developments in other parts of an increasingly globalized and digitally networked world.

References

Bosch, Marco. 2007. *Wahlkampagne 2.0, Politische Kommunikation im Web 2.0 – mehr Demokratie durch mehr Kommunikation?* Marburg: Tectum.

Brändli, Matthias, and Rouven Leuener. 2007. *Von 'Bunker-Mami' bis auf-nachbern.ch: Kandidaten und ihr Webauftritt im Schweizer Nationalratswahlkampf 2007.* Master's thesis, Zürich. (on file with authors).

Busch, Christoph. 2008. "Rechtsradikales eCampaigning am Beispiel der Anti-Islam-Kampagne." In Heinz-Gerd Hegering et al. (eds.), *Informatik 2008 – Beherrschbare Systeme dank Informatik* (pp. 443–8). Berlin: Gesellschaft für Informatik.

Gasser, Urs, James Thurman, Richard Stäuber, and Jan Gerlach. 2010. *E-Democracy in Switzerland: Practice and Perspectives.* Zürich: Dike.

Gerth, Matthias, Karin Puhringer, Urs Dahinden, Patrick Rademacher, and Gabriele Siegert. 2009. "Challenges to Political Campaigns in the Media: Commercialization, Framing, and Personalization." *Studies in Communication Sciences 9* (1): 69–89.

Graf, Joseph. 2008. "New Media – The Cutting Edge of Campaign Communications." In Richard Semiatin (ed.), *Campaigns on the Cutting Edge* (pp. 48–68). Washington, DC: CQ Press.

Hoffmann, Jochen, Adrian Steiner, and Ottfried Jarren. 2007. *Politische Kommunikation als Dienstleistung, Public-Affairs-Berater in der Schweiz.* Konstanz: UVK Verlagsgesellschaft.

Holtz-Bacha, Christina. 2000. "Entertainisierung der Politik." *Zeitschrift für Parlamentsfragen 31*: 156–66.

Holtz-Bacha, Christina. 2002. "Massenmedien und Wahlen: Die Professionalisierung der Kampagnen." *Politik und Zeitgeschichte* B15–16: 23–8.

Imhof, Kurt. 2006. *Politik im "Neuen" Strukturwandel der Öffentlichkeit.* fög discussion paper GL-2006-0010. Zürich: fög-Forschungsbereich Öffentlichkeit und Gesellschaft.

Jarren, Ottfried, and Patrick Donges. 2006. *Politische Kommunikation in der Mediengesellschaft, Eine Einführung,* 2nd ed. Wiesbaden: Verlag für Sozialwissenschaften.

Jun, Uwe. 2009. "Parteien, Politik und Medien. Wandel der Politikvermittlung unter den Bedingungen der Mediendemokratie." In Frank Marcinkowski and Barbara Pfetsch (eds.), *Politik in der Mediendemokratie* (pp. 270–95). Wiesbaden: Verlag für Sozialwissenschaften.

Lachmann, Günther. 2009, January 8. "Die SPD setzt im Wahlkampf auf Internet-Kampagnen," *Die Welt.* Retrieved from http://www.welt.de/welt_print/article2988992/Die-SPD-setzt-im-Wahlkampf-auf-Internet-Kampagnen.html.

Norris, Pippa. 2000. *A Virtuous Circle: Political Communications in Postindustrial Societies.* Cambridge: Cambridge University Press.

Plasser, Fritz, Günther Pallaver, and Günther Lengauer. 2009. "Die (trans-)nationale Nachrichtenlogik in Mediendemokratien – Politischer TV-Journalismus im Wahlkampf zwischen transatlantischer Konvergen und nationaler Divergenz." In Frank Marcinkowski and Barbara Pfetsch (eds.), *Politik in der Mediendemokratie* (pp. 174–202). Wiesbaden: Verlag für Sozialwissenschaften.

Schulz, Winfried. 1998. "Wahlkampf unter Vielkanalbedingungen. Kampagnenmanagement, Informationsnutzung und Wählerverhalten." *Media Perspektiven* 8: 378–91.

Vowe, Gerhard, and Marco Dohle. 2007. "Politische Kommunikation im Umbruch – neue Forschung zu Akteuren, Medieninhalten und Wirkungen." *Politische Vierteljahresschrift* 48 (2): 338–59.

Weinmann, Benjamin. 2009. *Die Amerikanisierung der politischen Kommunikation in der Schweiz.* Zürich: Rüegger.

Zittel, Thomas. 2007. "Lost in Technology? Political Parties and Online-Campaigning in Mixed Member Electoral Systems." *Paper presented at the ECPR General Conference*, Pisa.

SECTION III

CIVIC MOBILIZATION AND GOVERNANCE IN THE NEW INFORMATION AGE

7

Preaching to the Choir or Converting the Flock

Presidential Communication Strategies in the Age of Three Medias

Matthew A. Baum

On September 9, 2009, President Barack Obama delivered a prime-time television address on health care reform to a joint session of Congress. According to nielsenwire.com, more than 32 million Americans watched the president's appeal on TV. Less than two weeks later, on September 21, 2009, Obama took to the stage of the *Late Show With David Letterman*, only the second time a sitting U.S. president had appeared on a network late-night comedy show.[1] This appearance – Obama's fifth on the Letterman show – capped an intensive media push by the president to promote health care reform, a push that included interviews on five Sunday news shows the previous day, spanning ABC, NBC, CBS, CNN, and the Spanish-language network Univision. That same month, Obama's Internet team sent weekly e-mails on health care (followed by two per week in October) to the roughly 13 million individuals in its famed e-mail database.

Obama's media frenzy was notable not only for the sheer number of public appeals but also for the diversity of outlets to which he carried his message. In addition, Obama's messages had quite different tenors, depending on the outlet audience to whom he was communicating. In his nationally televised address to the nation, the president was, to borrow a phrase, a unifier, not a divider, offering a solemn appeal for national

---

[1] Obama also made the *first* such appearance, on *The Tonight Show with Jay Leno*, six months earlier, on March 18, 2009. In most other respects, however, these were not exceptional events. For instance, nine different presidential candidates appeared on Letterman during 2007 (see fn. 20). This show was only one of many soft news outlets – primarily daytime and late-night talk shows – to attract presidential candidates in the 2008 election cycle.

unity. He thus observed, "In 1965, when some argued that Medicare represented a government takeover of health care, members of Congress – Democrats and Republicans – did not back down. They joined together so that all of us could enter our golden years with some basic peace of mind.... I still believe we can replace acrimony with civility."[2]

Obama's e-mail appeals took a different tack, inviting direct action from recipients – in the form of making donations, joining discussion groups, participating in rallies, watching a video clip, visiting Obama's "Organizing for America" website, submitting homemade videos, or calling members of Congress – to support the president's health care reform effort. They were also far more aggressive in their appeals, delivering messages like the following: "Those who profit from the status quo – and those who put partisan advantage above all else – will fight us every inch of the way.... The stakes are too high to let scare tactics cloud the debate" (barackobama.com e-mail, 9/9/09).[3]

Finally, in his Letterman appearance, Obama lightened his tone. For instance, in response to a question about allegations that racism motivated the anti-health care reform movement, he quipped, "I think it is important to realize that I was actually black before the election." While Obama offered a variety of policy-related observations, he also took time to comment on his daughters' transition to the White House. No mention of political parties or partisanship crossed the president's lips during the Letterman appearance, with the sole exception of a single comment aimed at dismissing partisan debate over his policies by proclaiming that "it doesn't matter" if you are a Democrat or a Republican.

The liberal blogosphere dutifully replayed video highlights from all of Obama's appearances, thereby magnifying his message and delivering it directly to the president's base. For instance, on September 21, Huffingtonpost.com featured "Highlights from Obama's Sunday Show Blitz," inviting readers to "vote for the best clip." The next day the site featured video clips from Obama's Letterman appearance.

Taken together, the public appeals arguably represent an unprecedented – at least in its diversity – presidential media blitz aimed at a single

---

[2] For a full copy of President Obama's remarks see http://www.presidentialrhetoric.com/speeches/09.09.09.html.
[3] Other Internet appeals are overtly partisan, such as one from January 19, 2010, supporting Martha Coakley's failed Senate bid. The e-mail, in part, warned that if recipients did not vote for Coakley, "the Senate can get one more person already walking in lockstep with Washington Republicans."

policy initiative. It raises the question of why President Obama pursued such a strategy and in such starkly different manners across different media outlets. The answer, I argue, is that a combination of fragmenting media and fragmenting media audiences has forced President Obama to adopt a complex and multitiered communication strategy aimed at reaching, in the aggregate, an audience comparable in numbers and partisan diversity to those his predecessors from the 1960s through the 1980s were largely able to take for granted virtually any time they appeared on national TV (Baum and Kernell 1999). The changing media landscape means that presidents, and politicians in general, need to work much harder to communicate with the American people and to be far more precise in tailoring their messages to particular subconstituencies who might otherwise tune them out entirely. As Blumler and Kavanagh (1999) argue, "The presumption of mass exposure to relatively uniform political content, which has underpinned each of the three leading paradigms of political effect – agenda setting, the spiral of silence, and the cultivation hypothesis – can no longer be taken for granted" (221–2).

In this chapter, I argue that presidents, and political leaders in general, have two primary leadership strategy alternatives. The first, which I term "preaching to the choir," entails reaching out to one's political base to excite core supporters so they will show up in large numbers on Election Day as well as enthusiastically support the leader on major policy issues. The second, which I term "converting the flock," consists of reaching out beyond one's base to recruit additional supporters and thereby expand one's support coalition. Neither strategy is new; presidents have long pursued both, frequently varying their emphasis from issue to issue, depending on which groups supported or opposed a given policy initiative. However, the ground underneath which presidents have stood while pursuing these strategies has shifted dramatically in recent years. This in turn has altered the strategies' relative costs and benefits, as well as their efficacies.

The first decade of the 21st century has been characterized by a unique historical circumstance in which three distinct types of media – each appealing to quite distinct audience types – coexist, cover news and politics, and compete for the attention of the American public. These are the traditional news media, dominated by the major broadcast networks and national newspapers; the so-called new media, most notably cable TV news and the Internet; and the soft news media, consisting of daytime and late-night talk shows, as well as entertainment-oriented and tabloid news magazine programs.[4] The audiences for these three media differ in important ways, with profound implications for their place in modern presidential communication strategies.

In the remainder of this chapter, I discuss each of the three media, considering their potential role and implications for presidential efforts to preach to the choir or convert the flock. I then consider the broader implications of the changing media landscape for the future of presidential leadership. Through this analysis, I hope to shed light on several of the central questions guiding this volume, including the effects of the evolving media and information environment on American political discourse, governance, and government accountability.

TRADITIONAL NEWS MEDIA

For nearly four decades, the traditional news media in general, and network television in particular, were the primary vehicles through which presidents sought to convert the flock. The decline of the traditional news media since the early 1990s is well documented and widely reported (Baum 2003; Baum and Kernell 1999, 2007; Hamilton 2003). The combined ratings for the evening newscasts of the "big three" broadcast networks (ABC, CBS, and NBC) have fallen from about 58 in 1969 to a little more than 16 in 2008.[5] Indeed, according to a 2008 Pew survey, the percent of Americans indicating that they regularly watch cable news now exceeds the percentage regularly watching network news (by 39% to 29%).[6]

Not only has the overall audience for network news declined dramatically but the demographics of network news viewers have also shifted starkly. Where the typical network news viewer was once comparable to the median television viewer (after all, the networks enjoyed an oligopoly for nearly four decades), by 2008 the network audience was notably older (with a median age of 61.3[7]) and, according to the Pew Center, composed

---

[4] One could include political talk radio in the "new media" category. Although talk radio can be an important media player, because this medium is in key respects comparable to partisan political blogs, I do not focus on it in this chapter. However, many of the arguments I make apply to political talk radio as well.

[5] Baum and Kernell (1999); http://www.stateofthemedia.org/2009/chartland.php?id=1008 &ct=line&dir=&sort=&col1_box=1&col2_box=1&col3_box=1.

[6] Pew Research Center for the People and the Press, "Biennial Media Consumption Survey," 2008.

[7] See http://staging.stateofthemedia.org/2009/narrative_networktv_audience.php?cat=2& media=6.

of more Democrats than Republicans by more than a 2-to-1 ratio (45% vs. 22% "regular" viewers).[8] These figures suggest that nationally televised presidential addresses are unlikely to reach the same cross-section of Americans as they did in earlier decades.

Of course, as the number of television networks broadcasting presidential addresses has increased (according to nielsenwire.com, 7 networks covered George W. Bush's first State of the Union Address in 2001, compared to 11 covering Obama's first State of the Union address in 2010), presidents presumably reach at least some members of the public who have abandoned the networks. However, according to the aforementioned Pew Center (2008) survey, cable news viewers are considerably more educated and politically knowledgeable than network news viewers, or the general public for that matter. Combined with the rise of a vast number of alternative, entertainment-oriented outlets, this makes it seem quite unlikely that cable news has entirely filled the void created by the mass exodus from the big three networks (but see Prior 2007).

Typical ratings for presidential addresses have fallen along with the network news audience. For instance, the televised addresses and press conferences of Presidents Nixon, Ford, and Carter each averaged audience ratings of about 48 (where each point represents 1% of U.S. households owning televisions). The corresponding averages for Presidents Clinton and George W. Bush were about 30, only slightly below the 32.5 rating for President Obama's first national address to the nation on February 24, 2009.

Moreover, the news values of the traditional news media have made it a particularly difficult environment for presidential communications. Baum and Groeling (2008, 2009a, 2009b) document the tremendous network news bias toward negative, hostile coverage of presidents and their policies. They report that across 42 foreign policy rally events between 1979 and 2003, nearly 80% of all rhetoric from members of Congress (MCs) appearing on the evening news within 61-day periods surrounding the events was critical of the president and his policies. The ratio was far more favorable on network Sunday morning talk shows (Baum and Groeling 2009b; Groeling and Baum 2009), where MCs had the opportunity to speak in their own voice in an unfiltered "open mike" format. This suggests a strong network negativity bias on the heavily edited network news.

---

[8] Pew Research Center, "Biennial Media Consumption Survey."

News coverage of the president in the traditional media has also shifted in form, with the president's own words supplemented, and increasingly supplanted, by the interpretations of journalists. The length of an average presidential sound bite on the evening news – that is, a president speaking in his own words – declined from about 40 seconds in 1968 (Hallin 1994) to 7.8 seconds in 2004. This means that journalists' relatively negative coverage of the president increasingly dominates news broadcasts.

Where network television once afforded presidents an ideal opportunity to communicate with a broad cross-section of the public, today, whenever a president takes to the airwaves he must compete with a myriad of alternative media for the public's attention. Indeed, broadcast networks have grown increasingly hesitant to surrender their airwaves for presidential communication. According to one report, network executives lost roughly $30 million in advertising revenue in the first half of 2009 due to preemptions for Obama news conferences.[9] This concern, in turn, prompted one of the "big four" networks (Fox) to decline the president's request for airtime for a presidential press conference on April 29, 2009.

Taken together, these patterns paint a picture of an increasingly inhospitable environment for presidential communication. The major networks no longer offer presidents access to a common civic space where all Americans gather on a routine basis. When presidents seek airtime for national addresses, they must first persuade skeptical network executives that their address will be newsworthy. As one network executive commented, "We will continue to make our decisions on White House requests on a case-by-case basis, but the Fox decision [to not broadcast Obama's 4/29/09 press conference] gives us cover to reject a request if we feel that there is no urgent breaking news that is going to be discussed."[10]

When presidents or their lieutenants *do* appear in traditional news environments, they can usually count on skeptical reporters challenging the merits of their policies and often even the motives behind them. Consequently, in an era in which presidents arguably depend more than ever before on "going public" (Kernell 2006) as a core leadership strategy (Baum and Kernell 2007), one of their principal avenues for doing so over the past half-century is becoming increasingly foreclosed. When recent presidents have attempted to speak to the entire nation, their audiences

---

[9] John Consoli, "Obama Drama: Nets Take a Stand against Primetime Pre-Emptions." *The Hollywood Reporter*, May 7, 2009. Retrieved from http://www.hollywoodreporter. com/hr/content_display/news/e3i4e17d68abb9787337186a5038618057a?pn=1.
[10] Ibid.

are far smaller than those enjoyed by their predecessors in earlier decades, even after accounting for viewers from cable news outlets. In fact, President Obama's State of the Union address on January 27, 2010, earned a combined rating of only 11 across the big three broadcast networks.[11] This suggests that the networks no longer afford presidents the capacity to reach out to a broad cross-section of the American people. Instead, they are able to offer a far smaller and more ideologically and generationally narrow segment of the population. For instance, according to data reported by Kernell and Rice (Forthcoming), the partisan gap in audiences for presidential television addresses has increased substantially over time. Across the 18 prime-time presidential addresses they investigated between 1971 and 1995, the gap in audience between members of the president's party and opposition partisans averaged 2.6%. Between 1996 and 2007, the average partisan gap across the 14 appearances for which data were available increased more than fourfold, to 11.8%. In short, over time the audience for presidential addresses has increasingly come to be dominated by his fellow partisans. This combination of audiences smaller in size and narrower in breadth, along with generally skeptical treatment by reporters of nearly any presidential statement or policy proposal, means that traditional news outlets have lost much of their utility to presidents as vehicles for converting the flock.

NEW MEDIA: CABLE NEWS AND THE INTERNET

The so-called new media, by which I refer primarily to cable news channels and the Internet, differ in important ways from their traditional media cousins. Most notably, nearly all such outlets self-consciously seek to appeal to relatively narrow and presumably more loyal niches of the public. Rather than seeking to be all things to all people – as the major networks did during their heyday – new media outlets try to provide a product that more closely fits the preferences of a particular subset of people. In news and politics, the primary dimension along which new media outlets have sought to differentiate themselves is ideology. Most notably, in 2010 there are prominent cable news channels aimed primarily at liberals (MSNBC), conservatives (Fox), and moderates (CNN). Similarly, on the Internet, the political blogosphere is dominated by ideologically narrow websites like Huffingtonpost.com on the left and Michellemalkin.com on

---

[11] See   http://tvbythenumbers.com/2010/01/28/tv-ratings-obama-state-of-the-union-address-american-idol/40398.

the right. As the range of options available to consumers seeking political information has expanded, making available media environments that closely match their personal political preferences, audiences have increasingly availed themselves of the opportunity to self-select into ideologically friendly political news environments.

Cable News

Figures 7.1 and 7.2 show the trend, from 2000 to 2008, in the partisan makeup of audiences for CNN and Fox (Fig. 7.1) and for CNN, Fox, and MSNBC (Fig. 7.2). The first graphic is based on self-reports in surveys by the Pew Center (2009),[12] whereas the second is derived from pooled national surveys conducted by a market research firm (Scarborough), representing more than 100,000 interviews for each period included in the graphic (Kernell and Rice 2010).[13]

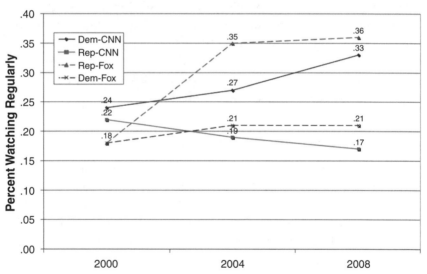

FIGURE 7.1. Trend in Partisan Preferences for CNN vs. Fox

The curves in Figures 7.1 and 7.2 are derived from quite distinct data sources, yet they paint a similar picture. In 2000, the audiences for Fox, CNN, and MSNBC consisted of similar proportions of Democrats and Republicans. In the Pew data, an identical proportion of Democrats and

[12] Pew Research Center for the People and the Press, "Partisanship and Cable News Audiences," October 30, 2009. Retrieved January 7, 2010, from http://pewresearch .org/pubs/1395/partisanship-fox-news-and–other-cable-news-audiences.
[13] Feltus (2009); Kernell and Rice (2010).

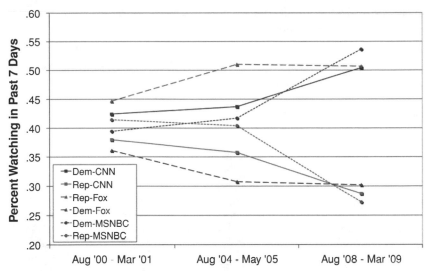

FIGURE 7.2. Trend in Partisan Viewing of CNN, Fox, and MSNBC.
Sources: Feltus (2009) and Kernell and Rice (2010).

Republicans reported "regularly" watching Fox, whereas only 2 percentage points separated "regular" partisan viewers on CNN. In the Scarborough data, the partisan gaps for viewers of CNN, Fox, and MSNBC in 2000 were 4, 8, and 2 percentage points, respectively. By 2008, these gaps had expanded considerably, as partisans increasingly sought out ideologically friendly media environments. In the Pew data, corresponding partisan gaps in 2008 were 15 and 16 points for CNN and Fox, respectively. In the Scarborough data, the gaps in 2008–09 stood at 30, 20, and 27 points for CNN, Fox, and MSNBC, respectively.

The partisan gaps reported by the Pew Center are even larger when we focus on a question asking respondents about their "main source" of news. In their July 2009 "News Attitudes" survey, Pew reports that, among Republicans, 38% chose Fox as their main sources of news, compared to only 13% who chose CNN. Conversely, among Democrats 46% chose CNN compared to only 18% who selected Fox. Independents were nearly evenly divided, with 38% choosing Fox and 35% choosing CNN. If Independents who leaned toward one or the other party are added to the mix, the figures are even more stark: 63% to 25% in favor of Fox among Republicans, and nearly the precise opposite – 63% to 22% in favor of CNN – among Democrats.[14] The figures are similar when one

---

[14] See http://pewresearch.org/pubs/1395/partisanship-fox-news-and–other-cable-news-audiences.

focuses on viewers' preferred sources of campaign news. As Figure 7.3 indicates, in 2008 Democrats were far more likely to turn to CNN or MSNBC and somewhat more likely to turn to network news for information about the presidential campaign, whereas Republicans were far more likely to turn to Fox.

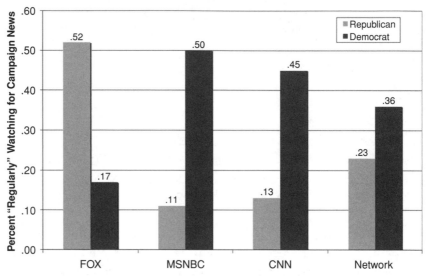

FIGURE 7.3. 2008 Partisan Profile of Regular Campaign News Sources

Although it is certainly the case that some partisan overlap remains (Kernell and Rice 2010; Prior 2007) – with potentially important implications for presidential communication (see the later discussion) – these data clearly suggest a fairly strong tendency toward partisan filtering on cable news.[15]

Internet

If niche programming has emerged as an important competitive strategy for television news, it is arguably the most consequential such strategy on the Internet. Research has shown that a stunningly small number of political news-oriented outlets dominate news and public affairs traffic on the Web (Hindman 2007). Although some of the most heavily trafficked sites – such as CNN.com, MSNBC.com, and Yahoo News – remain predominantly audience aggregators, rather than disaggregators, the political blogosphere functions primarily as an arena for partisan and ideological self-selection.

[15] See Feltus (2009).

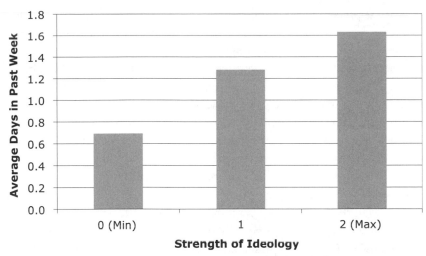

FIGURE 7.4. Average Days in Past Week Accessed Political Blogs on Internet, as Strength of Ideology Varies

There are a variety of well-documented digital divides online, including by age, gender, race, and socioeconomic status. Some – particularly gender and race – have receded somewhat in recent years. In each case, the net effect is that some Americans are systematically more likely than others to rely on the Internet for political news. Most of these divides are exogenous to the preferences and policies of individual Internet outlets. However, political ideology remains a key *proactive* filter that political news websites, in general, and blogs, in particular, frequently use in seeking to build a loyal niche audience.

Along these lines, Baum and Groeling (2008, 2009b) report that left-leaning political blogs like DailyKos.com are disproportionately likely to cover news that favors Democrats over Republicans, whereas right-leaning blogs like FreeRepublic.com are disproportionately likely to feature news favorable to Republicans over Democrats. Perhaps not surprisingly, given the ideological and partisan slant on political blogs, users of these sites are, on average, more likely than typical Americans to prefer news that reinforces their preexisting preferences (far more so than, say, viewers of network news), more likely to discuss political news with family and friends (Baum and Groeling 2008), and, as shown in Figure 7.4, more ideologically extreme.[16]

---

[16] Cooperative Campaign Analysis Project (CCAP), 2007–8 Panel Study. Simon Jackman and Lynn Vavreck, Principal Investigators. University of California, Los Angeles, Stanford University, and Yougov/Polimetrix. In Figure 7.4, 0 = moderate, 1 = liberal or conservative, and 2 = very liberal or very conservative.

Not surprisingly, the audiences for such outlets are highly skewed based on party affiliation. For instance, according to an April 2007 Nielsen report, 77% of HuffingtonPost.com readers were registered Democrats, and only 3.8% were registered Republicans.[17] Although, as with cable news, some Internet consumers seek out news from across the ideological spectrum – and some evidence (Gentzkow and Shapiro 2010) suggests they do so to a greater extent on the Internet than on cable – the Internet is nonetheless a particularly amenable environment for ideological self-selection, and the aforementioned evidence from political blogs suggests that many politically oriented news consumers engage in such self-imposed ideological segregation.[18]

Although the audience for political news on the Internet does not yet approach that for television news (Baum and Groeling 2008), it is by no means trivial. Figure 7.5 presents the percentage of survey respondents who reported getting news about the 2008 presidential campaign from the

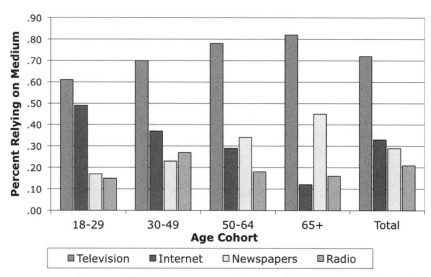

FIGURE 7.5. Percent of Public Relying on Medium for News about Campaign 2008

---

[17] "Is Yahoo!'s Online Debate Going to be Fair and Balanced?" Retrieved from http://techpresident.com/blog-entry/yahoo's-online-debate-going-be-fair-and-balanced (CCAP 2008).

[18] Along these lines, Baum and Groeling (2009b) report evidence that some ideological news blogs cover the "other side" primarily to set the stage for making their own political argument, in effect using "opposition" political blogs as straw men. It seems likely that at least some politically sophisticated Internet news consumers are similarly motivated when "crossing over" to ideologically hostile news sources.

Internet.[19] The results indicate that, among respondents under age 50, the Internet was the second most important source of campaign news, trailing only television. Among respondents under age 30, nearly half reported relying on the Internet for campaign news.

Turning from the Internet news in general to political blogs in particular, according to comScore.com, in September 2008 the total number of unique visitors to the top 15 political blog sites was approximately 206 million. This represents about a 10% increase over the prior year.[20] Survey data in roughly the same period indicate that 37% of Americans reported going online for news at least three times per week, an increase of 19% from 2006.[21] This percentage compares to 39% and 29% of respondents who claimed to regularly watch cable and network news, respectively.

New Media and Leadership

Taken together, these data suggest that the new media are becoming an increasingly central presence in the American political news landscape. They are doing so primarily by appealing to relatively narrow segments of the overall audience who self-select into news environments where they are disproportionately likely to encounter news and information that reinforces, rather than challenges, their preexisting political beliefs.

These patterns hold important implications for presidential leadership. The new media are ideal vehicles for preaching to the choir. Increasingly sophisticated communication methods – such as Obama's targeted e mail campaign on health care reform described in the introduction – combined with partisan self-selection by consumers, allow political leaders an unprecedented opportunity to reach out to their core supporters. By providing so-called red meat to the base, presidents can rally supporters to organize in their communities to support policy proposals, as well as to turn out on Election Day. In turn, more effective local organizing of core supporters can indirectly enhance presidents' capacities to convert the flock, by transforming their core supporters into messengers charged with reaching out beyond the base. Indeed, much of the aforementioned Obama e-mail campaign was aimed at inspiring core

[19] Pew Research Center, "Biennial Media Consumption Survey."
[20] See http://www.comscore.com/Press_Events/Press_Releases/2008/10/ Huffington_Post_ and_Politico_Lead_Political_Blogs/(language)/eng-US.
[21] Pew Research Center, "Biennial Media Consumption Survey."

supporters to become active advocates of his health care reform policy in their communities. Also worth noting, core supporters are far more likely than typical individuals to contribute money to the president's causes. Obama's health care e-mail campaign thus also served as a potentially potent fundraising vehicle. Similar types of appeals seem likely to be effective in the partisan blogosphere and, to some extent, on cable news channels.

All that said, it is important to also recognize that new media do offer some opportunities for presidents to directly convert the flock. Although opportunities to do so may be relatively rare, they can sometimes be particularly effective. For instance, if a president is able to gain a sympathetic audience from an outlet widely perceived as ideologically hostile, consumers of that outlet are likely to view his message as considerably more credible – given the costly signal made by the ideologically hostile outlet in airing the president's message – than they would in virtually any other context (Baum and Groeling 2009b).

Along these lines, Baum and Groeling (2009a) found, in an experiment, that consumers were more persuaded by criticism of President George W. Bush when it appeared to emanate from Fox News than when it appeared to have originated on CNN, while finding the precise opposite pattern for praise of President Bush. They report similar patterns in national survey data regarding the war in Iraq.

This logic may explain President Obama's decision to submit to an interview on Fox News on November 18, 2009, soon after a verbal joust between Fox News and the White House, in which White House Communications Director Anita Dunn called Fox a "wing of the Republican Party."[22] Such a strategy holds potential twin benefits for the White House. First, to the extent that it can undermine Fox's status as a legitimate news source, it can reduce the ability of political opponents (conservative Republicans) to use the outlet as a vehicle for converting the flock by appealing to, say, Independent viewers (either by persuading them not to watch the network or by reducing the credibility of the information they encounter if they continue to watch). Second, it maximizes the potential credibility boost that the president gains from an appearance on the network. After all, Fox's decision to afford the president a relatively civil venue for promoting his policies may appear as a costly signal that he is to be considered seriously, if not necessarily supported. The more hostile the venue, the costlier the signal it sends.

---

[22] See   http://www.huffingtonpost.com/2009/10/11/anita-dunn-fox-news-an-ou_n_
316691.html.

Although for many issues such a strategy is unlikely to result in significant persuasion of the opposition base, it may help the president persuade marginal viewers, such as Independents (the least hostile portion of "the flock"). Moreover, on some issues – where policies do not fall out along clear partisan lines – the president may be able to communicate effectively to the opposition, thereby, in effect, further converting the flock. One case in point is the Obama administration's policy of escalating the U.S. conflict in Afghanistan, a policy that majorities of both Republicans and Democrats support.[23] Obama succeeded in increasing Republican support for the policy by emphasizing traditional national security concerns rather than, or at least in addition to, the core concerns of more liberal internationalist voters, such as human rights and democracy (Baum and Nau 2009). Nonetheless, with the latter caveat, it seems reasonable to conclude that the new media are better suited for preaching to the choir than for converting the flock.

SOFT NEWS

Millions of Americans who eschew most traditional news outlets, at least most of the time, and who rarely if ever read political blogs or other Internet news outlets are nonetheless exposed to at least *some* political news via the so-called soft news media, including daytime and late-night talk shows, as well as entertainment-oriented news outlets and tabloids.[24] President Obama's aforementioned September 21, 2009, appearance on the *David Letterman Show* was his fifth on the program. Obama was by no means alone in courting Letterman during the 2008 election cycle. Nine presidential candidates appeared on the show during 2007.[25] Letterman is only one of many soft news outlets – primarily daytime and late-night talk shows – to attract presidential candidates in the 2008 election cycle. In fact, during the 2000, 2004, and 2008 primary and general

---

[23] According to Gallup, as of early December 2009, 58% of Democrats favored Obama's Afghanistan policy, compared to 55% of Republicans. The corresponding percentages opposing the policy were 35 and 37% (http://www.gallup.com/poll/124562/obama-plan-afghanistan-finds-bipartisan-support.aspx).

[24] Zaller (2003: 129) states that, "soft news is information that is either personally useful or merely entertaining." Borrowing from Patterson (2000), I define "soft news" similarly, as a set of story characteristics, including the absence of a public policy component, sensationalized presentation, human-interest themes, and emphasis on dramatic subject matter. In my 2003 book, I refer to those media outlets that focus *primarily* on such material – including entertainment and tabloid news shows, network newsmagazines, and daytime and late night talk shows – as the soft news media.

[25] "TV Become Essential Stops on the Presidential Trail to Reach 'Regular Folks'," *New York Times*, September 20, 2007.

presidential election campaigns, virtually every candidate appeared on daytime and late-night entertainment-oriented talk shows. According to a study by the Center for Media and Public Affairs, presidential candidates made a total of 110 appearances on late-night talk shows in the runup to the 2008 presidential election,[26] which represents more than a fourfold increase from the corresponding total of 25 in 2004. Figure 7.6 tallies the appearances by those individual candidates who accounted for the bulk of these numbers.[27]

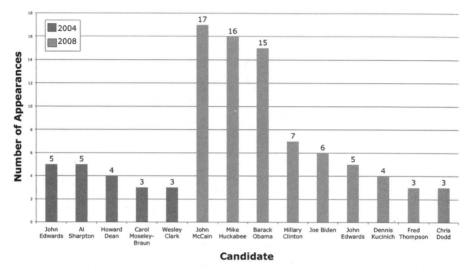

FIGURE 7.6. Number of Late-Night Talk Show Appearances by Presidential Candidates, 2004 vs. 2008

Why would any politician, let alone a sitting president, choose to add a late-night comedy-oriented talk show to an already crowded weekend media itinerary of five appearances on traditional news and political interview shows? One obvious answer concerns the magnitude of the audience. Nearly 7.2 million Americans tuned in to watch the president defend his health care proposals on Letterman, as well as exchange one-liners with the host and describe his daughters' transition to life in the White House. This was the largest audience for the show in four years and represents more than double the 3.1 million who tuned in to Obama's

26 Center for Media and Public Affairs (CMPA), "Late-Night Talk Shows Were Road to White House: Study Finds Candidates Appeared over 100 Times," December 29, 2008. Retrieved January 7, 2010, from http://www.cmpa.com/media_room_comedy_12_29_08.htm.
27 The several appearances not included in Figure 7.6 include those by candidate family members.

more traditional news interview the day before on ABC's *This Week with George Stephanopoulos.*[28]

A second, perhaps slightly less obvious answer concerns the *nature* of Letterman's audience. Compared to the typical audience for traditional news shows such as ABC's *This Week*, Letterman's audience is less politically engaged, less ideologically extreme, and less partisan (Baum 2003, 2005; Baum and Jamison 2006). Consequently, Letterman's viewers are more likely to be persuaded by a presidential appeal than the relatively more partisan and ideologically extreme audiences of typical traditional news venues (Baum 2003; Zaller 1992). Given the relatively stronger partisan and ideological orientation of typical political Internet blog readers, this persuasion gap is presumably even larger relative to these latter outlets.

Finally, such interviews tend to present candidates in a more favorable light than traditional political interview shows. For example, commenting on a different 2008 presidential candidate's talk show appearances, Gold (2007) observes, "John and Elizabeth Edwards got substantially gentler treatment from Leno on 'The Tonight Show' than they did from Katie Couric on '60 Minutes.'" In short, appearances on daytime and late-night entertainment talk shows, or on other soft news programs, afford politicians one of their best opportunities to reach a large group of potentially persuadable voters in a relatively sympathetic venue (Baum 2005). Therefore, such appearances arguably represent one of the *last* and perhaps the *best* opportunity for political leaders to convert the flock.

The current political environment, in which the major parties compete for an ever-smaller proportion of the voting public that remains persuadable – or, stated differently, an ever-shrinking flock – inflates the political significance of soft news venues. It is thus unsurprising that both political candidates and sitting presidents court the attention of the soft news media. They do so not only by appearing on soft-news-oriented interview shows but also by emphasizing soft news themes in their rhetoric, as well as by associating themselves with personalities who appeal to entertainment-oriented media.

The 2005 State of the Union address offers an example of the pattern of emphasizing soft news themes. In the runup to the address, President

---

[28] Appearances by presidential aspirants on *daytime* talk shows have also attracted large audiences. For instance, a decade ago, 8.7 million households watched Al Gore's September 11, 2000 appearance on the *Oprah Winfrey Show*; even more households tuned in to George W. Bush's appearance eight days later (Baum 2005).

Bush presented a major speech outlining an ambitious agenda for space exploration. The issue, however, failed to capture the public's interest. In contrast, a second apparent pre-address "trial balloon" focusing on steroid abuse *did* capture the public's imagination. Consequently, at the last moment, the president altered a substantial segment of his address to drop any mention of space exploration in favor of condemning steroid abuse among professional athletes.[29]

The president's focus on steroid abuse – which necessitated reseating California Governor Arnold Schwarzenegger, an admitted steroid user, away from First Lady Laura Bush – paid political dividends. The nation's sports media (TV, radio, and print) covered the story extensively. Taking up the president's call to arms, Congress quickly arranged a series of high-profile hearings on the subject. These hearings, involving some of the nation's most celebrated athletes, generated a feeding frenzy of media coverage. By focusing on steroids, the president reached a vast audience of sports enthusiasts who might otherwise have never heard about his State of the Union address. He also generated considerable post-address attention by continuing to promote the issue, even as his allies in Congress arranged public hearings on the subject – hearings that attracted a nationwide audience thanks to predictable media fascination with the lifestyles (and foibles) of America's rich and famous celebrities, including star athletes. By reaching out beyond his live television audience – which consisted mostly of his core supporters[30] – President Bush and later the Republican congressional leadership sought to use the soft news media as a means of reaching and thereby converting the flock.

Illustrating the pattern of associating with compelling personalities, Baum (2007) notes that, when former Secretary of State Condoleezza Rice traveled abroad, she often arranged airport photo opportunities with local celebrities. In Tokyo, she posed for photographs with a popular Japanese American sumo wrestling champion; in Romania, she met with Olympic legend Nadia Comaneci. Rice intended these "photo ops" to attract the local media, so that they would pay more attention to her visit and, in doing so, transmit her messages to segments of the local population that might otherwise ignore her visit. One official predicted that Romanians "will go crazy" over the secretary's meeting with Comaneci (Brinkley 2005).

---

[29] I thank Sam Popkin for calling my attention to this anecdote.
[30] See Kernell and Rice (2010).

In the runup to the March 2003 U.S. invasion of Iraq, in turn, the Pentagon granted coveted reporting slots "embedded" within U.S. combat units to such decidedly apolitical media outlets as MTV, *Rolling Stone*, and *People* magazine. Bryan G. Whitman, Deputy Assistant Secretary of Defense for Media Operations, explained as follows the Pentagon's rationale for doing so:

> It is a recognition that not everyone gets their news from *The Washington Post* and *The Wall Street Journal*.... We consciously looked at those news organizations that have reach and impact and provided them with the greatest possible opportunities.... Each of them [embedded reporters] reach a different audience. Our goal was to dominate the information market.[31]

Not only did the Pentagon embed soft news reporters with U.S. troops in Iraq but it also fed them regular doses of soft news friendly topics and themes, such as defining the U.S. conflicts in Iraq and Afghanistan in stark, moralistic terms emphasizing heroes and villains. In the heroism camp are the narratives of Pat Tillman – a college football star who volunteered to forego a lucrative NFL contract to serve in the military after 9/11 and who was later tragically killed by friendly fire in Afghanistan – as well as Jessica Lynch, a soldier captured by enemy forces in Iraq and subsequently freed in a daring military raid. In both cases, the soft news media offered saturation coverage of these classic stories of heroism, one tragic and the other more uplifting, both turning out quite differently from the original administration narrative as portrayed in the media.

In the case of villains, successive U.S. presidents have routinely cast America's adversaries – from Saddam, to Milosevic, to Aideed of Somalia – as the embodiments of evil, frequently likening them to Adolf Hitler (Baum 2003). This labeling transforms arcane foreign policy conflicts into dramatic soap operas, thereby appealing to soft news sensibilities. In this one respect, American adversaries share in common the fate of spoiled millionaire athletes on steroids: senior American officials have cast both as the villains in classic American morality plays.

Of course, not all soft news outlets are the same. Some, such as *The Daily Show with Jon Stewart* and *The Colbert Report*, cater to more politically sophisticated and partisan audience niches (Jamison and Baum 2011). When presidential candidates or other politicians appear on these venues, they are more likely to be preaching to the choir than converting the flock. Yet, with these noteworthy exceptions, soft news outlets

---

[31] David Carr, "War News from MTV and People Magazine," *New York Times*, March 27, 2003.

remain predominantly a venue for converting the flock. It is consequently unsurprising that presidential candidates appearing on daytime and late-night talk shows typically offer almost no mention of political parties or partisanship (Baum 2005). Such rhetoric might offend the sensibilities of the relatively less partisan audiences of such venues (relative to those of other, more traditional news or new media outlets).

CONCLUSION

The picture I have painted of the contemporary media landscape is in some respects overly stark. For one thing, there is certainly overlap between the three types of media, both in terms of content and audience. Viewers of traditional news media, especially network news, are more left-leaning than in the past, whereas arguably the fastest growing segment of the soft news media – satirical political news shows like *The Daily Show with Jon Stewart* – caters less to nonpartisan viewers than to politically sophisticated ideologues. Some Democrats consume conservative media, and some Republicans consume liberal media. All three media, in turn, continue to afford presidents at least *some* capacity both to preach to the choir and convert the flock. Political messages frequently cross the boundaries of the three media, as exemplified by the Obama media blitz described at the outset of this chapter. Hence, the media commons, and the common civic space for public affairs dialogue it created, has not entirely disappeared, nor has the capacity of presidents to use the media as a tool for building broader support constituencies via converting the flock.

That said, current trends toward ever more consumer self-selection and increasingly sophisticated information filtering and media targeting of consumer preferences all portend greater audience fragmentation and hence continued shrinking of the media commons. It seems inevitable that news providers will increasingly apply to news and public affairs content the same filtering technologies that allow media content distributors like Netflix and iTunes to determine the types of movies or music a customer is likely to prefer. The end result may be what Cass Sunstein (2009) terms "cyberbalkanization," in which the media commons is largely replaced by the "Daily Me" in which consumers encounter only the news and information they want, most of which tends to confirm rather than chal-lenge their preexisting attitudes. Whether or not the media commons disappears entirely, there is little question that technological innovations and shifts in audience behavior are changing the organization of news consumption, with content growing increasingly personalized and subject to consumer preferences regarding what, when, and where they entertain themselves or expose themselves to politically themed news.

This shift represents both a challenge and an opportunity for political leaders. It is a challenge in that reaching beyond one's base is becoming increasingly difficult and may perhaps become mostly limited to soft news appeals. After all, the soft news media remain arguably the best avenue for reaching relatively persuadable voters. Even there, some scholars have speculated that as filtering technologies that consumers can use to set their own daily news menus grow increasingly adept, they will preempt much of the incidental political learning associated with soft news consumption by relatively inattentive and apolitical citizens (Parkin 2010; Xenos and Becker 2009).

In contrast, this trend represents an opportunity, because preaching to the choir is in many respects easier and more effective than ever before, as new media technologies allow leaders to first identify and then communicate more directly with their core constituents. A case in point is the Obama administration's frequent appeals to 13 million Americans via its e-mail database, through which it raised record campaign contributions in 2008 and has since regularly sought to rally the Democratic base in support of the president's policies.

Of course, effective presidential leadership requires combining both strategies – that is, exciting the base while building coalitions – and there is no reason to suppose that future presidents will succeed, at least over the longer term, by emphasizing one over the other. Along with and perhaps in part *because of* the three medias, politics in America is at a crossroads. Traditional communications channels are increasingly foreclosed, even as new ones emerge. Different channels, in turn, reach different audiences and so privilege different communication strategies, different forms of leadership, and ultimately, different policies (Popkin 2006). Given the enormity and speed of the changes in this marketplace, and their potential consequences for democratic participation and the strategic landscape for politicians, this is a key area for future scholarly research.

References

Baum, Matthew A. 2003. *Soft News Goes to War: Public Opinion and American Foreign Policy in the New Media Age.* Princeton, NJ: Princeton University Press.
Baum, Matthew A. 2005. "Talking the Vote: Why Presidential Candidates Hit the Talk Show Circuit." *American Journal of Political Science* 44 (April): 213–34.

Baum, Matthew A. 2007. "Soft News and Foreign Policy: How Expanding the Audience Changes the Policies." *Japanese Journal of Political Science* 8 (1): 109–38.

Baum, Matthew A., and Tim Groeling. 2008. "New Media and the Polarization of American Political Discourse." *Political Communication* 25 (4): 345–65.

Baum, Matthew A., and Tim Groeling. 2009a. "Shot by the Messenger: An Experimental Examination of the Effects of Party Cues on Public Opinion regarding National Security and War." *Political Behavior* 31 (June): 157–86.

Baum, Matthew A., and Tim Groeling. 2009b. *War Stories: The Causes and Consequences of Citizen Views of War*. Princeton, NJ: Princeton University Press.

Baum, Matthew A., and Angela Jamison. 2006. "The Oprah Effect: How Soft News Helps Inattentive Citizens Vote Consistently." *Journal of Politics* 68 (November): 946–59.

Baum, Matthew A., and Samuel Kernell. 2009. "How Cable Ended the Golden Age of Presidential Television: From 1969–2006." In Samuel Kernell and Steven S. Smith (eds.), *The Principles and Practice of American Politics*, 4th Edition, Ch.7.4: 311-26. Washington, DC: CQ Press.

Baum, Matthew A., and Sam Kernell. 1999. "Has Cable Ended the Golden Age of Presidential Television?" *American Political Science Review* 93 (March): 1–16.

Baum, Matthew A., and Henry Nau. 2009. "Foreign Policy Views and U.S. Standing in the World." Paper presented at the annual meeting of the American Political Science Association, Toronto.

Blumler, Jay G., and Dennis Kavanagh. 1999. "The Third Age of Political Communication: Influences and Features." *Political Communication* 16 (3): 209–30.

Brinkley, Joel. 2005. "The Man behind the Secretary of State's Rock Star Image." *New York Times*, Dec. 5, A3.

Feltus, Will. 2009. "Cable News Bias? Audiences Say 'Yes'." *National Media Research, Planning, and Placement*. October 29. nmrpp.com/CableNews BiasAudiences.pdf.

Gentzkow, Matthew, and Jesse M. Shapiro. 2010, January 7. "Ideological Segregation Online and Offline." NBER Working Paper 15916. Retrieved from http://www.nber.org/papers/w15916.pdf.

Gold, Matea. "Candidates Embrace the Chat: Daytime Gabfests and Latenight Comedy TV Become Essential Stops on the Presidential Trail to Reach 'Regular Folks'," *New York Times*, September 29, 2007.

Groeling, Tim, and Matthew A. Baum. 2009. "Journalists' Incentives and Coverage of Elite Foreign Policy Evaluations." *Conflict Management and Peace Science* 26 (November): 437–70.

Hallin, Daniel. 1994. *We Keep America on Top of the World: Television Journalism and the Public Sphere*. London: Routledge.

Hamilton, James T. 2003. *All the News That's Fit to Sell: How the Market Transforms Information into News*. Princeton, NJ: Princeton University Press.

Hindman, Matthew. 2007. *The Myth of Digital Democracy*. Princeton, NJ: Princeton University Press.

Jamison, Angela, and Matthew A. Baum. 2011. "Soft News and the Four Oprah Effects." In Lawrence Jacobs and Robert Shapiro (eds.), *Oxford Handbook of American Public Opinion and the Media*, Ch.8: 121–37. Oxford: Oxford University Press.

Kernell, Samuel. 2006. *Going Public*. Washington, DC: CQ Press.

Kernell, Samuel, and Laurie L. Rice. Forthcoming. "Cable and Partisan Polarization of the President's Audience." *Presidential Studies Quarterly*.

Parkin, Michael. 2010. "Taking Late Night Comedy Seriously: How Candidate Appearances on Late Night Television Can Engage Viewers." *Political Research Quarterly* 63: 3–15.

Patterson, Thomas. 2000. "Doing Well and Doing Good." Research Report. *Joan Shorenstein Center on the Press, Politics and Public Policy*. Cambridge, MA: Harvard University.

Popkin, Samuel. 2006. "Changing Media, Changing Politics." *Perspectives on Politics* 4 (June): 327–41.

Prior, Markus. 2007. *Post-Broadcast Democracy: How Media Choice Increases Inequality in Political Involvement and Polarizes Elections*. Cambridge: Cambridge University Press.

Sunstein, Cass. 2009. *Republic.com 2.0*. Princeton, NJ: Princeton University Press.

Xenos, Michael, and Amy Becker. 2009. "Moments of Zen: Effects of *The Daily Show* on Information Seeking." *Political Communication* 26 (July): 317–32.

Zaller, John. 1992. *The Nature and Origins of Mass Opinion*. New York: Cambridge University Press.

Zaller, John. 2003. "A New Standard of News Quality: Burglar Alarms for the Monitorial Citizen." *Political Communication* 20 (April/June): 109–30.

8

Twitter and Facebook

New Ways for Members of Congress to Send the Same Old Messages?

Jennifer L. Lawless

Former White House Press Secretary Robert Gibbs made news in February 2010 when he officially entered the social networking universe. With a username of @PressSec, he solicited advice – in fewer than 140 characters – about how best to use a new medium of communication: "Learning about 'the twitter' – easing into this with first tweet – any tips?"[1] Mr. Gibbs would soon learn that he would have no trouble acquiring the tricks of the trade; indeed, many of his colleagues in the White House and on Capitol Hill were already proficient users.

Consider the bipartisan congressional Twitter response to revelations about South Carolina governor Mark Sanford's extramarital affair. On June 25, 2009, Congressman Bob Inglis (R-SC) took to the keyboard to comment on the governor's personal transgressions: "Not one of us is capable of fully living the truths we proclaim. Each of us is dependent on grace. I'm praying Psalm 51 for Mark Sanford."[2] U.S. Senator Claire McCaskill (D-MO) wrote, "This place loves to dwell on tragic comedy of infidelity. I feel for this man's family. What are these guys thinking of? I truly don't get it." Congressman Jared Polis (D-CO) took the news more

---

[1] Martina Stewart, "Top Obama Spokesman Joins Twitter," CNN *Political Ticker*, February 13, 2010.

[2] Unless otherwise noted, the tweets and Facebook posts presented as examples in this chapter are drawn from a unique dataset I compiled from June 24, 2009–August 18, 2009. They contain the exact language (including spelling and grammatical errors) transmitted by the members of Congress. See "The Dataset" section of this chapter for a detailed description of the dataset and the data-collection process.

Thanks to Gene Goldstein-Plesser and Alyssa Mowitz, both of whom collected and coded thousands of tweets and Facebook posts.

personally, tweeting, "I got bumped from *Hardball* tonight because Gov Sanford had an affair with a woman in Argentina."

Salacious details surrounding politicians' lurid escapades are not the only topics motivating representatives and senators to communicate through new media like Twitter and Facebook. U.S. Senator John Cornyn (R-TX) called his Facebook friends' attention to a culinary wonder: "A 151-pound cupcake in Minneapolis has been certified as the world's largest. The 1-foot tall, 2-foot wide cupcake on display Saturday at the Minneapolis Mall of America had 15 pounds of fudge filling and 60 pounds of yellow icing." Congressman Greg Walden (R-OR) wondered on his Facebook page, "When will family dogs learn that a skunk will always win?! Short night after neutralizing odor." U.S. Senator Charles Grassley (R-IA) took the time to let his Twitter followers know that he was "enjoying thick chocolate malt at North English Malt Shop." Congressman Todd Tiahrt (R-KS) could not resist sharing his personal frustration with his followers: "I cannot find my iPod. Driving me nuts!" And whereas Congressman Solomon Ortiz (D-TX) announced that he was "getting started with [his] Facebook page," Congressman Peter King (R-NY) proudly posted, "Gone over the 2,500 friend mark!!"

Members of Congress, of course, also use Twitter and Facebook to convey political news. As he awaited President Obama's first address to a joint session of Congress, for example, Congressman Jason Chaffetz (R-UT) tweeted from the House floor: "One teleprompter appears broken. Still 1.5 hours to go but I bet they are nervous."[3] Others sent messages to their followers as the president approached the podium. Congressman Earl Blumenauer (D-OR) wrote, "One doesn't want to sound snarky, but it is nice not to see Cheney up there."[4] Senator McCaskill typed, "I did big woohoo for Justice Ginsberg. She looks good."[5] Senator McCaskill's incessant tweeting, however, did draw some criticism, to which she responded – via Twitter, naturally: "Ok ok. Mom's upset that I was rude at Pres speech re: tweets. For the record I tweeted bfor, at very begining, & after speech."[6] Moving beyond the halls of the Capitol, Congressman Pete Hoekstra (R-MI) tweeted from the Green Zone in Baghdad. Interestingly, his visit to the U.S. Embassy in Iraq was almost

[3] Peter Hamby, "Members of Congress Twitter through Obama's Big Speech," *CNN.com*, February 25, 2009.

[4] Sarah Abruzzese, "The Twittering Class," *Politico Live*, February 24, 2009.

[5] Peter Hamby, "Members of Congress Twitter."

[6] David Goldstein, "High Tech Tool Has Members of Congress all A-Twitter," *McClatchy Newspapers*, March 8, 2009.

canceled because of the security risks Hoekstra generated by alerting his Twitter followers to the trip in advance of his departure.[7]

The advent of Twitter and Facebook affords politicians new means of communicating directly with their constituents. They can tweet in real time, post regular updates to their Facebook pages, and impart to their "followers" and "friends" information about legislative goals and accomplishments. Indeed, journalists, pundits, and bloggers regularly comment on the proliferation of the use of social media inside the Capitol: "Lawmakers Tweet up a Storm in D.C." graced the front page of the *Los Angeles Times*; "Congress's New Love Affair with Twitter" occupied space in *Time* magazine; the *Washington Post* accused members of Congress of "Tweeting Their Own Horns;" and *The Hill* recognized the phenomenon when it ran a story entitled, "Congress 'Friends' Facebook."[8] Yet academics have devoted relatively little attention to these new media. The two systematic analyses that do exist – neither of which was conducted by political scientists – are quite limited in scope (Glassman, Straus, and Shogun 2009; Golbeck, Grimes, and Rogers 2009). At the most fundamental level, we know little about the members of Congress who opt to use these new media and even less about the content of the messages they transmit. Has the new media environment altered the tone or substance of political discourse? Does the instantaneous transmission that these media allow elevate political debate and deliberation? Do Facebook and Twitter provide citizens with new political knowledge and information that can affect political norms, practices, and government accountability? These remain largely open questions.

Based on a detailed analysis of every tweet and Facebook post issued by a member of Congress over an eight-week period in summer 2009, this chapter provides the first nuanced assessment of the new media habits of members of Congress, as well as the content of the messages they transmit. In terms of the extent to which members embrace social media, the results reveal few demographic differences, but a significant party gap: Republicans are more likely than Democrats to communicate through Twitter and Facebook and to use them regularly. When I turn to the content of the tweets and posts, though, the data indicate that Twitter

---

[7] Michael Choy, "Some in Congress all a 'Twitter" with New Media," February 9, 2009. Retrieved from http://www.cbs4denver.com.

[8] Faye Fiore, "Lawmakers Tweet up a Storm in D.C.," *Los Angeles Times*, February 22, 2010; Jay Newton-Small, "Congress's New Love Affair with Twitter," *Time*, February 11, 2009; Daniel de Vise, "Tweeting Their Own Horns," *Washington Post*, September 20, 2009, p. A13; Kris Kitto, "Congress 'Friends' Facebook," *The Hill*, March 10, 2008.

and Facebook serve, for the most part, as two new ways to send the same old messages. Nearly four decades ago, David Mayhew (1974) posited that, as single-minded seekers of reelection, members of Congress tend to engage in three types of activities: advertising, position-taking, and credit-claiming. Since then, political scientists have relied on Mayhew's framework to shed light on congressional communication and behavior (e.g., Bovitz and Carson 2006; Evans 1982; Maltzman and Sigelman 1996). The results of my analysis indicate that, although many members of Congress (and their staffs) have adapted to the new media, the content of their communication through Twitter and Facebook tends to be consistent with Mayhew's thesis. Therefore, it is unlikely that the technological revolution surrounding political communication will fundamentally affect congressional communication or governing. Of course, there is little reason to expect that it would. Members of Congress are engaged in a permanent campaign; Twitter and Facebook provide representatives and senators with two new useful tools to pursue the electoral connection.

BACKGROUND: THE EFFECTS OF NEW TECHNOLOGY ON POLITICS AND GOVERNMENT

Thirty-five percent of American adult Internet users have a profile on at least one social networking site, marking a fourfold increase since 2004.[9] As of January 2010, roughly 24 million Americans had Twitter accounts (three times the number with Twitter accounts in March 2009),[10] and when Facebook celebrated its sixth anniversary in February 2010, it boasted 400 million users.[11] It should come as no surprise, therefore, that politicians have also taken to cyberspace. Since the advent of the Internet, candidates and elected officials have adapted to new media and quickly learned the advantages, as well as the disadvantages, associated with direct and immediate communication. In perhaps the most high-profile, recent example of the potential costs associated with social media, Anthony Weiner (D-NY) was forced to resign his seat in the U.S. House of Representatives in June 2011 after mistakenly sending to his

---

[9] Amanda Lenhart, "Adults and Social Network Websites," Pew Research Center, January 14, 2009.

[10] Sharon Gaudin, "Twitter Now Has 75M Users; Most Asleep at the Mouse," *Computerworld*, January 26, 2010.

[11] Sharon Gaudin, "Facebook Celebrates Sixth Birthday with Re-Design," *Computerworld*, February 5, 2010.

thousands of Twitter followers an explicit photo of himself. He intended to send the tweet to only one woman with whom he communicated via Twitter regularly.[12]

Political scientists have tried to keep apace, producing a growing body of literature that identifies the potential effects of the new media and assesses the manner in which new technologies transform politics. Perhaps the most highly publicized way that politicians rely on new media is in the campaign environment. Howard Dean's 2004 presidential campaign made clear the power of the Internet as a tool for fundraising (Hindman 2006; Mayer and Cornfield 2008), organizing and energizing campaign supporters (Bimber and Davis 2003), and facilitating communication between citizens and candidates (Mayer and Cornfield 2008). Congressional candidates followed suit in 2006; more than 30% of U.S. Senate candidates and roughly 15% of U.S. House candidates in that election cycle actively posted to Facebook during the campaign (Williams and Gulati 2007). Candidates also took advantage of YouTube to achieve greater access to voters, broader message dissemination, and heightened fundraising ability (Gueorguieva 2008). By the 2008 presidential election, all of the major candidates on both sides of the political aisle directed voters to their highly interactive websites, all of which included links to Facebook, Twitter, YouTube, MySpace, and a plethora of other social networking options (Compton 2008).[13]

The manner in which the new media affect campaigns, however, transcends levels of political participation; they can also influence political outcomes. The newfound ability to take their message directly to the American people enables candidates and their supporters to highlight their opponents' comments and gaffes that might not have traditionally garnered attention. Consider former U.S. Senator George Allen's (R-VA) comments at a 2006 campaign rally in southwest Virginia. Allen pointed to an Indian American man in the crowd and explained his presence to the audience: "This fellow here, over here with the yellow shirt, macaca, or whatever his name is. He's with my opponent. He's following us around everywhere. And it's just great.... Let's give a welcome to macaca, here. Welcome to America and the real world of Virginia."[14] Depending on the spelling, "macaca" means either a monkey that inhabits

---

[12] Raymond Hernandez, "Weiner Resigns in Chaotic Final Scene," *New York Times*, June 17, 2011, p. A1.

[13] Early research suggests, however, that social networking cites are not, necessarily, very effective in increasing levels of political participation (Baumgartner and Morris 2010).

[14] Tim Craig and Michael D. Shear, "Allen Quip Provokes Outrage, Apology," *Washington Post*, August 15, 2006.

the Eastern Hemisphere or a racial slur against African immigrants. When Allen's infamous remark went viral within a matter of minutes, no apology could compensate for what was perceived as a racially insensitive comment. Allen lost not only his 2006 reelection bid, but also his viability as a 2008 presidential candidate (Rosenblatt 2010). The Internet also allows interest groups to launch far-reaching campaigns to affect legislation. Jeremy Mayer and Michael Cornfield (2008, 323) point to the defeat of the 2006 and 2007 immigration reform bills, which were initially supported by Congress and the Bush administration, as an example of the manner in which "populist uprising spurred through talk radio and executed through email" can sink legislation.

Moving beyond the campaign environment, new technologies have also fundamentally changed the legislative process. From the production and distribution of legislative documents to the supply of data and information necessary for policy formulation, the Internet has improved the efficiency of the internal operations of Congress (Evans and Oleszek 2003; Thurber and Campbell 2003). It has also helped bridge the communication and information gap between legislators and their constituents; legislative activities, floor speeches, bill sponsorships, press releases, and information about constituent services are easily accessible on member, committee, and caucus websites (Campbell and Dulio 2003; Dreier 2003). As a result of these developments, some scholars argue that the roles of network news and newspapers in linking citizens to their government are now so tenuous that democratic participation and governance no longer depend on them (Picard 2008).

When we turn to elected officials' use of new media to communicate more actively with their constituents, however, the academic research is scant. Indeed, turning specifically to Facebook and Twitter – the two most popular and fastest growing social networking sites – only two systematic analyses even begin to shed any light on patterns of congressional use and content. Jennifer Golbeck, Justin Grimes, and Anthony Rogers (2009) analyze the tweets sent by 69 members of Congress in February 2009. They conclude that members of Congress use Twitter to promote themselves, rather than engage in a dialogue with the public. Eighty percent of the tweets they coded are links to news articles, press releases, or information about the members' activities and events. Matthew Glassman, Jacob Straus, and Colleen Shogun's (2009) analysis of 158 members' Twitter content for two week-long periods in July and August 2009 confirms the finding that press-related tweets are most common. These analysts for the Congressional Research Service report also that Republicans are more likely than Democrats to send messages.

Yet neither study offers an analysis – beyond party affiliation – of the predictors of Twitter use, nor links content to any member-level characteristics, such as age, sex, race, party, or seniority. In addition, no scholars assess patterns of Twitter use or content relative to other social media, such as Facebook.

There is no question that the new media environment has the potential to engage, inform, and empower the public to address political issues and events (Neuman 2008). Similarly, elected officials now have unprecedented opportunities to circumvent the media – and any concomitant media bias they perceive (Bennett and Lawrence 2008). Yet the little research that exists pertaining to Facebook and Twitter only begins to scratch the surface in terms of which members of Congress rely on new media, what messages they send, and whether their communications carry implications for political knowledge, debate, and deliberation. This chapter offers preliminary answers to these questions.

THE DATASET: COLLECTING INFORMATION FROM FACEBOOK POSTS AND TWITTER FEEDS

I base this chapter's analysis on a unique dataset of all Facebook posts and Twitter feeds generated by members of Congress from June 24–August 18, 2009. I chose this eight-week period because it allowed for an assessment of congressional communication both while Congress is in session and while members are at home in their districts and states. Specifically, Congress was in session for six of these eight weeks, but out of session from June 29–July 6 and then again from August 10–August 18. The dataset includes the 7,043 Facebook updates (posts) and 7,668 Twitter messages (tweets) sent by the 186 members who tweeted and the 291 members who posted to Facebook during this eight-week interval. The accounts tracked and content coded are the members' official congressional Twitter and Facebook sites, not their campaign accounts. After all, the purpose of this analysis is to investigate how legislators use the new media to convey political information and knowledge, not engage in overt campaign activities, although the distinction can often be amorphous.

To track congressional use and content on Twitter, I began with tweetcongress.org's list of all tweeting members of Congress.[15] I then

---

[15] The website, tweetcongress.org, was created when its founders searched for their local congressmen on Twitter and were "amazed at how many folks on the Hill aren't

supplemented this list with the results from a search of the names of each member of the U.S. House of Representatives and U.S. Senate in twitter .com. In cases in which an account seemed less than official, I called the member's congressional office to verify the account's authenticity and to confirm that it was not a campaign account. Every two weeks, for the duration of the eight-week data-collection phase of the project, I repeated this procedure and added new accounts to the database. I then subscribed to the RSS feed broadcast by each Twitter account, so as to capture and import into the database every tweet sent by each member of Congress dating to June 24, 2009.

Turning to the Facebook data, I relied on Facebook's search tool to identify congressional profiles. Once again, in cases of questionable profile authenticity, I contacted the congressional office for verification. Every two weeks, I completed a new search of all members of Congress without an active profile in the database and added new accounts to the database. Because Facebook profiles do not broadcast RSS feeds, I collected all posts manually, dating to June 24, 2009.

For each observation, I coded two sets of variables: (1) the characteristics of the member of Congress issuing the message, and (2) the content of the tweet or Facebook post. More specifically, I coded each member's sex, race, age, party affiliation, vote share in the previous election, seniority, and state. In terms of content, I relied on David Mayhew's (1974) well-known theory that members of Congress are single-minded seekers of reelection who engage in advertising, position-taking, and credit-claiming. I coded as "advertising" all content that calls attention to an activity, event, appearance, or meeting that positions the representative or senator in a favorable or impressive light. "Position-taking" occurs when tweets or posts include an explicit political position, either framed as something the member supports or opposes. Instances of "credit-claiming" involve a member of Congress reporting on a political accomplishment, such as passing a piece of legislation, successfully opposing a bill, or securing funding for the district. In addition to coding for these three types of content, I tracked whether the tweet or post included the dissemination of neutral information, mentions of the member's personal life, or attention to the procedural or internal operations of Congress.

tweeting. This site is a grass-roots effort to get our men and women in Congress to open up and have a real conversation with us." Retrieved February 27, 2010, from http://tweetcongress.org/about. The two academic studies that focus on Twitter also built their datasets from tweetcongress.org (Glassman, Straus, and Shogun 2009; Golbeck, Grimes, and Rogers 2009).

Finally, I coded whether the message or post contained an audio or visual component or a link to an external source.[16] I arranged the data so as to facilitate analysis at both the candidate and tweet/post levels.

FINDINGS AND ANALYSIS

Who Uses Facebook and Twitter? A Profile of Members with Active Accounts

Perhaps the best place to begin the analysis is with a general profile of Facebook and Twitter users within the U.S. House and Senate. Overall, 35% of members of Congress have "active" Twitter accounts, compared to 55% of members with "active" Facebook accounts. For the purposes of this analysis, an "active" account includes any Twitter feed or Facebook profile with at least one message posted during the eight-week period of this study. The larger proportion of Facebook accounts, relative to Twitter, is likely the result of the fact that Facebook has existed three times as long as has Twitter.

When we turn to demographic and institutional variation among members, we can identify several patterns of usage, most of which apply to both of these social media. Table 8.1 presents the percentage of members of Congress, broken down by a series of demographic and political variables, with active Facebook or Twitter accounts. Turning first to basic demographics, whereas female members are only slightly less likely than men to have Facebook accounts, they are more than 25% less likely than their male colleagues to have Twitter accounts. Racial and ethnic variation emerges at the bivariate level, too, with black and Latino/a members of Congress least likely to communicate through Facebook and Twitter. Not surprisingly, the average Twitter and Facebook user is four years younger than the average nonuser. By no means are these new modes of communication restricted to "young" members of Congress, however: The average user was born in 1952, making him or her nearly 60 years of age.

---

[16] The first 1,000 Tweets and 1,000 Facebook posts were coded independently by two research assistants with 95% intercoder reliability. I then resolved the discrepancies on a case-by-case basis. The remaining cases were divided evenly between the two research assistants, and I checked a random sample of them for accuracy and comparability. The "Findings and Analysis" section of this chapter provides detailed examples of each type of content.

TABLE 8.1. *Who Uses the New Media? A Profile of Members of Congress with Active Facebook and Twitter Accounts*

	Twitter (%)	Facebook (%)
Member Demographics		
Men	37	55
Women	27	52
White	36	58
Black	28	31
Latino	24	44
Asian	33	56
Political Factors		
House	35	57
Senate	36	45
Unopposed	37	51
Challenged	20	55
Democrat	24	45
Republican	51	69
Total	35	55
N	533	533

Notes: Entries indicate the percentage of members of Congress within each demographic or political group who have an active Facebook or Twitter account. "Active accounts" include any Twitter feed or Facebook post with at least one message.

The data presented in the bottom half of Table 8.1 reveal politically relevant patterns of usage. Members of the House are more likely than U.S. senators to use Facebook, although there are no chamber differences in the likelihood of having a Twitter account. Members of Congress who ran unopposed in their last election are nearly twice as likely to communicate via Twitter, but not more likely to use Facebook, as compared to members who faced an opponent in the last election cycle.[17] And the average Twitter and Facebook user was elected in 1997, one cycle later than the average nonuser. The most striking finding to emerge from Table 8.1, however, is the party affiliation usage gap: Republican members of

[17] When we break the data down in a somewhat more nuanced fashion, though, an important pattern emerges. In terms of margin of victory (including members who ran unopposed), the average Twitter user won his or her last election by 35 points, and the average Facebook user defeated his or her opponent by 31 percentage points. Nonusers experienced somewhat higher margins of victory; members without Facebook accounts won their races by 40 percentage points, and non-Twitter users won their races by 39 percentage points. Nonusers may have less of an incentive to adopt new modes of communication because their electoral viability is so solid.

Congress are 53% more likely than Democrats to have a Facebook page and more than twice as likely to have a Twitter account.

The party gap is actually more significant than it might initially appear because it also drives many of the other user differences identified in Table 8.1. Table 8.2 presents a multivariate model that predicts whether a member of Congress has a Facebook or Twitter account. The equations include key demographic variables (sex, race, and age), as well as key political variables (chamber, seniority, margin of victory in the last election, and party affiliation). The multivariate results are striking in that most of the bivariate differences fail to achieve levels of statistical significance when we control for party identification. Indeed, with the exception of age, which continues to exert an effect on the likelihood that a member of Congress has an active Twitter account, the only statistically significant predictor of Facebook and Twitter use is party identification. All else equal, Republicans are not only substantively, but also significantly, more likely than Democrats to use Facebook and Twitter.

The partisan gap in new media usage may result from the different attitudes Democrats and Republicans hold toward the mainstream media, such as newspapers and television networks. Republicans distrust the mainstream media in far greater proportions than do Democrats (Graber 2010). The same attitudes that Republicans at the mass level hold regarding ideological biases in the mainstream media's filtering of news, therefore, may spur Republican elites to avoid the filtering process altogether and take their messages directly to the voters. In other words,

TABLE 8.2. *Multivariate Analysis: Member Demographics and Political Factors as Predictors of Twitter and Facebook Activity (Logistic Regression Coefficients and Standard Errors)*

	Active Twitter Account	Active Facebook Account
Sex (Female)	−.292 (.278)	.018 (.250)
Race (White)	−.402 (.326)	.552 (.291)
Year of Birth	.028 (.013) *	.018 (.012)
Seniority	.013 (.014)	.023 (.013)
Chamber (House)	.292 (.272)	−.294 (.257)
Margin of Victory in Last Race	−.007 (.004)	.003 (.004)
Party (Republican)	1.195 (.207) **	.942 (.201) **
Constant	−80.791 (24.026) **	−80.992 (21.895) **
Pseudo-R^2	.130	.160
% Correctly Predicted	60.3	70.9
N	529	529

Note: Significance levels: $**p < .01$; $*p < .05$.

these technologies allow members of the opposition party to coordinate their message and generate direct public support.

Somewhat surprisingly, we do not see a similar pattern regarding gender differences in use. After all, a wide body of literature provides compelling evidence that women are more likely than men to receive media coverage and commentary that are based on their appearance, "feminine" traits, and ability to handle "women's issues" (Braden 1996; Bystrom et al. 2004; Carroll and Schreiber 1997; Norris 1997a, 1997b). After the 2008 presidential election, scholars also identified egregious examples of overt sexism in media coverage (Carlin and Winfrey 2009; Carroll 2009; Lawless 2009). Yet female members of Congress are no more likely than men to have a Facebook or Twitter account, suggesting that women do not take advantage of these new media to sidestep the gendered media coverage they often receive.

Magnitude of Use: Levels of Facebook and Twitter Activity

Examining which members of Congress have active Twitter and Facebook accounts offers a broad overview of the extent to which the new media have infiltrated Capitol Hill. Yet only with a more nuanced assessment of the frequency with which representatives and senators use their accounts and the size of the audiences they attract can we fully understand the reach of these new tools. We can begin to gauge the extent to which members of Congress use Facebook and Twitter by counting the number of messages the average member transmits. Overall, throughout the eight-week period between June and August 2009, the average member of Congress sent 14 messages via Twitter and posted 13 updates to Facebook. Levels of activity at the aggregate level, therefore, translate into the average member transmitting fewer than two messages per week.

When we break the data down by party, though, we see clear differences in levels of activity between Democrats and Republicans. The top half of Table 8.3 presents the range and the average number of tweets and posts issued by members of Congress during the eight-week period of this study. The average Republican sent nearly four times as many tweets as did the average Democrat; Republicans outpaced Democrats on Facebook, too, posting at nearly three times the rate.

These results are not simply an artifact of Democrats being less likely than Republicans to have active accounts. Indeed, when we restrict the analysis only to the 186 members with active Twitter accounts and 291 members with active Facebook profiles, we see that party differences

TABLE 8.3. *Magnitude and Intensity of Twitter and Facebook Activity*

	Democrats	Republicans
Among All Members of Congress		
Average Number of Tweets	6.62	25.44
Range	0–193	0–416
N	317	216
Average Number of Facebook Posts	7.32	20.75
Range	0–139	0–231
N	317	216
Among "Active" Users		
Average Number of Tweets	27.99	49.50
Range	1–193	1–416
N	75	111
Average Number of Facebook Posts	16.22	30.08
Range	1–139	1–231
N	142	149

Notes: The top half of the table reports the mean number of Facebook posts and tweets among all 533 members of Congress. The bottom half of the table restricts the data analysis only to representatives and senators with "active" Facebook pages or Twitter accounts.

persist. The bottom half of Table 8.3 reveals that, even among active users, the average Republican used Twitter and Facebook nearly twice as often as his or her Democratic counterpart. Moreover, the data reveal that even the most active Democrats paled in comparison to their Republican counterparts. Fourteen of the 15 most active Twitter users and 13 of the 15 most active Facebook users were Republicans (see Table 8.4).

Gauging Facebook and Twitter activity allows us to determine the number of messages the members send. But we can assess the reach of the message only by turning to the size of the audience that receives the tweets and posts. When data collection commenced in late June 2009, 1.26 million women and men were "friends" with a member of Congress. Eight weeks later, the total number of Facebook friends that House members and Senators could boast had risen to 1.44 million. In other words, in the course of eight weeks, members of Congress acquired 177,138 new friends. A similar pattern emerges when we turn to Twitter. In June 2009, members of Congress had a combined 1.14 million followers. By mid-August 2009, that number increased by 476,590 individuals.

Once again, however, party differences that advantage the Republicans surface among active Facebook and Twitter users. Figure 8.1 graphs

TABLE 8.4. *Maximum Usage of New Media: Top 15 Twitter and Facebook Users*

Twitter Activity (Member of Congress and Total Tweets)		Facebook Activity (Member of Congress and Total Posts)	
Mike Pence (R-IN)	416	Blaine Luetkemeyer (R-MO)	231
Michael Burgess (R-TX)	228	*John Cornyn (R-TX)*	166
Claire McCaskill (D-MO)	193	Joe Sestak (D-PA)	139
Ileana Ros-Lehtinan (R-FL)	182	*Orrin Hatch (R-UT)*	131
Robert Wittman (R-VA)	171	Doris Matsui (D-CA)	127
Kay Bailey Hutchison (R-TX)	163	William Shuster (R-PA)	122
Steve King (R-IA)	159	Tom Price (R-GA)	100
John Culberson (R-TX)	159	John Fleming (R-LA)	94
Darrell Issa (R-CA)	156	*John McCain (R-AZ)*	88
Jason Chaffetz (R-UT)	135	Cathy McMorris Rodgers (R-WA)	88
John McCain (R-AZ)	124	Mike Pence (R-IN)	87
Roy Blunt (R-MO)	123	John Shimkus (R-IL)	85
Orrin Hatch (R-UT)	117	Jason Chaffetz (R-UT)	84
Jim DeMint (R-SC)	102	Greg Walden (R-OR)	83
Bill Posey (R-FL)	101	Kevin Brady (R-TX)	83

Note: Italicized names are senators; nonitalicized names are members of the House of Representatives.

the average member's total number of Facebook friends and Twitter followers, by party. The data reveal that, each week, the average Republican member of Congress had roughly three times as many Facebook friends and five times as many Twitter followers as the average Democrat. The dip in the average number of Republican Facebook followers toward the end of the eight-week interval actually reflects increased Republican activity: During the interval between the seventh and eighth weeks of the study, 37 new Republicans began using Facebook, which decreased the average number of friends, because it takes some time to build a following.

What Are They Saying? A Content Analysis of Tweets and Facebook Posts

The final part of this analysis moves from data about the members of Congress who use Twitter and Facebook to the content of the messages they tweet and post. Based on a nuanced coding of the 14,711 tweets and Facebook posts transmitted during this eight-week period, we can begin to gain a better understanding not only of what members of Congress say when communicating directly with their friends and followers, but also whether any important demographic or political differences affect the content of the messages. The content analysis takes into account not only

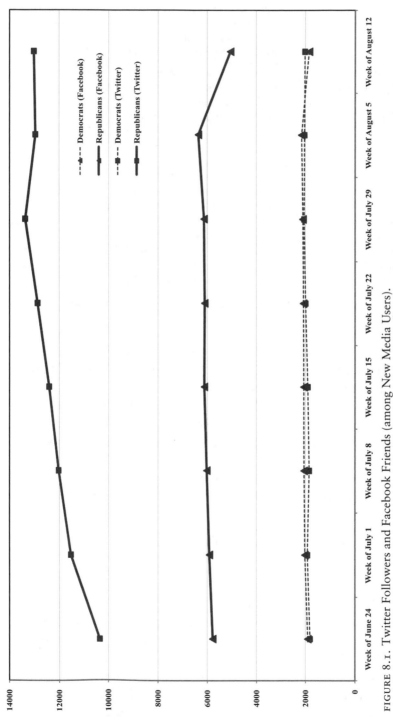

FIGURE 8.1. Twitter Followers and Facebook Friends (among New Media Users).

Note: The number of Democrats using Twitter increased from 57 to 75 over the course of this eight-week period. Republican users increased from 87 to 111. Similar growth occurred in terms of Facebook use. Whereas only 52 Democrats actively posted to Facebook during the week of June 24, 142 posted by mid-August. Republican Facebook users increased from 82 to 149 over the same eight-week period. Accordingly, the dip in the average number of "Followers" and "Friends" is due, in part, to the new users and the time it takes to build a base of supporters.

the members' words, but also the substance included in any external links or audio and visual components to which their message refers. These links are not incidental, because they were included in a substantial number of tweets and posts (see Table 8.5).

Turning first to the aggregate-level data, Figure 8.2 provides the percentage of tweets and posts that fall into each of the content categories introduced in the "Dataset" section of this chapter. Most observations include references to more than one category, so the percentages add up to more than 100%. As we might expect, although Facebook and Twitter represent new media through which to transmit messages, the content is strikingly similar to that which David Mayhew (1974) posited nearly 40 years ago and what congressional scholars have consistently identified in patterns of congressional communication. That is, members of Congress devote the bulk of their communications to advertising, position-taking, and credit-claiming.

Approximately three-quarters of all tweets and posts include some degree of advertising by the member of Congress. Mentions of Congressman John Adler's (D-NJ) address to the Fort Dix community, Congressman Todd Akin's (R-MO) appearance on C-SPAN, Congresswoman Michele Bachmann's (R-MN) conversation with Glenn Beck, as well as photos of Congresswoman Judy Biggert's (R-IL) local stops in August 2009 and Congressman Artur Davis's (D-AL) speech to the incoming class at the University of Alabama School of Medicine, were among the activities advertised by members on Facebook. Twitter advertising was similar. Followers of Congresswoman Ileana Ros-Lehtinen (R-FL) learned that she was "Driving to ocean drive. To help cleanup beach. South tip of beach." Men and women following Congressman Mike Honda (D-CA) found out that he would be nominating a new congressional page for the fall 2009 semester. Congressman Steve Israel (D-NY) called his followers' attention to the new video blog posted on his website, in which he discussed federal support for veterans programs. And Senator Susan

TABLE 8.5. *Dissemination of Information via Twitter and Facebook*

	Twitter (%)	Facebook (%)
Includes Link to Another Source	12.7	43.4
Includes Audio or Visual Component	15.9	25.6
Number	7,650	6,757

Note: Entries indicate the percentage and number of tweets and posts containing links to other sources or audio or visual materials.

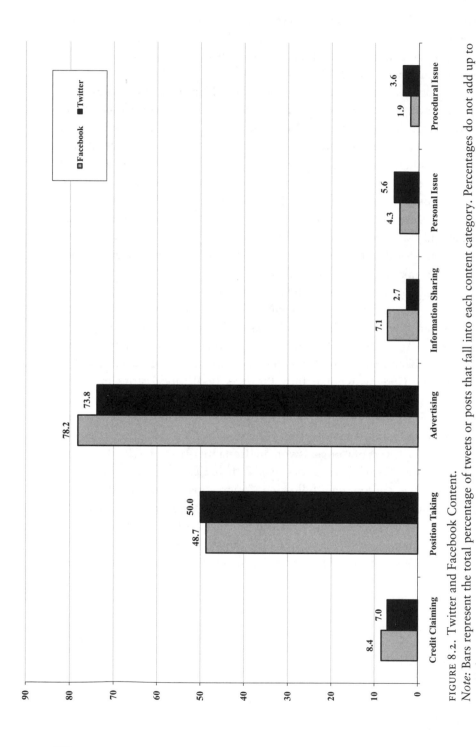

FIGURE 8.2. Twitter and Facebook Content.

Note: Bars represent the total percentage of tweets or posts that fall into each content category. Percentages do not add up to 100% because one tweet or post often includes more than one type of content. For Facebook, N = 7,043; for Twitter, N = 7,668.

Collins (R-ME) tweeted from a juvenile diabetes hearing, where she was "listening to testimony from sugar ray leonard."

The second-most transmitted content on both Twitter and Facebook centers around position-taking: Approximately half of the tweets and posts include an explicit political position. Congressman Mike Doyle's (D-PA) vote to "improve health care for our veterans," Congresswoman Mary Fallin's (R-OK) statement that women in Congress must work to "stop Obama's bid for tax-funded abortions," Congressman Randy Forbes' (R-VA) mention that he was "headed to the floor to fight for new Manhattan Project and oppose Cap-and-Trade national energy tax," and Senator Kay Bailey Hutchison's (R-TX) announcement that she planned to vote against confirming Sonia Sotomayor because of her "liberal stance on the Second Amendment" were prominently displayed on these members' Facebook pages. Senator Barbara Boxer's (D-CA) support of the Matthew Shepard Hate Crimes Act, Senator James Inhofe's (R-OK) support of a bond rescission amendment, Congressman Jason Chaffetz's (R-UT) floor speech "challenging Congressman Whitfield's (R-KY) earmark for $250k for a farmer's market in Monroe County," and Congresswoman Mary Bono Mack's (R-CA) meeting with Nancy Pelosi to "stress the need to push for nuclear power. A strong push, not a wink-and-a-nod approach" all merited a tweet.

Credit-claiming represents the third most frequent type of content, although the dropoff from advertising and position-taking is significant: Fewer than one in 10 tweets or posts involve a member of Congress taking credit for a legislative success or delivering money, programs, or publicity to the state or district. This is not to say that members do not highlight their accomplishments. When Senator Jeff Bingaman's (D-NM) "comprehensive, bipartisan, and forward-looking energy bill . . . cleared its first hurdle: the American Clean Energy Leadership Act was approved by the Senate Energy and Natural Resources Committee," he let his Facebook friends know. When the U.S. House of Representatives passed Congresswoman Suzanne Kosmas's (D-FL) bill that would "provide assistance to small businesses affected by the retirement of the Space Shuttle so they can commercialize their products and preserve jobs," her Facebook page touted the accomplishment. And Senator David Vitter (R-LA) was quick to inform his 1,914 Twitter followers that his "hurricane protection, pump to the river language passed tonight on the senate floor. Will help protect SE LA against future storm surge."

The relatively small proportion of tweets and Facebook posts dedicated to credit-claiming activities likely reflects the fact that these new media are not geography bound (see also Campbell and Dulio 2003). Members of Congress communicate not only with their constituents, but also with a national audience that is less impressed by or interested in district- or state-level accomplishments. The issues that members address through Twitter and Facebook serve as additional evidence for this claim. Whereas more than one-quarter of tweets and posts address health care – an issue of national significance and a source of national debate – fewer than 10% of the messages focus on any local issue or event (see Table 8.6). The old adage that "all politics are local" is severely undercut when friends and followers represent a nationally distributed group of political junkies.[18]

The remaining types of content that members of Congress send via Twitter or post on Facebook are relatively rare. Information sharing, in which a member neutrally calls attention to a current issue or event, occurs more often on Facebook than Twitter, but still not frequently. Congresswoman Marsha Blackburn's (R-TN) post that "the markup has

TABLE 8.6. *Top 10 Issues Mentioned in Twitter Feeds and Facebook Posts*

Twitter (Issue and Percentage of Tweets in which it is Mentioned)		Facebook (Issue and Percentage of Posts in which it is Mentioned)	
Health Care	27.9	Health Care	27.6
Energy	9.4	Trade Policy	6.5
Local Event	5.4	Stimulus Package	4.9
Local Issue	4.0	Local Event	4.4
Stimulus Package	3.8	Budget	3.7
Budget	2.8	Local Issue	3.5
Financial Regulations	2.3	Financial Regulations	2.4
Supreme Court	1.9	Military	1.6
Defense Policy	1.7	Energy	1.5
Iran	1.5	Veterans	1.2
N	7,668	N	7,043

Note: Entries indicate the percentage of tweets or posts in which the issue is mentioned. In the case of health care, for example, roughly 28% of tweets and posts included some mention of the issue.

[18] This is not a new problem for members of Congress. Indeed, Congressman David Dreier (2003, 62), a Republican member of the U.S. House of Representatives from California, recounted a similar issue when e-mail became the preferred means by which to communicate with members of Congress: "Short of the constituent including his or her street address within the email, there is no viable way of confirming whether or not he or she is an actual constituent. In addition, the creation and use of distribution lists easily supports the practice of spamming and other activities that make managing these communications difficult at best."

begun. It is being broadcast on C-SPAN 3," Senator John Cornyn's (R-TX) announcement that "the Sotomayor floor debate begins today," Congresswoman Chellie Pingree's (D-ME) tweet that "The House is swearing in our newest member, and the first Chinese-American woman, Judy Chu. She replaces Hilda Solis, now secy of Labor," and Congresswoman Eddie Bernice Johnson's (D-TX) mention of the U.S. House of Representatives' tribute to Michael Jackson fall into the information-sharing category. Overall, however, members tend not to spend much time providing relatively neutral information, even if it relates to their legislative and political activities.

Members also spend relatively little time writing about the inner workings of Congress or the procedural aspects by which a bill becomes a law. And when they do, they tend to frame their messages in terms of positions on the issues. Congressman Todd Akin, for instance, posted to his Facebook page, "I am currently on the floor of the House and our Minority Leader, Representative Boehner is reading the 300 page amendment to the disasterous [sic] Cap and Tax bill that threatens to destroy our economy. If you can, tune into C-SPAN and hear for yourself this proposed historic over reach by the Majority." Congressman Dean Heller (R-NV) shared that he was "extremely disappointed that the majority party has refused to allow consideration of my amendment to curb congressional spending." Congressman Steven LaTourette (R-OH) posted this message:

> Received an invite from Speaker Pelosi to attend a meeting about energy on Wed. I'm wondering if they are short votes on the cap-n-trade legislation or if they are just trying to siphon off a couple of Republican votes to make it appear that it is a bi-partisan piece of legislation. Obviously, I'm not going as I'm voting against this tax increasing and business killing legislation.

Congressman John Carter (R-TX) tweeted to his followers that he would "use every parliamentary rule available to at least let there be an open debate on runaway spending." Senator Claire McCaskill was one of the only members to send a positive message: "I'm gonna faint. Commerce Com mark up, Ds and Rs working together. FAA reauthorization. Wish we could do this on everything."

Ninety-five percent of the Tweets and Facebook posts also lacked mention of the members' personal thoughts, feelings, and experiences, the very topics that tend to garner the most attention in journalists' accounts of congressional use of Facebook and Twitter. In fact, Father's Day and Fourth of July greetings comprised the largest proportion of this category, followed by commentary on the congressional baseball game.

Congressman Jason Chaffetz's affection for Ben Stein, Congressman Darrell Issa's (R-CA) tribute to his nephew, Congressman James Oberstar's (D-MN) love of cycling, and Congresswoman Dina Titus's (D-NV) amazement that she acquired 3,000 Facebook friends, therefore, are rare examples of personal content posted to Facebook. Senator McCaskill's, "oh no, UP is a tear jerker? I cry so easily... even at commercials. And I get it from my mom. I better bring a box of Kleenex," as well as Congresswoman Gabrielle Giffords' (D-AZ), "Newest member of the Giffords family is my sisters son Fraser James Giffords!" serve as rare personal content sent through Twitter.

The frequency of content that we observe at the aggregate level is generally consistent within demographic and political subsamples. The entries in Table 8.7 indicate the percentage of tweets or posts within each demographic or political group that fall into the various types of content. Regardless of sex, race, chamber, opposition in the last election, or party affiliation, members of Congress use Twitter and Facebook most often for advertising, followed by position-taking and credit-claiming. Personal and procedural content is relatively rare across all demographic and political categories.

Two notable findings do merit additional attention, though. First, men's tweets and posts are nearly 25% more likely than women's to contain position-taking language. The gap nearly doubles when we compare white members of Congress to racial and ethnic minority members. In contrast, women, as well as racial and ethnic minorities, are more likely than their male and white counterparts to send messages and post content that includes advertising or credit-claiming. Gender, race, and ethnicity may not predict whether members of Congress have Twitter and Facebook accounts, or whether they use them frequently. But the data suggest that members of underrepresented groups are particularly likely to use these new media to prop themselves up and call attention to their successes. They are less likely to state their positions, a finding that suggests they might be attempting not to ruffle feathers or motivate their opponents.

Party differences emerge as the second key finding. Democratic content is more likely than Republican content to include credit-claiming and advertising. The messages sent and posted by Republicans are more likely than those transmitted by Democrats to fall into the position-taking category. Status within each chamber likely accounts for the party gap. As members of the majority party, Democrats are far more likely than Republicans to achieve legislative successes, so it follows that their content is

TABLE 8.7. *Twitter and Facebook Content, by Member Demographics and Political Factors*

	Credit-Claiming (%)		Position-Taking (%)		Advertising (%)		Personal Issue (%)		Procedural Issue (%)	
	Twitter	Facebook	Twitter	Facebook	Twitter	Facebook	Twitter	Facebook	Twitter	Facebook
Men	7	8	52	50	74	77	5	4	4	2
Women	7	11	37	38	77	37	10	4	3	1
White	7	8	52	50	72	78	6	4	4	2
Nonwhite	13	17	30	27	93	88	3	3	1	1
Unopposed	9	12	40	49	85	82	6	4	0	2
Challenged	7	8	50	49	73	78	6	4	4	0
House Member	7	9	50	48	73	78	5	4	4	2
Senator	8	8	50	51	77	8c	9	5	1	1
Democrat	13	13	41	36	81	87	5	5	2	0
Republican	5	6	53	51	71	74	8	4	4	3

Notes: Entries indicate the percentage of tweets or posts within each demographic or political group that fall into each substantive category. Using sex as an example, the data indicate that 52% of men's tweets, compared to 37% of women's tweets, include some degree of position-taking. Percentages do not add up to 100% because one tweet or post often includes more than one type of content. For Facebook, N = 7,043; for Twitter, N = 7,668.

227

twice as likely to contain mentions of credit-claiming. By contrast, Republicans must rely on highlighting the strengths of their policy proposals and the problems with Democratic bills to garner support. Accordingly, the content they post and tweet is more likely to include position-taking. In essence, the minority party uses Twitter and Facebook to challenge the majority party's positions and version of events, which tend to be what the mainstream media most often report (see Bennett and Lawrence 2008).

Overall, the great majority of the content transmitted by members of Congress falls within the broad categories of advertising, position-taking, and credit-claiming. We cannot make direct comparisons between these findings and the ratios of each type of activity in traditional congressional communications because no such data exist. In all likelihood, however, franked newsletters sent within the district contain more examples of credit-claiming than do tweets and Facebook posts transmitted through cyberspace. Moreover, even limited attention to procedural maneuvers, as well as personal information, likely do not emerge as frequently in more traditional modes of communication with constituents. Thus, even though the findings are consistent with patterns of more traditional congressional communication, the data suggest that the new media allow for somewhat more than simply a new way to send the same old message.

DISCUSSION AND CONCLUSION

Based on the results of the first detailed and thorough analysis of Facebook and Twitter activity by members of Congress, this chapter provides strong evidence that these new media are commonly used and growing in popularity. Not all members of Congress are equally likely to adopt these new technologies, though. Regardless of whether we examine the existence of a Facebook or Twitter account, the intensity of use, or the size of the audience, Republicans outperform Democrats. They are more likely to have active accounts, transmit messages, and attract a broad following. To the extent to which incumbents' use of new media will ultimately pay dividends for campaigns, elections, and governing, the data suggest a Republican advantage. When we turn to the content of the Tweets and Facebook posts, some party differences persist, but broadly speaking, the representatives and senators who use Twitter and Facebook tend to engage in the classic incumbent activities of advertising, position-taking, and credit-claiming. Thus, members of Congress have found new ways to transmit effectively the types of messages that will help propel them to reelection.

These findings are important because they demonstrate that technological advances and active social media use, alone, are insufficient for the transmission of new political information and knowledge. Studies of media content tend to coalesce around the premise that different media provide coverage of similar content because of selection and production biases toward commercial concerns (see Gaunt 1990; McManus 1993; Picard 2008). Because social media do not require filtered content, tools like Facebook and Twitter afford politicians the ability to communicate substantive policy goals, issue preferences, and political positions with more nuance and in more than a sound bite, if often only through links to more information. Members of Congress, however, have not fully realized these opportunities. Rather, they tend to employ social media as a new method by which to convey the same content they would in newsletters, franked mail, and media appearances, albeit perhaps more casually, personally, and in different ratios.

Granted, the degree to which members of Congress are failing to realize the opportunity to impart new information is contingent on the profile of their audience. We know little about the women and men who subscribe to representative and senators' Twitter feeds or who regularly follow congressional status updates on Facebook. If political junkies are the ones taking advantage of these new media, as is the case with general Internet use (see Norris 2001), then the content of the politicians' posts is somewhat less relevant than if new audiences are logging in and gaining information they might not have previously accessed. Should new media begin to supplant more traditional means of communicating with constituents, however, then the majority of the public – people who are not hyperpolitically interested – may find themselves even less informed. After all, many might argue that the act of reading a congressional newsletter differs fundamentally and qualitatively from perusing a Facebook page.

Even if the content of their messages does not differ from that given in the traditional ways in which they present themselves to their constituents, we must not discount the ease with which members of Congress can now communicate with the American public. The potential to disseminate information, clarify positions, publicize events, and hold opponents accountable cannot be overstated. Whether representatives and senators will fully use Twitter and Facebook to achieve these goals and elevate political knowledge, debate, and deliberation remains to be seen. But the pace at which they are acquiring the ability to do so is an essential first step. Indeed, Robert Gibbs – in a matter of just two short weeks – "tested out Twitter from [his] blackberry," succeeded in the endeavor, and quickly came to consider it "very handy for trips!"[19] His 32,625 followers likely agreed.

References

Baumgartner, Jody C., and Jonathan S. Morris. 2010. "MyFaceTube Politics: Social Networking Web Sites and Political Engagement of Young Adults." *Social Science Computer Review* 28 (1): 24–44.

Bennett, W. Lance, and Regina G. Lawrence. 2008. "Press Freedom and Democratic Accountability in a Time of War, Commercialism, and the Internet." In Doris Graber, Denis McQuail, and Pippa Norris (eds.), *The Politics of News, the News of Politics* (247–67), 2nd ed. Washington, DC: CQ Press.

Bimber, Bruce A., and Richard Davis. 2003. *Campaigning Online: The Internet in U.S. Elections*. New York: Oxford University Press.

Bovitz, Gregory L., and Jamie L. Carson. 2006. "Position-Taking and Electoral Accountability in the U.S. House of Representatives." *Political Research Quarterly* 59 (2): 297–312.

Braden, Maria. 1996. *Women Politicians in the Media*. Lexington: University of Kentucky Press.

Bystrom, Dianne G., Mary Christine Banwart, Lynda Lee Kaid, and Terry A. Robertson. 2004. *Gender and Candidate Communication*. New York: Routledge.

Campbell, Colton C., and David A. Dulio. 2003. "Campaigning along the Information Highway." In James A. Thurber and Colton C. Campbell (eds.), *Congress and the Internet* (11–30). Upper Saddle River, NJ: Prentice-Hall.

Carlin, Diana B., and Kelly L. Winfrey. 2009. "Have You Come a Long Way, Baby? Hillary Clinton, Sarah Palin, and Sexism in 2008 Campaign Coverage." *Communication Studies* 60 (4): 326–43.

Carroll, Susan J. 2009. "Reflections on Gender and Hillary Clinton's Presidential Campaign: The Good, the Bad, and the Misogynistic." *Politics & Gender* 5 (1): 1–20.

Carroll, Susan, and Ronnee Schreiber. 1997. "Media Coverage of Women in the 103rd Congress." In Pippa Norris (ed.), *Women, Media, and Politics* (131–48). New York: Oxford University Press.

Compton, Jordan. 2008. "Mixing Friends with Politics: A Functional Analysis of '08 Presidential Candidates Social Networking Profiles." *Paper presented at the annual meeting of the NCA Convention*, San Diego, November 20.

Dreier, David. 2003. "We've Come A Long Way . . . Maybe." In James A. Thurber and Colton C. Campbell (eds.), *Congress and the Internet* (52–77). Upper Saddle River, NJ: Prentice-Hall.

Evans, C. Lawrence, and Walter J. Oleszek. 2003. "The Wired Congress: The Internet, Institutional Change, and Legislative Work." In James A. Thurber

[19] See http://twitter.com/PressSec, February 27, 2010.

and Colton C. Campbell (eds.), *Congress and the Internet* (99–122). Upper Saddle River, NJ: Prentice-Hall.

Evans, Diana. 1982. "House Members' Communication Styles: Newsletters and Press Releases." *Journal of Politics* 44: 1049–71.

Gaunt, Philip. 1990. *Choosing the News: The Profit Factor in News Selection.* Westport, CT: Greenwood Press.

Glassman, Matthew Eric, Jacob R. Straus, and Colleen J. Shogun. 2009. "Social Networking and Constituent Communication: Member Use of Twitter during a Two Week Period in the 111th Congress." *CRS Report R40823.* Washington, DC: Congressional Research Service.

Golbeck, Jennifer, Justin Grimes, and Anthony Rogers. 2009. "Twitter Use by the U.S. Congress." Unpublished manuscript. College Park: University of Maryland.

Graber, Doris A. 2010. *Mass Media and American Politics.* Washington, DC: CQ Press.

Gueorguieva, Vassia. 2008. "Voters, MySpace, and YouTube: The Impact of Alternative Communication Channels on the 2006 Election Cycle and Beyond." *Social Science Computer Review* 3: 288–300.

Hindman, Matthew. 2006. "Reflections on the First Digital Campaign." In Doris A. Graber (ed.), *Media Power in Politics* (192–201), 5th ed. Washington, DC: CQ Press.

Lawless, Jennifer L. 2009. "Sexism and Gender Bias in Election 2008: A More Complex Path for Women in Politics." *Politics & Gender* 5 (1): 70–80.

Maltzman, Forrest, and Lee Sigelman. 1996. "The Politics of Talk: Unconstrained Floor Time in the U.S. House of Representatives." *Journal of Politics* 58: 819–30.

Mayer, Jeremy D., and Michael Cornfield. 2008. "The Internet and the Future of Media Politics." In Mark J. Rozell and Jeremy D. Mayer (eds.), *Media Power, Media Politics* (319–38), 2nd ed. Lanham, MD: Rowman & Littlefield.

Mayhew, David. 1974. *The Electoral Connection.* New Haven, CT: Yale University Press.

McManus, John. 1993. *Market-Driven Journalism: Let the Citizens Beware?* Thousand Oaks, CA: Sage.

Neuman, W. Russell. 2008. "Globalization and the New Media." In Doris Graber, Denis McQuail, and Pippa Norris (eds.), *The Politics of News, the News of Politics* (230–46), 2nd ed. Washington, DC: CQ Press.

Norris, Pippa. 1997a. "Introduction: Women, Media and Politics," In Pippa Norris (ed), *Women, Media, and Politics* (1–18). New York: Oxford University Press.

Norris, Pippa. 1997b. "Women Leaders Worldwide: A Splash of Color in the Photo Op." In Pippa Norris (ed), *Women, Media, and Politics* (149–65). New York: Oxford University Press.

Norris, Pippa. 2001. *Digital Divide: Civic Engagement, Information Poverty, and the Internet Worldwide.* New York: Cambridge University Press.

Picard, Robert G. 2008. "The Challenges of Public Functions and Commercialized Media." In Doris Graber, Denis McQuail, and Pippa Norris (eds.), *The Politics of News, the News of Politics* (211–29), 2nd ed. Washington, DC: CQ Press.

Rosenblatt, Alan. 2010. "Dimensions of Campaigns in the Age of Digital Networks." In James A. Thurber and Candice J. Nelson (eds.), *Campaigns and Elections American Style* (207–26), 3rd ed. Philadelphia: Westview.

Thurber, James A., and Colton C. Campbell. 2003. "Introduction: Congress Goes On-Line." In James A. Thurber and Colton C. Campbell (eds.), *Congress and the Internet* (1–10). Upper Saddle River, NJ: Prentice-Hall.

Williams, Christine, and Girish Gulati. 2007. "Social Networks in Political Campaigns: Facebook and the 2006 Midterm Elections." *Paper presented at the annual meeting of the American Political Science Association*, Chicago: August 30.

9

The Dog That Didn't Bark

Obama, Netroots Progressives,
and Health Care Reform

Matthew R. Kerbel

By late summer 2009, some of the people who had worked hardest to elect Barack Obama were beginning to doubt whether they believed in the changes the new president was advancing. The topic was health care reform, and what had started out in early spring as an exciting venture to restructure the health care system according to progressive principles had become, to some reformers, an increasingly bitter exercise in the disparity between words and deeds. In a *Washington Post* opinion piece, Peter Dreier and Marshall Ganz, who helped engineer Obama's grassroots campaign strategy, lamented how the president seemed to have forgotten his admonition made as a candidate that the only path to enduring social change was to organize against entrenched interests.[1] Disappointed and worried progressive activists like Mike Elk, who had worked around the clock for months to help Obama carry Pennsylvania, echoed this sentiment in the blogoshere. Writing in *The Huffington Post* on behalf of hundreds of former campaign staffers, Elk implored the president not to drop a proposal for a publicly run health care option that would compete against private insurance plans, because doing so would amount to a major victory for the insurance industry and a stinging defeat for the progressive goal of affordable health care. Referencing the millions who worked to put Obama in office, Elk wrote, "Mr. President, we are here to say that there is only one force in this country more powerful than the insurance industry and its corporate allies – us! During the campaign, we defeated two of the strongest machines ever assembled in the primary and

[1] Peter Dreier and Marhsall Ganz, "We Have the Hope. Now Where's the Audacity?" *Washington Post*, August 30, 2009.

general election [Hillary Clinton and John McCain]. We can beat these guys too."[2]

Concordant voices could be heard at *Daily Kos*, the largest progressive community weblog and a hub of pro-public option activism. "Boy, oh, boy do I remember the fight to get President Obama elected," blogged a former campaign organizer with the screen name HRCDemographic4Obama. "My experience working on President Obama's campaign teaches me he needs a strong reaction from Progressives. He needs to know we are willing to fight everyone, including him, for what is a moral obligation in a nation such as ours, universal health care."[3] While still regarding Obama as an ally, these individuals who had worked so hard to elect him were preparing to mobilize against him as they watched the president's rhetorical call for transformational change diverge from a governing strategy built around conventional politics. As Dreier and Ganz note,

> Once in office, the president moved quickly, announcing one ambitious legislative objective after another. But instead of launching a parallel strategy to mobilize supporters, most progressive organizations and Organizing for America – the group created to organize Obama's former campaign volunteers – failed to keep up.... The administration and its allies followed a strategy that blurred their goals, avoided polarization, confused marketing with movement-building and hoped for bipartisan compromise that was never in the cards. This approach replaced an "outsider" mobilizing strategy that not only got Obama into the White House but has also played a key role in every successful reform movement, including abolition, women's suffrage, workers' rights, civil rights and environmental justice.[4]

The frustration felt by these activists stemmed from Obama's choice not to view his administration as a movement as he did his improbable campaign, which likely would have failed without a paradigm-challenging organizational model built on engaging and empowering ordinary citizens through the Internet. Where underdog candidates have to roll the dice, incumbent presidents face a decidedly different risk environment and have to navigate a wide set of entrenched political and economic interests. As president, Obama faces a sprawling Democratic Party establishment composed in part of individuals whose interests would be directly threatened by the type of activism his most energized partisans expect. His ability to

[2] Mike Elk, "I Am a Former Staffer of the President's and I Want Him To Fight Like He Promised Us." *The Huffington Post*, September 4, 2009.
[3] HRCDemographic4Obama, "Former Obama Staffers Are Standing up for a Robust Public Option." *Daily Kos*, September 7, 2009.
[4] Dreier and Ganz, "We Have the Hope."

influence those individuals during his tenure in office – his political capital – is built on his success at governance, on being able to claim credit for advancing the ambitious menu of domestic initiatives he promised as a candidate.[5] Failure early leads to paralysis later, so he had to tread carefully.

It is understandable that those who witnessed the effectiveness of Obama's grassroots efforts, as well as the progressives dedicated to causes like affordable universal health care, would see a replay of the Obama campaign's movement politics model as the most likely path to their goals. Indeed Obama did incorporate some of his successful Internet campaign tactics into his governing strategy. Yet campaigning is not governance, just like movements are not presidential administrations. Movements articulate and advance a set of goals; administrations bend to accommodate broad coalitions. Campaigns appeal to the dreamer; governance is the jurisdiction of the pragmatist. Movements are about single-minded advocacy; administrations have to deal with disparate party caucuses and legislators with their own sources of authority. Movements and campaigns unify and inspire; partisans in the act of governing make deals and, in the process, create winners and losers. Turning health care reform into an Internet-driven movement would require the administration to believe it could assemble a winning congressional coalition using the tools so skillfully employed by Internet activists. In 2009, that was a long-shot proposition.

So it was that as campaigning turned to governing and the rhetoric of hope met the implacable boundaries of change, Internet politics proved ready for advocacy if not yet for governance. In a seamless extension of their campaign role, the broad, horizontally organized structures of the netroots (or "Internet grassroots"), on offense for the first time, emerged as the progressive home base in the health care reform debate – cajoling, pushing, threatening, and screaming (virtually and literally) at recalcitrant Democrats while pressuring their allies to stay firm in support of the more progressive elements of the legislation, notably a public plan to compete with private insurance companies. Not so with the remnants of Obama's campaign operation, now renamed Organizing for America (OFA) from its previous incarnation as Obama for America. Although present in the debate, OFA was a supporting player in a traditional game of deal

---

[5] This is essentially Richard Neustadt's (1991) formulation that "Washingtonians" respond to presidents who demonstrate the ability to use the advantages afforded them by the office, operating within the political circumstances that define their time.

making rather than the transformative presence it had been in 2008, when an otherwise underfunded and inexperienced candidate leveraged his Internet presence to best whatever the Clintons and the Republicans threw his way. The netroots and the administration chose their different paths, the former conducive to movement organizing and the latter to transactional politics. In the process, they widened the cracks between them that were evident even as they were fighting for a common electoral goal one year earlier, when there was already evidence suggesting that the Obama campaign was not integrated with and could be at odds with netroots objectives.

The fissures between the netroots and the campaign were rooted in the power struggle between an online progressive elite and established political interests – a struggle that the Obama campaign never embraced. As a political movement, the netroots are focused on wresting power from a political class that includes some of the Democratic officials who were instrumental in advancing Obama's health care initiative. Their aim is to replace the agents of a system built around big-money television politics – including entrenched officials backed by wealthy interest groups, Washington-based political consultants, and old-school journalists – with a communitarian politics that rekindles the connections between officials and citizens through social networking and Internet discourse (Kerbel 2009). The Obama campaign, of course, was focused on winning an election, and although the netroots could be useful in that pursuit, the campaign had independently constructed an online operation under its control. "For the life of me, I cannot figure out why he hasn't pursued a blog outreach strategy," wondered Jerome Armstrong on MyDD.[6] However, given the divergent objectives of the campaign and the netroots, and the fact that close coordination would saddle the campaign with responsibility for anything that might be posted in the blogosphere that could undermine the campaign's electoral strategy, it is not entirely surprising that Obama for America would want to remain a distinct entity.

A hint of the difficulties the netroots could cause the candidate – and a foreshadowing of the cracks that would develop in 2009 – occurred with the appearance of a grassroots movement to use the campaign's own Web tools to protest the candidate's position on the Foreign Intelligence Surveillance Act (FISA). This movement spread online from a single *Daily Kos* reader to 17,000 people within one week (Kerbel 2009). The impetus

[6] Jerome Armstrong, "Obama Operating." *MyDD*, August 20, 2008.

for this act of rebellion was Obama's announcement that he would not block the FISA bill in the Senate even if it protected telecommunications companies from prosecution for monitoring customers' conversations in the name of national security. From a netroots perspective, this online protest was true to the spirit of the Obama campaign and consistent with progressive goals, both because Obama's position protecting telecommunications companies from having participated in illegal spying activities was at odds with a key netroots objective and the candidate himself had spoken at length about the importance of grassroots organizing in the defense of core values. Although this protest split those in the netroots who wanted to hold the candidate accountable for undermining progressive ends from those who preferred to remain silent in order to defeat John McCain, the primary fault line was between a campaign (and some bloggers) willing to manage relations with entrenched interests like telecommunications firms in order to win the election, and those netroots activists who wanted to use the campaign as a vehicle for advancing social change by confronting powerful elites. This sort of division would reemerge one year later in the debate over the public health care option.

The new media environment was permitting a self-selected group of ordinary citizens to organize and assert their influence over the policy process in a manner without parallel during the decades when television reigned supreme in our politics, and in a way reflective of the democratic ideal of citizen engagement in politics. During the health care battle of 2009–10, netroots activists challenged a philosophically compatible president and congressional leadership with a new way of organizing, keeping the pressure on them in an attempt to win Democratic support for a progressive agenda. This chapter recounts their efforts to mobililze in ways previously reserved for organized interest groups, contrasting netroots activists' embrace of the Internet as a vehicle for movement politics with the cautious approach of the administration, demonstrating the netroots' sophisticated understanding of how to work the political system from inside and out. We will see how ordinary citizens with an extraordinary interest in politics found each other online, produced leaders, and developed organizing strategies through the constant discussion and refinement of a wide range of ideas. Although they did not realize their goal of progressive health care reform, their advocacy attracted the notice of the professional political class as they demonstrated the promise and potential of Internet politics in policy making.

MONEY, POWER, AND OUTCOMES

The predominant netroots narrative about the administration's role in the health care initiative placed in sharp relief the difference between passing legislation (the administration's political objective) and challenging powerful interests (Obama's rhetorical campaign position and the netroots' political objective). As the legislation became increasingly soft on insurance and pharmaceutical interests as it worked its way through Congress, prominent voices in the blogosphere loudly accused the administration of trading away progressive ends and protecting the status quo in the interest of expediency. At issue was the administration's willingness to co-opt the interests that progressives believed needed to be undermined instead as a prerequisite to making health care universally available and widely affordable.

Noting that the White House had repeatedly pressured congressional progressives while protecting centrist and conservative Democrats, Glenn Greenwald blogged at Salon.com that the rationales offered by the administration for giving up on proposals for a strong government presence in health insurance markets – the inability to get the necessary votes to end a Senate filibuster, the desire for elusive bipartisan support – were smokescreens for an approach that sold out progressive objectives to placate the very interests Obama had suggested he would take on:

> The Obama White House isn't sitting impotently by while Democratic Senators shove a bad bill down its throat. This is the bill because this is the bill which Democratic leaders are happy to have. It's the bill they believe in. As important, by giving the insurance and pharmaceutical industries most everything they want, it ensures that the GOP doesn't become the repository for the largesse of those industries (and, conversely, that the Democratic Party retains its status). This is how things always work. The industry interests which own and control our government always get their way. When was the last time they didn't?[7]

Jane Hamsher, who emerged as one of the leading netroots activists in support of progressive health care policy through her blog *FireDogLake*, suggested that the White House was following a deliberate and carefully crafted strategy aimed at keeping monied stakeholders like the pharmaceutical lobby, hospitals, health insurance corporations, and the American Medical Association from using their clout to advertise against health

---

[7] Glenn Greenwald, "Why the Health Care Debate Is So Important Regardless of One's View of the 'Public Option'," *Salon.com*, August 19, 2009.

care reform and to replenish the coffers of a Republican Party reeling from two devastating electoral cycles. She charged the administration with reneging on a campaign promise to conduct transparent health care negotiations in order to cut private profit-protecting deals that sacrificed progressive objectives. "People make a mistake when they think the battle for health care reform is about ideology," she blogged in an argument reflective of the broader progressive netroots power struggle. "It's about who controls K Street [lobbyists] and the cash that flows from it, which could fund a 2010 GOP resurgence – or not."[8]

THE NETROOTS: HORIZONTAL ACTIVISM

With a Democratic-controlled Congress and a Democratic president ostensibly aligned against them, netroots activists leveraged the decentralized advantages of their medium to battle on behalf of progressive health care reform. Their efforts were extensive and demonstrated a sophisticated appreciation of how to use the Internet to advance political objectives. Without the centralized planning that characterizes presidential campaigns and administration policy initiatives, collective action evolved spontaneously and organically on the Web in the form of an intricate inside/outside strategy. A constellation of websites served as the neural center for this effort, led by a few self-selected activists surrounded by an energized community of committed bloggers.

The Players

In keeping with the horizontal, decentralized structure of the progressive blogosphere, it would be misleading to say there was a single locus of netroots activism. Rather, there were several prominent nodes linked to one another, as well as a few highly engaged individuals working in tandem with a cluster of professional writers and amateur bloggers. The structure of this web of activity resembled netroots activism during past electoral cycles, anti-Iraq War organizing, and lobbying for less prominent policies like Internet neutrality; it even reflected the collaborative manner in which the first Netroots Nation conference (called "Yearly Kos") was planned and implemented (Kerbel 2009). The common thread is that individuals were empowered to self-select what they wanted to do

---

[8] Jane Hamsher, "The Baucus Caucus: PhRMA, Insurance, Hospitals and Rahm." *FireDogLake*, August 19, 2009.

and how engaged they wished to be. This is the signature characteristic of Internet activism, the feature that makes the Internet a democratizing medium and an ideal medium for movement politics (Anderson and Cornfield 2003; Blumenthal 2005; Bowers and Stoller 2005; Johnson and Kaye 2004; Trippi 2004).

Along with Hamsher, *Daily Kos* bloggers slinkerwink (Noelle Cigarroa Bell) and nyceve (Eve Gittelson) emerged as frontline activists who designed, coordinated, and enacted key strategic plans and also blogged incessantly about the daily machinations of policy making. In addition to Hamsher's *FireDogLake* blog (and the sites she created to facilitate action on health care, such as publicoptionplease.com and Blue America Pac for soliciting contributions), the progressive blogosphere discussed health care almost obsessively during the second half of 2009. For example, on the activist-oriented *Open Left* blog, Chris Bowers and Mike Lux engaged in an ongoing interactive strategic analysis of the process with the site's readers. Writers like Greenwald at *Salon*, Digby at *Hullabaloo*, Marcy Wheeler at *FireDogLake*, and a battery of *Daily Kos* bloggers contributed to the planning and assessment of efforts to move health care policy in a progressive direction.

Horizontal links between blogs and other progressive sites served to multiply the force of blog activism. Among those sites was Progressivecongress.org, the online home of the American Progressive Caucus Policy Foundation, a nonpartisan 501(c)(3) organization that was deeply involved in pressing for progressive health care policy. Its executive director, Darcy Burner, is a netroots favorite who received extensive support from the progressive blogosphere in two unsuccessful congressional campaigns. Progressivemajority.org, which identifies and recruits progressive candidates around an agenda that includes universal, affordable, high-quality health care, was also involved.[9] Democracy for America (DFA), the organizational heir to Howard Dean's online presidential operation, is a million-member progressive political action community dedicated, according to its mission statement, to changing "our country and the Democratic Party from the bottom-up."[10] Although Dean himself no longer runs the organization he founded, in September 2009 he teamed up with DFA to form America Can't Wait (americacantwait.com), on which signatures were gathered online to petition Congress to include a public option in the final version of health care legislation.

---

[9] See http://www.progressivemajority.org/MissionAgenda/.
[10] See http://www.democracyforamerica.com/about.

Other arms of the far-flung grassroots progressive constellation include relatively old organizations like MoveOn.org (which traces its roots to the Clinton impeachment era – prehistoric in blogging terms); Drinking Liberally (drinkingliberally.org), a Web organization that helps progressives find each other so they can meet in the bricks-and-mortar world and discuss politics and political action; and ActBlue (actblue.com), a website that serves as a central clearinghouse for campaign contributions to progressive politicians. Progressive television and talk radio hosts, such as Keith Olbermann, Rachel Maddow, and Ed Schultz on MSNBC, contributed to blog discussions of health care reform and featured principal online progressive activists on their programs, thereby linking traditional and new media.

Inside Strategies

Despite being situated on the outside, netroots activists ran an extensive and creative set of inside strategies designed primarily to unify the Congressional Progressive Caucus behind the public option. They understood that House progressives had been disorganized in the past and were unable to serve as a counterweight to a smaller group of "Blue Dog" conservatives, who therefore held the balance of power in the Democratic caucus. To alter this dynamic, they coordinated their efforts with progressive caucus leaders, engaged in a sustained effort to rally progressive members behind the public option, briefed members and their staffs, and participated in the markup of the House bill.

- *Coordinating with House progressives.* Netroots activists recognized that, in tandem with online progressive organizations, they could communicate to sympathetic officials the acceptable parameters of progressive health care policy while amplifying the messaging of progressive officials through a two-way communication flow between officials and bloggers. Darcy Burner of the American Progressive Caucus Policy Foundation regarded this interplay as a system that married the organizational and communication strengths of the netroots and affiliated organizations with the numerical advantages of a large but heretofore ineffectual progressive congressional bloc.[11] As the blogger mcjoan explained on *Daily Kos*, "As part of the progressive movement,

---

[11] mcjoan, "The Netroots and the House Progressives: Toward More Progressive Policy." *Daily Kos*, June 28, 2009.

[bloggers] are in a sort of a feedback loop with the [House Progressive] Caucus, working on both the policy formation and policy framing efforts – sort of the stick part of the process, as well as the 'amplification' side – the more carrot part where we do our best to shore up their efforts, provide them with the public support, the financial support and, frankly, the ongoing pressure they need to become what will essentially be a progressive stop to the Senate."[12] Chris Bowers of *Open Left* credited this strategy with keeping the public option viable deep into the Senate negotiating phase of the process, even though it lacked the 60 votes necessary for cloture and Senate approval. Blogged Bowers, "Cooperation and coordination between Congressional Progressives and outside grassroots progressive groups [maintained] a large enough bloc of Progressives to defeat the bill [in the House] if the demand [for a public option] is not met [in the Senate]."[13]

- *Taking "the pledge."* To this end, bloggers led by Jane Hamsher worked for months to whip the votes of House progressives, encouraging, cajoling, and figuratively bludgeoning them to sign a pledge that they would vote against any health care initiative without a public option. Simultaneously, Bowers maintained a close whip count of Senate Democrats. The goal of the whip effort was to present congressional leadership with a credible threat that no health care legislation could pass the House without a public option, thus applying pressure from the left to force conservative Senate Democrats to compromise. A key instrument in this endeavor was the Public Plan Whip Tool, a netroots community action site designed by Hamsher to exert visible pressure on progressives to hold firmly to their beliefs. Readers could link to the site through *FireDogLake*, where they would find the names and phone numbers of 100 House progressives in a chart indicating whether the member had committed to the pledge and containing space for recording the name of the member or members called and the results of the contact.[14] A string of diaries on *FireDogLake* and *Daily Kos* implored readers to use the tool ("Please, for the love of Jesus," blogged Eve Gittelson, "commit to making at least one Whip

[12] Ibid.
[13] Chris Bowers, "Progressive Block Forced Public Option into Senate Bill." *Open Left*, October 26, 2009.
[14] See Jane Hamsher, "FDL Action: Let's Whip the Public Plan!" *FireDogLake*, June 23, 2009; and the Public Plan Whip Tool, at http://action.firedoglake.com/page/s/publicoption.

Count call every day."[15]), and Hamsher regularly updated the results on her blog and on Twitter.[16]

- *Briefings.* As a result of their online leadership efforts, Gittelson and Hamsher were invited by Rep. John Conyers' staff to brief a gathering of congressional staffers on health care reform. In turn, Gittelson blogged to her *Daily Kos* readers that she wanted to put a human face on the problems caused by the health insurance industry by sharing their stories in her briefing. Her diary received 763 comments filled with firsthand accounts of denied or insufficient coverage, along with pointers on how to speak in front of a large audience.[17] After the briefing, Gittelson acknowledged the community effort that enabled her to make the trip to brief the staffers:

  > I want to thank Cedwyn and KStreetProjecter for helping me with this presentation, I really couldn't have done it without their wisdom, guidance and hard work. And a huge hug of gratitude to all those who emailed with heartfelt offers of office space, copying services, sleeping accommodations, whatever I needed. Also, this actually brings tears to my eyes, one Kossack [Daily Kos blogger] even sent a $50.00 Paypal donation to cover some of my expenses, and he refused to take it back![18]

- *Freezing out professional lobbyists.* In advance of the markup sessions for the committee versions of the House bill, Hamsher and Gittelson issued an all-points bulletin to blog readers living in the Washington, DC, area to go to the Hill and wait in line for the meetings so that lobbyists would be denied access to the proceedings. Their rationale was that lobbyists use these sessions as an opportunity to influence the legal language of legislation during markups and that small changes in wording could easily fly under the public radar but have an enormous influence on how the legislation works. Noting that lobbyists will pay people to wait in line to assure them a place in the room, Gittelson reasoned that if netroots activists arrived first, they could freeze out at least some lobbyists.[19] She provided readers with the locations of the Education and Labor, Energy and Commerce, and Ways and Means

---

[15] nyceve, "Give Yourself a Hand, Hagan's on Board, Whip Count Holdout Takes the Pledge." *Daily Kos*, July 2, 2009.

[16] See, for instance, Jane Hamsher, "16 Down, 24 to Go: John Conyers Takes the Pledge." *FireDogLake*, September 8, 2009.

[17] nyceve, "I Was Asked to Come to Washington and I Need Your Help." *Daily Kos*, June 4, 2009.

[18] nyceve, "Eve and Jane Bring Healthcare Hell to Capitol Hill." *Daily Kos*, July 9, 2009.

[19] nyceve, "All Hands: Help Coax a Whip Count Holdout, Urgent Plans, Updates, and More." *Daily Kos*, July 10, 2009.

markups, the times people were needed to report, and instructions on what to do: "If you can be there, please organize on the spot. Introduce yourself and try to ascertain whether others [i]n line are also waiting for our side. If there appear to be a good number of people, then go to one of the other locations and scout out the situation. Give your cell phone number to whomever can be helpful in sorting out where volunteers are needed."[20] Then, it was in the hands of others to let blog-based activism carry the plan forward.

Outside Strategies

A broader range of netroots voices participated in a complementary set of outside strategies geared toward bringing public pressure on congressional Democrats. In addition to around-the-clock blogging about health care reform developments, these strategies included fundraising to support cooperative progressive officials; recruiting progressive candidates to run in primaries against liberals in safe seats, should they abandon the public option; efforts to deny funds to Democratic Party organizations that were not working for a public health care option; phone calls, e-mails, and faxes to pressure conservative Blue Dog Democrats; online petitioning; running netroots-backed advertisements; online social networking; and local organizing.

- *Raising and Denying Money.* The now well-established ability of the Internet to serve as a source for big-dollar fundraising was put to good use by the netroots, primarily as a carrot to reward what Jane Hamsher called "good behavior" by progressive Democrats who pledged to hold the line on a public option (there was even a Facebook link to an Act Blue health care contribution page adorned with a picture of carrots).[21]

In late August 2009, the blogger Dante Atkins posted on *Daily Kos* that "the combined efforts of this community, of all the state-based blogs, of the activist bloggers at *FireDogLake* and BlueAmerica, of MoveOn, and of concerned grassroots progressives everywhere in support of the public option" had generated more than $100,000 a day for the previous four days to reward progressives who had fallen in line with netroots efforts.[22]

[20] nyceve, "In Washington: Making the Powerful Uncomfortable." *Daily Kos*, July 15, 2009.
[21] Jane Hamsher, "Rewarding Good Behavior." *FireDogLake*, August 18, 2009.
[22] Dante Atkins, "Think You Can't Compete with Big Health? THINK AGAIN." *Daily Kos*, August 21, 2009.

Citing an *Economist* article listing the average HMO contribution to Blue Dog Democrats at $4,400 per member, Dante Atkins calculated that the netroots push had produced enough cash to best that in their support of progressives. "Now, don't get me wrong," he added soberly. "AHIP, PhRMA, and their allies still have the ability to dump a cool million or two into TV advertising during election season whenever they want. But in this fight right now – when it comes time for members of Congress to determine who they're going to be loyal to when push comes to shove – these contributions are difference-makers."[23] This sentiment was reiterated by the blogger thereisnospoon, who wrote, "You beat the insurance industry at its own game. You've made standing up for a public option a stronger incentive, financially, than standing against it. That's nothing short of amazing."[24]

As a complementary strategy, netroots activists alerted each other to the importance of withholding money from any Democratic Party-affiliated political group that was not completely behind the public option. Again, thereisnospoon blogged,

> The DSCC [Democratic Senatorial Campaign Committee] is making fundraising calls today, one of which I just received on my cell phone. I told them in no uncertain terms that I was not happy with how the Democrats in the Senate were behaving, that Harry Reid seemed completely unable to hold his caucus together, that the elevation of the Senate Finance Committee in its importance was very disheartening.... Money talks louder than words. If the DSCC hears a near-unified front in this regard when making their fundraising calls, I guarantee you it will make a difference.[25]

- *Recruiting primary opponents.* As a short-term strategy for advancing progressive health care objectives and a long-term strategy for advancing a broader progressive agenda, the blogger Kid Oakland recommended canvassing the safe electoral districts of progressive Democrats for potential challengers serving in state and local offices. "The process," he explained, "is a win-win":

> Nothing offers a clearer wake up call to an elected official than to realize that there's a popular, progressive elected official who *shares voters with you.* If that progressive official can raise funds, deliver results and organize support in your district then they can easily *replace you someday* if the voters so choose. And, yes, if that progressive, local

[23] Ibid.
[24] thereisnospoon, "OMG, What Have You People Done?" *Daily Kos*, August 21, 2009.
[25] thereisnospoon, "Just Got a Call from the DSCC Today." *Daily Kos*, September 16, 2009.

elected is an outspoken advocate of true health care reform, then it is all the more powerful. This reality is a natural part of politics in the USA and it doesn't take a primary for that pressure to be felt. In fact, the impact can be quite immediate.[26]

Jane Hamsher quickly amplified the idea of identifying a "progressive bench" with a "help wanted" post for new progressive leaders,[27] supplemented later with a Blue America outreach effort to put proponents of single-payer health care on the ballot in every congressional district.[28]

- *Phone calls, e-mails, and faxes.* Repeated requests to contact members of Congress directly complemented the online fundraising strategy, and no one was more persistent in making calls for action than the blogger slinkerwink. "Right now, we need you to CALL the White House and tell them that the conservative Democrats must UPHOLD the majority view of Americans who need a strong, robust Medicare-like public option," she blogged on *Daily Kos* in early July.[29] "I want you guys to burn up the phone lines to the House tomorrow!" she added in late September. "They need to know just why we want a public option, and that there will be consequences to pay if they don't support the public option."[30] Long comment threads followed these posts, with people blogging about actions planned or taken, while venting their frustrations about a Byzantine policy process that seemed stacked against their efforts to translate their achievements in the 2006 and 2008 elections into strong progressive policy.

- *Online petitioning.* A petition on an action page at *FireDogLake* implored readers to add their names to the thousands (65,500 by September 2009) urging House progressives to remain firm in their commitment to the public option. With an embedded YouTube video of Jane Hamsher discussing the petition drive on *The Rachel Maddow Show*, the page permitted signees to add personal messages for the House progressive delegation.[31] The petitions, which were delivered to

---

[26] Kid Oakland, "Two Petitions and a Call to Action." *Daily Kos*, September 3, 2009. Emphasis in original.

[27] Jane Hamsher, "Help Wanted: New Progressive Leaders." *FireDogLake*, September 4, 2009.

[28] Jane Hamsher, "Blue America or Single Payer." *FireDogLake*, December 4, 2009.

[29] slinkerwink, "Obama Doesn't Want Us to Attack Blue Dogs on Public Option." *Daily Kos*, July 4, 2009.

[30] slinkerwink, "We've Lost a Battle for the Public Option but Not the War!" *Daily Kos*, September 29, 2009.

[31] See http://action.firedoglake.com/page/s/keepthepledge.

progressive Representatives Keith Ellison (D-MN) and Raul Grijalva (D-AZ), supported the netroots' inside strategy of coordinating with House progressives while keeping public pressure on them.

- *Advertising.* At several points in the process, bloggers and online progressive organizations ran ads against Senate Democrats who opposed the public option, including an ad sponsored by MoveOn.org against Democrat Mary Landrieu.[32] Subsequently, *FireDogLake*'s Blue America Pac supported ads against Blanche Lincoln and other conservative Democrats.[33]

- *Social networking.* In addition to regular postings of YouTube videos with blog posts, and the use of Facebook and Twitter to supplement blog-centered political action, at one point in late summer the effort to move health care reform in a progressive direction went viral, with large numbers of Facebook users posting the same message on their site: "No one should die because they cannot afford health care. No one should go broke because they get sick, and no one should be tied to a job because of pre-existing conditions. If you agree, please post this as your status for the rest of the day." Commented Jonathan Singer at MyDD: "What amazes me is not only the size of the movement (it appears to be in the thousands, perhaps tens of thousands) but rather the faces behind it. . . . What is remarkable here is that these status updates containing a strong and clear message in favor of health care reform are coming not only from the political community but also from those whose lives are not immersed in these fights."[34] Matt Singer at WireTap Blog concurred: "While some of my friends who have put [the message] up are either dedicated activists or work professionally for progressive organizations, I've also seen it posted by, for example, two philosophy graduate students I know from my undergrad days, a high school friend, fundraisers for local charities, etc."[35]

- *Local organizing.* During the August congressional recess, when conservative Tea Party activists flooded constituent town meetings to protest the Obama initiative, progressive bloggers responded by targeting those same gatherings to make the case for progressive reform. *FireDogLake* posted an Action Event Tracker to help direct readers

[32] slinkerwink, "Obama Doesn't Want Us to Attack Blue Dogs on Public Option!" *Daily Kos*, July 4, 2009.

[33] nyceve, "We're Targeting Blue Dogs with Ads." *Daily Kos*, September 18, 2009.

[34] Jonathan Singer, "Health care Reform Goes Viral on Facebook." *MyDD*, September 3, 2009.

[35] Matt Singer, "Facebook Explodes with Healthcare Meme." *WireTap Blog*, September 3, 2009.

to as many meetings as possible. "With clammyc's wonderful help," blogged Eve Gittelson, "I intend to be with my FlipCam at three in New Jersey next week."[36] Simultaneously, *FireDogLake* worked the local angle with DFA, Drinking Liberally, and other progressive organizations to have their local chapters pass resolutions demanding a strong public option in the final health care bill.

THE ADMINISTRATION: PLAYING FROM THE INSIDE

While the netroots were implementing a far-reaching inside/outside strategy from their position outside the power structure, the Obama administration was conducting an outside strategy in support of intensive inside negotiating from their vantage point in the White House. In keeping with its campaign approach, Organizing for America provided users with a slick array of networking tools designed to build momentum for reform and keep pressure on Congress. Yet in contrast to the campaign, OFA's use of the Internet was a secondary component of this strategy, as the primary plan centered on bringing the relevant stakeholders to the table. Whereas the campaign was a movement, the administration's effort to reform health care was not.

OFA was used to advance the president's bottom-line objective: getting a health care reform measure through Congress. Because it was not employed as an activist site to shape the contents of the legislation, its efforts were at odds with what was happening in the blogosphere, where energy was directed at opposing some of the interests Obama was bringing into the negotiations. The difference is evident in the petition on the site's homepage, where users were asked to urge their member of Congress to "please support President Obama's plan for health reform in 2009. We need to bring stability and security to those who currently have insurance, affordable coverage to those who don't, and rein in the cost of health care."[37] Absent is any reference to a public option or to holding insurance companies accountable, the centerpiece of netroots efforts. A link to the details of the president's plan does list a public option among a broad set of principles – security and stability, quality, affordable choices, and cost control – but as only one element of affordability among several

---

[36] nyceve, "All Hands: YOU are the Little Mouse That's Roaring (and Hate Pays Me Many Visits)." *Daily Kos*, August 19, 2009.

[37] Organizing for America Health Care Action Center, at http://my.barackobama.com/page/content/health-care-action-center/?source=feature.

bullet points. Contrast this with the *FireDogLake* War Room, with its petition to stop the Stupak anti-abortion amendment, its tool for pressuring progressive members to pledge their support for a public option, and its advocacy for removing individual mandates from the final bill if a public option is excluded.[38] Because the administration's negotiating strategy entailed giving Congress latitude to negotiate the specifics, the president's plan per se was not articulated in a detailed manner on the OFA website, and the site was not revised to keep pace with the changes that emerged as the legislation worked its way through Congress. Instead OFA users were encouraged to advocate for whatever version of these principles happened to be under discussion at any given moment.

So it was with the other elements of the site, which were familiar to anyone who frequented OFA in its campaign iteration. There was a health care blog, a local event finder, and tools for tweeting senators and representatives, downloading graphics and posters, and e-mailing links to the Health Care Action Center to family and friends. Customizable, action oriented, and localized, the site contained all the key features that made OFA such a powerful campaign social networking tool. Passing health care legislation had simply replaced electing Barack Obama as its primary purpose.

As in the campaign, social networking was integrated with community events around the country. During a "Week of Action" in midsummer, OFA organized phone-banking events, door-to-door canvassing, and roundtable discussions geared toward building visible grassroots support for reform.[39] In mid-November, OFA set a goal of having its supporters make 100,000 calls to Congress in one day – a goal they surpassed in hours and ultimately trebled.[40] At the same time, OFA continued to train new supporters in community organizing techniques and expanded its donor base – one in four contributions to OFA came from people who did not contribute during the campaign.[41] Other metrics were as impressive: volunteers and staff in every congressional district, 2.2 million supporters working expressly on health care reform, more than 1.5 million declarations of support for Obama's priorities, more than 230,000 letters to the editor submitted to newspapers, and 238,000

---

[38] See *FireDogLake* War Room, at http://action.firedoglake.com/page/content/warroom/.
[39] See Greg Sargent, "Obama's Political Operation Set to Launch Health Care Events in All 50 States." *The Plum Line*, July 16, 2009.
[40] Christina Bellantoni, "Inside DNC's Organizing for America." *Talking Points Memo*, November 11, 2009.
[41] Ibid.

personal health care stories shared online – all accomplished within nine months.[42]

Still, with all that grassroots firepower, there was a strong sense in the blogosphere that the effort was too generic and not focused sufficiently on the content of reform. David Dayen at *FireDogLake* expressed a sentiment that was widely echoed on progressive blogs:

> The campaign arm of the DNC, Organizing For America, has delivered over 150,000 phone calls, at last count, in favor of health care reform. The President himself will deliver remarks at a "Time To Deliver" call party tonight. Less clear is what these callers are actually asking for in the health care reform currently working its way through Congress. The President has resisted at almost any opportunity delivering specific instructions on what he wants out of health care, particularly with respect to the high-profile provision of a public option. And now, Sam Stein [of *The Huffington Post*] is reporting that Democratic aides are worried that this lack of insistence will end up squandering the opportunity to include a public option in the bill.[43]

These different strategic objectives – passing a bill versus passing a progressive bill – sometimes flared into open disagreement between the administration and the netroots. In early July, when MoveOn.org was running its ad against Senator Mary Landrieu, Obama huddled with Democratic congressional leaders in an attempt to put a stop to the ads and convince progressive groups to fall in line behind his strategy of pursuing legislation that met the goals outlined on the OFA website.[44] Progressives pushed back, asserting that the struggle for a public option was also a test of their influence in Obama's Washington. "Unless progressives in Congress actually demonstrate they have a spine on this issue," blogged Jed Lewison at *Daily Kos*, "nobody will ever take them seriously – nor should they. But if progressives in Congress do put up a fight, . . . then they will have won a major victory that goes beyond just the issue at hand."[45] In response to continued netroots resistance, Obama made gestures toward accommodating some version of the public option in the final Senate bill.[46] However, the compromises he discussed – a triggered option, a provision for states to opt out of the

---

[42] Christina Bellantoni, "OFA Metrics Nine Month In." *Talking Points Memo*, November 11, 2009.

[43] David Dayen, "Door Open on the Public Option, President Obama Need Only Walk through It." *FireDogLake*, October 20, 2009.

[44] Ceci Connolly, "Obama Urges Groups to Stop Attacks." *Washington Post*, July 4, 2009.

[45] Jed Lewison, "Why the Public Option Matters." *Daily Kos*, September 13, 2009.

[46] See Greg Sargent, "Obama's Political Operation Pressuring Congress to Back Public Option." *The Plum Line*, November 3, 2009; Jane Hamsher, "And Oh, by the Way, We Blew up the White House Deal with AHIP." *FireDogLake*, October 12, 2009.

plan – were regarded in the blogosphere as window-dressing for a plan that would not fundamentally weaken the power of private insurance companies.[47]

OUTCOMES

By mid-October, the netroots inside/outside strategy had succeeded in pressuring Senate Majority Leader Harry Reid into including a compromise version of a public plan in the merged bill he took to the full chamber. Still ahead lay debate on that measure and the prospect that a single defection from the Democrat's 60-member caucus could derail the legislation by preventing a vote. Several senators opposed to the public plan had the incentive to defect and with it the power to hijack the process, putting progressives in a precarious strategic situation despite having advanced the public option so far against powerful opposition. In addition, the public option still had to survive a conference committee and a final vote of both houses. "The preliminaries are finally over," blogged Mike Lux, a veteran of the Clinton administration's failed health care reform effort, and despite the challenges he was feeling pretty good about what the netroots had accomplished:

> It is only because of the progressive movement that health care has been on the agenda, and only because of that movement that the debate has not drifted inexorably to the right. We have a shot at passing a strong bill that will actually cover Americans and create competition and a check on the power of the insurance industry. We have a shot at making history. Let's stay on the court until the victory is won.[48]

Lux was not alone in this assessment. Ohio Sen. Sherrod Brown, a progressive ally, credited the inside/outside strategy with keeping the public option afloat: "We were pounding on the inside, the progressives in the Senate, and you [the netroots] all were writing and calling and engaging in activism from the outside and that's what made the difference."[49] Blogger AdamGreen expressed a similar sentiment from his vantage point in the trenches, citing the collective efforts of

> Democracy for America, MoveOn, Blue America, FDL, Credo, OpenLeft, and others. National and state bloggers – and progressive media voices like

47 See slinkerwink, "Are Senate Moderates Falling in Line on Public Option?" *Daily Kos*, October 5, 2009; mcjoan, "Public Option Battle Won, Now We Have to Win the War." *Daily Kos*, October 5, 2009.
48 Mike Lux, "Prelims Finished, the Big Battle is Joined." *Open Left*, October 14, 2009.
49 Quoted in David Dayen, "Sherrod Brown Praises "Inside/Outside" Progressive Strategy on Public Option." *FireDogLake*, October 29, 2009.

The Young Turks – have pushed politicians and gotten facts out there that the mass media consistently missed. And many local activists have started their own grassroots efforts to pressure their senators. Sometimes we get discouraged. This fight has been long. It's not over yet. But it's important to take note of progress along the way and recognize that grassroots pressure works.[50]

Then, in a matter of days, a delicately calibrated Senate compromise unraveled. Negotiations on an alternative to Reid's bill among several Senate holdouts had appeared to yield an agreement capable of winning 60 Senate votes without alienating House progressives. The public option would be negotiated away to satisfy its Senate opponents, to be replaced with a limited extension of Medicare eligibility to people over age 55. The netroots response was generally positive. Chris Bowers wrote of "meaningful concessions" brought about by the larger campaign for a public option.[51] Howard Dean liked the deal. Then Sen. Joseph Lieberman had a change of heart, pulled his support from the compromise, and insisted he would filibuster a final bill with either a public option or a Medicare extension. Without the possibility of Republican support, Lieberman's position amounted to a veto of everything the netroots had worked for. Congressional leaders, including netroots allies, began imploring activists to settle for what they could get: a bill that would establish health care as a right without addressing the wealth or power of insurance companies.

The angry and divided response that ensued resembled a fiery replay of the telecommunications tussle. Jane Hamsher forcefully advocated for House progressives to hold to their pledge and kill the bill. Dean originally said the bill should be jettisoned, then shifted his position to support letting the process continue, thereby allowing the bill to be improved in conference committee. Indeed, this rift between progressives resigned to taking what they could get from governing elites and those determined to challenge them posed a test for the netroots in the days after the Lieberman defection. Movement objectives were colliding with governing possibilities, forcing an assessment of where the netroots stood in the wake of the administration's failure to support it.

Although sober, David Sirota was upbeat. Sirota, a long-time vocal progressive movement advocate, stated plainly what the netroots had going against them – and in their favor. Progressive activists do have allies

---

[50] Adam Green, "Grassroots Pressure Works." *Open Left*, October 23, 2009.
[51] Chris Bowers, "Some More Details on the Compromise – Franken Amendment in Bill!" *Open Left*, December 9, 2009.

in Washington, he wrote, and it should be acceptable for progressives to have honest disagreements over whether the health care bill should be scrapped or supported. However, it is equally important for the netroots to keep pressing against an entire establishment of individuals who would otherwise have the final say over the process. "These Establishment voices in the coming weeks will do whatever they can to make the progressive movement feel marginalized," he warned. "They are not interested in movements because movements are a threat to the status quo, their personal legitimacy and, quite often, their own hidden agendas."[52] Nate Silver, of the data-oriented progressive website FiveThirtyEight, had a complementary take on the situation. From a strategic vantage point, he argued, the public option may never have been viable.

> Progressives did just about everything in their power to try to get a decent public option into the bill. They threatened. They bargained. They complained. They organized. They persuaded. They begged. There was the opt-in, the opt-out, the trigger, the Medicare buy-in. There was no lack of initiative or creativity. And they actually had quite a bit of success: from 43 [Senate] votes in August, they got up to perhaps as many as 48–52 for a strong-ish public option, and 57–59 for a weak-ish one. People like Kay Hagan, Tom Carper and Kent Conrad, to varying degrees, came on board. But just because you perceive yourself as being in a negotiation with another party doesn't entitle you to win that negotiation, or even to split things halfway. Sometimes your adversary doesn't think there's anything to negotiate at all.[53]

Silver recounted an abundance of obstacles: the relative unpopularity of the public option and the overall health care bill in districts and states represented by conservative Democrats, the value of a bill without a public option to progressive representatives and the accompanying hollowness of threats to take it down, the absence of a credible, low-risk legislative alternative to finding 60 Senate votes for cloture, and the ability of corporate campaign contributions to move policy in a conservative direction – a point Darcy Burner acknowledged by recognizing that, notwithstanding the netroots fundraising prowess, the Blue Dog PAC had doled out more contributions than any other politician-controlled PAC in 2009, almost all of it originating as corporate money.[54] Under this difficult set of circumstances, Silver felt the progressive movement had

52 David Sirota, "The Establishment Backlash." *Open Left*, December 24, 2009.
53 Nate Silver, "The Public Option Fight May Not Have Been Winnable." *FiveThirtyEight*, December 14, 2009.
54 Ibid., and Darcy Burner, "Why the Blue Dogs Are Eating Our Lunch." *Daily Kos*, January 1, 2010.

acquitted itself well: "[T]hey set a *very* high bar, worked their butts off, and just barely failed to clear it."[55] Still, they were left with a nagging sense of what could have been had the administration used its Internet presence to work with them.

Ironically, in the health care reform endgame a large portion of the netroots activists climbed on board with the administration to push for passage of a bill that lacked the key characteristics they had fought so hard to include – the opposite dynamic to the kind of cooperation the netroots long sought from the administration. Republican Scott Brown's January 2010 victory in a special election to fill the Massachusetts Senate seat held by the late Edward Kennedy upended the administration's legislative strategy of negotiating compromise language for the House bill – absent a public option – that could win 60 Senate votes without sacrificing House support. Netroots activists continued to voice their opposition until Brown's victory stripped Democrats of their 60th Senate seat, leaving them scrambling for an alternative as they debated among themselves whether it was feasible or politically desirable to push forward.

As the political question changed overnight from whether Congress should pass a progressive bill to whether it should pass a bill at all, many – although certainly not all – online voices concluded that it would be devastating to walk away with nothing after investing so much in health care reform, and that a defeat under these circumstances, which would be attributed to voters at the ballot box rather than activists, might disable efforts to reform the health care system for years to come. A consensus began to build around using the reconciliation process to get modifications to the House bill through the Senate with a simple majority. With the administration and congressional leadership joining this consensus, the primary health care reform stakeholders found themselves working for the same objective for the first time. Although there was a fair amount of online agitation for including a public option provision in the reconciliation package (if there were more than 50 Senate votes for a public option before, the reasoning went, there should be 50 votes now), there was more acceptance than pushback when the White House and congressional leadership insisted that including a public option would only complicate what was already a complex legislative dance. The result was a measure that was embraced as an accomplishment by some of the same people who were poised to oppose it had it been passed through regular procedures with a 60-vote supermajority. For the netroots, the measure

55 Silver, "The Public Option May Not Have Been Winnable," emphasis in original.

would serve as a step in what they regarded as a long power struggle – yet it was not the step many thought they would be able to take when an Internet-savvy president first made the call for health care reform.

ALTERNATIVES

In a postmortem on the public option advocacy effort appearing on *Daily Kos*, thereisnospoon did not hold back: "I am your enemy. That you don't know this is understandable: after all people like me prefer it that way. But until you understand just what you're up against and why, you're going to continue to lose, and look like fools in the process."[56] He is a qualitative research consultant, thereisnospoon explained, whose job it is to manipulate public opinion so that "we can take sugar water and sell it back to you as a health drink, and even Whole Foods shoppers will believe it."[57] With a tiny investment of pharmaceutical or insurance money, he continues, it would be easy to turn the public against health care reform and against the Democratic Party through a campaign of persuasion. Obama had two ways to prevent this effort: co-opt drug and insurance interests through negotiation or fight them along with his allies. Fighting was risky: Industry contributions to fellow Democrats would temper the allegiance of some would-be congressional allies, and the Internet, to date, has not proved to be a reliable vehicle for launching counternarrative campaigns effective enough to compete with the mainstream media (Kerbel 2009).[58] This made negotiation appear to be the better choice. "Barack Obama has indeed sold you out," thereisnospoon continued. "He hasn't done it because he's a bad guy. In fact, he's a great guy. I think he's doing pretty much the best job he can. He's sold you out because he's not afraid of you."[59]

Indeed, the Democratic nominee in 2008 spoke like someone who understood the forces aligned against progressive change, but seemed in word and deed ready to man the trenches with the netroots. Obama was quoted as saying then, "One of my fundamental beliefs from my days as a community organizer is that real change comes from the bottom up. And there's no more powerful tool for grass-roots organizing than

[56] thereisnospoon, "No One Is Going To Save You Fools." *Daily Kos*, December 16, 2009.
[57] Ibid.
[58] Of their three primary objectives – influencing political outcomes, building online and virtual communities, and shaping media narratives – the netroots have been least effective at influencing mainstream news frames.
[59] Ibid.

the Internet."[60] The structure of the movement that would propel him to the White House reflected this belief. Yet Obama chose to abandon movement politics in office in pursuit of his highest profile domestic objective.

It was not an irrational choice. However, consider for a moment how the other option – to fight entrenched interests – might have played out. Instead of blurring his goals, seeking compromise, and relying on marketing techniques, the president would have been free to draw the line in the sand that bloggers were repeatedly clamoring for, proclaiming what he would and would not accept in a final package. With insurance companies as his adversaries, he would have been free to consider all options, including a single-payer approach that was always the first choice of progressives but was pulled from consideration before the process began to keep insurance companies at the table.

Had Obama viewed health care reform as a movement objective the way Dreier and Ganz did – as the latest struggle in a line dating back to abolition and women's suffrage – he would have approached it as he did his campaign; in fact, it would have become an extension of his campaign, with high-profile campaign-style events designed to build a narrative in support of transformational reform. Obama's rhetoric would have lined up with his actions. The netroots would have been engaged, albeit cautiously, as allies, and the Democratic base would have been energized.

In that scenario, the inside/outside strategies employed by the netroots would have complemented rather than competed with the work of OFA, which in turn could have countered the corporate money being spent against it by seeking small-dollar contributions as Obama had done so successfully during the campaign and on a larger scale than what the netroots could accomplish alone. Taking a page from the Dean campaign – where the candidate, to demonstrate the power of online fundraising, raised $50,000 in a single day for an Iowa congressman whom most of his supporters did not know[61] – Obama could have spearheaded a drive to raise money for members of Congress who otherwise would have no counterweight to industry contributions. In other words, the health care campaign could have looked a lot like the Obama campaign.

[60] Quoted in Brian Stelter, "The Facebooker Who Befriended Obama." *The New York Times*, July 7, 2009.

[61] The beneficiary was Rep. Leonard Boswell. See http://www.democraticunderground .com/discuss/duboard.php?az=view_all&address=104x821791.

Doing this would have been a high-risk, high-reward gamble. If successful, Obama would have been able to claim an accomplishment on par with his own election and consistent with what his candidacy represented to some of his supporters. Yet a lot of things could have gone wrong. The public response is untested in a policy campaign such as this, and far fewer people pay attention to policy making than to presidential politics. Would enough people engage or stay with it when things got difficult or when the inevitable compromises had to be made? Could enough money be raised to combat the deep pockets of industries that would be fighting for their existence? Could the president, even with the bully pulpit at his disposal, succeed in framing the debate? If he could not – if the initiative failed – Obama's political capital would be gone. Just getting *any* health care legislation was a goal that had eluded his predecessors. Did he want to risk his presidency on the larger objective of transforming health care policy? Internet technology may make collective engagement possible on a mass scale, but it does not guarantee that people will show up or follow through.

Nor was the left operating in a vacuum. As progressives were demonstrating a sophisticated understanding of Internet politics built on several years of grassroots activity, conservatives were gearing up to do battle as well. The Internet connected some of the August 2009 protestors who flooded congressional constituent meetings to shout down their representatives in anger over what they felt was a government takeover of the health care industry. Although what would come to be known as the Tea Party movement is not entirely a bottom-up entity, it boasts echoes of the protest politics that initially animated progressives along with, in some quarters, a recognition of the advantages offered by emerging media technologies. Had the administration and the netroots pursued an Internet-based health care campaign, there is no guarantee they would have had the field to themselves.

As the netroots continue to organize and as the Internet grows in strength relative to television, it is conceivable that the risk-reward ratios will change in their favor. They have already demonstrated the ability of Internet organizing to exert citizen influence on a process long dominated by organized special interests. They now seek to amplify that influence, and it is apparent from the health care experience that the activists operating in cyberspace would be helped immensely by leadership on the inside willing to view governing in movement terms, because the horizontal structure of the Internet is best suited to advancing a movement, whether it be online progressives or the Obama campaign. Securing leadership on the inside will require electing more officials through Internet-based campaigns. Even to the degree that Obama's campaign was powered by savvy social networking and small-dollar contributions, he still had to work with a Congress that largely was not. Progressives will benefit from getting behind candidates who approach elections like Alan Grayson of Florida, a first-term congressman from a swing district who, although unsuccessful in a difficult year for Democrats, ran an Internet-based campaign for reelection because, in his words, "If we can demonstrate a new model, a model where you get your campaign support on the basis of people-power, then we'll be much more likely to be able to implement the progressive agenda, and show America what a party with a conscience actually can do for America."[62] If there is one lesson for the netroots to take away from their health care efforts in 2009 about the potential of an Internet-engaged citizenry, this is probably it.

References

Anderson, David M., and Michael Cornfield (eds.). 2003. *The Civic Web: Online Politics and Democratic Values*. Lanham, MD: Rowman & Littlefield.

Blumenthal, Mark M. 2005. "Toward an Open-Source Methodology: What We Can Learn from the Blogosphere." *Public Opinion Quarterly* 69 (5): 665–9.

Bowers, Chris, and Matthew Stoler. 2005. *Emergence of the Progressive Blogosphere: A New Force in American Politics*. Washington, DC: New Progressive Institute.

Johnson, Thomas J., and Barbara K. Kaye. 2004. "Wag the Blog: How Reliance on Traditional Media and the Internet Influence Credibility Perceptions of Weblogs among Blog Users." *Journalism and Mass Communication Quarterly* 81 (3); 622–42.

Kerbel, Matthew R. 2009. *Netroots: Online Progressives and the Transformation of American Politics*. Boulder, CO: Paradigm Publishers.

Neustadt, Richard E. 1991. *Presidential Power and the Modern Presidents*. New York: Free Press.

Trippi, Joe. 2004. *The Revolution Will Not Be Televised: Democracy, the Internet, and the Overthrow of Everything*. New York: Regan.

---

[62] Cited in Paul Rosenberg, "Alan Grayson – Why His Moneybomb, Why Now." *Open Left*, November 2, 2009.

10

New Media and Political Change

Lessons from Internet Users in Jordan, Egypt, and Kuwait

Deborah L. Wheeler and Lauren Mintz

The other chapters in this volume consider the impact of new media environments on Western democratic societies. Because culture and context in part construct the meaning and implication of technology diffusion, one might wonder how new media and information capabilities will affect citizens in non-Western, nondemocratic societies (Chen, Boase, and Wellman 2002; Ess, Sudweeks, and Herring 2001). The key questions posed by this edited volume take on new significance when applied to the Middle East because, as a study of the Arab blogosphere observes, "in a part of the world where print and broadcast media traditionally have been controlled by the government, digital networked spaces offer the possibility of a much richer public sphere than existed before" (Etling et al. 2009: 46). Thus new media networks in the Arab world have the potential to reshape relations between citizens and the state. However, will new media environments produce a more informed and active citizenry in authoritarian, non-Western contexts? More specifically, will new information environments change political norms and practices in the Arab world? Will new media capabilities affect government accountability in the region? Answers to these questions are considered in more detail in this chapter in light of empirical research conducted between 2004 and 2009 in three Arab countries: Jordan (2004), Egypt (2004), and Kuwait (2009).

The primary argument developed in the following pages is that the Internet and social media are being used in the Arab world to mobilize the masses to demand better governance. The data analyzed in the case studies are clear evidence both of changing norms and social practices and of a better informed and active citizenry. These findings help explain the foundations of the 2011 "Twitter revolutions" in the region. This chapter explores reasons for expecting more citizen participation in government in the Middle East and North Africa, although they are tempered by cautious realism.

COMPETING EXPLANATIONS IN CONTEXT

Since the earliest Internet connections were established in the Middle East in the mid-1990s, commentators have been promising more transparent, accountable, democratic, participatory governance in the region. The argument is that with increased public voice and abilities gained by network interests, authoritarian states would "slowly retreat" (Norton 1999: 20). Yet, until the recent uprisings and unrest in Tunisia and Egypt, the expected "wave of democratization" promised by the Internet revolution's earliest prophets did not seem to apply to the Middle East.[1] To understand the unrest and potential for political change in the increasingly wired Arab world, we must probe the emancipatory potential of new media tools (Murphy 2009: 1131).

In the early months of 2011, masses of disenfranchised Arab citizens used Facebook, Twitter, blogs, and other forms of new media to push for regime change (Tunisia and Egypt) and political reform (Jordan, Yemen, and Algeria) with mixed results. As Asef Bayat observes, "[R]eform of authoritarian states would require distinctly laborious struggles, the significance and difficulties of which one cannot discount" (Bayat 2010: 248). A more nuanced and realistic view of political change in authoritarian contexts is one that acknowledges the importance of social norms, whereby "change in society's sensibilities is a precondition for far-reaching democratic transformation" (248). From this perspective, significant political and social change can emerge from "the exchange of ideas, information and models" that create and sustain "an active citizenry" (247). In Bayat's view, "an active citizenry" is "the most crucial element for democratic reform" (249). The argument of this chapter is along the same lines – that the ground for significant political change in authoritarian contexts can be readied by people using new media tools

---

[1] John Perry Barlow, "Declaration of the Independence of Cyberspace," 1996. Retrieved from https://projects.eff.org/~barlow/Declaration-Final.html; Al Gore. "Information Superhighways Speech," delivered March 21, 2004, at the World Telecommunications Development Conference, Buenos Aires, Argentina. Retrieved from http://vlib.iue.it/history/internet/algorespeech.html.

"to discover and generate new spaces within which they can voice their dissent and assert their presence in pursuit of bettering their lives" (ix).

Much of the attention concerning the power of new media to transform authoritarian societies comes from recent U.S. government policy. In response to clear evidence from China and Iran that new media tools help mobilize public dissent, the United States has made promoting Internet access and freedom of use a top foreign policy goal in the expectation that Internet diffusion and enhanced citizen communication capabilities will help open up "closed societies."[2] In a January 2010 speech at the Newseum in Washington, DC, Secretary of State Hillary Clinton stated that "Internet freedom had become a fundamental principle of American foreign policy."[3] Moreover, Clinton observed, "Even in authoritarian countries, information networks are helping people discover new facts and making governments more accountable."[4]

TECHNOLOGY DIFFUSION IS KEY

If people in the Middle East do not have access to the Internet, how can it be emancipatory? It cannot be, because access is a key factor in being ready to play the game. As late as 2005, Internet access was "growing and spreading more slowly in the Middle East and North Africa than any other place in the world" (Wheeler 2006b: 31). In 2001, Egypt was among the countries with the lowest Internet diffusion rates, with less than 1% of the population having access. Even Kuwait, an oil-rich country, only had 8.9% Internet penetration in 2001, whereas less than 4% of Jordan's population had Internet access. Yet, this was soon to change. As a result of increased state and private sector investment in IT in all three of these countries, the prices for access dropped, making more Arabic content available online. By 2008, as depicted in Table I.1 in the Introduction, the Internet was spreading more quickly in the Middle East than anywhere else. With Internet access increasingly reaching a critical mass of citizens in the region (as depicted in Table 10.1), expectations for Internet use to

[2] Mark Landler, "US Hopes Exports Will Help Open Closed Societies," *New York Times*, March 7, 2010, p. A4. Online version available at http://www.nytimes.com/2010/03/08/world/08export.html.
[3] Hillary Clinton, "Remarks on Internet Freedom." Speech delivered at the Newseum, Washington, DC, January 21, 2010. Retrieved April 2, 2010, from http://www.nytimes.com/2010/03/08/world/08export.html.
[4] Ibid.

TABLE 10.1. *Internet Penetration Rates for the Middle East and North Africa,*
2009

Country	Population 2009 Est.	Internet Usage, 2000	Internet Usage, 2009	Percent Population (penetration)	Percent Growth 2000–9	GDP Per Capita (PPP) in US$*
Algeria	34,178,188	50,000	4,100,000	12.0	3,740.0	7,200
Bahrain	728,290	40,000	155,000	21.0	287.5	39,400
Egypt	78,866,635	450,000	12,568,900	15.9	2,693.1	6,000
Iran	66,429,284	250,000	32,200,000	48.5	12,780.0	11,000
Iraq	28,945,569	12,500	300,000	1.0	2,300.0	3,600
Jordan	6,269,285	127,300	1,500,500	23.9	1,078.7	5,200
Kuwait	2,692,526	150,000	1,000,000	37.1	566.7	51,900
Lebanon	4,017,095	300,000	945,000	23.5	215.0	13,300
Libya	6,324,357	10,000	323,000	5.1	3,130.0	13,600
Morocco	31,285,174	100,000	10,300,000	32.9	10,200.0	4,700
Oman	3,418,085	90,000	465,000	13.6	416.7	25,400
Qatar	833,285	30,000	436,000	53.3	1,353.3	122,800
Saudi Arabia	28,686,633	200,000	7,700,000	26.8	3,750.0	23,700
Syria	21,762,978	30,000	3,565,000	16.4	11,783.3	4,700
Tunisia	10,486,339	100,000	2,800,000	26.7	2,700.0	9,300
UAE	4,798,491	735,000	2,922,000	60.9	297.6	40,600
Yemen	22,858,238	15,000	370,000	1.6	2,366.7	2,600

Note: The three countries studied in this chapter – Egypt, Jordan, and Kuwait – are in boldfaced type.
Source: Internet World Stats, see www.internetworldstats.com; CIA World Factbook, see www.cia.gov.

matter in some detectable way politically are also on the rise, giving new meaning and importance to empirical data on the subject.

Why focus on Kuwait, Jordan, and Egypt? According to Table 10.1, the three countries are not regional leaders on IT variables. None of them have the highest Internet penetration rate (United Arab Emirates is the highest at 60.9%), the highest GDP in the region (Qatar is the highest at $122,800 ppp [purchasing power parity]), or the fastest growing Internet penetration rates (Iran is the highest at 12,780%). What makes these three countries a good choice to study is that they represent a middle ground for the region. Moreover, each country comes from a distinct regional subculture: the Gulf (Kuwait), the Fertile Crescent (Jordan), and North Africa (Egypt). Given that these three countries are not outliers, their data can be interpreted as more representative of what might be general trends for the region. Moreover, by drawing a case from each of the subregions, we also obtain a more representative sample of

Internet cultures than if we just focused on countries from the same subregion.[5]

Because very little empirical data on the Internet's impact in the Middle East exist, any starting point is a step in the right direction, especially in light of the recent Facebook- and Twitter-supported unrest in the region. President Obama and members of Congress recently criticized the intelligence community for missing the widespread impact that new media and its ability to mobilize the masses could have on the regimes of the United States' close allies in the region. As Sen. Dianne Feinstein (D-CA) observed during a recent meeting of the Senate's Intelligence Committee on which she serves, "There should have been much more warning of the revolts in Tunisia and Egypt, because demonstrators were using the Internet and social media to organize. Was someone looking at what was going on the Internet?"[6]

THE SURVEYS AND DATA COLLECTION

The data for this chapter were collected during trips to the Arab world in 2004 (Jordan and Egypt) and in 2009 (Kuwait). The reason for conducting the comparative case studies was to understand where people in the Arab world get access to the Internet, how often and for what amount of time they go online, for what purposes they use the Internet, and, most importantly, whether using the Internet had changed their lives, local politics, and/or society in any way. Although there were a common set of questions designed to obtain data with which to answer our initial questions, some minor adaptations of the 2009 survey instrument were made to reflect the different context and time frame. Nonetheless, 24 questions were asked of all 517 participants across the cases (see Appendix A).[7]

[5] Another not so obvious reason for using these cases is that these are the countries for which the lead author got funding to study; Kuwait (1997, 1998, 2009. and 2010), Egypt (2000 and 2004), and Jordan (2004).

[6] Kimberly Dozer, "US Intelligence on Arab Unrest Draws Criticism," *Associated Press*, February 4, 2011. Retrieved February 8, 2011, from http://www.valleynewslive.com/Global/story.asp?S=13968896.

[7] The first data were collected in Jordan. Funds for the surveys were provided by a research grant the lead author (Wheeler) obtained from the Oxford Internet Institute (OII). The survey questions were designed and refined while Wheeler was in residence at the OII (2003–4) before heading to the field. Some adaptation of the survey questions to be more "contextually appropriate" were made in consultation with the Jordanian research assistant hired to assist with data collection (hiring a research assistant was necessitated because locals were reluctant to participate in an American survey research project in

The Jordanian survey included a total of 48 questions, which collectively addressed basic demographic information, level of education, employment, and other issues related to social class and upbringing as well as questions probing Internet uses, patterns, and habits; and open-ended questions. The surveys were conducted between February and April 2004; they were administered in Arabic and translated into English. There were 100 men and 100 women surveyed, ranging in age from 15 to 47 years old.

Even though the surveys were conducted in a representative sample of neighborhoods with Internet cafés in Amman and Zarqa – the two largest urban areas in Jordan where more than three-quarters of the Jordanian population live – the results of the case study are not representative of the population of Jordan as a whole. Because all surveys were conducted in an array of Internet cafés, the survey does not reflect those who would be unlikely to be in an Internet café, including the very rich and the very poor. The dataset is large for an ethnographic study and small for a quantitative study. However, given the scant empirical research on the development and impact of the Internet in the Arab world, this study makes an important first step in that direction.

The Egyptian case study was conducted between April and May 2004 by the same Jordanian research assistant, who by then had great familiarity with the survey instrument and also had lived in Cairo for several years. In Egypt, conducting survey research is not allowed without government approval, and approval is rarely given to foreign researchers. Given the logistical challenges of working around the state in Egypt, we asked fewer questions (28 instead of 48) and interviewed fewer participants (50 instead of 200). The data-collection method was a combination of participant observation and interview format. Follow-up research was conducted from June through August 2004 during which data were gathered based on participant observation and interviews with Internet café users and managers throughout Cairo.[8]

---

light of the U.S. invasion of Iraq). Under these circumstances, participants were more forthcoming when speaking to a Jordanian than to a foreigner. In addition to the data collected by the research assistant, Wheeler engaged in participant observation in Internet cafés throughout Jordan and discussed her research findings with Internet café managers and users when opportunities emerged.

[8] In 2000 Wheeler conducted research on the diffusion and impact of the Internet in Egypt, with a focus on claims that IT would support economic, social, and political development in Egypt. The results of this earlier research were published in an article and a book chapter (Wheeler, 2003a, 2003b).

The Kuwait survey was conducted by students at American University in Kuwait in June–July 2009.[9] The survey instrument included 29 questions, in addition to the 24 core questions that are common across the three case studies. It included questions about whether someone had a Facebook page, blogged or visited blogs, and thought the Internet was having an impact on Arab society and politics. These new questions were introduced to reflect new communication tools emerging in the five years since the Jordanian and Egyptian case studies had been conducted (Facebook, Twitter, blogs), as well as to reflect the growing expectation that, as Internet access and use reached increasingly critical mass in the region, some detectable impact on state and social practices would be demonstrated. We wanted to obtain local voices to comment on social media platforms and ascertain the extent to which they mattered in the region.

Only Kuwaiti nationals were interviewed for the study.[10] Moreover, given the nature of Kuwaiti society, whereby people tend to interact most frequently within tight friend and family networks, the survey data were not random, but rather constitute a purposive sample: Kuwaiti citizens who use the Internet and are identified by the individual students who conducted the survey. The students were told to try to get a "representative sample" of Kuwaitis to interview, including young and old, male and female, rich and poor, highly educated and not so well educated. In all, 139 men and 128 women were surveyed. Participants ranged in age from 15 to 61 years of age.

Again, the findings are not representative of Kuwaiti society as a whole, especially because two-thirds of Kuwaiti residents are non-Kuwaiti, the sample size was relatively small, and participants were not randomly selected. Nonetheless, this study provides some of the only current empirically based research on Internet use and impact in Kuwait (see also Wheeler 2006b). It indicates how Kuwaiti Internet practices have changed over the years and provides an additional case study with which to compare the earlier Jordanian and Egyptian studies.

---

[9] The course was entitled Arab Human Development, taught by Deborah Wheeler.
[10] Because the surveys were conducted by students as a part of a class assignment, no funding was needed to support the research. Indirectly, the research was supported by American University in Kuwait (AUK), because they were paying Wheeler's salary and hosting her in Kuwait.

BACKGROUND ON JORDAN, EGYPT, AND KUWAIT

Before proceeding with the analysis, it is helpful to provide background information about the three countries. In the 2011 *Freedom in the World* report, the annual survey by Freedom House, Jordan and Egypt are ranked as "not free," whereas Kuwait is ranked as "partially free" given recent advances in women's rights and a relatively free and open press.[11] Moreover, all three countries are known to be "semi-democratic" with active, popularly elected parliaments, which provide a weak check, if any, on the power of the ruler. The fact that, in each country, the ruler can suspend or dissolve parliament at will means that the head of state's power grossly outweighs public consent. There is little accountability between ruler and ruled in any of these countries, especially because the head of state is not popularly elected, but also because there are few if any checks on the power of the head of state, outside of revolution, of which there have been many in the Middle East.

If rulers in Jordan, Egypt and Kuwait do not like the pressure they are getting from public representatives, they just dissolve parliament. For example, Jordan's king dissolved parliament in 2009 and decided not to allow elections until the end of 2010. The move was designed to check the rising voice and power of Islamist elements in Jordanian politics. Jordan also has some of the strictest press laws in the region and has used them to prosecute people who are too free with their oppositional words in print and online. Jordan also has a high rate of honor killings for the region, which implies that women who experiment with cyberdating, as was found to be common among Internet users, take big risks, given tribal norms and laws that do not effectively protect women from threats from family members if they act in ways that are perceived to "tarnish" family honor.

In spite of clear constraints on democratic politics in Jordan, recent scholarship suggests that significant processes of change are occurring at the grassroots level. For example, King Abdullah's "Jordan First" initiative aims "to increase political participation" and "to advance democratic dialogue" (Baylouny 2005: 40). Part of the Jordan First initiative is a USAID-sponsored project to make Jordan a regional IT hub. Computers and e-learning are being introduced to the educational curriculum at all levels (kindergarten through college) in order to prepare youth for

[11] Freedom House, "Freedom in the World 2010." Retrieved from http://www.freedom house.org/template.cfm?page=505.

the digital economy. Telecenters, which provide low-cost Internet access and training, have been built throughout the country, including poor and rural areas.[12] State efforts to diffuse new media technologies throughout Jordanian society are having an impact on social and political behavior in Jordan, as examined in this chapter.

Egypt is also rated as "not free" politically by Freedom House, at the same time that the diffusion of new media is giving Egyptians alternative forms of political and social agency.[13] Egypt had an active parliament that has only been dissolved twice by the ruler, once in 1987 and again in 1990.[14] However, President Husni Mubarak had other ways to manipulate politics: His National Democratic Party controlled four-fifths of all the parliamentary seats, and he suppressed opposition politicians by making their movements illegal. This suppression was applied especially to the most popular and best organized opposition movement, the Muslim Brotherhood; the number of opposition politicians in prison, especially from the outlawed Muslim Brotherhood, always rose before elections, even when such candidates tried to run as "independents." After the 1981 assassination of President Anwar Sadat, a state of emergency rule was instituted and not lifted until February 2011. These emergency laws were used by President Mubarak to suppress press freedom, freedom of association, and freedom of speech, even online.

However, despite state repression, and an entire branch of the Ministry of the Interior dedicated to policing cyberspace, activism in Egypt had been on the rise before the collapse of the Mubarak regime. Increased economic instability and hardships for the majority of Egyptians fueled that activism. When this economic unrest was combined with a state policy to introduce IT access and training to most Egyptians as a means to stimulate foreign direct investment and increased economic opportunity, the stage was set for a revolution (Wheeler 2003a).[15]

---

[12] Jordan is also in the Guinness Book of world records for having the most Internet cafés on a single street, University Avenue, which is across the street from Yarmouk University.

[13] Ibid.

[14] Adam Morrow and Khalid Moussa al-Omrani, "Father Still Knows Best," *IPS*, July 17, 2009. Retrieved from http://ipsnews.net/news.asp?idnews=47700.

[15] These words were written in April 2010, several months in advance of the "Twitter revolution" in Egypt. As this chapter goes to press, it is not yet clear what the outcomes of the popular uprising for change will be. Observers conclude that Egypt will never be the same, implying that changes toward better governance and more equitable distribution of state resources and opportunities will emerge. Others are not so optimistic. Only time will tell.

In Egypt, the public has been increasingly making demands for greater government accountability and more economic opportunities, using the Internet as a vehicle for their voices and emerging social networks. For example, it is not surprising that "although the Muslim Brotherhood is technically illegal in Egypt, it has a very active presence in the blogo-sphere" (Etling et al. 2009). Similarly, in an analysis of the role of blogs and social networking technologies in Egyptian politics, David Faris argues that new media technologies reshape public discourse by making what is fit to print in the official press broader and less muz-zled by censorship. As a result, social media networks have "placed new tools and resources in the hands of the political opposition" (Faris 2010: 22). Faris demonstrates ways in which new media break stories, stimu-late mobilization, and sometimes encourage government reform in cases of torture, sexual harassment, land grabs, and human rights abuses of Sudanese refugees. Although he is careful not to exaggerate the impact of social media, he does skillfully demonstrate how new media prac-tices "change the context of the relationship between the regime and its people" in Egypt (Faris 2010: 78).

Before the Twitter revolutions in Tunisia and Egypt, Kuwait seemed to be the case that held the most promise for democratic change, as indicated both by the data yielded by the 2009 study and by the impact of Internet use on government policy. For example, in 2006, the Orange Movement, a government reform initiative, used the Internet "to convey unfiltered news, discuss, agitate, expose corruption, mobilize" making it possible to "engage each other in ways impossible offline" (Nordenson 2010: iv). Its main political impact was to persuade the Kuwaiti government to reduce the number of electoral districts from 25 to 5. This reduction was said to favor women's chances of getting elected to parliament (indeed, four women won seats in the 2009 elections after redistricting) and to reduce the possibilities of corruption through vote buying.[16] Similarly, in the 2009 Kuwaiti elections, many candidates used the Web to campaign and to widen their base of support.

The 2009 data on Internet influence in Kuwait documented for the first time perceptions about the political impact of Internet use. The earlier research in Jordan and Egypt showed that, as early as 2004, people surveyed were articulating how Internet technologies opened their minds,

---

[16] Henry Bowles, "Kuwait's Women's Rights Pioneer Talks Religion and the Future" *Kuwait Times*, November 30, 2007. Retrieved from http://www.kuwaittimes.net/read_news.php?newsid=MTAxNzI5MDkwMw==.

changed their views, and encouraged them to be more actively engaged with the world around them, but they were a minority voice within the dataset: only 34% of those surveyed. In the Kuwait case, however, more than 80% of those surveyed told us in their own words exactly how the Internet matters politically. Collectively these narratives suggest that "political change doesn't always begin with a bang; it often starts with just a whisper" (Goldfarb 2006: 1). It is not by accident that, as Goldfarb observes, "the Internet favors a democratic politics of small things" (141). It allows for the pooling of whispers, the collective yet often uncoordinated redefinition of new information relationships, and new forms of power – localized in individual lives, solidifying changes in norms and behaviors one click at a time.

SURVEY ANALYSES

Ethnographic and survey data on Internet activity in Jordan, Egypt, and Kuwait identify five general areas in which the Internet is having an impact by opening up Arab lives to new experiences with emancipatory potential: social networking, access to uncensored information, civic engagement, pathways out of boredom, and ease-of-life factors. As described earlier, these data were collected at different times, in different geographic locations, and in different situations. For example, research in Egypt and Jordan was confined to Internet cafés where an estimated 80% of the Internet-using population goes online (Rochidi 2004). In Kuwait, however, research was based on a purposive sampling of Kuwaiti Internet users as a whole, because most Kuwaiti Internet usage does not occur in a café. Nonetheless, the findings yield clear patterns in regional use and impact across the cases.

As described earlier and as seen in Table 10.2, the Jordan and Egypt datasets were gathered in 2004 via surveys conducted at Internet cafés by a Jordanian research assistant. Every respondent was an Internet café user, and thus the data apply to a very specific type of person, not the general population as a whole. However, the finding that the majority of the people using the Internet in 2004 in Cairo and Amman did so in a café suggests that the data collected accurately represent the Internet users in these cities. Yet the small number of interviewees in the Cairo case study does not allow us to make any sweeping conclusions about Internet use in Egypt.

Despite these limitations, several patterns emerge from the 2004 data. These café users were generally young: The average age for both datasets

TABLE 10.2. *Egyptian and Jordanian Survey Results Summary Statistics (2004)*

- Information Savvy:
  - 87% read daily newspaper
  - Overall hrs online weekly: 14.13 (avg)
  - Men online 19.3 hrs weekly (avg)
  - Women online 9.2 hrs weekly (avg)
  - 80.3% own mobile phone
  - 98% of cell phone owners send texts daily (avg daily = 9.5)
- Generation Gap:
  - Average age started using Internet: 21
  - 71%: Neither parent uses Internet
- Internet Accessibility:
  - 9.6% home
  - 27% school
  - 17% work
  - 100% café

N = 250

was 24.65 years old. Respondents were much more technologically savvy than stereotypes would assume. Even though the digital gap between male and female Internet use was still quite large, women were using the Internet far more than one might expect. The study also reveals that using the Internet helps people break through social and cultural barriers and that it transforms people's lives by enabling increased information access, increased social networking opportunities, expanding views, and encounters with other cultures and different political perspectives (see also Wheeler 2006a). In addition, many also cited that they use the Internet simply to reduce boredom.

The Kuwait dataset included a few extra questions that were not present in the 2004 case studies, mostly reflecting the new media technology's evolution. As mentioned earlier, there were new questions on blogging, Facebook, and MySpace use and the perceived political impact of such tools. Two things are surprising about the 2009 data. First, the gender gap has disappeared. In fact, often women reported more political activity or technology use than the men. Second, despite the passage of time, the patterns observed in the 2004 study about Internet use patterns and perceived impacts remained the same, although with an intensification of trends over time. For example, hours of Internet use per week, the number of people accessing Internet from home, and the number of people surveyed whose parents also use the Internet all increased.

TABLE 10.3. *Kuwait Survey Results Summary Statistics (2009)*

Information Savvy:
- Hours spent online weekly: Men, 20.67; Women, 20.04
- Read a daily newspaper: 60.6%
- Own a cell phone: 98.5%
- Average number of SMS sent daily – 34
- Prefer to visit websites in English: 92.7%
- Read blogs: Women, 36.5%; Men, 24.4%
- Write blogs: Women, 5%; Men, 4%
- Have a Facebook/MySpace: Women, 64%; Men, 68%

Generation Gap:
- Average age started using Internet: 15
- 70%: One or both parents use the Internet

Internet Accessibility:
- Home: 99.6%
- Work: 55.8%
- School: 76.8%
- Mobile: 74.9%

N = 267

A comparison of the summary statistics of the 2009 Kuwait dataset (see Table 10.3) with the 2004 Jordanian and Egyptian findings highlights these changes. In the 2004 dataset, women spent an average of 9.24 hours online weekly, and men 19.13 hours weekly. The Kuwait data show no significant difference between the genders, with women spending 20.04 hours and men 20.67 hours online weekly. The education levels are similar between the datasets, although slightly lower in the 2004 data (36.95% high school, 14.86% community college, 48.19% BA/BS degree) than in the Kuwait 2009 data (46.77% high school, 0.76% community college, 51.33% BA/BS degree, 1.14% MA degree). The increase in technology use is vast: 98.5% of the Kuwait respondents own a cell phone, and they send on average 34.38 texts per day, in contrast to 80.32% owning a mobile and sending on average only 9.45 texts daily in 2004. Even more telling is the fact that nearly 75% of the respondents in 2009 primarily access the Internet on their cell phones. Whereas the 2004 dataset represented people who frequented Internet cafés, 78% of the Kuwait respondents mostly used the Internet at home (with 99.6% having Internet access at home, compared to only 9.64% having home Internet access in the 2004 data).

The reasons why people use the Internet remain stable through both datasets as seen in Figures 10.1 and 10.2. The top three uses of the

Internet Uses

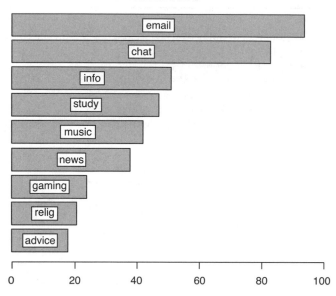

FIGURE 10.1. Internet Uses in Jordan and Egypt, 2004. Percentage of those who use the Internet for that particular activity.

Internet in all three countries are e-mail, study, and music, followed by chat and news. Strikingly, religious uses of the Internet are the lowest reported category for both datasets. One might assume from a "clash of civilizations" perspective that religious use of the Web would be more significant for conservative Muslim societies than suggested here (Huntington 1998). What is surprising about these reported uses is that there is nothing contextually distinct about use patterns: Internet activity in Jordan, Egypt, and Kuwait mirrors other cosmopolitan societies in the West. For example, the Pew Internet and American Life project reports that "89% of Americans use the Internet for e-mail, 88% get information online, 75% shop online, and 72 % get news online, whereas only 28% use the Web for spiritual or religious purposes."[17] One clear regional difference is the fact that only 22% of Americans surveyed use the Internet for chat, whereas in the three Middle Eastern cases studies explored here, the percentage of people surveyed who chat is close to 80%.

[17] Pew Internet and American Life, "Online Activities Total," 2009. Retrieved from http://www.pewinternet.org/Static-Pages/Trend-Data/Online-Activites-Total.aspx.

Internet Uses

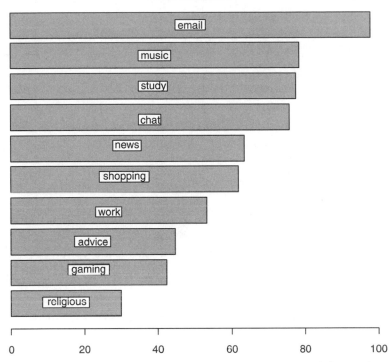

0	20	40	60	80	100

FIGURE 10.2. Internet Uses in Kuwait, 2009. Percentage of those who use the Internet for that particular activity.

The generation gap of Internet use seems to be closing, as emphasized by the Kuwait data. In the 2004 dataset, only 28.9% of respondents had a parent who used the Internet, in contrast to 70% in the 2009 Kuwait data. Also interesting is that the age when people began using the Internet has decreased from 20.94 in the Jordan and Egypt cases to 15.74 in the 2009 Kuwait study. This finding suggests that, over time, people are on average beginning to use the Internet at a far younger age.

In contrast to the prominent transformations resulting from Internet usage found in the 2004 dataset, the Kuwait data, although also showing common themes representing these four categories (information, networking, political change, and boredom), yielded a fifth category: simply that the Internet makes life easier. This general response encompasses the others, because it implies that using the Internet has made it easier to find information, network with people, find out about other societies, and fill one's time. More than 46% of the Kuwait respondents gave this

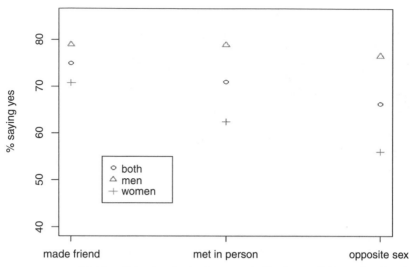

FIGURE 10.3. Making Friends via the Internet in Jordan and Egypt by Gender, 2004

response, which may account for the lower percentages for the other four categories when compared to the 2004 data.

Another contrast between the 2004 and 2009 data related to women's use of the Internet. One of the most interesting findings of the 2004 study related to women breaking social barriers through the Internet, anonymously meeting both men and women online and then in person. What is surprising is that there are fewer women meeting men online and subsequently in real life in Kuwait 2009 than in Jordan and Egypt in 2004.

Figures 10.3 and 10.4 suggest that society in Kuwait is more open and free than that of Jordan or Egypt, so that the Internet is not as important a tool in breaking down gender barriers. Overall, 60.7% of the Kuwait respondents made a friend online, with 68.3% of these then meeting them in person and 63.8% of these friends being of the opposite gender. The percentages for the women are interesting: More women than men made a friend online (62.5% vs. 59.1%), but more men then met the friend in person, with a higher percentage of those friends being of the opposite gender (men: 71.6% of those who made a friend online met them in person, with 72.5% of these friends being women; women: 65% met an online friend in person, with 55% of these friends being men). Comparatively, in the 2004 data, 74.9% overall (regardless of the gender

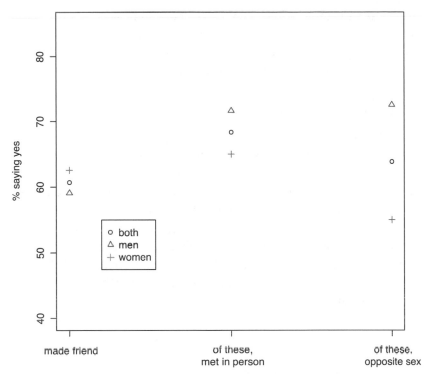

FIGURE 10.4. Making Friends via the Internet in Kuwait, by Gender

of the respondent) made a friend online, with 71% meeting the friend in person and 66.3% of these cases being friends of the opposite gender. One finding of the survey is that Internet access intensifies social interaction, and often against the grain of cultural norms.

POLITICAL MEANING AND INTERNET USE: NARRATIVE ANALYSES

For the purpose of this chapter the most interesting findings are the political meanings attributed to Internet use. Given that the Kuwait data (2009) showed a majority of those interviewed (more than 80%) felt that the Internet was having an impact on politics, this narrative analysis focuses mostly on their explanations for this phenomenon. These explanations can be linked, however, with observable patterns in the earlier Jordanian and Egyptian cases, just with different intensities, building over time (Wheeler 2006a). These socio-political impacts are observable across the cases in at least three realms: an increased ability to network for information and opportunity, to access uncensored information and develop new opinions, and to exercise freedom and engage in civic activities. It is in these three areas especially that we see hints of new forms of civic engagement emerging with emancipatory potential in Kuwait, Jordan, and Egypt, as explored more carefully below.

Networking for Information and Opportunities

Our earliest sense that the Internet could build civic engagement by bringing people together for conversations beyond the narrow conscripes of their regular life came from interviews with Internet café users in Jordan and Egypt in 2004. For example, a 17-year-old female from Zamalek neighborhood in Cairo observes, "On the net I have made many friends in other countries. We exchange viewpoints and ideas. It is better than pen pal friendship" (interview, May 2004). Similarly, a 25-year-old female from Amman explains, "Of course the Internet has changed my life. If I don't go to the Internet café, I'll die of boredom, especially now that I am not working, and have nothing to do. I enjoy my time online and make new friends and talk and exchange ideas" (interview, April 2004).

In terms of networking for opportunities, a 19-year-old male from Cairo observes, "The Internet has helped me to make many new friends. Some of the ones here in Egypt are trying to get me a job. They are good contacts. It's fun to chat and get to know people. It helps me not to think about my daily problems and helps me to do something in the long free time that I have" (interview, May 2004). A female from Cairo captures the ways in which Internet access allows for the subversion of communicative norms and how national identity bounds information flows when she observes,

> I love the Internet. It has made a huge difference in my life. It is a world of its own, and has its own particular charms including abundant information, the chance to know people from all over the world, having all kinds of discussions from politics to social issues to religious debates to fun and easy going topics. It is interesting to chat and to make friends. I like talking to foreigners. I am not that keen on the closed Arab mentality. I like people who are themselves in chat . . . no masks. In person they have to put on masks. (interview, May 2004)

Whereas the 2004 data reveal the ways in which the young in particular are leveraging the Internet to find new chatting companions and new jobs and opportunities, especially for the unemployed, the 2009 Kuwait data link these same processes of searching for information and opportunities with politics. These following responses were all taken from the

Kuwaiti Internet survey conducted in July 2009. One Kuwaiti says that the Internet affects local politics because online "people mix, opinions spread." Another Kuwaiti claims that online, he "got to know many new people." One respondent says that the result of such expanded social networks is that "it makes the world feel like a small continent." Another observes that "the Internet is one of the biggest political tools. Just go to Paltalk and see what the chat subjects are and what they talk about in the Arabic rooms." Another Kuwaiti says that blogs "change the political situation by making it easier to reach more people."

Given the fact that Middle Eastern societies are highly stratified along gender, ethnic, religious, and class lines, the Internet has the ability to support progress in civic engagement because it encourages people to interact with those not within their trusted social networks.[18] All of these "norms" of engagement can be subverted online, as evidenced by the narratives cited earlier. Building on this process of enhanced citizen awareness, the following section discusses how the Internet enables users to subvert state attempts at withholding and filtering information that might be politically sensitive.

"On the Internet I Get Access to All the Information I Want"

Arab countries are known as some of the most restrictive in the world in terms of information access and flow. Countries in the region, including Jordan, Egypt, and Kuwait, have restrictive press laws that draw red lines for oppositional discourse. Highly publicized arrests and prosecution of those who transgress these "no say" zones send a clear message to potential activists – resistance is futile, and opportunity costs are too high. In Kuwait, for example, although most newspapers are privately owned, it remains illegal to publish any material that criticizes the ruling family or insults the religion of Islam. Jordan and Egypt's press laws are even more restrictive.

In a context of media repression, citizens of the Arab world have found that the Internet provides pathways to new information resources and means of self-expression. A growing expectation for instant information, on demand, and tailored to one's interests is changing information environments and citizen engagement in the region, as evidenced in the following user testimonies.

---

[18] Several centuries ago, John Stuart Mill observed that when communication happens "with other persons dissimilar to oneself," this has been "one of the primary sources of progress" (quoted in Sunstein 2001: 191).

Once again, our first sense of the importance of the Internet for improving information flows in the Arab world comes from narratives collected in Jordan and Egypt (2004). For example, a 38-year-old Muslim female from Jordan observes, "The Internet is a beautiful thing. I can see and know about the world outside. It is fun for people who have more free time to use it. It gives me access to more news" (interview, April 2004). Similarly, an Internet café manager in Egypt observes,

> In terms of the Internet as a force for change, we see that it is a great source for people to get information and add to their knowledge. It helps students with school/university assignments; it helps researchers find any info they need.... It's opening people's minds to new things, trends of thought and adding to their awareness about things around them here and in the world. (interview, May 2004)

Another Internet user in Cairo reinforces this view that the Internet allows users to expand their knowledge beyond the normally accessible press when he observes,

> The Internet is a great way for communication and info access. I'm not that into chat and silly things, but I find the Internet a great device to improve oneself and to add to my knowledge and education, to keep up with the changes around us, in business and all aspects of life. It's also a great tool with which to know what's going on in the Arab world and all over the world with better coverage than TV and newspapers that don't provide enough detailed information. (interview, May 2004)

These observations – that the Internet provides greater access to information, tailored to an individual's needs, with a clear impact on citizen engagement – are replicated, and linked with political impacts in the Kuwait data (all these responses come from the Kuwait Internet survey, July 2009). For example, one Kuwaiti observes, "The Internet is like a massive database." Moreover, in another Kuwaiti's view, the Internet "allows communication from different places around the world, to meet people, and for news." Another Kuwaiti reinforces this view when he observes that, when online, "I can communicate with the world." One Kuwaiti sums up what makes the Internet especially transformative in Middle East media environments: "The Internet allows me to stay connected, up to date with news that are not allowed to be viewed or are censored in Kuwait. I think that the Internet has allowed me to expand my knowledge because not many books are available in Kuwait." Another Kuwaiti surveyed for this study links greater access to information online with activism when he observes that, because of the Internet, "people are more aware now about what is going on in the world around them – take a look at Iran."

Some Kuwaitis highlighted how increased access to information enhanced political awareness. For example, one Kuwaiti female states, "People are getting more educated through the Internet and now they know more about politics." What this means is that, according to another Kuwaiti, "in terms of politics, it [the Internet] made it easier to say your opinion and spread an idea or information." In other words, the Internet provides a new public sphere: "It's the place where you can express your opinion freely and widely." The cumulative impact of this process is that "the Internet has made the Arab world more open to discuss political views freely with use of anonymity; also it made them aware of current affairs as soon as they occur." As a result, one Kuwaiti explains, "People are more informed, organized." One of the reasons for these changes is put quite simply by another participant: "No Censorship." Moreover, the Internet is "keeping people up to date and aware of situations that are normally censored," especially because "[t]here is more freedom of speech on the Internet." The end result is that in the Middle East, "now the government can't hide anything. The people know everything."

"It Seems Like They Have More Freedom"

Emma C. Murphy, a Pulitzer-Prize-winning journalist, assesses the impact of "free-wheeling political discussion and debate in digital space" on "real-life politics" in the Middle East. Her conclusion is that "the virtual world is offering new opportunities for political expression and communication" (Murphy 2006: 1). In a later article, she argues that "across the region, legions of bloggers are mouthing off as never before. And ordinary folk are having their say in chat rooms, forums and online newspaper sites."[19] She points to concrete examples of how new media technologies affect political mobilization – "Lebanon's 2005 Cedar Revolution, Egypt's Kifaya movement and Kuwait's successful campaign to grant women the vote" – noting that all of these movements for political change "tapped the Internet's powers of mobilization and information dissemination."[20] Most importantly, Murphy argues, the huge 2009

---

[19] Caryle Murphy, "Arab Facebook: The Internet's Role in Politics in the Middle East," *The Majalla*, November 13, 2009. Retrieved from http://www.majalla.com/en/cover_story/article10699.ece.

[20] Ibid.

"street protests against election results in Iran – the so-called 'Twitter Revolution'... underscored the Internet's ability to virally connect people around the world."[21]

As discussed previously in the statistical overview, 80.5% of respondents in the Kuwait study answered "Yes" to the question whether the Internet is having a political impact on Arab society. As another indication of activism, 30.4% overall admitted to reading blogs: Broken down by gender, 36.5% of women and 24.4% of men responded yes. Similarly, more women than men were writing a blog themselves (5% vs. 4.1%). A 2009 study of the Arab blogosphere observes that most Kuwaiti blogs "focus heavily on domestic news and politics... and are more likely to advocate reform and discuss economic and women's rights issues when the blog is in English" (Etling et al. 2009: 3). Given the context, it is surprising that the women admit to being more politically active than the male respondents.

Across the data, those who were surveyed stated that the Internet "expanded their horizons" in key ways, bringing them into contact with new information, opinions, and other cultures, and that this new awareness made them more actively engaged as citizens. In the Kuwaiti case, 41.7% of women described such a transformation resulting from their Internet use, in contrast to only 25.5% of men. In the Jordan and Egypt case studies, an inverse relationship exists, with more men (41.9%) than women (26.4%) stating that the Internet has expanded their horizons.

To go beyond the numbers, the rest of this section illustrates, using the words of the participants, how Internet use across the case studies has expanded their political horizons (all Kuwaiti responses are from the July 2009 Internet survey). In Egypt, one respondent explains that chatting with citizens from Western societies helped her realize how life in societies that value individual liberties and freedom is different from her own. A second participant from Egypt notes that his Internet use helps him formulate dreams for a better future:

> The Internet made my free time more fun, exciting and enjoyable. I made many new friendships. It is interesting to know people from all over the world, not just here in Egypt. People really are different and they think in different ways in different countries. I wish I could travel, but they don't give us visas. [If I could go abroad], I am sure my life would be different if I could work at a different job, make money, finish university and have a better life... but these are just all dreams.

[21] Ibid.

Using the Internet to network for a better future is a common theme in the surveys. In part this process shows how the Internet, in the words of a Kuwaiti participant, enables a "more informed public, with more choices." Another Kuwaiti expands on this view when he explains that the Internet "makes Arabs more active in reaching others to find ways to express freedom. It taught Arabs a lot about the values of democracy and freedom." This is because, "online there is democracy and you can say whatever you want." And "the Internet is spreading democracy and new information about countries."

For those searching for any link between Internet use and enhanced citizen engagement, the 2009 Kuwait Internet study provides illuminating evidence. Whether or not the Internet actually does spread democracy and more accountable governance is difficult to decipher, but it is encouraging to have locals on the ground tell us that such processes are occurring. Stated concisely, a 40-year-old Kuwaiti female explains that the Internet "is opening the eyes of the younger generation and they are exercising more freedom. They can compare freedom in their countries with other countries and push for change to get more freedom at home." In the following section, we try to make sense of all of these voices, changes, prospects, and promises. What does the Internet mean for polity and politics, state and citizen in the Middle East?

THE FUTURE OF POLITICAL CHANGE AND THE INTERNET IN THE ARAB WORLD

A Cairo Internet café manager interviewed for this study explains the importance of the Internet for Arab audiences when he observes,

> There is no way to compare the Arab world before or after the net, of course it has made a huge difference, especially for the younger generations. The Internet is a door to the outside world. If we cannot have the chance to travel and live abroad, at least through the net people have access to get in touch with the world through chat discussions. These discussions are making people in the Arab world more open-minded, regardless of the negative influence of chat and porn sites. It's also educating people, adding to their knowledge and exposure to new ideas. In chat people have the freedom to express themselves. (interview with an Internet café manager in Zamalek, May 2004)

No matter how "different" Arab societies are now that the Internet is fully entrenched and growing, enhanced state repression of public expression and activism online suggests that a tug of war between state and society will inevitably result. It is not surprising to us that nearly half of the countries listed as "Internet Enemies" in a 2009 report by Reporters without Borders are Middle Eastern, including Saudi Arabia, Egypt, Iran, Syria and Tunisia.[22] Each of these countries is notable in terms of regional Internet use patterns (see Table 10.1). For example, Iran's population constitutes most of the region's Internet users: 56.1%. Moreover, the Internet is spreading more quickly in Iran than in any other country in the region: Usage has increased 12,780% between the years 2000 and 2009. Iran also has one of the regions highest per capita Internet penetration rates at 48.5%. At the same time, according to Reporters without Borders, "Iran leads the way in the Middle East in repression of the Internet, with 5 million webs sites blocked and 4 bloggers in prison."[23] Saudi Arabia has the second highest concentration of the region's Internet users, at 13.4%. It also has the third highest diffusion rate, with a growth rate of 3,750% in the number of users between the years 2000–9. At the same time, Saudi Arabia actively censors the Web and in 2008 imprisoned two high-profile bloggers. Egypt has the second highest number of Internet users in all of Africa and a growth rate of 1269.3% in the number of users between 2000–9. Currently, two cyber dissidents are in jail for antigovernment opinions they posted online.[24] Tunisia has one of the highest Internet penetration rates in Africa, at 26.7%; yet, the president of Tunisia continues to enforce an active campaign of Internet filtering, and self-censorship is the norm for the local blogging community.[25]

Sorting through these ironies and what the future may hold for the region as Internet access and repression seem to grow simultaneously will be an important topic of future research. The tug of war between net-enabled citizens and well-armored states is likely to be a feature of the Middle East for the foreseeable future, and who will win this contest remains to be seen. It could be that it is just a matter of time until

---

[22] Reporters without Borders, "Internet Enemies 2009," RSF. Retrieved from http://www.scribd.com/doc/13239325/Reporters-Without-Borders-Internet-Enemies-2009,
[23] Ibid.
[24] Ibid.
[25] These words were written six months in advance of Tunisia's Twitter revolution. As this chapter goes to print, former Tunisian president Ben Ali has been deposed and a new government is emerging, one more reflective of a broader base of society's concerns, needs, and demands. In this case nearly 30% Internet penetration, severe repression, high levels of unemployment and hopelessness, and a young man's desperate act of self-immolation were enough to create a revolution. Internet use created some of the conditions necessary for such change to emerge. Sorting through exactly what, when, and how social media helped create this revolution is a topic for future research. Moreover, comparing the surprising results in Tunisia and the less surprising results in Iran and Egypt is also an interesting topic for future research.

more accountable governance emerges in the region, based on IT-enabled public demand for it. Or perhaps the region will produce a hybridized version of an "information revolution" in which the public's capacity for civic engagement with the world and each other will grow, while formal, institutionalized power remains firmly in the grasp of an increasingly insulated state. This well-armored state, protected by formal institutions that discourage accountability to the public, will use repression in attempts to deter networked publics. When it is in the state's best interests (as when millions of people pour into the streets for protests), small openings of new spaces for political engagement will likely be tolerated, but not to the degree that such openings would result in a loss of state power, as we have seen most recently in Tunisia.

Given the tug of war between state and society in the region, many Internet users are careful, as explored in this chapter, to couch their resistance practices in ways that remain just below the state's radar (Wheeler 2009: 305, 319). This means that emerging changes may be occurring under our noses, affecting individual lives at this stage more than formal political institutions, yet gathering steam for future confrontation, as we are seeing in Tahrir Square in Egypt. In this way, new media environments "reveal the interactive constitution of an emerging alternative public and politics" in the Arab world (Goldfarb 2006: 12).

Participants in the studies presented in this chapter say that the results of online experiments in communicative action are increasing their political consciousness, global awareness, and self-confidence and producing other signs of enhanced citizen engagement. What happens over time when these small changes in individual lives congeal into a sea change of new attitudes and ways of being vocal? Inspired by Asef Bayat's study of nonmovement politics, we argue that, through new mediated forms of social networking and digital activism, "ordinary people, the subaltern" in the Arab world "affect the contours of change in their societies by refusing to exit from the social and political stage controlled by authoritarian states" (Bayat 2010: ix). This "art of presence," as Bayat calls it, enables people in the region to reshape the contours of their everyday life and to slowly eat away at the hegemony of authoritarian states (1). Although organized activism invites state repression and is relatively easy to target and diffuse, as Bayat observes, states "are limited when it comes to stifling an entire society, the mass of ordinary citizens in their daily lives" (249).

Increasingly, Internet users in the region are forming a critical mass. They are using technology to network, learn, develop, express, resist, challenge norms, engage new local and global publics, risk, and strategically enhance their lives – whether escaping boredom or looking for a spouse, a new job, education, or a visa to a new world. All of these everyday activities make more engaged citizens, more aware publics, and enhance individual agency. A state cannot stop such processes because providing society access to new media tools is a characteristic of good governance and is a requirement for economic growth and development opportunities. Moreover, a state cannot repress millions of people at a time for behaving in ways that are not a crime, but are just going about their everyday lives online.

Nonetheless, as suggested by this study, new digital publics pose a threat to the status quo. Internet practices in the Middle East prepare citizens for more active civic and political engagement both online and off. Members of these new publics are waiting for a chance to engage a more tolerant and responsive state. Until formal arenas of power are more open to Arab publics, the Internet gives citizens an arena in which to train as they engage one another, sharing their dreams for a more democratic and opportunity-rich future.

APPENDIX A: THE 24 SURVEY QUESTIONS ASKED IN JORDAN, EGYPT, AND KUWAIT

1. Gender
2. Age
3. Religion
4. Marital Status
5. Highest level of education obtained
6. Age when started using the Internet
7. Who taught you to use the Internet?
8. Have you ever taught anyone to use the Internet; if so, whom?
9. Do you have Internet access at:

   Home?
   Work?
   School/University?
   Café?
   Mobile?

10. Where are you most likely to use the Internet?
11. Are you employed; if so, in what job?
12. Number of hours per week you use the Internet?

13. What do you use the Internet for?

   E-mail
   Chatting
   Gaming
   Health-related concerns
   To get advice
   For religious purposes
   Music Downloads
   News sites
   For study/research
   For work/business
   For shopping
   Other: _____

14. Has the Internet changed your life? If so, how?

   _____

   _____

   _____

15. Do you read a daily newspaper; if so, which one?
16. Are you comfortable using English?
17. Do you prefer to visit websites in Arabic or English?
18. Do your Mom or/and Dad use the Internet?
19. What are your favorite websites?

   _____

   _____

   _____

20. Have you ever made a friend online?
21. Were they your same gender?
22. Did you ever meet them in person?
23. Do you own a mobile phone?
24. About how many text messages do you send per day?

References

Bayat, Asaf. 2010. *Life as Politics: How Ordinary People Change the Middle East*. Stanford: Stanford University Press.

Baylouny, Anne Marie. 2005. "Jordan's New 'Political Development' Strategy." *Middle East Report* 236: 40–3.

Bellin, Eva. 2002. *Stalled Democracy: Capital, Labor and the Paradox of State Sponsored Development*. Ithaca, NY: Cornell University Press.

Bellin, Eva. 2004. "The Robustness of Authoritarianism in the Middle East: Exceptionalism in Comparative Perspective." *Comparative Politics* January: 139–57.

Bimber, Bruce. 1998. "Internet and Political Transformation: Populism, Community and Accelerated Pluralism." *Polity* 31 (1): 133–60.

Brownlee, Jason. 2007. *Authoritarianism in an Age of Democratization*. New York: Cambridge University Press.

Chen, Wenhong, Jeffry Boase, and Barry Wellman. 2002. "Global Villagers: Comparing Internet Uses and Users around the World." In Carolyn Haythornthwaite and Barry Wellman (eds.), *Internet and Everyday Life* (pp. 74–113). London: Blackwell.

Ess, Charles, Fay Sudweeks, and Sandra Harding, eds. 2001. *Culture, Technology, Communication: Towards an Intercultural Global Village*. Albany: State University of New York Press.

Etling, Bruce, John Kelly, Robert Faris, and John Palfrey. 2009. *Mapping the Arabic Blogosphere: Politics, Culture and Dissent*. Cambridge: Berkman Center for Internet and Society.

Faris, David. 2010. *Revolutions and Revolutionaries: Social Media Networks and Regime Response in Egypt*. Ph.D. thesis, University of Pennsylvania Department of Political Science.

Goldfarb, Jeffrey C. 2006. *The Politics of Small Things: The Power of the Powerless in Dark Times*. Chicago: University of Chicago Press.

Huntington, Samuel. 1998. *The Clash of Civilizations and the Remaking of World Order*. New York: Simon and Schuster.

Murphy, Emma C. 2006. "Agency and Space: Information Technology and Political Reform in the Gulf Arab States." *Third World Quarterly* 27 (6): 1059–83.

Murphy, Emma C. 2009. "Theorizing ICT's in the Arab World: Informational Capitalism and the Public Sphere." *International Studies Quarterly* 53 (4): 1131–53.

Nordenson, Jon. 2010. *We Want Five! Kuwait, the Internet and the Public Sphere*. Master Thesis in Arabic Language, Department of Culture Studies and Oriental Languages, University of Oslo.

Norton, Augustus Richard. 1999. "The New Media, Civic Pluralism, and the Slowly Retreating State." In Dale E. Eickelman and Jon W. Anderson (eds.), *New Media in the Muslim World: The Emerging Public Sphere* (pp. 19–28). Bloomington: Indiana University Press.

Rochidi, Naijat. 2004. Personal interview. UN Headquarters, World Trade Center Bldg. Cairo, Egypt, August.

Sunstein, Cass. 2001. *Republic.com*. Princeton, NJ: Princeton University Press.

Wheeler, Deborah. 2003a. "Egypt: Building an Information Society for International Development." *Review of African Political Economy* 30: 627–42.

Wheeler, Deborah. 2003b. "Living at E.Speed: A Look at Egypt's E.Readiness." In Imed Limam (ed.), *Challenges and Reforms of Economic Regulation in MENA Countries* (pp. 129–57). New York: American University in Cairo Press.

Wheeler, Deborah. 2006a, July. *Empowering Publics: Information Technology and Democratization in the Arab World – Lessons from Internet Cafes and Beyond*. Research Report No. 11. Oxford: Oxford Internet Institute.

Wheeler, Deborah. 2006b. *The Internet in the Middle East: Global Expectations and Local Imaginations in Kuwait.* Albany: State University of New York Press.

Wheeler, Deborah. 2009. "Working around the State: Internet Use and Political Identity in the Arab World." In Andrew Chadwick and Philip N. Howard (eds.), *Routledge Handbook of Internet Politics* (pp. 305–20). London: Routledge.

Index